FEELING, IMAGINATION, AND THE SELF

FEELING, IMAGINATION, AND THE SELF

Transformations of the
Mother-Infant Relationship

William Willeford

Northwestern University Press
Evanston, IL

Northwestern University Press, Evanston, IL 60201

Copyright 1987 by William Willeford

Printed in the United States of America

Library of Congress Cataloging-in-Publication Data

Willeford, William.
    Feeling, imagination, and the self.

    Includes index.
    1. Self.   2. Mother and infant.   3. Personality.
4. Psychoanalysis and culture.   I. Title.
BF697.W4937   1987   155.2   87-24805
ISBN 0-8101-0762-7
ISBN 0-8101-0763-5 (pbk.)

Acknowledgments

I am grateful to the John Simon Guggenheim Memorial Foundation for a Fellowship that enabled me to complete the first draft of this book.

Elizabeth Tachikawa navigated intricacies of the library, contributed valuable queries and suggestions, and checked and rechecked countless details. Her sensitive and meticulous help for the last years of my work on the book has been an exemplum of *gift* as understood in these pages.

WITHDRAWN

Portions of this book—here revised—have been published previously: Section 3 in *Chiron* (1985), Section 4 in *The Journal of Analytical Psychology*, Vol. 26, No. 4 (October 1981), Section 5 in *The Journal of Analytical Psychology*, Vol. 29, No. 4 (October 1984), and Part 6.3 in *The Journal of Analytical Psychology*, Vol. 12, No. 2 (July 1967).

Grateful acknowledgment is given for permission to quote from the following.

William Carlos Williams, "To Waken an Old Lady," from *Collected Poems, Volume 1: 1909–1939* (New York: New Directions Publishing Corporation, 1938).

Wallace Stevens, "Gubbinal," from *The Collected Poems of Wallace Stevens* (New York: Alfred A. Knopf, Inc., 1954).

Robert Frost, lines 1–8 and 14–20 of "The Most of It," from *The Poetry of Robert Frost*, ed. Edward C. Lathem (New York: Holt, 1969).

Contents

Illustrations

Author's Note

Parts 1 and 2 lay out my concerns in this book and my way of approaching them. Part 6 draws my discussion of them to a close in ways largely requiring an understanding of matters treated in various places earlier. Parts 3, 4, and 5, originally written as self-contained essays on interrelated themes, have been revised with the overall argument of the book in mind. They retain enough of their independent character, however, that the reader who has reason to read them out of order should be able to do so with profit but should know that parts 4.3 and 4.4 (pp. 148–56) take up theoretical topics basic to the whole, and so supplement the definitions in part 2.5 (pp. 36–49).

Biblical citations are from the Authorized Version unless otherwise indicated.

Shakespeare citations are from *The Complete Signet Classic Shakespeare*, gen. ed. Sylvan Barnet (New York: Harcourt Brace Jovanovich 1972).

References to C. G. Jung are to *The Collected Works of C. G. Jung*, 20 vols., trans. R. F. C. Hull (except vol. 2, trans. Leopold Stein in collaboration with Diana Riviere), edited by Sir Herbert Read, Michael Fordham, and Gerhard Adler (New York: Pantheon, 1953–1966; Princeton: Princeton University Press, 1967–79, including revised editions), hereafter CW.

1 Baby, the Given, and Doing Theory

Near the beginning of Shakespeare's *The Winter's Tale*, the insanely jealous King Leontes wrongly accuses his queen, Hermione, of adultery, and has her cast into prison, where she gives birth to a baby girl. The queen's waiting-woman, Paulina, acts to avert worse disaster by taking the baby to the king and showing it to him. She does this on the assumption that the sight of the baby will touch something in him deeper than his deluded ego: her appeal is to feeling, imagination, and the self. That the king responds by condemning the baby to be taken to some desolate place and left there to die shows that she underestimated the magnitude of his insanity. Still, her action originated in a sound psychological understanding of important matters. This book explores the implications of that understanding, concerned as it is with feeling, imagination, and the self, and their bearing upon the experience of the ego.

The *feeling* to which Paulina appealed is a capacity of the ego but is also ego-transcending, entailing a special mode of relationship to the emotional substrate of conscious experience and to the self. Also ego-transcending, and yet a capacity of the ego, *imagination* creates images and symbols as constituents of essential meaning. By the *self* I mean, to begin with, the person regarded as a more comprehensive entity than that centered in the conscious ego. I also mean, within the person, a principle of organization (and disorganization) supraordinate to the ego. This principle I take to be personal but also transpersonal, including contents and processes such as the physiological changes marking the stages of life—in which one participates but which one does not originate and cannot possess, except by means of the conscious attitude one adopts toward them. (Self will be defined

1

more fully in part 2.5 and elsewhere.) By the *ego* I mean, most briefly, those psychic elements infused with the felt sense of "I" and "mine." (At least implicitly, this term, too, will receive further definition later, especially in places where I discuss the self, distinguishing it from the ego, with which the self is not identical—except in unusual cases, most often pathological. I am for now disregarding the special problem of the relations between ego and self in infancy.)

Such terms as ego and self, and to a lesser extent feeling and imagination, name what could be called experiential concepts: they are useful not so much for talking about things that can be clearly defined as for suggesting qualities of lived experience in the hope that persons addressed will recognize them—much as they would, one hopes, understand *home* as distinct from the more clearly definable *house*. Though the qualities of lived experience named by such terms as ego and self may in some measure be examined empirically, they retain links with phenomena named by such terms as *soul* and *spirit*, which, while less susceptible of such examination, may for many people be utterly real in what C. G. Jung called "the reality of the psyche," in which soul and spirit may be as substantial as the table upon which one cannot, by the nature of things, place them for study.

Such entities as soul or spirit are products of imagination, which — though it may take the form of listless fantasy or Leontes' raging delusions—ideally mediates between ego and self in a constructive and synthetic way. Thus, not only is Leontes' feeling deranged, so also is his imagination, and Paulina's appeal to feeling is also an appeal to imagination, with which feeling is intimately connected.

Though the baby is Leontes' own child, it is also a symbol. Christian churches contain representations of the Christ Child partly for the same reason that Paulina presents the baby to Leontes, and for the same reason that many mythologies focus on the extraordinary infancy and childhood of their gods and goddesses: the divine child is a mythical form in its own right, and not simply the child-stage of the mature divinity.[1] Part of the significance of the mythic or poetic image of the child is expressed by saying that it is symbolic of the self, not yet constrained by the ego's attitudes and purposes, and holding potentialities for further development of the personality in such a way that the ego may actively participate in their realization. We relate to the self in part as we relate to a baby, whose intentions we try to read as we seek to make a place for it in our lives that will further its unfolding and development. In this sense, the ego is the bearer of the self, as Saint Christopher is the bearer of the Christ Child on his shoulders. (See fig. 1.)

Owing in part to the status of feeling as a capacity of the ego, the infant, real and symbolic—we *feel* about babies—plays an important role in adequate ego-functioning. Thus, Leontes' rejection of the baby is a measure of the impairment of his ego. This is to speak of the baby as an object of awareness. Turning to the baby as a subject, we recall the common assumption that a baby has an ego only in germinal form, and that when its ego is securely established, infantile modes of behavior are relegated to the unconscious and, in waking life, to moments of regression. This assumption, however, ignores ways in which interactions between mother and infant provide the model for important aspects of differentiated ego-functioning. This model will be stressed at various points in the following pages.

The mother-infant relationship of my subtitle is not so much that of mother and infant now, the infant being still an infant; it is, much more, that relationship as it remains dynamically implicit in larger developments of the individual personality and in cultural life.

To know what feeling is, one must feel; to know what imagination is, one must imagine; to know what the self is, one must have experiences of the self. To express these psychic processes and structures in terms other than their own is partly to falsify them. And yet there are things to be gained by such translation. The resulting mixture of truth and falsehood may be suggested by analogy with the term *psychic androgyny,* which acknowledges the presence in everyone of contrasexual psychic components derived in part from one's experiences of one's parent of the opposite sex. The term, however, opens the door to nonsense if one forgets that the lived experience of living in a female body and that of living in a male body are in important respects irreducibly distinct, so that there is a distance to be imaginatively overcome if I am to know what it is to give birth to a baby and nurse it; and the resulting knowledge must be in the manner of a translation, however successful. With respect to the realities named by such terms as feeling, imagination, and the self, it is useful to reflect that they

3

Fig. 1. The ego, symbolized by Saint Christopher, as the bearer of the self, symbolized by the Christ Child. This representation of the pair (by Meister von Messkirch [?], active around 1540) implies that wholeness, balance, and completion as desiderata of the self require the efforts of the mature ego for their realization. Further, the image of the vulnerable baby evokes an opening of ourselves in a receptive mode derived from that so important to both partners in the early mother-infant relationship. And so this representation also implies that such receptivity is essential for the differentiation of the adult personality under the aspect of individuation.

4

fall within the domain of "psyche," the mythical emblem of which is a butterfly. To ignore the flickering, fluttering, now-you-see-it-now-you-don't quality of their manifestations is to falsify them. And yet there are things to be gained from reasoning about them.

Since what follows is less the unilinear, systematic argument some readers might expect than a personal, essayistic treatment of various subjects related to my main themes, I wish to comment on *facts, data,* and *theory* as they bear on my procedure.

It is commonly thought that psychology develops in this way: facts are used, in clear awareness, as data leading to the establishment, rejection, or refinement of concepts. This view needs to be qualified by a recognition that facts—Lat. *facta,* from *facere,* "to make"—are *made,* that data—Lat. *data,* from *dare,* "to give"—are *given,* and clear awareness is a specialization, in many respects a falsifying one, of the more fundamental form of awareness of which the butterfly is an emblem.

Data of science and technology—for example, data fed into a computer—would seem to comprise a rationally definable category. *Giving* does not comprise such a category, at least not exclusively, for two main reasons. First, when a nine-month-old baby offers one a mangled, spittle-soaked piece of bread in the hope that one will eat it with relish, the action shows that the baby has taken an important step toward grasping the reciprocity and turn-taking it must understand if it is to master language and acquire other forms of participation in social and cultural life.[2] But the knowledge of giving demonstrated in the infant's offering of its bread is prelinguistic, something on the order of a mimed gesture of what the philosopher and phenomenological psychologist Maurice Merleau-Ponty calls the "body-subject."[3] Even if language presupposes such knowledge of giving, it is not simply translated *into* language and out of its original prelinguistic, extrarational, experiential mode. And second, giving is an action the meaning of which has been elaborated in mythologies, in magical and religious practices, and in literary and artistic creations. (As creatures we are given life by God; Hermione's baby is a gift; Paulina's presentation of the baby to Leontes was a gift; his rejection of it was the refusal of a gift; to sacrifice—perhaps the fundamental religious act—is to give; Christians believe that Christ gave his life to save them.)

5

The giving imagined in these modes is that of a volitional agent. Paradoxically, to speak of scientific or technological "data" is to divorce them from any such agent: they are, the word *data* tells us, "given," but have no relation to a giver or to an act of giving.

To be given to (by someone or something that gives) is occasion for gratitude. (One thanks Baby for the soggy bread one pretends to eat.) And gratitude is, not only etymologically, linked with grace. God's grace, Christians say, is not merited but freely given (gratis and gratuitously), and it leads to freedom (from sin and death). That freedom is not, however, license; it is, rather, a certain attitude of acceptance as one lives an ordered life. Grace as an aesthetic quality has similar connotations of freedom within constraints. A graceful brushstroke in a painting or a graceful movement of a dancer looks effortless. This is not because it is undisciplined but rather because it is executed as though there were, with respect to the intention expressed in it, no obstacles that could not be easily surmounted, as though there were ample time and space for the execution. A graceful gesture is economical, a minimal use of power that one nonetheless senses to be there in ample reserves. The freedom of grace is an unforced accommodation to limits within a context of plenitude, of more than enough. Thus, Saint Bernard of Clairvaux (1091–1153) preaches that true charity "does not flow outwards until it abounds within," that its gifts are the results of an overflowing. "Help me out of your abundance if you have it," he remarks; "if not, then spare yourself the trouble."⁴ And thus, Baby does not offer the piece of bread unless she can assume that there would be more if she wanted it. To give and to be given to is to be receptively open to the world.

Sections that follow are concerned with what might be called the giving of the fundamentally given, and the receiving of it, with *giving* and *given* to be understood in the broad sense I have just sketched. Giving and being given to—unlike scientific and technological "data"— are forms of interaction between volitional agents. A gift is alive with the life of the giver. (Baby gives not bread but *her* bread; to give and to be given to in the religious sense—for example, in the Christian collection of offerings and Eucharist—is to participate in the larger life of a community and a relation to a living God, a God of Life.)

Milton's Satan understood these relations, and the bearing of gratitude upon them, in a way that illustrates my argument. Speaking of how God created him "In that bright eminence" of Heaven, Satan asks, "What could be less than to afford him praise, / The easiest recompense, and pay him thanks, / How due!" but then goes on to ponder "The debt immense of endless gratitude, / So burdensome, still paying, still to owe." Yet Satan must acknowledge himself "Forgetful what from him I still receiv'd"; and must admit that he "understood not that a grateful mind / By owing owes not, but still pays, at once / Indebted and discharg'd," so that he is left with the question, "What burden then?"⁵

Envy, competition, and covetousness are realities that must be dealt with by the maturing person; one must acknowledge, as Satan does ruefully, their capacity for impeding gratitude. But to use such a term as *narcissistic supplies* (to be encountered in psychoanalytic literature) is to assume that one pays for what one gets, either legitimately or by robbing Peter to pay Paul—that any advantage is balanced by a disadvantage, any profit by a loss. Yet without advocating deficit spending and the reckless use of plastic charge cards, one can counter that a sense of more-than-enough is prior to such realities. The nine-month-old baby has an understanding of envy, but its offering of squashed-up bread reflects an understanding that giving and being given to are more basic than the economics of mutual depredation. And giving and being given to remain basic to the maturing person in the sense of being essential to one's receptivity to the life revealed especially by feeling and imagination as originating in the self. Speaking of narcissistic supplies mistakenly implies either deriving self from ego or equating them in a way that reduces self to ego.

Sections that follow are also concerned with how exceptional minds and hearts have comprehended the giving and being given to with which I am now concerned—with what they have thus *made* of it—and with how we, partly aided by them, may further reflect upon it.

This is a book of reflections. It is theoretical in relation to the original sense of *theory* as mental viewing or contemplation. (The Greek root of the word means "looking at," and is related to the root of *theater.*⁶) In emphasizing the action of looking at with a contemplative cast, I am taking a stand with respect to a widespread understanding of theory.

Many mental-health professionals—psychiatrists, clinical psychologists, analysts, psychotherapists—take theory to be a body of explanatory ideas about what people are and do, a system or model, which guides their practice. They serve this model as practical technicians: they apply their theory—and in a few years suffer from what they call "burn-out." In the field of mental health—as in such fields as literary criticism and theology—system follows upon system, wave upon wave, foredoomed. Surely, coherent ideas need to guide practice, and in principle such ideas can be improved upon; yet the transience of many such systems is remarkable. They pass in part because their inadequacies are in time revealed—indeed, some shine with what should be seen at the outset as the glamor of fads. But such rapid obsolescence also, I believe, expresses an unacknowledged but rightful dissatisfaction with the role of practical technicians serving a theory by applying it, as though following a factory manual.

Such a distinction between theory and practice is in many ways artificial and self-defeating. General principles need specification, but the activity of specifying them may also be part of theory. In Anglo-Saxon case law, for example, cases are decided on the basis of precedent; and general principles acquire real character through reflection on individual instances.

To apply theory is to assume that it is preset, self-complete; to *do* theory is to assume that it is open and in process. The openness and process I have in mind are suggested by the butterfly spontaneously marking out its unpredictable course and thus being emblematic of everything psychic.

Remarks by the French poet and orientalist René Daumal (1908–44) and by the novelist Marcel Proust (1871–1922) illumine the distinction between the application and the doing of theory. "The Modern Man," Daumal writes, "believes himself adult, a finished product, with nothing to do for the rest of his life but alternately earn and spend material things (money, vital forces, skills), without these exchanges having the slightest effect on the thing called 'I.' The Hindu," on the other hand, "regards himself as something still to be formed, a false vision to be corrected, a composite of substances to be transmuted, a multitude to be unified."[7] To apply theory as one might follow a factory manual is to be "adult" in the sense of Daumal's modern man, and to be "adult" in that sense is to be cut off from the baby presented to Leontes.

Similarly concerned with the need for each person, at least on some level, to forge the truth for himself, Proust observes that "by a singular and moreover providential law of minds (a law that possibly signifies that we can receive the truth from no one else and must create it ourselves), the final achievement of . . . [the] wisdom [of others] appears to us as only the beginning of our own, so that it is just when they have told us everything they can that they awake in us the feeling that they haven't yet said a thing."[8] Thus, even to accept received truths in a personal way that makes them one's own is to continue the process of reflection through which they were discovered. Such truths have their fullest meaning, not divorced from that process, but as part of it.

This view has its inevitable qualification in our being born to community, without which there is no self, and in our creatureliness—which means, among other things, that persons are not the creation of ego-consciousness. This can be taken to mean that we are inert matter, divorced from the active power that regrettably does not inform us, pots of a remote potter. Such a view has been an unfortunate by-product of the elaboration of the metaphor of God as creator. But it can also be taken to imply the presence, now, of a creative God in nature, in history, and in the self, a God calling ego-consciousness to be aware of dependency and interconnectedness, and to remain open to the unknown depths of the unconscious self. I have this implication in mind when I speak of creatureliness. It is disastrous to try, as Shakespeare's Coriolanus vowed to do, to "stand / As if a man were author of himself / And knew no other kin" (*Coriolanus* V.iii.35–37). And Shakespeare's Richard of Gloucester proclaims the perversion of his will when he declares, as he kills the king, "I have no brother, I am like no brother, / . . . I am myself alone" (*Henry VI, Part III* V.vi.80–83). Rather, in the words of John Donne (1573–1631), "No man is an island, entire of itself; every man is a piece of the continent, a part of the main. . . ."[9]

Ego-consciousness has the responsibility of playing as well as it can a hand of cards it most often did not deal in a game in which every move is in relation to the moves of all the other players. Though various egos may take turns dealing, the self is always manifest in the order of the shuffled deck, and every move in response to the other players alters the ego's relation to the self.

9

Feeling, Imagination, and the Self

As responsible agents of the natural world we are called upon to be as aware as we can of further and further levels of ecological interconnectedness. In precisely the same way, we are called upon to relate the self as known by the ego to the self supraordinate to it. Early interactions of Mother and Baby are implicit in this later awareness and relating.

Though literature and other imaginative products, analytic practice, and everyday life provide my subject matter, in this book I am, then, not primarily applying a theory to them; nor am I opposing this or that theory to modify it with another. Rather, I am recording a process of reflection, the conclusions of which are sometimes clearly separable from the process but also sometimes not.

Conscious as we may try to be, what lives our lives is to a large degree unconscious, often problematically so. We are thus self-divided, usually having some reason to doubt whether our right hand knows what our left hand is doing. To disclose and constructively alter this state of affairs, reflection must be something more personal than the application of a theory.

A good example of the self-division and self-deception with which I am concerned is offered by the consummate jazz alto saxophonist Art Pepper, who, when released from prison after a lengthy stay for crimes related to heroin addiction, was—though with no clear conscious purpose—immediately ready to do again the things for which he had been arrested. I will let him serve for a moment as my instance of Everyman, because various features of his story touch on themes treated in the following pages—though some of those features make him, like Leontes, an example more cautionary than worthy of emulation. Neither Pepper's able mind nor his opportunity for sustained reflection saved him from doing things grossly opposed to his best interests. The discrepancy between the feeling expressed in the conduct of his life and that expressed in his music is striking. One may describe much of that discrepancy by saying that his ego—with its mode of feeling—was largely inadequate to his genius on the level of the self—with its mode of feeling and its mode of imagination.

In Pepper's early childhood he was deprived and abused, with results to his person that might lead one to ponder the effects of separation, loss, and abandonment on the self-esteem and integrity of the personality—though pondering them would also require one to marvel at how hard it is to kill the will to survive and the capacity for self-affirmation. I also want to contrast his story,[10] thus sketched, with that of an analyst, "Dr. Edgar Smile," ostensibly in a better position to profit from psychological theory. Dr. Smile brings us to the role of such theory in analysis.

The activity of what is not very helpfully called "analysis" can be either the applying of theory or the doing of theory, that is, reflection. If it is the doing of theory, it proceeds in contemplative awareness that it is going out from what is given, that there is nothing else for it to go out from; that whatever insight is achieved into patterns of behavior, and whatever images arise to guide understanding and action, are part of the apprehension of a subtle essence, in which the configuration of this person's life at this moment may be glimpsed; that this apprehension is personal knowledge, and that the subtle essence thus apprehended has its own freedom and cannot be willfully secured, and will inevitably give way to other such essences inviting apprehension; and that impersonal theory is always modified and transformed in our personal knowledge of the kinds of contents with which it purports to be concerned.[11] What I am now saying about theory may be illumined—as may the plight of Leontes and that of Art Pepper—by a consideration of the way in which Dr. Smile's attempts to do theory, in principle laudable, went awry.

Conducting a seminar for analyst-trainees, Dr. Smile described a hypothetical situation in which a woman begins taking her clothes off in the presence of her male analyst. The task for the trainees was to try to think of appropriate responses, after Dr. Smile had assured them that the notions they offered as to what might be done would be less important to the discussion than their reasoning about the problem. This is analogous to an examination in English literature in which the right answer—"this unidentified poem is by Abraham Cowley"—is justifiably treated as of less importance than the candidate's sensitivity in talking about style. Though Dr. Smile was seemingly intent on doing theory in the way I have been proposing, he shortly thereafter was brought before the ethics committee of his professional organization owing to real situations in which he and women presumably in analysis with him were without clothes. Members of the ethics

11

committee were less immediately interested in Dr. Smile's reasoning about these situations than in his actions within them, as those actions violated ethical and therapeutic principles, and in how they would sound when described in a court of law or in a newspaper. Why had his psychological sophistication given him no more practical wisdom than Art Pepper displayed when he left San Quentin, and, within a short time, with no hesitant soul-searching, was again using heroin?

For the relationship between ego and self to be dynamic in such a way that the ego is revivified and finds new meaning through that relationship, while putting itself in the service of the self, the ego must itself be open to the self, as Paulina demanded that Leontes open himself to the sight of the baby. Of course, the ego is not always in as urgent need as Leontes was of the sight of his baby daughter; and manifestations of the self are seldom as clear in their purpose and meaning as that apparition. Indeed, much of what there is to work with in the analytic enterprise comes with no overt indication of what it means and what should be done with it. For example, dreams may be useful in analysis; some are very like Paulina's showing of the baby to Leontes; there is reason to assume that many dreams meaningfully represent the workings of the self. Still, many do not in any discernible way, and cannot be made to do so by bringing a preset theory to bear upon them.

By challenging the applicability of an accepted theory, however, puzzling dreams may help to keep theory as reflection alive, and thus serve the intentionality of the self. But this is to reach from rigorous method to the kind of fleeting, uncomprehended, sometimes chaotic psychic stuff out of which poetry is sometimes made. The movement is to receptivity—and dependence—and possible abandonment.

When Paulina shows the baby to Leontes, one of the things she is doing is reminding him of all the possible things it can mean to be utterly dependent. He responds by ordering the baby to be abandoned, an act equivalent to decreeing the abandonment of the self. (Later, we see the baby grown to adulthood; she has qualities of royalty and near-divinity expressive of the self as the larger personality, far transcending Leontes' conscious viewpoint.) To disavow receptivity by abandoning the self is to be abandoned by the self. The willfulness manifested by Leontes in his denial of the baby as a symbol of dependency is purely and narrowly egoistic, with the ego deprived of access to sources of self-correction and transformation. Thus, Leontes can be wrongly proud of his clear judgment, as he declares himself to be, while we see him as delusional in an unconsciously motivated way.

This brings us again to the question of why Dr. Smile could reason so adeptly about psychological matters without dispelling his own confusion—why, with the resources of psychological understanding at his disposal, he could have been as shortsighted as Art Pepper was in using his new-won freedom to get himself put back in prison.

When consciousness is narrowly egoistic, without access to the supraordinate self, it can use virtually any materials to express and enact its unconscious motives. Just as those materials can include religious injunctions to humility and charity, so they can include theorizing about the supraordinate nature of the self with respect to the ego. For this book to be understood properly, its essence—like the subtle essence of a valuable analytic interview—must be heard *through* and not *in* my reasoned arguments about such matters. This is not to say that the ego lacks powers of self-monitoring, self-reflection, and self-correction: it has them, and they are precious. It is to say, however, that to be true to oneself, one's ego must see beyond its own vested interests and unconsciously motivated charades, and must be receptive to the self on which it is dependent. Imagine the moron in the old gag who holds his right thumb with his left hand—right thumb in a ring formed by left thumb and forefinger—and then snatches with his right hand at the spot where his right thumb had been, but fails to catch it, because it is no longer there, and because the snatching action involves the use of the hand to which the thumb remains stubbornly attached. Thinking that his failure is due to his not being fast enough, the moron loses himself in efforts to speed up the snatching. So it is with attempts of the ego to solve its own problems using only its own resources.

It is possible that the theory Dr. Smile had learned failed to provide him with what he needed in the way of practical guidance because he has only a rudimentarily developed capacity for feeling in certain of its aspects: feeling as a personal, responsible, differentiated conscious concern with gradations, transitions, continuity, and coherence. He rather acted out of *disordered feeling* (explored in part 6.10). That Art

Pepper's personal life should show a similar incoherence of feeling is not surprising in view of the bleakness of his childhood. It is also not surprising that, apart from his music, his imagination should often take the relatively passive and low-grade form of sexual voyeurism and fantasies of being a Hollywood-movie gangster. (Though I call such fantasies passive, I grant that they may be busy: there is much busy passivity in the world—in the form, for example, of people working at jobs that awaken in them neither interest nor commitment.) Still, in his music he in part explored the emotional implications of the incoherence of feeling he knew so well—while also yielding to the need of the self for felt authenticity—and in so doing, created beauty, order in process, coherence. His doing so shows that the psychic depths may prove to have resources for reparation and self-balancing. That in his case these resources turned out to be accessible, whereas for many other people they do not, and that his personal life should continue to be a shambles, shows precisely the disjunction between ego and self I want to stress.

The problem created by this disjunction is so basic to the human condition that no received theory can guarantee a solution to it. Yet the example of Socrates might remind us that it is possible to theorize, to do theory, without falling into the kind of moral confusion that beset Dr. Smile. Indeed, Socrates is a model of the personal integrity that is compatible with an alert willingness to question all general truths.

The ambiguous relation of the ego to the self also finds exalted expression, and an admission of its unavoidability, in the prayer of Jesus at Gethsemane: "O my Father, if it be possible, let this cup pass from me: nevertheless not as I will, but as thou wilt" (Matt. 26:39). This utterance could be taken as a weighing of the prerogatives of the ego under the dominion of the self. If Socrates offers one model of openness, Jesus offers another, related to it, manifest in many aspects of his life, but dramatized with special clarity in this moment, as he passed through doubt to assurance, by reflecting, in the moment, and by grasping the moment imaginatively.

In speaking positively about receptivity and dependency, I am not pardoning the sponging and clinging discernible in many bad human relationships, any more than I am pardoning the willfulness of pseudoindependence and pseudointegrity. It is precisely the possibility of

14

such untoward developments that makes the relation of ego to self a religious problem. Many religions teach that we are to become receptive only to that which is worth receiving, and dependent only on that which is truly dependable, and that access to such a bountiful, reliable good is humanly possible, or at least possible with divine help. That this teaching is compromised and perverted by egoistic vested interests is a problem that must be dealt with day by day, hour by hour, in continual acts of discrimination the nature of which, the object of which, often is unclear, since there is no factory manual to guide the process. (Think of dreams, as puzzling at the end of a long analytic discussion of them as they were at the beginning.) Still, though infantile forms of dependency must be left behind for more mature forms, our relation to the latter is impeded insofar as we fail to acknowledge the importance of the mother-infant relationship in our most refined assessment of who we are and what our lives are about.

We might say about someone, "This person is a creature of the Lord," or, with equal justice, "This person is or was the infant of a mother." Since the levels implied by the two statements are distinct, one cannot in a blanket fashion reduce religious experience to vestiges of infantility, as psychoanalysts have done. Though distinct, the two levels are nonetheless interrelated, so that there is something of the mother-infant relationship in the manifestations of the self to the ego, and in the functioning of the ego, both in apprehending the self and in its more ordinary workings. I am concerned with the complex interrelations between these two levels.

The mother-infant relationship appears in the subtitle rather than in the title of this book because this book is mainly about what comes of that relationship, reflected in qualities of the adult personality and cultural life. Among the issues treated are the ambiguous nature of the will, as experienced by an ego that needs control over itself and the world on the one hand, and that needs to be receptive on the other; abandonment and loss, wish and hope; and the nature of feeling, imagination, and the self. These issues are examined in their own right, and in their bearing on the mother-infant relationship and on the relationship between ego and self.

Delightful as babies may otherwise be, in their third year they are often enough manipulative and bullying; their relations to social rules

15

are inevitably marked by exaggerations and struggle, and they still need to consolidate their capacity to be alone and to bear loneliness. Moreover, the unresolved Oedipus complex is cripplingly real in many people who have advanced beyond childhood, and narcissistic personalities arrested at a developmental stage some time before the third year abound. These matters, important all, have been treated extensively elsewhere, and this book is not primarily about them—though it does touch on them in various places. It is rather—directly and indirectly—about residuals of the early mother-infant relationship in the realized psychological maturity of the individual and in cultural life. And it is especially about ways in which that relationship is implicit in experiences of feeling and imagination, some of them revelatory of the self. I take it that this view, at least as regards the ego, accords with that of the psychoanalyst Hans Loewald, who proposes that "the so-called fully developed, the mature ego is not one that has become fixated at the presumably highest or latest stage of development, having left the others behind it, but is an ego that integrates its reality in such a way that the earlier and deeper levels of ego-reality integration remain alive as dynamic sources of higher organization."[12]

Although this book does not argue a thesis, it treats interrelated themes amounting to a program of concerns and an affirmation of certain values, which I will briefly describe.

The mother-infant relationship gives the infant experiences of receptivity and mutuality that remain important in the later development of the individual and in cultural life, partly because the mutuality of that relationship reflects the self-balancing tendencies of the self, thus making them incarnate and giving them specific character, in personal lived experience. Within the mother-infant dyad, both mother and infant mediate experience of both ego and self for one another. The receptivity developed through such early experiences may assume a more active form in feeling and imagination as interrelated processes of the ego, processes that are also unconscious and ego-transcending. Such felt and imaginative active receptivity may figure valuably in the relations of the ego to the world of community and to the deeper regions of the psyche, as these relations reflect the workings of the self, often in ways that have emotional concomitants needing to be read. (See fig. 2.)

16

Fig. 2. Mother carrying baby. Openness of mother and infant to one another fosters openness of the maturing individual to self and world. Richness of their interaction fosters richness of feeling and imagination, and creates inner resources for dealing with pain and loss attendant upon such openness. Secure dependence of infant on mother fosters the kind of independence that entails recognition of our interdependence as members of community and parts of a larger, religiously and philosophically conceived whole. Later psychological developments, including differentiation to accommodate the Father World, imply this stage and draw on inner resources created during it, and do so without superseding it. The self importantly influences and is shaped by this early stage, which remains part of the dynamic pattern of individuation.

17

Since the mutuality of which I am speaking is also that of masculine and feminine, and since the interaction between these qualities is one of my themes, I add a comment on it.

The skyscrapers of downtown Seattle, a loveless clutter of arrogantly inert geometrical shapes, can be taken as representing a profusion of yang, or masculine energy, in a degraded and degrading form. Nor is it farfetched to presume a connection between the nuclear missiles poised to attack and defend the skyscrapers and a contest of eight-year-old boys to see who can pee the farthest. Conversely, ancient Chinese diviners were concerned with signs showing an improper prominence of yin, or feminine energy. Among these signs were the intrusion of frogs and snakes, yin animals, into the hall of the court; the apparition of dragons (also yin); and the arrogance of womanly power, as when a wife of a deceased emperor had her son enthroned and declared herself regent—acts which led to her being overthrown and killed.[13] Indeed, in 813 A.D. the T'ang empire suffered a severe flood, understood as resulting from an excess of yin, to which the reigning monarch responded by expelling from his palace two hundred wagonloads of women.[14] Male and female energies need to interact in some sort of balance. In developing this theme, I assume that the balancing of these energies is, on many levels, a never-ending process of redressing imbalances—much as, in analysis, one examines dreams and other details of one's life in the hope of making one's conscious attitude more balanced.

In talking first about the mutuality of mother and infant and then about that of masculine and feminine, I may seem to be conflating the two in a way that advocates Momism. On the contrary, I would observe that if the philosopher Nietzsche's Zarathustra was extreme in declaring that a man should take a whip when going among women, Dagwood Bumstead is as extreme, and considerably more dismal, in snoring on the sofa while relinquishing total control of the family's affairs to Blondie, and that perhaps Zarathustra's whip should be brandished at Dagwood to provoke him to deal with her. In any case, Dagwood is all infant, and Blondie all mother—with most of the masculine energy of the two. They illustrate, as negative examples, my concern with a balance of masculine and feminine energies and the persistence of the mother-infant relationship in adulthood.

Incidentally, though patriarchy is currently under massive attack, and though this book focuses more on Mother than on Father, it was

Baby, the Given, and Doing Theory

written in full awareness of how immensely important the paternal principle—as distinct from prevailing collective images of it—is. If consciousness undergoes the transformations which I feel are demanded of it, the paternal principle will, I believe, assume forms responsive to the concerns of this book.

Feeling and *imagination* name complex interrelated processes expressive of the "self" of the mature person. Yet these processes retain links to his earliest past, in ways suggested by Sigmund Freud's summary statement that "every earlier stage of development persists alongside the later stage which has arisen from it." Freud also remarked, near the beginning of his scientific work, that "the original helplessness of human beings is . . . the primal source of all moral motives."[15] These observations have important implications not exhausted within his special viewpoint.

Some of these implications, bearing on feeling, imagination, and the self, become apparent when one considers ambiguities of the term *egocentricity* applied to the early infant by the cognitive psychologist Jean Piaget and others. These ambiguities arise because the infant behaves as though it is the center of the world but does so in the absence of an ego consolidated as an organ of conscious life. Indeed, at the outset the infant's behavior is in many respects very poorly organized. (Thus any stimulation, including pinching the infant's toe or pulling its hair, elicits the sucking response, which, on the other hand, is not reliably elicited by stimulating its lips.[16]) But in other respects its behavior is well organized indeed. (Thus, a newborn may imitate its mother in sticking its tongue out or fluttering its eyelashes— showing that it recognizes some identity between itself and her. Or it may respond defensively to a representation of an approaching object, though not to one of an approaching hole—showing that the infant has a degree of intersensory coordination.[17]) And so the infant presents an overall picture of organization within disorganization, or disorganization within organization. About this picture it makes sense to say that there is, or has been, a self preceding the ego, though this self is not in the infant alone but is in the mother-infant dyad, within which the mother acts to complement the infant's "helplessness" and egolessness in a way that will help it to thrive.

It is obvious enough that the mother performs ego functions on behalf of the infant. Indeed, the developmental psychologist Kenneth

Kaye has offered a detailed account of the way in which the mother and other adults treat the infant as having more of an ego than it has and of being more capable of shared intentions than it is, as it serves an "apprenticeship" by means of which it is socialized into having a "mind." This occurs because "evolution has produced infants who can fool their parents into treating them as more intelligent than they really are." By playing out this fiction, the parents eventually cause it to become true, and so "the infant does become a person and an intelligent partner in intersubjective communication."[18]

Important as this apprenticeship is in cognitive development, attention to it should not mislead one into regarding "mind" as more conscious throughout all its ranges than it is, and into oversimplifying respects in which self is supraordinate to ego, and is from the outset not only social but also implicitly individual.

One may see the supraordinate character of the self in the way in which, as the analytical psychologist Michael Fordham puts it, "The wholeness of the self becomes represented in the ego in the achievement of unit status" at about the age of two.[19] Moreover, a powerful motive for the independence necessary to realize individuality may be found in the infant's original psychosomatic unity—the "original self" in Fordham's phrase—in which the infant is not related to its mother. "Growing independence can therefore draw on the earliest state of separation which, in spite of states of fusion and identity, persists throughout all maturation."[20]

It is thus an oversimplification to maintain, as some Jungians do, that the mother is a "carrier of the self" of the infant. On the other hand, in important ways creating its mother in its own image, the infant does make her a part of the infant's own self.[21] And the mother-infant relationship is thus the field in which archaic self-representations of various kinds are manifest to the infant. And though these entail separateness, they may give way to fusion again. By self-representations I mean a wide range of infantile experiences that have not reached expression in either image or symbol but that are felt both to be separate from ordinary experience and to refer directly or indirectly to the infant himself. These then "develop into the organized and essentially complex experiences known as self-reliance, self-confidence, self-esteem or the sense of being a person with a continuity and identity in space and time."[22] If such self-representations are treated as real and taken seriously, inferred though they must largely be, it is impossible to see how they can be regarded as the product of the socialization Kaye describes.

Further, the infant may at moments have for the mother the value of the divine child as an image or symbol amounting to a mature self-representation.

In such ways as these, then, self precedes ego and remains supraordinate to it, while fostering its development through the play of proactive unconscious forces.

The egoless egocentricity of the infant assumes an odd aspect in light of the often highly aggressive willfulness of the eighteen- to thirty-six-month-old (in the "terrible twos"). This is a time when the infant's egocentricity is reactively being challenged by its parents, as it challenges their authority. In a sense, its egocentric world is being replaced by a parent-centered one, with the parents serving as representatives of society in a broader sense. And the infant is developing its own resources of ego strength through its confrontations with the larger world it is in the process of joining. But an army cannot mount an attack based on nothing—it must have supplies, reserves, a strategy, and fall-back positions. In a related fashion, the assertiveness of the two-year-old does not emerge out of nowhere but is a culmination of many processes and many experiences making ego nuclei (focused on specific body functions, for example) into a coherent instrument for maintaining that "I am" and "I do"—a complex development involving phases and subphases that have been described and defined in various ways.

The assertiveness I have been describing implies trust—that the infant has a prospect of success or at least of breaking even in squaring off against authority, that it has a claim to a place in the world, and that it will be able to withstand its own aggression and that of others that its own might provoke. It has acquired resources for such trust through successfully mastered upsets of various kinds—as the infant, for example, realizes that it is still intact despite having emotionally fallen apart.

But experience of another, often altogether more peaceful, kind has also contributed. This experience, mediated by the affective climate shared by mother and infant, is of intercommunication, and mutual receptivity and accommodation. Such experience is an important theme of this book, especially as in important ways it points beyond two-year-old assertiveness and styles of later behavior based on it. Such experience fosters the openness necessary to mutuality. (When the prophet proclaims that "a little child shall lead them" [Isa. 11:6], he is surely extolling such openness, rather than asking us to imagine a procession led by a two- to three-year-old in an autocratic frame of mind.) Though Western technological society largely suppresses the capacity for such experience among its adults, adults of other societies retain it, and it is essential to important phenomena of adult life described in each of the following parts of this book.[23]

Part 2 is about the self as an inner authority providing an individual basis for values and valuing. As such a basis, the self enhances and is fulfilled, rather than annulled, by the mutuality and community that are major themes of this book. Concern with the self in this sense requires a discussion of several basic terms (among them *ego*, *self*, *feeling*, *imagination*, *passionate crisis*, and the *pathic ground*). The nature of feeling, in relation to both ego and self, is elucidated through an exploration of medieval concepts of affection.

The unfathomability of the self, of the unconscious, and of the "other"—touched on in my discussion of affection—is psychologically congruous with religious ideas of "the abundance of the heart" and abundant grace. Some meanings of *heart*, biblical and later, are discussed with a view to deepening the treatment of issues raised with regard to feeling as affection in the medieval sense.

Especially important are the seemingly contradictory views that the heart is volatile—emotion is overwhelming and disorienting—and that the heart is rational—emotion is continuous with feeling, which can be ordered and ordering. These views are examined in a way that notes the larger compatibility between them.

The early mother-infant relationship has a bearing on the religious and philosophical themes and the issues of cultural life discussed in part 2. Just as concern with abundance requires one to consider limitation and lack, so concern with the mother-infant relationship as fostering mutuality requires one to consider obstructions to mutuality

22

in the forms of envy, rivalry, and the Oedipus complex. Mutuality is treated as a fundamental resource for psychological development favoring self-validation and values and valuing based on the self.

The mutuality that is one of my main concerns is not, of course, everywhere apparent, also not among mothers and infants. Indeed, there are many disastrous mother-infant relationships that produce disastrous psychological results. But the larger picture of these results is somewhat less thoroughly appalling than one might expect, as they include the survivors of psychological atrocities, the almost-victims who when knocked down insist on getting back up, intent on living and even flourishing. This impression, which should not be romantically exaggerated, is consistent with my understanding of the self as knowing what is good for itself and as containing a disposition to optimal development. Benign fortune is in the ascendant when a "good enough mother," as that invaluable person has been called by the British pediatrician and psychoanalyst D. W. Winnicott, nurtures this self. The self that knows what is good for itself plays a mediating role in the mother-infant relationship. And that relationship, in turn, is essential in shaping modes of relationship between ego and self.

Part 3 is about the musical and poetic art form of the blues, which explores a number of issues raised or implied in part 2. These include the need to remain open to the world, feeling as an activity necessary to survival, and ways in which the mother-infant dyad may properly figure in art celebrating the triumph of individuality and community.

The pathos and irony of the blues, its engagement and detachment from the emotional reality of having the blues, are explored, as are the implications of this artistic process for an understanding of feeling and emotion more generally.

Though the blues is often concerned with such triangles as those created by an unfaithful lover, it is here shown to be ultimately more concerned with ambiguities between threes and kinds of twos that suggest the mother-infant relationship.

The blues is discussed as a form of "talk" in which extraverbal elements effect a transcendence of the verbal content.

A main theme of the blues is abandonment, which is considered in relation to self-alienation, so remote from the self-validation explored in part 2. Grief and rage as emotional responses to abandonment are examined, as is the revitalization of feeling achieved by the blues in a way that resists seduction by wish as false hope.

Part 4 is about psychological issues raised by the universal custom of feasts and feasting. Festival fosters mutuality, and its doing this is fundamental to its nature and to its meaning for those who participate in it. Such mutuality has its prototype in experiences in the mother-infant relationship that are relatively independent of the satisfaction of appetite.

In festival the satisfaction of appetite becomes part of a process of symbolic understanding, enhancing one's sense of mutuality and of the abundance discussed earlier. These qualities can be related psychologically to the self that knows what is good for itself, the characteristics of which are explored in part 4.

Part 5 is about several important psychological and cultural issues posed by the practice of magic of various kinds, and by the often ambiguous relation of magic to religion and science.

Although there are strong grounds for emphasizing the coercive intent of magic, one must also allow that much magic may be compatible with the contemplative aim of much religion—that there may be magical contemplation. Indeed, magic is psychologically important in occurring at the juncture between "participating consciousness"— imaginatively open to the structuring principles at work in the background of consciousness—and willed action. Moreover, magic as a special form of willed action concerned with matters of emotional import draws on resources of both dependence and independence. (One may be dependent upon a magical procedure to further an independent personal end.) In these and other respects the practice of magic elaborates upon concerns of the infant in the first years of life. Exploring the relation between magic and those concerns illuminates some of the strategies adult people develop for dealing with nonego psychic parts of themselves, experiences of destructive force, and the unmasterability of passionate crisis.

Part 6 is about receptivity, commitment, and detachment in the felt and imaginative relations between ego and self.

The African ideal of the cool heart provides an illuminating perspective on images and concepts of the heart discussed in part 2.

Consideration of this ideal leads to an examination of the important distinction between interest on the level of the ego and on that of the self.

Since deep interest has been shaped by mythic forms and images (or archetypes), their power to effect such shaping is treated, along with their frequent failure to effect it. This failure calls attention to relations between mythic forms and images and fantasy and imagination in the individual.

Implications of the cardinal numbers one through four with respect to the felt oneness of mother and infant, and to the relations between distance and distancelessness in the life of feeling, are discussed.

Simple and complex feeling-judgments are examined, especially in their bearing on feeling-toned complexes.

Finally, artistic representations both of disordered feeling and of receptivity are considered in the context of the mother-infant relationship, which remains implicit in our relations to the ego-transcending larger life.

25

2 Being True to Oneself in Abundance and Limitation

2.1 "I," Interconnectedness, and Intimacy

Who is the I that says "I," and how is it reduced, expanded, corrupted, fulfilled by being also the I that says "we"? In what sense is what I feel to be my inner life really mine, since to bring it to expression even to myself I must use shared means that allow communication even while distorting it—as when I just now wanted, but failed, to speak something more intimately myself and more open to relationship than the phrase "my inner life" serves to name?

Is there a form of sharing, of human association, that is neither degrading nor idolatrous, neither presuming indolence, envy, and the urge to depredation as basic to what we are, nor proclaiming the singularity and grandeur of *this* group—a monstrous collective "I"— as it severs itself from nature to become, for example, a community of saints?

How can I pay the price of my fate, treasuring my glimpses of it without being deceived that my transactions with priest, prophet, oracle, or gypsy fortune-teller have secured it as my fully knowable and masterable possession—without being deceived that the price of my fate has anything to do with fees paid such intermediaries, and that their readings of it are more than spottily accurate translation? How can I be imaginative enough still to know, when faced with issues of life and death, that not only the readings of my fate but also my fate itself are poetry—that the fullest apprehension of who I am and of what it means for me to be alive, here and now, is both personal, mine, and yet impersonal, as is a work of art presented not to this person but to a larger audience—indeed to a succession of audiences unimagined by its maker?

How can I remain aware that, despite the shabby compromises and falsifications of purpose made inevitable by my engagement in society, I am, even in and through that engagement, part of a living fabric of interconnectedness? How can I take responsibility for myself, even form myself, as I partly can and must, without coming to believe that I am self-created, and thus trying to tear myself from that living fabric?

How can I properly acknowledge that the truest expression of who and what I most uniquely am is a meeting with another, coming from a great distance, and that this meeting is thus inseparable from myself? How can I keep in mind that in our meeting, in an intimacy closer than I am to myself, this other—as parent, brother, sister, lover, spouse, child, friend, or newly met stranger—remains unnamed, unknown, living on in a knowledge of that distance otherwise closed to me? How can I prepare myself to remember, when doing so will make all the difference, that this meeting—a flower singled out by me alone, for me alone, among all the flowers soon to fade into the void—is the most precious portion of my fate?[1]

2.2 Polonius's Advice

A scheming old windbag exhorts his headstrong son to be true to himself—to be constant and self-consistent—assuring his son that such integrity will inevitably determine his relations with others: "To thine own self be true," and "thou canst not then be false to any man." In separating the two clauses with the grand-sounding but vapid—and oversimplifying—rhetorical flourish of "it shall follow as the night the day," he shows that he does not grasp the deeper meaning of what he is saying—even if his words convey a glimmering awareness that integrity and plain dealing somehow should be high values, despite his own inclinations to deviousness. Far from following as the night the day, the proper form of one's relations to others is partly dictated by one's understanding of one's own self and of how to be true to it, and such understanding is by no means simple and obvious.

Hamlet, who lived as though trying to follow the precept Polonius offered his son, found that he did not have a single self that supported a single course of action in a consistent way. He was true to himself; but he was true to himself in spite of himself, in spite of his wavering

28

understanding of which version of himself to be true to. He was true to himself in realizing that the self to which one should be true is not the complete, static entity assumed by Polonius, and that this self is not as governable by the conscious ego, and not as primarily and simply social, as Polonius took it to be. Rather, Hamlet knew the self to have hidden depths, made known in gradual disclosure, at its own time and in its own ways, a making-known to which the conscious ego must accommodate itself.

Though fully aware of his connectedness with others (mostly alien to him), and though for moments even comparing himself with his friend Horatio and the enigmatic interloper young Fortinbras, Hamlet knew that the self, whatever else it also is, is an individual essence, and that he could act meaningfully to realize that essence—to define it and bring it to expression—only by also contemplating it as a mystery inseparable from the larger mystery of things. He knew that to be true to oneself means to retain a sense of wonder at the fact of being alive, as one's life is made known to one in the reality of the psyche, governed by principles supraordinate to the conscious ego and only partly— although importantly—derived from society.[2] And so he knew that Polonius was right when he made being true to oneself primary and not being false to others secondary.

2.3 "The Natural Man"

Years ago in Himalayan India, where I had been frightened by encounters with roaming bands of bad-tempered, large black-and-white apes, I was returning to the plains on a clanking bus when the uproarious laughter of my Indian fellow-passengers called my attention to a striking sight. It was a man who had painted himself black and white and affixed to himself a rope for a tail, in imitation of the kind of apes that had menaced me. He was alone, trudging down the road, his facial expression betraying nothing about his intent. He was not part of a festival of the familiar kind in which people pretend to revert to their animal natures; surely he did not think that such apes were his totem animal; nor was he part of a circus performance. In the absence of any defining frame, one might guess that he had decided to resign from civilization and return to being what Saint Paul called "the natural man."[3]

Still, what he had done in converting himself into an ape was in the nature of a theatrical performance, even if primarily for himself. Shakespeare dramatized this ambiguity in act IV of *King Lear*. There the mad king encounters the naked Bedlam beggar, Poor Tom, and begins tearing his own clothes off, so that he too can be "the thing itself," "poor unaccommodated man." But the audience knows that this "thing itself" is part of a theatrical performance within which Poor Tom is really Edgar in disguise. Since even his nakedness is a disguise, it is impossible to know what it would mean, Shakespeare would seem to agree, to strip oneself down to the "natural man."

One way of describing this impossibility is to say that we are language-using creatures and that language places us in the world while removing us from it[4]—a formulation that could be extended to all our symbol systems. Still, nature is the source, scene, and context of our actions, and we are obliged to love and respect it—to listen to it and answer to it—if we are not, in our disdain of its fragile, all-embracing structure, to call elemental chaos upon ourselves. Moreover, considering what we are as natural creatures is an important part of defining our potentialities, limits, and aims. King Lear's concern with what he regarded as the natural "thing itself" was part of a process by which he came to a deeper understanding of the meaning of community.

We may translate this estrangement from nature into religious terms and say that it was a fall from grace, a falling away from God. But God is beyond creation and beyond nature in such a way that this translation may be thought to leave the problem created by the estrangement untouched. Estrangement from God, that is to say, is a figure of speech implying a disrupted personal relationship within a social framework. And in relation to that framework, nature is in important respects secondary—as is suggested, for example, when (in Gen. 2:19) God creates the animals and has Adam name them. But as the source, scene, and context of our actions, nature is also primary. As a form of social action, art transcends nature, but nature also transcends art. The storm on the heath is *within* the play *King Lear*— yet there were storms for eons before Shakespeare wrote his play. And art may become the means of our estrangement from nature, when we experience the "artificiality" of art as debilitating—when a landscape is portrayed as "enameled," say, but we need it to be wild and free. And though art molds and enhances feeling, like all other means of such molding and enhancement, art may be used to brutalize mind and heart. (Nazi architecture and socialist realist painting under Stalin explored these potentialities.) When Lear, thinking of the brutality of Goneril and Regan, calls them "unnatural" (II.iv.275), he implies that proper modes of feeling belong not only to our transcendence of nature, through religion and art, but also to our rootedness in it.

The philosopher Jean-Jacques Rousseau (1712–78) was greatly concerned with "the natural man," not in the sense intended by Saint Paul but in the sense of what man is *in* nature, loved and respected as the source, scene, and context of our actions. In a passage in his *Discours sur l'origine et les fondements de l'inégalité parmi les hommes* [Discourse on inequality] (1755), he elaborates on this theme in a way that raises issues of great importance. I will examine them briefly with a view to identifying the main theme of this book.

In a bit of fanciful but illuminating anthropology, Rousseau imagines savages just before they took the first step toward the inequality that characterizes all of the more complex societies. These people were accustomed to singing and dancing unselfconsciously in front of their huts or around a great tree. The step toward inequality came when each of them began to want to be admired by the others, with the result that his sense of self-worth came to be determined by public opinion as to who could sing and dance the best.[5]

Two centuries earlier, another penetrating psychologist, Michel de Montaigne (1533–92), also spoke about the kind of envious emulation that concerned Rousseau, and about its adverse effects on one's activity of valuing. Writing on the subject of "presumption," Montaigne spoke of his inclination to undervalue the things he possessed, simply because he possesses them, and to overvalue anything strange, absent, and not his. He called this inclination *une erreur d'âme*, a "soul error."[6]

From an orthodox Christian perspective, Saint John Chrysostom (345?–407) much earlier expressed a related idea when, in his comments on the prayer "Fill us with the Holy Ghost," he said that "it is not even possible to approve one's self as one ought" unless one is "filled with . . . grace," and that true followers of Christ have not the slightest regard "for the shame that proceeds from the many," though such Christians are greatly concerned to be unashamed and well-pleasing in the sight of the Lord.[7] Such thoughts obviously imply a theology of sin and grace foreign to Rousseau's respect for the "natural man." Still, for Chrysostom as for Rousseau, proper valuation of one's actions proceeds not from a consideration of "the many" but from the relation of the conscious ego to a more fundamental and embracing interior principle.

One cannot, as Lear wanted to do, strip oneself of the clothes of a corrupt and unjust society and thus be "the thing itself." We cannot simply go back to singing and dancing in front of our huts or around a great tree. But Rousseau's myth implies that there is a form of self-validation prior to the envious perversion of desire that came to afflict his singers and dancers, and that this fundamental form of self-validation has been, or could be, the basis of a community of more authentic individuals than they became and that most people now are. Despite the complexities of our lives, it is possible and imperative to know something about this being true to oneself, about the valuing based upon it, and about the kind of community made possible by such being true to oneself and to such valuing.[8] *Feeling* is the name I will use for the psychic process essential to this knowledge of one's individual essence and its reaching out into the world of others. In the following pages I will be concerned not so much with broad social issues as with individual psychology and with intimate interpersonal relations. I will illustrate my theoretical reflections by vignettes from everyday life and from analytic and psychotherapeutic practice, and by works of art and literature.

2.4 Self-Validation and Inner Authority

To validate oneself in the manner of Rousseau's uncorrupted savages is to be supported by an inner authority that is not simply an internalized image of something once imposed from without. It is to be supported by the self, and more specifically by what (in part 4.3) I will call the self that knows what is good for itself. Being aware of this inner authority can have important consequences for practical psychological understanding. This point becomes clear if one compares two possible interpretations of a dream of "Frank MacKay," a lay director of education for a Roman Catholic parish, whose duties include occasional preaching. His wife accuses him of "pontificating" in his interactions with her and with others, and, in his general propensity to feel guilty, he assumes that she is right. He dreams that he is in a pulpit preaching to a congregation that includes Pope John XXIII and Pope John Paul II, and that after the sermon Pope John XXIII comes up to him and greets him warmly. One might think that this dream presents Mr. MacKay as a superpontificator, so pontifical that he has two popes in his audience, and one might wonder about the deficient self-esteem that would call forth such grandiose over-compensation. This would be to regard the dream as concerned with the Father-World of authority and the exercise of power, and indeed Mr. MacKay has had problems with father figures, authority, and power.

If Mr. MacKay had been pontificating, however, the dream could have made clear that this was so, and it did not. The fact that it did not might encourage us to regard it rather as depicting his gaining access to his own inner authority. The popes, of course, are figures in the collective, social world. Still, their authority is spiritual, that is, based on their appeal to what one regards as the innermost and most valuable dimension of the human person, one's sense of that dimension being a primary component of whatever allegiance one feels toward those figures. The dream presents the possibility of a direct contact between Mr. MacKay and them, without mediation from the pastor, the head of the parish PTA, or the officious parish secretary, all of whom have figured in power problems causing Mr. MacKay to feel that the domain of his duties has been infringed upon, while they have felt that he has exceeded that domain. An analogy to the way in which the two popes could symbolize Mr. MacKay's own inner authority is offered by an occasion on which a normally quite good European orchestra played superbly, with its members knowing that Arturo Toscanini was in the audience. Although Toscanini, like the popes, was a figure in the collective, social world, he presumably had the effect of constellating in the orchestra members their best musical selves, from which and for which they then played.

The dream's duplication of the popes might represent a differentiation, a dawning awareness in Mr. MacKay that the authority he had assumed to be unitary (one pope), in actuality has more than one aspect (two popes). Significantly, one pope, John Paul II, is the current pontiff, whereas the other, John XXIII, is the pope Mr. MacKay finds most compatible with his own hopes for the Church. Thus John Paul II might represent Mr. MacKay's adaptation to the actual state of affairs, whereas John XXIII might represent Mr. MacKay's commitment to his own perspective on that state of affairs. The primacy of the value represented by Pope John XXIII is shown by his warmly greeting Mr. MacKay after his sermon. In a dream touching on issues of power and authority, the two popes are harmonious. And importantly in this regard, although they are patriarchs, they are servants of Mother Church, which has a stability and continuity expressive of the flow of life persisting steadily beneath perturbations of ecclesiastical politics and disputes about what the Church's teaching should be.

Is truth something personal that I find or claim using my own resources, my own experience—something of which I am in some sense the *author*, a word cognate with *authority*? Or is it something that I accept on the basis of my trust in an institution or another person? These questions are by no means mutually exclusive. The philosopher Michael Polanyi, for example, has remarked that in science opinion is "not held by any single human mind, but . . . is held by a multitude of individuals, each of whom endorses the others' opinion at second hand, by relying on the consensual chains which link him to all the others through a sequence of overlapping neighbourhoods."[9] Still, the issue of inner authority may assume forms that are clear indeed and very important, bearing as they do on the integrity of the self.

This was the case in the relationship between Freud and Jung insofar as it entailed questions regarding the final basis of the truth value of psychoanalysis.[10] Freud founded psychoanalysis to an important extent on the basis of his own fantasy experiences and his own interpretation of them (his "self-analysis"), and then elevated that interpretation to the status of an orthodoxy binding for all further interpretation of psychic life. Jung was compelled by his own powerful fantasy experiences to realize that their content was so unlike Freud's that they did not support Freud's interpretive argument, and indeed that their content demanded a different conception of the nature of fantasy. For Jung, fantasy became "the clearest expression of the specific activity of the psyche. It is, pre-eminently, the creative activity from which the answers to all answerable questions come; it is the mother of all possibilities, where, like all psychological opposites, the inner and outer worlds are joined together in living union. Fantasy it was and ever is which fashions the bridge between the irreconcilable claims of subject and object."[11]

That "fantasy" here is the bearer of qualities that I, and that Jung elsewhere, would attribute rather to imagination need not concern us, as the difference between the two terms must be relative. What is important in this passage is that fantasy-imagination is made basic to our experience in such a way that it is implicitly an expression of the self with its structuring and authenticating powers. By "authenticating" I mean that the self has an authority that can with no more legitimacy be abrogated by the will of another than it can by the will of one's own ego. While granting that many of Freud's insights are of fundamental importance, I am persuaded that with regard to this basic issue Jung was right and Freud was wrong.

Jung remarks, "The relationship of the individual to his fantasy is very largely conditioned by his relation to the unconscious in general, and this in turn is conditioned in particular by the spirit of the age."[12] Since fantasy and interpretation are linked—as both Freud and Jung make clear—theory must be allowed to develop in the way Polanyi describes as being governed by "mutual authority."[13] For Freud, authority could not be made mutual. I conceive of "self" as inseparable from "mutuality," and I take the self in mutuality as the deepest basis of what (in part 1) I called "doing theory" as distinct from applying it.

Freud, through his interpretations, tried to maneuver Jung into reenacting the oedipal parricide, with Freud as the victim—at least to the extent of revealing that Jung harbored parricidal impulses toward him. In refusing this interpretation and the authority seeking to impose it, Jung appealed to the deeper, preoedipal authority of the self as manifested in the mother-infant bond. The mutuality of this bond is the basis of all later experiences of mutuality. And one of the transformations of the mother-infant relationship is the mutual authority Polanyi deems necessary to empirical science.

The two popes of Frank MacKay's dream offer a telling image of Polanyi's "overlapping neighbourhoods" of mutual authority, while also implying that the principle of hierarchy—essential to language and inevitable in social life—may operate in ways that encourage the creation of complex feeling-judgments (discussed in parts 2.5 and 6.9)—John Paul II, representing current actuality, in conjunction with John XXIII, representing a "mythic" ideal. Significantly, too, the embodiments of this principle (the popes) support the workings of the ego (Mr. MacKay's preaching), not by inflating it but by reminding it of its responsibility to a wider and deeper order (the self), of which the dream gives a symbolic reminder sympathetic to the purposes of the ego in the world.

2.5 Some Terms Bearing on Feeling, Imagination, and the Self

A brief summary of some special terms used in this book—and others related to them—may help to clarify the concerns informing it.

In describing the "self" (in part 1) as a principle of organization (and disorganization) supraordinate to the ego, I implicitly attributed centrality to it—one possible meaning of "supraordinate" being more nearly central, or more expressive of what is central. Other metaphors for the self as thus supraordinate—for example, the self as the vital core of the personality—also imply centrality. And in describing the self (in part 1) as the person regarded as a more comprehensive entity than that centered in the conscious ego, I also implicitly attributed totality to it: the self is the whole person. This second way of speaking immediately requires the proviso that this totality cannot be bounded, except hypothetically. This is because dynamically real regions of the unconscious psyche (and of the body from which it is inseparable) are inaccessible to the conscious discrimination—at least by their personal subject—and because the self, as active principle, is oriented toward future developments that are part of the emerging totality but cannot now be known. Moreover, metaphors implying centrality, such as "vital core," might be thought to name something fixed and stable, which the self, in all the senses in which I use the term, is not.

To summarize my comments on the difficulties of the concept: the self, a transcendental postulate, is unknowable in itself; but it can be known directly through what are in German called *Hinweise*, hints, as to its character—as revealed in dreams, for example. Such knowl-

edge is for the most part nonempirical, uncertain, and provisional—
it is imaginative knowledge in process, always to be qualified by "as
if." And yet such knowledge is precious. Any reader discouraged by
my description of its seeming capriciousness would do well to recall
the remarks by Daumal and Proust (discussed in part 1) that would
dissuade one from trying to define the most central, deepest, or fullest
aspects of one's person in terms that would satisfy the rational intellect.
Daumal and Proust treasure the hints that make up the most that we
have of self-knowledge.

In lived experience the self has, at moments, the character of an
agent: the self acts upon one (while being the person it acts upon).
Further, the self is in important respects evaluative. The self as evaluative, in relation to conscious and unconscious feeling, is a major
theme of this book.

By "ego," as distinct from self, I mean (as I have remarked in part
1) those psychic elements to which the felt sense of "I" and "mine"
attaches. ("I am here"; "I perceive this"; "I understand this"; "I am
doing this"; "this is mine.") Yet this shorthand definition does not
accomplish very much, as is evident when one considers the seeming
contradiction that arises when one regards the ego in this way. (The
reader may recall what I said in part 1 about the ego as experiential
concept, not strictly definable.) Further, many workings of the ego
are not known to itself. (A pianist does not know exactly how he
plays the piano, and cannot directly communicate his knowledge of
piano-playing to a student.) One may say about this state of affairs
that the ego has unconscious regions, or that it knows certain things
"tacitly."[14] On the other hand, the ego in its developed form has the
capacity for responsible reflection. This seeming contradiction is in
some measure resolved, however, when one considers that though "I"
perceive, perception is largely an unconscious process. Both things
can be true: the feeling activity "I" do can retain connections with
more autonomous "feelings" and with emotional currents from the
pathic ground, and responsible reflection can open the ego to the
supraordinate self.

The relationship between ego and self is mutual and sometimes
manifestly dialectical. This means that what the ego thinks, feels,
decides, does, has reverberations within the psychic totality that issue

37

in some sort of response—for example, a dream that comments on the attitude of the ego in such a way as to replace it within a broader perspective. Ego and self may act on behalf of one another in various ways—for example, in the form of an "emergency ego"[15]—that may, without the person's conscious awareness, act to save his life (as we will see in part 4.4).

When I say that "I" am or do this or that, I am convinced that I know what I mean by "I," even though a depth psychologist, poet, Eastern metaphysician, or even a teacher of Philosophy 101 might instill doubt by persuading me that my conviction oversimplifies a complex state of affairs. This doubt would quickly fade, however, as I continued the business of living my life, unless the doubt ceased being a mere intellectual quandary and brought me to a different affective and emotional way of experiencing the world. In such ways "ego" is problematic. And "self" is vastly more so. Indeed, having called self an experiential concept, I must go far toward taking this assertion back—as I have already done in my comments on Daumal and Proust—by also insisting that the self is not experienceable in itself, but is known in intimations.

The ambiguity of the self has often been expressed in religious terms. Thus, Saint Paul declares, "For now we see through a glass, darkly; but then face to face: now I know in part; but then shall I know even as also I am known" (1 Cor. 13:12). I do not now see God face to face—do not have direct knowledge of the self—though signs of God's love, wrath, grace, etc., may be of paramount importance to me. I may honor those shifting patterns of events, dreams, quirks of fate that call to me as though from the hidden center of myself, requiring of me modification of consciousness in answer to a deeper questioning of who I am and what my life is about. The resulting knowledge cannot be called empirical, since it is qualified by the imaginative proviso "as if"—"I pledge myself to this or that bit of uncertainty as if it were certain"—though I may accept such knowledge as the soundest guide to how to live my life.

Further, as Jung has said, the self "is the smallest of the small, easily overlooked and pushed aside. Indeed, it is in need of help and must be perceived, protected, and as it were built up by the conscious mind, just as if it did not exist at all and were called into being only through man's care and devotion." On the other hand, "older than the ego . . . it is actually the secret *spiritus rector* of our fate." And manifest in "a situation within which the ego is contained . . . the self cannot be localized in an individual ego-consciousness, but acts like a circumambient atmosphere to which no definite limits can be set, either in space or in time."[16]

Such statements may seem regrettably paradoxical to logical reason; and indeed, Jung presents them as paraphrases of utterances employing the vocabulary of soul and spirit. But in lived experience, the self is not at special pains to accord with logical reason, and does participate in modes of reality that the vocabulary of soul and spirit was created to describe. The phenomenology of the self in lived experience is to be found in imaginative products that require imagination to apprehend them.

There is another reason, too, why one sees the self darkly. This is that the self, though it is the broadest organizing principle of psychic life, also manifests itself in disorganization. ("Deintegration" of the self will be discussed later in this section.) One can invoke another religious figure of speech to express the potentiality of the self for disorganization and for being known in disorganization: "The wind bloweth where it listeth" (John 3:8). The wind inspires, enlivens, but also blows things about and may indeed become the whirlwind used in various biblical texts to describe the sudden attack of an invader or the divine judgment.

Indefinite, shifting, and inexplicable as our emotional natures are in lived experience, it should not be surprising that theories of "feeling and emotion" make up the most confused subfield within psychology. Indeed, something of the current state of affairs may be suggested by the fact that the six authors of an excellent recent survey of the subject agree at the outset that their project would be foredoomed if they were to try to settle on a definition of "emotion," and despite their attempts at completeness, they forego consideration of some important views.[17] Therefore, in the following pages I do not try to employ a single, rigorously self-consistent vocabulary of terms for "feeling and emotion," for to do so would mean not making use of the views of some

important students of the subject, many of whom use terms in contradictory ways. Here I wish to comment on some of the relevant
terms only to the end of clarifying my own viewpoint.

Affect, affection, and *affectivity* are often used to name a mode of
mental functioning distinct from conation (impelling or directing mus-
cular or mental effort) and cognition (perceiving or knowing), and as
a class name for feeling, emotion, mood, and temperament. As the
form *affection* in everyday speech suggests, these words often imply a
reaction to something as liked or disliked. *Affectivity* may be used as
a synonym of *emotionality* or *emotion* as the general condition of being
emotional. Jung seems to have been using the word in this sense when
he wrote, in 1907, that the "essential basis of our personality is affectivity," "feeling, sentiment, emotion, affect"—remarking that he
was taking the term from the psychiatrist Paul Eugen Bleuler, for whom
it meant "not only affects in the proper sense, but the slight feelings
or feeling-tones of pleasure and unpleasure in every possible circum-
stance."[18] It makes sense that affectivity—with its implications of
liking and not liking—and emotionality or emotion should at least
overlap, since emotion plays an important part in the evaluative system
of the organism. (Rage or fear evaluate something as deserving to be
attacked or fled; disgust at the smell of spoiled food evaluates it as not
to be eaten.) The same reason may be presumed for Jung's frequent
use of the word affect to mean strong emotion, as in "a burst of affect."

"Affects" have been described as object-related, in contrast to
moods, which "seem to represent . . . a cross-section through the
entire state of the ego, lending a particular, uniform coloring to all
its manifestations for a longer or shorter period," unrelated "to a
specific content or object."[19] Still, even if the word *mood* is used in
this way, the ego does not create its moods. They are, rather, expressions of relations between the ego and affectivity as the "essential
basis of our personality." And moods do enter into our grasp of objects.
Even if certain qualities of emotional life may be "unintentional," to
use the expression of the phenomenological philosophers, these are
continuous with, and interrelated with, those that are "intentional,"
that are part of the way in which consciousness creates its contents.
I mean by these observations to deny that our experience of the world

is of some kind of objectivity to which we subjectively and emotionally respond in a secondary way.

"Feelings" I understand as emotional qualities experienced as ego-syntonic, or at least as nonthreatening to the ego, either because they are mild (a slight feeling of annoyance) or because they accord with values to which the person is strongly committed (a deep feeling of love for one's child, a strong feeling of revulsion against a murderer's callousness).

"Feeling" in the title of this book, however, has another meaning. I understand feeling as a distinct mode of consciousness—a *function* of consciousness, as Jung called it. It evaluates in the forming, maintaining, and breaking of relationships on behalf of the ego. I am here using *relationship* to mean eros-connectedness, and I am assuming that the ego can be related in this sense to intrapsychic contents and processes—including ideas—as well as to persons and objects in the outer world.

Since this use of the term *eros* makes love cognitive, I should point out that both Plato and Aristotle regarded desire or love as the basis of all cognition. Thus, in the first sentence of the *Metaphysics* Aristotle claims that "all men by nature *desire* to know" (italics added); indeed, in a passage presenting the basis of his theory of knowledge, he employs the term eros to describe the action of the First Mover, or God, in moving the universe as a whole—that is, in creating it and keeping it going.[20] Love plays a related role in Saint Thomas Aquinas's account of man's quest for the higher forms of truth, and Dante regarded love as the ultimate motive of poetic creation, which was a means of bringing to expression the essential forms of human experience. These views caution against relegating eros to biological drives and regarding feeling as merely idiosyncratically subjective. Rather, feeling can be thought to aspire, from the outset, to universal values known personally through love.

Feeling relates the ego to the pathic ground and so to self, its evaluative aspect. By "pathic ground" I mean the indissoluble rootedness of our experience in emotionality that is ultimately unconscious and always at least semiautonomous with respect to conscious volition. In being *unergründlich*, unfathomable, it is itself a ground. It is pathic because it is the basis of the unconscious empathy found among humans as well as in infrahuman species—as when a school of fish suddenly rush in the same direction. This empathy (which I refer to in part 5.4 as "the conviviality of the native mind") develops in turn into the less instinctive and more culturally molded process of sympathy. (Mothers sympathize with their infants; warriors and cannibals do and do not sympathize with their victims.) The pathic ground is the basis of emotional life. It is also a fundamental aspect of the self, since all knowledge of the self is emotional.

In some of its basic operations, the conscious ego aims at mastery; yet, in Freud's graphically simple formulation, it is not master in its own house. This means that the conscious ego must relate to vital currents impinging upon it or flowing into it from the pathic ground, but it cannot command them, cannot reduce them to static counters to be used in support of its own purposes, and may often be uncertain as to what these vital currents are about. Such ambiguity occasions passionate crisis. By "passionate crisis" I mean the play of vital currents from the pathic ground as these require the constant accommodation of the ego, entailing its partial disintegration and the sacrifice of some of its contents so that it can attend to others. This is analogous to the perceptual field, parts of which are constantly sacrificed or torn away in the process of attending to new contents. I intend the seeming paradox that passionate crisis is a continuous, sometimes acute, component of conscious awareness. (The night before the battle of Agincourt, described in Shakespeare's *Henry V*, was a time of crisis, though it consisted largely of waiting. The Cuban missile crisis of 1962 went on for several days of signaling and seeking to read intentions.) Passionate crisis is fundamental to the ego's structuring and restructuring of itself in some sort of felt or unfelt relation to the self.

Though with a somewhat different emphasis, much of what I mean by passionate crisis is what Fordham means by deintegration. Fordham hypothesizes a primary self that deintegrates at about the time of birth in a way that allows the infant to come into relation with its mother. This development lays down a pattern in which deintegrative and reintegrative phases repeatedly succeed one another—for example, in the deintegrative excitement of the infant in a vigorous feed, which is then followed by a reintegrative sleep.[21] In the course of this development (as I have maintained in part 1), the infant partly creates its mother in its own image. The mother thus becomes a "deintegrate" of the self.

One implication of this view is entirely and importantly in keeping with a main emphasis of this book: deintegration is a normal part of the life of the self, which means that the self implicitly suffuses dein-tegrative phases. Consequently these result only in extreme cases in what psychoanalysts, especially those influenced by the psychoanalyst Melanie Klein, call "splitting."[22] While concerned with these, pas-sionate crisis also calls attention to emotional phenomena perceived more microscopically. For example, I encounter someone who seems familiar, though I cannot remember when or where I have known him, and I am unaccountably troubled by something in his manner—is it malicious or simply bumbling? This perception might be regarded as a moment of passionate crisis, though not involving a larger move-ment of either ego or self. So, too, poetic metaphor might express passionate crisis without altering the position of ego or self in a fun-damental way. Thus, when King Lear's Fool remarks, "So out went the candle, and we were left darkling" (I.iv.218), he gives a glimpse of perhaps even universal dissolution, though his doing so is consistent with his banter throughout this part of the play, though Lear does not seem to notice the remark, and though it is not a particularly climactic detail for the audience.

An adept in one of the martial arts knows that life is full of potential and real danger demanding vigilance, that to hunch down centered within oneself is to be a sitting duck surrounded by hunters, that one must therefore constantly move or be ready to move, that to move is to enter disequilibrium, and that one must therefore also constantly find and lose and refind one's center in disequilibrium. By analogy, emotion—as passionate crisis expressive of the pathic ground—gen-erates life-furthering disequilibrium and is necessary to the finding and losing and refinding of one's center within it. Feeling in one of its fundamental aspects is the sensibility that values in a potentially dif-ferentiated way the finding, losing, and refinding of one's center in disequilibrium. This valuing extends with equal force to one's rela-tionship with the "other"—potentially both partner and opponent—inseparable from one's center, as the martial artist knows.

43

In view of these complexities, feeling is emotional but not syn-onymous with emotion. The expression *emotional intuition* used by some phenomenological philosophers to describe valuing—with emotion being a quality, perhaps in some senses secondary, of the process—may convey this distinction. There is, I assume, a distance, often slight, between feeling and emotion. The physiological psychologist Magda B. Arnold, concerned with such matters as brain circuitry, describes feeling as a "fruit of perception," an "affective experience," based on a form of sensory appraisal preceding evaluation and emotion.[23]

Attending not to physiology but to subjective qualities of lived experience, phenomenological philosophers and psychologists, among them Mikel Dufrenne, describe feeling as an ongoing process distinct from emotion.[24] Feeling, for example, reads a situation or event as horrible; the emotional reaction to this reading is to be horrified. I understand feeling as such an ongoing process.

Feeling is also concerned with the discrimination of emotional currents in relation to contents that can also be apprehended non-emotionally—for example, ideas. Such discrimination is necessary, first, because emotion can be blinding and confusing, and can over-whelm feeling as a capacity of the ego; and second, because emotion can supply feeling with valid information. (For some people in some situations, to know that they are angry is an accomplishment, if ru-dimentary, of feeling. To know what they are angry about, in its larger ramifications, is a further accomplishment of the same kind.) The reading accomplished by feeling also encompasses artistic and other expressive qualities—those of a spring landscape, for example—that are not emotional in any specifiable way.

Feeling aims at maintaining the integrity of the subjective sphere. By the "subjective sphere" I mean ego and self in relation to whatever psychic contents and processes are constellated as significant to them at a particular moment or over a period of time. In speaking of its "integrity," I pose this as a desideratum in relation to various forms of integration and disintegration discussed in these pages. (The reader may recall Rousseau's notion of self-validation.)

With the maintenance of this integrity as its aim, differentiated feeling as a function of the ego takes the requirements of community into account, though often ignoring or rejecting a specific form of community (as did Martin Luther [1483–1546] at Wittenberg, for example, with his theses).

It might be thought that any well-developed form of conscious functioning that smoothly serves adaptation would serve the integrity of the subjective sphere. Yet such a function may also be one-sided in a way that violates this integrity. When any form of conscious functioning—thinking, for example—is called upon and fails, emotion results, with implications for feeling that have already been suggested.

Feeling makes simple and complex feeling-judgments. Simple feeling-judgments are global. When feeling is differentiated, its simple feeling-judgments are adapted and appropriate, as when one simply loves someone or something worthy of love, with this worthiness determined by real qualities of the person or thing realistically assessed, and by an optimal relation between the ego and self of the loving subject. Such a simple feeling-judgment—made by differentiated feeling—must be contrasted with such a judgment as "my country right or wrong," though both express convictions. Complex feeling-judgments allow for various factors to be weighed in accordance with various scales within an attitude that is open yet self-consistent.

Complex feeling-judgments are not expressions of the feeling-toned complexes described by Jung, though these are important in psychic life (and will be discussed in part 6.9). A "complex" in this sense is a bundle of psychic material of various kinds—images, memories, ideas—bound together by a common feeling-tone. There is no danger of confusion, since in the following pages the adjective *complex* always means not simple, whereas the noun *complex* always means a feeling-toned bundle of psychic material. It should be noted that the "feeling-tone" of a feeling-toned complex has no direct relation to the function of feeling as described above.

In keeping with what I have said about the integrity of the subjective sphere, when feeling is differentiated it is especially concerned with gradations, transitions, continuity, and coherence. This is true in its aspects both of relationship and judgment. What I mean may be suggested by a negative example: a novelist stuck in her writing has a tantrum in which she burns her manuscript, then resentfully throws the books of other authors into the fire. The next day she reports what has happened matter-of-factly, though with a bid for sympathy, as though she were the victim of someone else's abuse. Despite what she takes to be the depth of her feeling, her actions are incoherent and disregard continuity, gradations, transitions.

Much of psychic life can be said to be intentional in the sense of being purposive, goal-directed. Feeling plays a special role in this intentionality and in our coming to conscious awareness of it. Our awareness of it is affective or affectional, and feeling plays an important part in registering it. (I will discuss "affection" in part 2.6.)

Affective awareness of psychic intentionality is grounded in the self as the ultimate source and agent of the homeostatic, self-balancing tendencies of the psyche. This assumes that the psyche is a communications system with various arrangements whereby feedback serves self-monitoring and self-correcting purposes, and that much communication within this system is affective. The system monitors itself to a great extent through what could be called a primitive and unconscious protoform of conscious feeling. (Thus the psychotic individuals to be considered in part 4.4, whose conscious egos are largely disintegrated, will be seen to behave in purposive ways defined by affective currents shaping what could be called global feeling-judgments.)

Such feeling on the level of the self is to be distinguished from feeling as a mode of conscious awareness, though self-feeling—part of the communications system of the psyche—is in important ways the basis of conscious feeling. I see no strong objection to using the same term, *feeling,* for processes on two levels, of ego and of self, that are in some manifestations very distinct. My reason for this lies in the special and ambiguous role that feeling—or affection—may play in conscious self-knowledge—knowledge in which there are intimations of the nature and purposes of the self. (That conscious feeling can develop, and that it can be differentiated, in ways that result in blindness to the self and in unrelatedness and blundering judgments of value, proves only that anything can be perverted, and that the same soil may nurture related but antagonistic developments.) In short, the self as the matrix of the ego is also the matrix of feeling as I have been using that term, and there are manifestations of psychic intentionality that in archaic ways (to be discussed in part 4.4) fulfill some important purposes of feeling, though in absence of a developed ego.

Being True to Oneself in Abundance and Limitation

The ultimate indistinguishability of feeling, emotion, and self in lived experience is well illustrated by the film *Invasion of the Body Snatchers* (1956), in which vegetable pods from outer space one-by-one form living replicas of individual human beings. These replicas have all the characteristics of the people they replace except genuine feelings and emotions and such signs of genuine individuality (and the self) as fingerprints. Imagination and feeling of the still fully human characters and audience are horrified (emotion) at the determined efforts of the pod people to reduce the human vital core to apathy and human freedom to the condition of a robot.

Here I would pause to note that individuality is rooted in a special way in the mother-infant relationship. For example, the wife of one couple who had for years wanted children had a miscarriage. And after they had in some measure mastered their hurt and disappointment, the husband wanted to regard their misfortune as a momentary setback and to go on trying to produce a baby. But she was restrained by her grief about the loss of what she felt to be not a fetus but the real, individual child she had been carrying. The husband recognized in his desire to press ahead undaunted an echo of the masculine biological strategy of emitting a rush of innumerable spermatozoa in search of a single ovum produced in the course of a month. And he recognized in the grief of his wife an affective awareness that for a woman each possibility of conception implies the possibility of years of commitment and personal relationship.

The husband of another couple, whose child died in its third year, also wanted to make up for the loss by trying immediately to produce another baby, but his wife, too, was restrained by her grief. The story of this second couple was recounted to a woman who spends every day and every night surrounded by babies, as she runs a day-care center and is herself the mother of four children and the grandmother of five. Generalizing from the story, she commented, "No single one of them can ever be replaced." The Father World shapes individuality in important ways, but it is nourished first by mothers who carry and care for their babies with the implicit feeling that no single one of them can ever be replaced. And so, although in important respects it originates in the infant, the self that knows what is good for itself (discussed in part 4.3) is also mediated by the mother feeling strongly about the individual value of her baby. (And this early nourishment of individuality presupposes, in turn, a woman's affective attunement to the reality of her own body.)

Since this book does not have as its main purpose a critical exposition of Jungian theory, I stress my agreement with Jung's views of these matters or my modification or restatement of his views only when such explicitness would further my discussion of the topic at hand.[25] My term *the pathic ground*, I should add, was suggested by the German psychologist Viktor von Weizäcker, who speaks of *das Pathische*, and whose description of it entails the notion of crisis.[26]

One may begin to distinguish between "fantasy" and "imagination" by saying that fantasy is present in states in which there is awareness of only a single reality—this being true of most dreams. Such states are conflict-free (though themes of conflict may be expressed in them). Imagination, in contrast, involves the interaction of conscious and unconscious processes, and of emotional urgency and such conscious functions as thinking and remembering, along with an awareness that we are living in a multidimensional world needing to be viewed in more than one perspective.[27] Imagination differs from fantasy, further, in being more pronouncedly an expression of the interaction between ego and self, and in more pronouncedly engaging feeling.

This view of imagination is congruent with the conflict model of psychic life dominant in the mainstream of psychoanalysis derived from Freud. And this model accords with the emphasis on deintegration and passionate crisis in this book and with Jung's own tendency (discussed in part 6.5) to think in polaristic terms. In much of his theorizing, however, Jung implies a model of psychic life better conveyed by the metaphors of growth and unfolding. Thus, for example, he speaks of the "evolving self" or the "entelechy" or formative disposition "of the self."[28] And he often describes fantasy or imagination in a way that emphasizes not conflict but self-expression and integration. Thus, for example, active fantasy is "the product of a conscious attitude *not* opposed to the unconscious, and of unconscious processes not opposed but merely compensatory to consciousness," and imagination is "not a special faculty," but "the reproductive or creative activity of the mind in general."[29] But division and unity imply one another, and the infant dreaming of threatening animals may at another time yield itself up to joy with Mother. And so these two ways of viewing imagination—focusing on conflict or integration—amount to complementary emphases. (These complementary aspects of imagination will be clearly evident in my discussion of fantasy, imagination, and symbol-formation in part 6.3.)

2.6 Affection, Will, and Imagination

In their use of the term *affectus,* related to our term *affection,* Saint Bernard of Clairvaux and his fellow ecclesiastic William of Saint Thierry (d. 1148?) call attention to important psychological phenomena neglected in recent discussions of feeling and emotion. Two implications of their use of the term are especially important.

First, Bernard's and William's use of the term *affectus* implies that emotional reality is fundamentally a matter of relations between ego and self—in the language of these writers, between the soul and God— and only then of relations between the person and "objects" of the real world. (Aware of the oddity of this way of speaking, I am for the moment following numerous psychoanalysts in employing the term "objects" to mean not only things but also persons important to one.)

To grant primacy to inner authority, as I do, and as I think Bernard and William do, is to assume that inner reality is in important respects nonderivative, and that persons important to one are not just value-invested "objects" but are, rather, fellow subjects with resources of value derived from what I have called the primarily given. That our relation to the world of other persons and things is also essential, and that what is given is given largely by and through them, does not diminish the primary importance of this inner authority and its activity of valuing.

Second, Bernard's and William's use of the term *affectus* implies something notable about the complex interrelations among feeling, imagination, and will, and between ego and self.

With these thoughts in mind, let us consider some shades of meaning these two writers seek to convey by means of a term that, owing to its subtlety and complexity, some translators of the writers have declined to translate.

Commenting on a verse from the Song of Songs, "My Beloved is mine and I am his" (2:16), Bernard remarks that "it is the *affectus,*

49

not the intellect, which has spoken, and it is not for the intellect to grasp," adding that currents of the *affectus* "have their own language, in which they disclose themselves." The *affectus* is the focus of such emotional states as grief and fear, originating in "spontaneous impulses" presumably not under the control of the will. Yet there is also an inward, supersensible, affective contemplation of God, which does involve the will.[30] Owing to this ambiguity, the relation of affection (*affectus*) to will is for Bernard of primary importance.

In Bernard's view will is essentially a rational faculty. Still, reason is not itself sufficient to prompt one to will the good. For this, grace is required, and grace touches on affection in a special way. Grace "sets in order what creation has given, so that virtues are nothing else but ordered affections," which, when ordered, are qualities of willing the good. This account accords with observations not difficult to make, that when the will is not overweening or deranged and defective it is likely to be feeble, and that it is difficult to do the good, however defined, without a wanting, striving, emotional commitment to it. One could say that to do the good it must engage one's feeling, or, with almost equal justice, that to do the good it must engage one's imagination. Thus it is not surprising that *affectus* embraces much of what we mean by feeling and imagination.

As Bernard points out, Christ taught men the proper form of willing by praying that the cup pass from him but then vowing submission to the will of God.[31] Though the will of God may seem irrational in the sense that it does not accord with the ego's unaided understanding of what is proper for it to desire, it is also rational in the sense that to conform to it is to order the affections.

Part of Bernard's meaning is captured in a psychological translation that takes grace and the will of God to be movements of the self, in response to which the ego must open. Indeed, the movement of the self and the opening of the ego are complementary aspects of the same process of understanding, since the ego must voluntarily open itself or forcibly be opened for movements of the self to be apprehended. As a result, the ego knows itself to be subordinate to something that exceeds its will and that may oppose its purposes.

One way to see how volitional tendencies opposing the purposes of the ego may represent movements of the self is to consider the "higher powers" represented by the relatively autonomous intrapsychic processes and contents called "complexes." As Jung remarks, "Everyone knows nowadays that people 'have complexes,' " but it "is not so well known . . . that complexes can *have us*," to which the analytical psychologist Jolande Jacobi adds, "And yet this is the crucial point on which we must gain clarity if we are to counter the prevailing smug faith in the supremacy of will and of ego-consciousness with the doubt it deserves."[32]

Complexes can create disturbances of will—for example, in slips of the tongue and other instances of what Freud called "the psychopathology of everyday life," and in a vast array of more strictly psychopathological symptoms. That complexes can do this should remind us that active and passive are in general ambiguously relative in lived experience. This is particularly true in the flow of imagination—a lifeless stone becomes a magical talisman, or a magical talisman becomes a lifeless stone—and in the flow of feeling. Of special significance are the ambiguous interrelations of active and passive in the receptivity of imagination and feeling that allow movements of the self to be glimpsed, or, in religious terms, allow the will of God to be known. The term *affectus* conveys an awareness of these ambiguous interrelations, which can be seen in its etymology.

Affectus can mean such things as "state, disposition, mood, feeling, passion, emotion." But it is derived from the Latin verb *afficere*—"to do to, to act on, to influence, to put to, to attach to." This verb derives from *ad* + *facere*—"to" + "to do" or "to make." Thus the noun (*affectus*, "affection") has a largely passive signification—it is formed from the past participle, "having been acted upon"—but its etymology highlights the active component in it, and suggests how *affectus* is linked with the doing, originating faculty of will.

We should not be surprised that *affectus* has both active and passive implications, since in much of lived experience active is transformed into passive and passive into active in ways that do not accord well with the syntactical form: subject / active verb / direct object. With regard to feeling, it would sometimes be preferable not to say "I feel this," but rather something like "I am being felt into this and it is being felt into me"—as when I am suffused by the "mood" of a tree or street. Imagination reveals the same ambiguity, as we see if we

51

compare a frightening obsessive fantasy—of which one feels oneself the passive victim—with glancing at a loved one and feeling the sight to be as freeing as it is compelling. (Note, incidentally, that I spontaneously used the word *feeling* in describing being imaginatively stirred by the glance.)

For William of Saint Thierry, *affectus* is the basis of what we would call mystical experience, as it is of the form of contemplation most highly favored by Bernard. Both writers describe an affective mystical union of the soul with God. In the broadest terms, according to one scholar, *affectus* is for William the "basic impulse to reach toward what is good." *Affectus* is regarded as being "at the center of human attitudes yet incorporating 'something more than,' 'something over and above' the human." "Because it is at the center of our life, [the *affectus*] can clothe itself in the various nuances of the powers (virtues) and faculties of our soul," so that "in its tending to goodness, the *affectus* can be a movement of piety, or perception, or faith, or hope, or love, or thought, or will, and so on."[33]

According to another commentator, "*Affectus* relates to the soul's ascent towards God (man is active)," but "it also serves to designate the condescending grace of God, who stoops to the soul . . . (so that man, in a sense, is passive)." Owing to the connection between the *affectus* and the Holy Spirit, "One may say that in the *affectus* God works in us and we cooperate in this divine action."[34]

This account strikingly suggests (in a rough psychological translation) that the most fundamental connection between ego and self is one of feeling and imagination, and that there is in this connection a striving for a realization of potentialities expressing the dynamism of a self that knows what is good for itself. That this realization comes about in ways that are anything but simple—indeed, that almost surely entail obstacles, setbacks, defeats, and forced detours—says nothing against the view that it originates in an intrinsic striving. An ailing friend maintains that one should ask of any illness not what caused it but what it is trying to make one do—how it is asking one to change one's life to the end of realizing neglected potentialities and thus of exploring new aspects of what is good for oneself. This prospective view of illness is every whit as "realistic" as that entertained, on the basis of a computer printout, by the employee of the medical conglomerate intent on finding the cause of what is wrong with one. And the prospective view is closer to that of William and Bernard.

The ambiguity of active and passive in the view of affection we have been considering bears on my understanding of feeling. We are in a measure passively *subject* to conditions named by the various terms for feeling and emotion, since such conditions always have a certain autonomy with respect to the ego. (One might recall Bernard's mention of fear and grief as movements of the *affectus*.) But the ego also, at least in principle, has a certain autonomy with respect to such conditions. The autonomy of the ego may assume more proper and less proper forms, which may be interrelated in complex ways.

Most properly, the ego maintains its autonomy by listening to the affectional language that Bernard describes—by attending to it—and by understanding it within a larger symbolic context offering a felt and imagined grasp of relations between ego and self. Religion offers such a context; so may individual symbol formation, resulting in such imaginative products as dreams. The ego is, however, subject to aberrations causing it to be inattentive to this affectional language. Taking comfort in the mastery it has achieved by painful trial and error and through the learning of hard truths, the ego is inclined to believe in its own self-sufficiency. As a result, the deluding sense of its own power that has presumably been sacrificed in the course of its growing accommodation with reality surreptitiously insinuates itself into its workings, distorting its relation to the self. With every intimation that it may indeed not be master in its own house, the ego is dumbfounded with disbelief. People return to their churches again and again, trying to learn the almost unlearnable truth that the "I" of each of them is not the center of the world. In this perspective the obstacles, setbacks, defeats, and forced detours of which I have spoken may have a positive value. In any case, they have meaning in relation to a dilemma of the human will that is crucial in the life of feeling.

Bernard's *affectus* corresponds to what I have called the pathic ground in generating, by its relative autonomy with respect to the ego, the passionate crisis that—to take a positive view of it—enables the ego to appreciate its own disorderedness, more specifically, the disorderedness of its affections. In Bernard's terms, without the freedom to will the bad, one would not have the freedom to will the good.

53

By the same token, without the potentiality for the disordering of the affections, there would be no potentiality for their ordering. Indeed, owing to the inclination of the ego to believe in its own self-sufficiency, one could speak not only of a potentiality but even of a disposition—a necessity—for the disordering of the affections, creating a condition from which deliverance is needed. Only through their ordering can this deliverance be achieved. (The infant achieves deliverance from its panic-stricken rages in part by coming to understand that, although whatever it is raging about is "bad," disintegration in rage is dangerous and in that sense also "bad," so that a more complex accommodation to the world is needed.) These reflections show how the pathic ground and passionate crisis are essential to differentiated feeling, which is concerned with ordering the affections.

Bernard employs the erotic symbolism of the Song of Songs to describe relations between God and the soul, including those relations in which the human will is "transformed" by becoming "conformed" to the will of God—a process also described by William. In expressing such receptivity to God in terms of sexual surrender, Bernard creates a perspective in which it is possible to discern significant patterns of relationship between receptivity and will, and between ego and self.

After commenting on a verse from the fourth Gospel, and on common strategies for dealing with what one takes to be one's inferiorities, I will suggest something of the nature of such patterns of relationship between receptivity and will, and between ego and self, by offering several vignettes from analytic practice. And I will comment on the political doings of Bernard, so different from his notions of affective contemplation. I will be concerned with the dark realm of one's inferiorities as the source and background of ordered affection, a realm that is seen as that source and background precisely when the ordering of the affections has failed. And I will be concerned with the mother-infant relationship as a primary model of the integrity that makes possible a superior relation to one's inferiorities and the ordering of one's affections.

According to the Authorized Version, "the light shineth in darkness; and the darkness comprehended it not" (John 1:5); one might imagine one's complexes and inferiorities as this "darkness." More recent translations prefer "master" or "overcome" to "comprehend" in their rendering of this verse: "The light shines in the darkness, and the darkness has not overcome it" (John 1:5 [Revised Standard Version]). Even if closer to the original, "overcome" loses the psychologically felicitous implication that a spiritual truth is what it is in relation to the condition of ignorance that created the need for it, that there is a dynamic interrelation between consciousness, on the one hand, and inferiorities in need of enlightenment and of being made compatible with the more justifiable beliefs and aspirations of the ego, on the other. But the biblical verse does not describe a dispelling of the darkness by the light. Rather, the verse suggests, the incomprehension of the darkness is part of the given state of affairs, which the conscious ego may nonetheless seek to alter.

Of a divided mind about the efficacy of will, most people who consult an analyst have long had reason to doubt that the ego is master in its own house. Yet they have persisted in trying to deal with this or that unwanted trait, inclination, or quandary by admonishing it, "Thou shalt not," or by declaring to it, "I divorce thee, I divorce thee, I divorce thee." Since prohibition is never an entirely conscious process, attempts to deal with one's inferiorities by means of it entail repression and denial (as unconscious components of conscious prohibition). And repression and denial create the condition for projection, by means of which the unconscious motives of one's inferiorities surreptitiously pervade the workings of consciousness. (Thus minimizing his own sexual perturbation, and to that extent dissociating himself from it, Dr. Smile can recognize that perturbation in projected form in women in analysis with him, with the result that he feels called upon to "save" them from their condition.) This is one reason why such strategies of prohibition do not work.

Another reason why such strategies do not work is that something in the person—the self—knows that the presumed inferiorities contain something of value that would be needed for a more adequate view of the person's life, and because the self, supraordinate to the ego, recognizes and sustains this value. (Though I will offer more attractive examples in a moment, I would for the sake of argument hold out at least this justification for Dr. Smile, that he was doing something— misguided—about his deep need for a better appreciation of eros, feeling, and the feminine.)

Feeling, Imagination, and the Self

Light shining in the darkness, which does not overmaster it but also does not comprehend it, is well illustrated by attorney "George Dempster," who defends business firms in lawsuits brought against them by people injured by products the firms have sold. He feels that he should be more successful in his profession than he is but is hindered in this ambition by what seem to him senseless anxiety attacks and bouts of depression. In a brief attempt at analysis, Mr. Dempster was disinclined to talk about anything other than his anxiety and depression and how to get rid of them. The attempt was to no avail, in part, presumably, because focusing willfully on the conflict inhibited the receptive awareness that might have allowed his symptoms to tell him something other than that he was not trying hard enough to achieve his conscious goals.

"Madeleine Long" ended a gluey, draining, self-confidence-depleting marriage with her passive, dependent, judgmental husband by divorcing him. Since then, another man has become attracted to her, but his interest is very disturbing to her—she weeps at the thought of it—because she is certain that if she gets to know him better, she will begin trying to understand and meet his needs and desires, as she did those of her former husband, and will remain as ignorant of her own as she has been till now. The thought of submitting to her new friend in this way awakens in her terrors of loss of self.

Though fond of her husband, "Susan Milstein" is incapable of sexual gratification unless she entertains fantasies of submission—of being tied up or whipped—or of forcing someone to do her sexual bidding. Sometimes she alternates between fantasies of submission and of domination. She insists that what matters to her is the *idea* of such actions, which she would not want to carry out in reality. Whatever these fantasies have to do specifically with sexuality, they undoubtedly have a great deal to do with will.

Sometimes "Linda Gayle" feels that her husband's sexual advances are unfeeling. She then makes herself able to respond anyway by imagining that their lovemaking is being watched. In early adolescence, after finding her clergyman father's cache of girlie magazines (such as *Playboy*), she developed the notion that a woman's sexual

56

role, and her feminine power, came from being looked at with desire. Thus, her fantasy of being watched in their lovemaking makes up for the self-esteem injured by her husband's unfeelingness.

University graduate student "Rhonda Stevens" suffers from powerful inferiority feelings which have as their main content her repeatedly being frightened into mute immobility by the prospect of writing papers and taking examinations. If she cannot break out of this problem, she will have to find some form of work beneath her considerable gifts. Still, her incapacitating fear knows something she needs to hear—in Bernard's language of the affections, a subversive part of her is right in insisting that she be loved for who and what she is rather than for achievement measured by grades on a transcript.

In his profound exploration of the reality and meaning of affective contemplation, Bernard created an invaluable body of knowledge, later drawn on by mystics of various nationalities, Goethe, Rousseau, a number of the romantics, and others concerned with the cultivation of a receptive mode of awareness and with kinds of truth knowable only in that mode. Nonetheless, in his conflict with his opponent Abelard, a powerful proponent of the rational intellect, he proved implacable in his hate, playing ecclesiastical politics in an unscrupulous way, and having Abelard's followers excommunicated and his books burned—Pope Innocent II himself prepared the bonfire at Saint Peter's—and in having Abelard banished to a monastery.[35] In so glaringly contradicting his professed conviction that love is the basis of intellect—and of human life—this explorer of the human soul and its affective nature may well remind us of Dr. Smile and other self-divided figures we have met and will meet.

Let us reflect a bit further on these vignettes.

Mr. Dempster's self-sabotage in his legal work by means of his anxieties and depression might remind us of the *affectus* as locus of feeling and emotion but also of aspiration to the good. In this perspective, ethical values are not simply internalized precepts from the social domain but are also an expression of the coherence of the self— and this by the very nature of the self. In any case, it is not alone the ego, surreptitiously motivated by inferiorities—such as Mr. Dempster's power drive—that determines the values by which one ought to live. What the ego can make in its dimness—Mr. Dempster's legal stratagems, for example—the self can break in its inscrutable darkness—his anxieties and depressions.

Mrs. Long is frightened by the man now attracted to her because she realizes that the relation of ego to self is primary and that of person to others is secondary. This means that if, as things stand now, her relation to him is to be the basis of her feeling-judgments, the value of her individual self will be lost, and with it her relationship with him. She also understands that arriving at some adequate form of self-knowledge will entail passionate crisis in which the unmasterable pathic ground will be manifest, and that the loneliness and fright of this prospect cannot be evaded by the consoling but for now disorienting companionship with him. Something in her knows that the possibility exists of a self-abandonment even more fundamental, and more disastrous, than abandonment by another.

Bearing in mind Bernard's accounts of the *affectus*, including its "spontaneous impulses," as well as what I have said so far about will, one might interpret Susan Milstein's sexual fantasies of submission and domination thus: "For sexual surrender to be possible, my egoistic will would have to open to admit affective currents recalcitrant to intellectual understanding and control. Being tied up or whipped provides an image of what would be required to bring my egoistic will to such surrender. Or else, my egoistic will would have to be so powerful that it would survive whatever reduction such surrender might entail. Forcing someone to do my bidding provides an image of such power."

Mrs. Gayle's fantasy of being watched in her lovemaking with her husband serves something of the same purpose, while giving glimpses of a further dimension. Egoistic will as the power to command desire becomes important when self-esteem—self in its knowing what is good for itself—has failed.

Rhonda Stevens's fear of failure—and, more deeply, of success—forces her to make "deals" with her professors. ("I didn't take the examination. What if instead I . . . ?" etc.) Thus what she regards as inferior secretly colors the workings of her ego. In their shabbiness and pleading for special treatment, these exchanges with her professors markedly compromise her perfectionism. Since in its present extreme form it is a crippling major ingredient in her problems, compromising it is, seen in one way, an expression of the self intent on undermining her egoistic will to the possible end of increased integrity of the personality.

Bernard's political machinations are also a reminder that spiritual truths arise from a real need on the part of the inferiorities they are intended to redeem and that these inferiorities—in Bernard's case power-driven bad feeling—remain the shadow and the context of such truths. Although one may regard the possession of such truths as transcendence achieved, with the original inferiorities forgotten, these inferiorities, once forgotten, may subvert the workings of the ego committed to the spiritual truths. (A slogan for this operation of Bernard's might be, "The aim of human life is not thinking about God but is rather the refinement of feeling. Whoever does not feel but thinks is to be condemned and destroyed.") In other words, possession of such truths is no protection whatsoever from the fundamental dilemma of the human will as I have been describing it. Such truths provide no certainty that they are being held in such a way that they are still true in one's holding of them.

Bernard belongs to one of those moments in Western civilization that have been characterized by the return of the repressed feminine, and which have seemed like eruptions, since existing cultural forms have not been conducive to the assimilation of these upsurges from the unconscious. It is thus not surprising that with one part of himself Bernard should declare loyalty to new currents of feeling, yet with another part of himself enact his ingrained commitment to the legalistic and militaristic strains within the dominant culture, including the Church. Another such moment of the returning feminine was that of romanticism; the severe psychic disturbances of many romantic artists might partly be accounted for in the same way. Still another such moment is represented by the psychology of Jung, reflecting his unsettling and profound experience of the feminine. A point of comparison between Jung and Bernard suggests itself.

After giving feeling an important place in his *Psychological Types* (1921), Jung devoted a great deal of attention to the mythic forms and images that he called archetypes. He was very concerned with the relations between strong emotion, mythic forms and images, and the imagination that produced them. (In the personal experience on

59

which his later theories were based, he was beset by tumultuous emotions from which he could free himself only by employing his imagination to bring forth the forms and images that were their content.) But he did not discuss in any detail the relationship between mythic forms and images and differentiated conscious feeling.

Speaking of poetry, Jung once remarked, "Whoever speaks in primordial images [or archetypes] speaks with a thousand voices; he enthralls and overpowers, while at the same time he lifts the idea he is seeking to express out of the occasional and the transitory into the realm of the ever-enduring."³⁶ This remark acknowledges that such forms have persuasive and formative powers partly independent of their concrete embodiment. (The Mass is nowadays thought to be the Mass, whether celebrated in Latin or in one of many vernacular languages. The death of any tragic hero partly reminds us of death as a general fact to which all individuality is subject. The marriages at the close of a Shakespearean comedy partly represent an elemental force to which the specific characters are subject. When one encounters an unknown infant, one reacts partly to the specific little person and partly to "Baby." Circles divided into quadrants have had religious significance in many times and places.) "Speaking with a thousand voices" might make us think of heroic symphonies and monumental architecture, which have been favored forms of art. Two reservations might be made about Jung's remark, however. First, much of what constitutes feeling is individual and personal, not a thousand voices but one; and much of what constitutes feeling is spoken softly. And second, the aesthetic was a problem for Jung in various ways, among them in representing a distraction from what he regarded as the most authentic kinds of spiritual experience.³⁷ Hence one might wonder whether the fantasy of speaking with a thousand voices might not partly reflect the same power component of inferiorities that we have seen in Bernard and in the contemporary people of whom I have offered glimpses.

My purpose is not to point out what Jung has never denied: that he, like everyone else, was capable of being less than perfectly self-consistent, and that unconscious motives sometimes played themselves out in his conscious utterances. My purpose is rather to raise an issue that is fundamental when such concepts as that of archetypes come, or deserve to come, into a consideration of imagination and feeling.

60

Being True to Oneself in Abundance and Limitation

The most authentic forms of spiritual experience were for Jung religious. They were concerned with mythic forms and images that were binding—giving structure and purpose to human life—because they were emotionally compelling. This brings us again to the juncture of emotion and feeling as a mode of consciousness, because religion has also served in many times and places as a primary cultural institution for the development of feeling. What is emotionally compelling can be apprehended—read—by feeling, or it can energize one in ways that leave one open to the willfulness of the inferiorities belonging to the power shadow of the vulnerable ego. (The ambiguities of power in religion will be considered more fully in part 5; feeling and imagination in relation to archetypes will be considered more fully in part 6.) To be receptive is to be vulnerable. Thus, it should not be surprising that Bernard, precisely owing to his cultivation of receptivity, should act in ways that show his receptivity to be compensated by a ruthless will rising through the ego from unconscious depths. And in our concern with mythic forms and images, we should keep in mind this caution: though they are in a qualified sense transpersonal, experience of them must be a form of personal—felt—knowledge if they are not to serve as the justifying guise of one's inferiorities—as when Bernard, intent on destroying Abelard, surely thought he was doing so out of selfless devotion to God the Father, the Son, the Holy Spirit, and the Blessed Virgin.

If the light of consciousness cannot simply dispel the darkness of the unconscious, if the darkness cannot overcome the light, if the darkness still needs to comprehend what it does not, and if the light can be self-deluded, the opposition between them needs to assume a new, more mutually responsive form. Such interaction may sooner or later lead to a new conscious attitude expressing values now known only fitfully and with little sense of how they relate to one another.

For example, not achieving, rather than achieving, might be for Rhonda Stevens a value in a new conscious attitude, though it conflicts with important values now defining for her a worthwhile life. Perhaps it is these values, in their bearing on the present and actual not-achieving, that need to be called in question. Perhaps the readiness to scold and cast away that serves to uphold them needs to be softened in a greater receptivity. But this would be to grant the existence of her inferiorities and also to grant their need for expression, not with a thousand voices and with papal denunciations, but more quietly and perhaps wordlessly, in the hope that what they utter will be heard with realistic compassion. There would have to be activated in Rhonda Stevens's psychic depths the good-enough mother in relation to the all-right (if sometimes fussy and sometimes incomprehensible) baby. And the activation of this psychic level would inevitably entail the deintegration and passionate crisis that characterize times in the mother-infant relationship when the self by and large continues to be felt as implicit even in the falling apart, and when the falling apart does not really seem the end of the world.

The self-expression of one's inferiorities as denunciations of an enemy, in the absence of the means to banish him immediately to eternal torment, is an "adult" equivalent of the screaming of a baby. But if the screaming of a baby could not be tolerated and got beyond by Mother and Baby and the household awakened at 3 A.M., if there were not a more embracing context of felt meaning to assimilate such deintegrative storms, and if this meaning were not by and large available, the human race would not have survived thus far. The baby's screaming can be heard as an appeal to the self in its knowing of the good—to the *affectus* of Bernard and William. The more "adult" and more culturally elaborated equivalents of such screaming—the back-handedly arranged papal denunciations—can also be heard as such appeals. To hear them as such is not to forgive evil in a cheerfully mindless way; rather, it is to remind oneself of the compassion or detachment necessary to keep such appeals within the domain of differentiated feeling.

That Baby may scream reminds us that Mother cannot—like light facing the uncomprehending darkness—tell Baby what Baby needs to know. Rather, there is between Mother and Baby a continuing, richly communicative interplay in which Mother is actively receptive to the possible meanings of Baby's actions. Mother assumes and goes out from what Baby is now, what Baby knows already, and what might be the next steps beyond Baby's present knowledge. Mother fosters the development of Baby by registering Baby's relatively inchoate strivings, assuming that they mean something, and wondering what they mean. Baby is not for Mother a tabula rasa, Baby is this person now and its potentialities. All further integration of the personality entails a recognition of the person one is now, including one's inferiorities. And this is a recognition that further development of who and what one already is can proceed only with and through one's inferiorities and not simply despite them. Mother's acceptance of Baby is a model of this. If Rhonda Stevens comes to accept herself, her doing so will recapitulate Mother's acceptance of Baby, perhaps allowing Rhonda's not achieving to assume a value it presently does not have: "Consider the lilies of the field, how they grow; they toil not, neither do they spin: And yet I say unto you, That even Solomon in all his glory was not arrayed like one of these" (Matt. 6:28–29).

The conscious and unconscious willfulness to be seen in Bernard's political machinations and in the vignettes of contemporary people we have considered is at the expense of the receptivity and the awareness of affective currents that are essential to feeling as I am concerned with it in this book. It is as the bride that the soul receives God as her beloved. And although the "conforming" of the human to the divine will may be in important respects an active process, it begins in yielding, in a movement of yin or feminine energy. Feeling is not the prerogative of the female person, but on a deep level feeling is and remains feminine because Mother is female and the receptivity of feeling is, to begin with, receptivity of Mother and Baby to one another.

The urgency of the infant's insistence that its needs and desires be met may at the moment create the impression that for the infant will is all. But the storms of rage and despair into which it falls when its efforts to impose its will are thwarted show that from the outset egoistic will is bounded, and is what it is only in relation to obstacles and to its capacity for dissolution, either in letting go, as in falling asleep, or in being overwhelmed, as in a tantrum. This is to say in another way that the integration of the developing personality has deintegration as its counterpart and countermovement.

Embracing the unstable infantile will, taking it up, molding it, acting on behalf of it, is the will of Mother and Baby in their interaction. This embracing will forms itself and lives itself in the mother's imaginative and feelingful understanding of her infant and in its responsiveness to her. Through their relationship the infant develops an ego trusting in the self to survive the ego's deintegration and to

63

gather the broken pieces of the ego together again. This tendency toward increasing inner stability is inseparable from the tendency of the infant to seek and find reliable forms of relationship to members of the larger community.

Insofar as the will is rational, as Bernard thought it to be, its rationality is realized in further developments based on the processes I have been describing. And Baby *is* rational, in that it does not just "behave" out into a cacophony of objects that it assumes is random. Rather it wants to understand and to be understood. Still, in all the actions of the will, both human and divine, there are elements that cannot be appropriated by *my* reason *now*. The disordering of the affections attendant upon recognition that this is so leads, by grace of either gentle insight or the stark overmastering of calamity, to a further recognition of the supraordinate nature of the self. Thus acknowledged, the self labors to reorder the disordered affections. And it behooves the ego to serve as active witness of this process. The self is, accordingly, our link with what we imagine as the divine will. Despite moments in which we seem to comprehend it rationally, the self is in lived experience finally akin to Schopenhauer's cosmic Will, unknowable in phenomenal representations because ultimately, and absolutely, beyond them. We know the self imaginatively and provisionally, under the aspect of "as if."

As Saint Thomas Aquinas (among others) has pointed out, the mystery of the Christian Incarnation implies that the Lord of Creation was once a "puling infant"—that a divine baby is nonetheless a baby, and babies cry a lot. One way to make sense of this strange notion is with reference to the prayer, "Thy will be done." The appeal is to the will of God, but to speak of the divine will is possible only if one understands distinctions among kinds and degrees of will in relation to lower and higher, more ephemeral and more enduring values. One must understand, too, that these distinctions can be grasped with only partial adequacy by the ego, and that insofar as the ego's grasp of them is adequate it is not once and for all but fitful, as life moves on and circumstances change and the ego falls prey to its characteristic delusions. To pray "Thy will be done" is thus partly to try to find one's way back to the psychic level of those formative experiences in which the incipient egoistic will of the infant was assimilated to the more embracing will of its relationship with its mother.

2.7 Abundance and the Heart

"You brood of vipers! how can you speak good, when you are evil? For out of the abundance of the heart the mouth speaks" (Matt. 12:34 [Revised Standard Version]). This text has implications bearing on central issues of these reflections.

Chrysostom remarks that in this biblical passage Jesus addresses his hearers as a "brood" or "generation" (Authorized Version) of vipers in order to deny them the descent from Abraham that they have prided themselves on, making them instead descendants of the vipers they are like.[38] Though the verse thus stresses the hypocrisy of apparently good words seeking to belie a bad heart, the heart is abundant in its goodness as well as its badness, so that Martin Luther can apply the same verse to words of Paul, precious to Luther, observing that though they are hard to understand, they were spoken out of the "abundance" of Paul's heart.[39]

Of the 851 occurrences of the word *heart* in the Old Testament, a third denote one's character or inner life as a whole; in a proportion of the remaining two thirds, the word denotes the emotional aspects of the personality, although in a large number of those occurrences the word stresses the intellectual and volitional functions of consciousness.[40] In Hebraic thought man is regarded as an existing totality, and various words may designate the totality of conscious life. When parts of the body, such as the bowels (often meaning the seat of emotion), the eye, or the heart are made the subject of vital acts, the whole person is identified with the organ as a focus of psychic energy.[41] Thus, "The 'heart' is in biblical diction man's total identity and existence described under the aspect of his vital intelligence, will, decision."[42] And, like *countenance* as distinct from *face*, the term belongs to a class of "total-human words" naming the human person as a whole without regard to a possible separation between "soul" or "spirit," on the one hand, and "body," on the other.[43]

The circulation of the blood, incidentally, was not understood until Sir William Harvey discovered it in 1651. This should caution us, in dealing with such archaic linguistic phenomena, against assuming that language is primarily the product of instrumental, as distinct from poetic, intelligence: *heart* was "person" long before it was "pump."[44]

Importantly, the biblical heart can denote an essential human quality hidden to the eye; this hiddenness is one aspect of the heart's

65

abundance. Indeed, the heart is "deep" (Ps. 64:6), even the unfathomable essence of the person—"the hidden man of the heart" (1 Pet. 3:4). In the view of Aquinas, it is precisely the heart that affords the unique person his individuality, one characteristic of which is "incommunicability."[45] And the novelist Herman Melville (1819–91) remarks, "Deep, deep, and still deep and deeper must we go, if we would find out the heart of a man; descending into which is as descending a spiral stair in a shaft, without any end."[46] Still, and also importantly, although the heart is finally incommunicable and inaccessible to other men, there are various relations, direct and indirect, between it and God, who can know it fully: "the Lord searcheth all hearts" (1 Chron. 28:9).

Old Testament authors sometimes clearly link the heart with feeling and emotion. Paul sometimes follows them in this, though for him Greek *kardia* ("heart") has its meaning in relation to other terms naming aspects of man's relation to God: *soma* ("body"), *sarx* ("flesh"), *psyche* ("soul"), and *pneuma* ("spirit")—to give approximate translations of words that are not always clearly distinguishable. Thus *kardia*, "heart," is often little different from *nous*, which seems to describe the human person as a knowing, judging subject, capable of understanding, decision, and planning. Where there is a distinction, *kardia* would seem to name the more emotional reactions of the intelligent self, which can love (2 Cor. 7:3, 8:16), grieve (Rom. 9:2), lust (Rom. 1:24), and suffer (2 Cor. 2:4).[47]

Paul frequently mentions joy or sorrow without situating them in the heart, and when in 2 Cor. 6:11–12 he speaks of the emotive capacity of the heart, he adds a reference to "bowels" (or "compassion"). Still, Luther, powerfully committed to the genius of the Bible, points out that the Hebrews used *bowels* to mean emotionality, but then translates the term as "heart," which is for him highly emotional.[48] Thus, when he speaks about the hidden activity of the heart, not yet given outward expression, he focuses on emotional stirrings of love and anger.[49] And this implies, in the world shaped by the Bible, an important indirect connection between the heart and God, since the relations between God's wrath and his love, and of both to man, are important biblical and theological themes.

That a person speaks out of the abundance of the heart implies that outward speech is a secondary and late manifestation of an inner process, that it is an overflowing of the heart. Indeed, one translation (New English Bible) speaks not of the heart's "abundance" but of its "overflowing." While we must read the contents of one another's hearts in the remote medium of outward speech, God, alone, can see directly into the heart. Thus, according to Chrysostom, it is as Christ, and hence as God, that Jesus can see into the hearts of his hearers and know to address them as a brood or generation of vipers. [50]

The idea of the human heart's abundance uttered in speech implies various contrasts between human and divine speech and between human and divine abundance more generally—implications explored by such writers as Luther, John Bunyan (1628–88), Chrysostom, and Bernard.

According to Luther, following various church fathers, there is in God, as in man, a "word of the heart." Just as a person may carry on a long inner conversation while devising a plan of action, so—in a clearly inadequate analogy—may God. The divine "word of the heart" is not directly knowable by man, owing in part to the incommensurability of the human person and God, and in part to the impossibility of any human person's seeing into the heart of another. Indeed, as a measure of this incommensurability, the word of God is coeternal with God and precedes the creation. "The human word does not carry with itself the essence or the nature of the heart; . . . it is only able to signify or to act as a sign," much like a statue, not carrying the essence of the person it portrays. But "in God, the word brings not only the sign and representation, but also the whole being and it is as full of God as he whose image or word it is." [51]

Certainly God may fill the human heart with the kinds of speech that will express his majesty, and will persuasively prescribe to an audience the right forms of relationship to him. Such Christian writers as Bunyan have been greatly concerned with the nature of this kind of grace as distinct from human gifts and arts of eloquence. And concern with the grace necessary for one to express in human terms the nature of the divine is closely related to concern with whether one may obtain grace sufficient for salvation. Thus Bunyan describes pondering the words, "My Grace is sufficient," and throwing down his book, feeling that the sentence "was not large enough for me; no, not large enough; but now it was as if it had arms of grace so wide, that it could not only inclose me, but many more besides," so that he

67

"was sustained, yet not without exceeding conflicts . . . because *for thee* was left out." As he despaired, "these words did with great power suddainly break in upon me, *My grace is sufficient for thee, my grace is sufficient for thee, my grace is sufficient for thee;* three times together; and, O me-thought that every word was a mighty word unto me; as *my,* and *grace,* and *sufficient,* and *for thee;* they were then, and sometimes are still, far bigger than others be."[52] In its abundant capacity for good as well as for evil, and for expressing good as well as evil, the heart is thus unable to utter the saving word that must come from God. Freely translated into psychological terms, this could be taken to mean that the ego cannot solve its sorely besetting problems without considering the fantasy-images, thoughts, and quirks of fate by which the self makes its deeper purposes known.

Proceeding in the opposite direction from Bunyan in his concern with one's personal relation to grace, one may ask whether grace is sufficient in the larger scheme of things. This question has been answered theologically in arguments based on the contrast between Adam and Christ, and between sufficiency, on the one hand, and abundance and even "superabundance" (in Paul's characteristic phrase), on the other. Both the question and the answer bear on the evaluative self, and on mutuality as entailing not sufficiency but abundance.

Chrysostom elaborates upon the idea that "Adam is a type of Christ," so that Adam is the cause of the deaths of those descended from him, though they did not eat of the forbidden tree, whereas Christ is the provider of righteousness to those descended from him through faith, though they did not earn that righteousness themselves. Despite the parallel, "sin and grace are not equivalents, death and life are not equivalents, the Devil and God are not equivalents, but there is a boundless space between them." Chrysostom cites Paul as claiming that "if through the offense of one many be dead, much more the grace of God, and the gift by grace, which is by one man, Jesus Christ, hath abounded unto the many." Thus Paul speaks of a "superabundance" of grace, which Chrysostom explains on the analogy of someone thrown into prison, with his wife and children and servants, because he owed ten mites, and who is saved by someone who not only pays the ten mites but also gives him ten thousand talents of gold, and leads the prisoner to the throne of the highest power and makes him partake of the highest honor and every kind of magnificence: would he then remember the ten mites? Chrysostom further explains this abounding grace on the analogies of someone not only freed of a disease but also given beauty, strength, and rank, and of a hungry person not only fed but given great riches and set up in the highest authority.[53]

Luther comments on the Pauline text and Chrysostom's exposition of it that the gift of Christ's grace "is given even to His enemies out of His mercy, because they were not worthy of this gift unless they were made worthy and accounted as such by the mercy and grace of God."[54] Indeed, it is some measure of the abundance of grace that it should be held out even to those intent on denying it.

As Luther was well aware, the abundance of God also raises the complex issue of how knowable God is, and in what way he is known, an issue having profound significance with regard to the heart as the emotional core that it so importantly was for Luther. He speaks of people who pray asking for things that are "too little, things that are too lowly or insignificant in comparison with what God wants to give them. . . . It is as if a person should write his father asking for silver, but the father is disposed to give him a thousand pieces of gold. The father throws away the letter and disregards it, and when the son learns of this and realizes that the silver is not coming to him as he requested, he is made sad."[55]

These thoughts remind us that the ego needs continually to revise its understanding of its intentions and desires by due consideration of the more embracing self, that the ego needs to remain skeptical regarding its ability to comprehend the self as a more embracing order of vitality and meaning, to which the ego must nonetheless commit itself. Luther's description is especially valuable in implying the rich play of emotionality in the relations of ego and self.

Even if *serenitas cordis*, "serenity of heart," is taken to be a goal of religious life, it is difficult to see how such a state could have religious value—and not be a form of self-deception—if divorced from one's tacit knowledge of the full range of emotional life, including the doubt, fear, anxiety, depression, bewilderment, and remorse that the son might feel upon failing to receive an answer to his letter to his father. Luther would place such distressing emotions within the larger context

69

of assurance, as though we are to believe that beyond any present situation evoking despair there are abiding grounds for hope.

Luther's insistence that we are disposed to ask God for too little implies that we are constitutionally able to receive God's greatness into us. And we have already considered Bernard of Clairvaux's affective contemplation, in which God as the bridegroom enters the soul, which thus must have the capacity to respond to the divine abundance. Augustine, too, has described the vision of God as an experience of "plenitude."

Hindu contemplatives have described experiences of bliss so superabundant as to be cosmic. And there are nontheological parallels to God's abundance. Thus, Rousseau used Augustine's word "abundance" to describe moments of especially rich subjective experience. And as Blake remarked, "If the doors of perception were cleansed every thing would appear to man as it is, infinite. / For man has closed himself up, till he sees all things thro' narrow chinks of his cavern": our sensory apparatus is a system of selection, radically reducing the richness of what is there to be perceived.[56] In a similar vein, the Swiss poet-novelist Gottfried Keller in *Abendlied* ("Evening Song") implores his eyes to drink in as much as their lashes will hold of the golden profusion, or overflowing, of the world: *"Trinkt, o Augen, was die Wimper hält, / Von dem goldnen Überfluss der Welt!"*[57]

Further, in functioning to master ambiguity, our conscious values and attitudes may impoverish imagination, an impoverishment readily seen in configurations of collective values. For example, the trillions of dollars a year now being spent on arms would provide vast resources toward mitigating pressing social problems that, unsolved, will directly or indirectly lead to war. The mounting stockpiles of weapons, in effect, consume many other forms of abundance waiting to be made known through an expansion of imagination in new directions.

Luther's analogy of the son seemingly unheard by his father also expresses the thought that that abundance may remain unperceived and thus untaken. When it so remains, the result may be that one feels grounded not in abundance but in the lack of it, not in grace but in the sin and death of Adam—as Bunyan did before hearing the assuring voice. Though fostering a proper vigilance concerning one's own attitudes and motives, the sense of lack may create tensions—as one tries not to be the Adam one palpably is—rendering one unreceptive to the abundance that one can have only by being receptive to it. Thus the prescribed cure may exacerbate the ailment.

This paradoxical effect is especially clear in certain kinds of symptomatic behavior consisting of magical operations (discussed at greater length in part 5.10) to assure that the good and bad things in one's life are balanced in such a way that the good ones do not become a threat. Thus, for example, "Natalie Rose," a young concert pianist, "pays for" the striking success of her musical career by phobically imagining disasters to herself and her husband, and by letting herself be drained by presumed friends who, on the pretext of seeking her advice, dump their tawdry troubles on her. She thus assures that there is sufficient gray misery in her life that the good things can be dispersed in it and thus not pose the issue of abundance raised by Luther. For to be grounded in abundance, to be related to a dependent source, is to be dependent upon it. But tolerating this dependency requires trust. Little in her family background gave her much reason for trust; but since she could not rely on others, she did learn to rely on herself, though her self-reliance entails the magical operations I have described. Her self-induced gray misery is entirely compatible with her in some ways fragile self-esteem, as the good things in her life are not. Trust is inseparable from self-esteem.

Paul, Chrysostom, Luther, and Bunyan were convinced that there could be a sufficiency of the good they called grace only because there was an abundance of it independent of their merit, that there could be no movement from their lack of merit to that sufficient good without invoking and contemplating the abundance of which that good was a sign. Natalie Rose partly seeks to move from what she feels as her lack of merit not to abundant but to merely sufficient good, which remains a sign of that lack. (Thus, when people whose judgment she respects praise her musical performance, she is sometimes unable to feel that the praise is deserved, whereas if an envious fellow musician offers criticism of her, she sometimes dwells on it at length, even while her better judgment tells her it is groundless.)

On a very deep level—of the self—there is something in Natalie Rose that wills good things for her, but this beneficent force must work with and around deficits of trust and self-esteem. These make gray misery seem to her deserved. And if such misery is available for contemplation as a deserved sign of deprivation, she can treat the good things in her life as happy accidents rather than as signs of an abundance that would challenge her understanding of deserving.

The condition of being closed to abundance is placed in another light by passages in the ancient Chinese oracle book, the *I Ching*, and by the late medieval emblem of the wheel of fortune. The arguments of Chrysostom and Luther based on Paul dramatize a causal sequence: Adam caused our sinfulness and death; Christ caused the righteousness of grace available to us. The hexagrams of the *I Ching*, in contrast, are intended acausally to represent the quality of a certain moment, that quality making itself known through the presumably random pattern resulting from the fall of tossed coins or the dividing of a bundle of yarrow stalks. Two of the hexagrams are *Sun* (or "Decrease") and *I* (or "Increase"), with Decrease leading inevitably to flowering, and Increase to decline, as opposites meet or turn into one another. Neither Decrease nor Increase is necessarily good or bad, each coming in its own time as moments in the life of the natural-supernatural cosmos. Rather than seeking to fix responsibility for these conditions in a causal way, the hexagrams seek to state both limitations and potentialities of the conditions, and to prescribe modes of conduct appropriate to each. For example, if in Decrease, "a time of scanty resources brings out an inner truth, one must not feel ashamed of simplicity. For simplicity is then the very thing needed to provide inner strength for further undertakings." And: "The time of INCREASE does not endure, therefore it must be utilized while it lasts."[58] Significantly, how to get the abundance lacking in a time of decrease is not posed as an appropriate problem. The quality of such a time is a just-so story.

The attitude of the oracle-book toward human responsibility may be clarified if we think again of Luther's analogy of the son writing to his father for silver and receiving no answer. This analogy conveys a meaning to us, Luther's readers—who are asked to think the chagrined son ought to trust his apparently hardhearted father—but that meaning is practically unavailable to the son. This is so even though it is available to him in principle, and though he is in principle responsible for his incomprehension of the true state of affairs. The hexagram of Decrease, however, might help him not to despair but to make sense of his situation and to act responsibly until his father's abundance is revealed.

The emblem of the wheel of fortune, presided over by the goddess of fortune, often depicted as blindfolded, portrays abundance and lack, since fortune means possessing life's material and spiritual goods, and misfortune means being deprived of them. In the emblem there is some sort of balance between fortune and misfortune, as some figures are rising on the wheel while others are descending. But this balance is being created and recreated within an overall process presumably experienced by the rising and descending figures as having something of the fortuitousness of tossed coins. Much as the *I Ching* asks us to understand that decrease and increase come in their own time, the emblem implies that we would be better advised to identify with the hub of the wheel than with the figures rising and descending on the rim. If we take the hub as the self, the process of individuation in later stages of life could be imagined as one of lessening one's sense of identity with the figures and increasing it with the hub. It might well be that Natalie Rose would find this more comprehensible and practically doable than the exhortations of Chrysostom and Luther.

In basic agreement with Chrysostom, Bunyan, the *I Ching,* and the emblem of the wheel of fortune, Luther insisted that the abundance of the good that he called grace was unknowable by reason. This conviction contradicted, however, a powerful strain of rationalistic theology having its source in Plato and continuing in various forms for the better part of two thousand years. This theology focuses on God's plenitude—compare my emphasis on abundance—and argues that owing to God's goodness and lack of envy, he allowed that plenitude to overflow in the creation of a world of being that, though less perfect—indeed, defective—stands in essentially intelligible relation to him. This theology thus has as a necessary component "the principle of sufficient reason," according to which, as stated by Spinoza in the seventeenth century, "a cause or reason must be assigned" to everything "alike for its existence or its non-existence," the cause being "the intellect of God, in so far as it is conceived to constitute the divine essence."[59]

Though coherent and intellectually dependable, a rational world of this kind is static and inert—a "block-world," as William James later called it, in which nothing is contingent, and everything is

73

determined by "necessary truths." In such a world, as summarized by Arthur O. Lovejoy, who has masterfully analyzed this complex of ideas, "everything is so rigorously tied up with the existence of the necessarily existent Being, and that Being, in turn, is so rigorously implicative of the existence of everything else, that the whole admits of no conceivable additions or omissions or alterations."[60]

The internal contradiction in this scheme of ideas was at last well stated by the philosopher F. W. J. von Schelling (1775–1854) at the beginning of the nineteenth century when he denied that prior to the world of things there was an all-perfect being that actually had the perfections of all other things in itself. "To believe that it did," said Schelling, "is difficult for many reasons, but first of all for the very simple one that, if it were in actual possession of the highest perfection [or completeness], it would have had no reason (*Grund*) for the creation and production of so many other things, through which it—being incapable of attaining a higher degree of perfection—could only fall to a lower one."[61] The product of the view Schelling is criticizing is "a God who is alien to nature and a nature that is devoid of God."[62]

This split between nature and God is implicit, incidentally, in a beautiful passage in which Luther earlier contemplated the image of Mary pondering in her heart the words of the annunciation, having within her the word of God but continuing to be in the eyes of others a simple peasant girl milking the cows and washing pots and kettles, "as though she cared nothing for such great gifts and graces."[63] Though Luther's meditation on Mary expresses the mysterious abundance of God's grace, it is important to his vision of it that he assume the physiology of Aristotle and Aquinas in regarding the woman as merely the natural vessel of the male procreative seed developing into an embryo. The passage, that is to say, gains its force precisely by dissuading us from imagining that Mary, through her earthly femininity, gave the word of God a natural form as necessary to the fulfillment of God as to that of nature. As Schelling realized, however, there is much to be said for the conception of such an unfulfilled or incomplete God.

In opposition to the tradition of rationalistic theology, Schelling proposed a God-in-the-making, gradually becoming manifest in the world in a process of self-realization that is a struggle against opposition: "Since the full possibilities of being were not realized all at once, and are not yet realized, there must in the original nature of things be some impediment, some principle of retardation."[64] This is a God of Becoming, destined to triumph in manifesting the full range of being, but doing so in a process of momentary defeats. The rationalistic theology derived from Plato is thus stood completely on its head. Nonetheless, as Lovejoy remarks, "the insatiable generativeness, the tendency to produce diversity, the necessity of the realization of the greatest possible 'fullness' of being—these attributes of the Platonistic world are still the attributes of the world of the Romantic philosopher. But the generativeness is now that of an insufficiency striving unconsciously for richer and more various being; and the fullness is not the permanent character but the flying goal of the whole of things."[65]

Owing to the internal contradictions in the Platonistic scheme and its incongruence with important facts of common experience and of the natural world, including the facts accounted for by the theory of natural evolution, the antirationalist theologians and philosophers through the ages—those who have grounded the created world in God's will rather than in his intellect, or in the prototypes of eternal Ideas—have, I believe (with Lovejoy), had the better of the argument. These thinkers include in the twentieth century the philosopher Alfred North Whitehead (1861–1947), who—in an assertion that would have profoundly shocked Plotinus or Spinoza—gives the name of God not to Infinite Fecundity but to "the supreme ground for limitation." By "limitation" Whitehead means such matter-of-fact determinations as the dimensions of the spatiotemporal continuum which "are inherent in the actual course of events, but which present themselves as arbitrary in respect to a more abstract possibility."[66] For this attribute of limitation, Whitehead avers, "no reason can be given: for all reason flows from it. God is the ultimate limitation, and His existence is the ultimate irrationality. For no reason can be given for just that limitation which it stands in His nature to impose. . . . No reason can be given for the nature of God, because that nature is the ground of rationality."[67] Instead of a Prime Mover, Whitehead's God is a God of Concretion—not concrete in himself but the ground of concrete things—and "actuality" is conceived "as in essential relation to an unfathomable possibility"[68]—in essential relation to another form of abundance.

A salutary quirk of language enables us to call this contingent world a "given," since what is thus "given" is a *gift* reminding us of our creatureliness and of the gratitude appropriate to the gift. But neither creatureliness nor the appropriateness of gratitude requires us to think that the world is what it is because reason and the goodness of God require it to be so: just as I may call the world as it happens to be a gift, I may also designate as a gift something that baffles my understanding and thus requires me to open myself to new possibilities.

Though we did not create the world and have not created ourselves, the relation of actuality to possibility is "essential" in the directions both of the actual and the possible: possibility is "unfathomable" but becomes actual in relation to what is already actual, now. We are agents of this actualization, and presumably, possibilities related to the actual and available for us to actualize remain forever unactualized if we do not actualize them. Actualizing them, moreover, amounts to actualizing the God-in-the-making propounded by Schelling, who (following Revelations) described God as the First and the Last, the Alpha and Omega, but insisted that the first, unevolved, implicit God is not in the same sense the last, evolved, explicit God—this last God clearly bearing a relation to God as "the supreme ground for limitation" described by Whitehead.[69] An overwhelmingly important corollary of this view is that we creatures of this world play a role in the explication and actualization of the implicit God of possibility. We help make God what he is becoming.

These thoughts bear on the development of the personality under the aspect of individuation. An adequate definition of this development might describe it in part as the actualization of unfathomable psychic potentiality within a contingent world that, so far as we know, simply happens to have the character it has. We happen to have capacities of various kinds including our physical constitution and predisposition to certain diseases and psychopathologies. We live in a certain social setting at a moment in history, and our life experience has marked us in many ways, thus realizing various potentialities with the result of making us what we now are. There are many constraints in what we now are psychologically, as anyone who has struggled with such psychological problems as those of Natalie Rose will attest. We actualize the possible, but the possible always reaches beyond the actual. In actualizing the possible, we play a role in the emergence of the self analogous to the role we play in the evolution of Schelling's God as Omega.

We have a measure of choice, but exercising it does not mean—in a psychological equivalent of the religious sense—that we create ourselves, since what we are and do is basically always subordinate to the self out of which our conscious lives are developing, the original self corresponding to Schelling's God as Alpha.

Though in Schelling's terms we may play a role in actualizing that God, it does not follow that without us God as Alpha is inert. On the contrary, he is a will exercised in relation to us. In analogous fashion, the original self corresponding to God as Alpha initiates, alters, hints at new directions, always in relation to what we have become, including what we take to be shackling restraints. Natalie Rose cannot directly, by conscious effort, solve her problems, because they constitute a pattern of fate as decreed by the wheel of fortune or as described by the *I Ching*. But such a pattern may gradually change, owing to the movement of the self in disclosing further possibilities related to the pattern. Conscious awareness helps to reveal those possibilities and make them actual, and so ego and self interact in the realization of the original self.

In this process subject stands over against, but also blends with, object in the ultimate unknowability of each. The unfathomable heart meets what it knows as the mystery of God, and ego and self interact in accordance with an intentionality that the ego can discern only in glimpses. The unknownness of these relations keeps active the play of emotion originating in the also unknown pathic ground. It is most importantly through imagination that this unknownness becomes known. And imagination entails a quality of consciousness in which the play of emotion attendant upon these relations is taken up and contained in feeling. Mary pondering in her heart the astonishing, even potentially terrifying message of the angel to her is an image of this containment.

Finally, taking as my point of departure the notion that the heart is the source and receptacle of love—as it was for Bernard, for example—I wish to comment briefly on the special role of feeling in the process of individuation.

Consideration of the heart as the source and receptacle of love may lead in two directions. One, as we have seen, is toward love as an experience of abundance. Thus, in the love poems of Donne, the love of the lovers often constitutes an entire world, and ages would be required for the lover to explore, and love adequately, the delightful attributes of his beloved. The other direction is toward love as the experience of lack, toward love as desire.

To speak of love not as overflowing but as desire is to remind ourselves that human beings are also defective creatures at war with themselves, wanting what they do not have or what they had but have no longer, or wanting contradictory things, or wanting things that cannot give the satisfactions they are impelled to seek in them; creatures constantly in need of a degree and quality of consciousness of which they are incapable, while having to discover that the consciousness they do have impairs the functioning of processes vital to them.

Overflowing love is allied with the kind of contemplation envisaged by Bernard; love as desire is allied with instrumental intelligence (as I will argue at greater length in part 5). And both are subject to aberrations. Thus, with respect to feeling as a theme of this book, there might be little to choose between the (contemplative) Jaina holy man pulling out all the hairs of his body to escape their impurity, and the (instrumental) computer specialist who wears headphones at the dinner table so he will not have to hear the conversation of his wife and children. The relations between the contemplative and the instrumental ways of living our lives are inescapably intertwined: a master potter may use the instrument of a wheel to make, contemplatively, a pot intended for use.

Like the small-minded, self-limiting people described by Chrysostom and Luther, we lack in the midst of abundance. And perhaps we may deal with our lack by opening our minds and hearts and imaginations. Or then again, perhaps that lack is, as the I Ching hexagram of Decrease or the emblem of the wheel of fortune might remind us, a just-so story, about which nothing can be done, at least now. Perhaps, at least now, we must with King Lear learn patience. The simplicity forced upon us by straitened circumstances may lead to, or may even be, an enrichment, and may be conducive of an attitude in which we contemplatively see the large in the small, or the small in relation to the large. And even if, in the broadest terms, there is an abundance of the good, discrimination is required, since, as Schelling might put it, not even God is free of error and can avoid impediments to his most enlightened strivings.

What such discrimination means with respect to feeling is well understood by the philosopher Franz Brentano, who speaks of "right hating" as well as "right loving," suggesting that one should, in the right way, hate and love the things that are right for one to hate and love.[70] This right hating and right loving entails knowing which objects are to be shunned and which striven toward, and such knowledge may be the result of a process of discovery for which there is no simple guiding recipe. It should be noted, however, that right loving and right hating may interact within the kind of complex feeling-judgments mentioned earlier. Thus, in the Second World War a Dutchman gave refuge and succor to thirty-two Allied soldiers stranded behind enemy lines. Did he do so out of his love for humanity or the Allied cause, or out of his hatred of Nazism and the Nazis? His actions could be said to exhibit either "singleness of heart" (Acts 2:46), or the simplicity recommended by the *I Ching* hexagram of Decrease, which might well describe life in a country occupied by an enemy army, but they surely also exhibit an accommodation to complexity.

The self aims at accommodation to complexity and to the resultant differentiation of psychic functions. Such differentiation requires limitation, which begins at the beginning, along with abundance. Certainly we learn about limitation soon, and continue having to learn about it: when the infant realizes that it wants the pleasure of eating, the meals become in its view sporadic. As soon as it begins trying to stand up, it falls down. School and work impose schedules and regulations. Criminals are fined or incarcerated. The book of life closes with a shocking thump. The Dutchman accepted limitations and remained committed to the abundance of the Good—committed to the realization of the Good that would make it more abundant because actual rather than merely potential. While surrounded by Nazis, living hopefully and cunningly true to biblical values of justice and compassion, doing this out of the core of himself, he exemplifies a fundamental quality of feeling in its more differentiated forms. In so doing, he perhaps pondered in his heart some of the same matters that Mary did.

79

2.8 The Volatile Heart and Its Reasons

A diagram illustrating a work by the sixteenth-century alchemist-philosopher-mystic Jacob Boehme suggests further implications of the heart as a symbol of the whole human person, especially when, shortly, we come to consider the diagram in relation to a drawing of a mother and her infant feeding one another.

Within the quadrated circles of the diagram (fig. 3) are two semicircles, one dark, one light, arranged back to back. Superimposed upon the intersection of the cross dividing the larger circle in four, and at the junction of the semicircles, is a heart. It is the center of what are designated as four interrelated principles: Father, Son, Holy Ghost, and Earth or Earthly Man (the human person). That is, the symbols of the design depict a larger order of meaning, having its own logic. The design implies that man's relationship to that meaning accords with what I shall here call "the reasoning of the heart," following Blaise Pascal (1623–62), who maintained that "the heart has its own reasons which Reason does not know."[71]

The quadrated circle of the design is characteristic of the mandalas used in Eastern meditation, and it appears in countless other products of the human imagination, including ground plans of archaic cities and temples, and drawings of psychotics and others faced with the task of integrating the disparate tendencies of the personality.[72]

The equilateral cross implies that the order of meaning depicted in the design is stable, and the words of the design imply that the meaning is in some sense knowable. Yet the junction of the two semicircles is infinitesimal, without extension. Their meeting-point is thus, in effect, All or Nothing, or both. The heart is accordingly, in this design as in some of the biblical utterances we have considered, unfathomable.

Moreover, if one disregards the cross, the form composed by the meeting of the two semicircles is unstable, since only the infinitesimal junction holds them together. This impression of instability is borne out by Boehme's writings, where the junction is described as a volatile, eruptive, evanescent "flash." This is the passionate crisis that is our link with the pathic ground. Further, if it were not for the outer circle we would have the impression that the contents of the semicircles were spluttering out into the blank margin of the page. I will return to this outer circle in a moment.

80

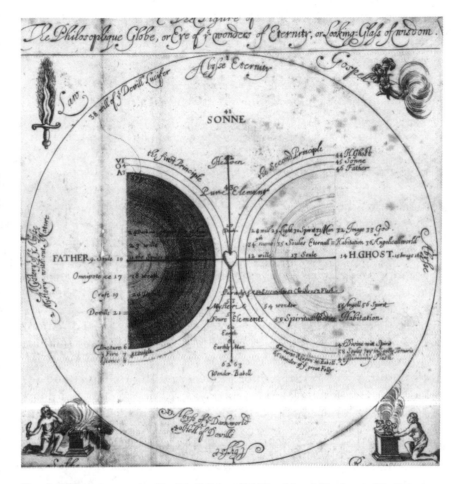

Fig. 3. Illustration to the English Edition (1647) of Jacob Boehme's *XL Questions Concerning the Soule (1620)*. At the center of the diagram is the human heart both as the symbolic seat of feeling and emotion, and as an organ of knowledge. The content of that knowledge is the intellectually articulated world-view summarized in the diagram, but if the heart knows what intellect knows, the heart knows its own version of it in its own mode. (In the words of Pascal, *"Le coeur a ses raisons,"* "The heart has its reasons.") The circle divided into quadrants suggests a wholeness and oneness, the back-to-back semicircles opposition and self-division; these are fundamental qualities in the life of feeling and emotion.

81

Feeling, Imagination, and the Self

The crossing of the horizontal and vertical lines and the meeting of the semicircles is essential to the meaning of the diagram; but significantly, the point of their crossing and meeting is obscured to the viewer by the heart. This implies that this point is not directly accessible to the eye studying the page, or to the intellect used as I am using mine now, and that the heart knows what it knows in its own manner.

Pascal's reference to the heart's "reasons" gains its effect by playing upon the deeply ingrained assumption that "reasons" and "heart" diverge or conflict. But the design, with its words and geometric shapes, implies that what the heart knows is at least in part of the same order of meaning as what is known by sense and intellect, even if an essential part of that meaning is known only by the heart, in its own way. If the heart is an organ of knowledge, how are we to reconcile this fact with the unpredictability and lack of self-control suggested by the diagram's equation of "Heart" and "Flash"?

That the heart, like the lungs, the diaphragm, and the chest generally, can be a seat of consciousness is an ancient and widespread conception met also in the form of the biblical "understanding heart." And as has been said of the mental functioning of the ancient Greeks, the consciousness thought to be localized in this bodily region is not only intellectual but also involves feeling, emotion, even conation (or willing and striving) in more immediate and diffuse interrelations than we nowadays would assume to be true of such processes.[73] We distinguish between perception or thought and the feeling attendant upon it, regarding the feeling as subsequent. But "the emotion may precede the idea, may be vaguely felt before taking definite shape in consciousness and being 'intellectualised'. A man," for example, "meets another or is brought into less direct relations with him, e.g. by being told about him. According to what he learns, so he feels towards him, and his emotion takes on intellectual definition and is realised in idea." Just as the subject has its activity, "the object, the 'idea', has quality and may be characterised according to its emotion and the action to which it tends." Survivals of this kind of mental functioning in our time are acknowledged "by the 'ideo-motor' theory of modern psychology which asserts that 'every "idea" is . . . also a tendency to movement,' " and that " 'systems of ideas . . . have their conative

82

aspect. Each system of ideas is a general tendency to feel and act in certain ways under certain circumstances.' "[74]

This form of consciousness could be called mythic in that its acts are experienced as originating sometimes in the human subject but sometimes also in gods and other spirits acting upon the human subject through inspiration and in other ways. But if Boehme was obsessed by the sort of visionary imagination that populates the world with angels, devils, and arcane forces, he was also obsessed by the need to articulate his visions in logical form. This is understandable, since if myth is in one sense more archaic than critically logical reasoning, myth and such reasoning are in another sense interrelated from the beginning, deriving from a common nexus, and retaining the capacity for implying one another. Thus, for example, a theology may be made out of a myth, but a myth may also be a dramatic expression of logical relations, as we see when gods mythically epitomize the values of a complex social organization.

Philosophers, concerned with large issues of meaning, sometimes employ such expressions as "rounding out" to describe their enterprise. For example, philosophical intelligibility has been said to arise "out of the demand to round out our experience and to make it meaningful as a whole."[75] The circle bounding the illustration to Boehme can be regarded as illustrating the rounding out by which a universe of discourse is created.

This rounding out, however, engages not only the logical mind but also the heart, which needs to be delivered from the instability that can lead to flashes of emotion. This happens as a coherent set of emotionally apprehended values in the form of attitudes, sentiments, and beliefs and comes to provide the person with an embracing and enduring order of meaning. The mythic consciousness of which I have spoken is alive in the discovery of such values and in continuing commitment to them. Yet the form of consciousness thus achieved is subject to various aberrations; order may destroy vitality, and in any case, order establishes the precondition for the conflict and disorder suggested by the "Flash" and the back-to-back black and white semicircles of the diagram. When order destroys vitality—and in consequence becomes itself meaningless—it must be dissolved.

2.9 The Reasoning of the Heart More Closely Considered

A few further comments on Pascal's reference to the heart's "reasons" may help to clarify the ambiguities with which I am now concerned, including those having to do with the *kind* of reasoning the emotionally flashing heart may reveal.

To begin with an important qualification, Pascal's attribution of "reasons" to the heart cannot be taken to mean that all of emotional life is propositional, designed to be translated into rational statements. It cannot be so taken because emotion transcends reason in two interrelated senses: first, emotion comprises a special, partly extrarational mode of experience constituting a felt relationship to the pathic ground; and second, emotion often disrupts reason, sometimes simply foiling it, but often through the disruption saving reason from its own complacency, opening it to neglected information, and thus revitalizing it.

Since it is the reason-disrupting—and in this sense "negative"—manifestations of emotion that are most commonly thought to make it a problem, I pause to offer examples suggesting the knowledge-creating, prospective thrust of many such manifestations. My examples are meant to offer glimpses of such disruption in its bearing on community, individuation, and realistic adaptation.

A and B quarrel in tears and anger; as a result they understand that the issues dividing them are slighter than they thought, and that they had been imagining one another's motives in ugly caricature. C and D quarrel in tears and anger; as a result they gird themselves even more defensively in resentful and implacable opposition. Even if C and D are now veiled to one another in mutual ignorance, that is not necessarily the end of the matter with respect to their emotional state as potential knowledge. For (as will become clearer in part 6.10) E might create a poetic or dramatic portrait of their conflict that would for audience F enhance the kind of emotional understanding from which C and D have cut themselves off.

Among the dreams a certain author has while writing a book is this: "I am living in a small house like one—next door to a nosy, envious couple—that I occupied in my twenties. An arsonist wads newspaper against the back door and sets it afire. I put out the fire, and then consider various plans, such as getting a fire extinguisher, to keep such an event from recurring; they all seem futile. All the windows are uncovered, and my wife and I and the contents of the house, including valuable art objects, are exposed to anyone who wishes to look in. Noticing an unknown man lurking outside one of the windows, I wake up in a cold sweat."

To write a book is an act of self-exposure; the finished work may invite envy and malice. Few books are of more than momentary significance, most being destined for oblivion, as very probably are the art objects in the house in this dream. The author should write his book, the dream suggests, despite these sad truths, simply because doing so interests him. The frightfulness of the dream and his corresponding fear thus encourage a complex feeling-judgment.

The foregoing qualifications notwithstanding, attribution of "reasons" to the heart can and should be taken to mean that in the larger view, and in much of our lived experience, the logical and the emotional are traceably interrelated.

W. W. Fortenbaugh has lucidly explicated Aristotle's view of these interrelations.[76] For Aristotle, the human soul is divided into logical and alogical halves, emotion being consigned to the alogical half. Still, these two halves interact in such a way that the experience of emotion is a complex cognitive process, always entailing a thought, which must be part of the essential definition of any emotion. Thus, for example, anger is a desire for revenge accompanied by pain owing to an unjustified apparent slight to oneself or one's own. This thought of personal insult is the efficient cause of the emotion, and is what allows Aristotle to draw the logical boundaries between the emotions of anger and hate. It is disagreeably true that such a thought as that of personal insult may be mistaken, but this entails the possibility that the thought may be corrected.[77]

Indeed, emotional response can be explained syllogistically, with the thought-component of the emotion, its efficient cause, serving as its middle term. This may be seen in a course of reasoning going out from the question, Why did war befall the Athenians? and from the answer, Because they attacked Sardis. If A stands for war, B for unprovoked aggression, and C for the Athenians, one may say that B (unprovoked aggression) applies to C (the Athenians), and A (war)

85

applies to B (unprovoked aggression). If the middle term—or efficient cause—"war" is replaced by "anger," and if "unprovoked aggression" is replaced by "apparent insult," we have a general explanation of all kinds of angry response.[78]

According to Aristotle, the logical half of the soul may appeal to the alogical half through reasoned rhetoric and such arts as drama and music because the alogical half has *logos* within it. Such constraints of reason upon emotion find their reversal, however, in the constraints of emotion upon reason. Thus, for example, Medea's wrath against her unfaithful husband leads her to kill her children, an act not in her best interest, though within that important larger limitation she carries out her plan with considerable cleverness.[79]

Psychoanalysts, too, assume that interrelations between the logical and the emotional can be traced even if they are lost from consciousness. (As an example of such loss, "Lenore Gallagher" wonders why it occurred to her only many years later, and then to her extreme consternation, that the reason her father ended up asleep on the floor so many evenings when she was a child was that he was drunk. Weeks of rainy weather depress her slightly; is such weather also the reason— she can think of no other—for the agitated dread into which her depression has recently issued?) Practically, such logical-emotional connections cannot always be traced and, one must allow, may not even be there. This is true especially in some states of extreme psychopathology—for example, severe chronic endogenous depression— though in these states, too, there may be unexpected success in tracing such connections.

Kinds of experience in which no connection can be traced between the logical and emotional bring us to a point at which order dissolves into randomness or chaos, or in which randomness or chaos become apprehensible order. This ambiguity characterizes our relation to the pathic ground of psychic life. If the practical tracing of all interrelations between the emotional and the logical could be assured even in principle, we would be on the way to plucking the heart of Hamlet's mystery. For, whatever else that mystery may be, it is surely a sense of the pathic ground in its bristling, ensnaring opacity. (T. S. Eliot felt this when he complained that *Hamlet* made reference to emotional concerns that did not find adequate expression—their "objective cor-relative"—in the actual play.)

"The reasoning of the heart" implies that there are appropriate and inappropriate emotions. Feeling, as I am using that term, plays a primary role in determining their appropriateness or inappropriateness.

"The reasoning of the heart" can and should be taken to mean, further, that skill in knowing what to feel is possible, as is suggested by the observation that "Aristotle is clearly not the only philosopher who has thought that the important thing if one is to lead a fulfilled and proper life is to feel the right emotion, on the right occasion, toward the right object and in the right degree."[80] And the phrase can and should be taken to mean that this skill can be educated, that there is an education of the heart.

"The reasoning of the heart" also can and should mean that the exercise of this skill is both highly individual and highly communal. For example, when I respond with the proper play of emotion to "Elizabeth," I must have seen, and must now vividly know, something of her individual essence. That essence must have been conveyed to me in a way that makes it, now, as cherished knowledge, part of my person. And when, in the tenth book of the *Odyssey*, Elpenor pleads with Odysseus to perform the proper burial rites for him, Elpenor is drawing upon a culturally given understanding of a network of forms of relationship and obligation, of the emotions proper to these, and of the rituals requisite to assure that such emotions are generated.[81]

"The reasoning of the heart" can and should mean, finally, that the objects of such heart-knowledge are both concrete and specific, on the one hand, and abstract and universal, on the other. For ex-ample, I disapprove of "Edward" for qualities of cowardice and men-dacity that would provoke my disapprobation of anyone in whom I met them. No amount of sympathetic understanding of how and why Edward became the wretch that he is will change my judgment and emotional response to these qualities, though I may achieve a complex feeling-judgment that does not assume these qualities to be identical with Edward's person as a whole. I grant that I know worse qualities, and that with different life experience—for example, if I were to spend much time in the company of rapists and murderers—I might be more

87

sharply aware than I am that there are much worse qualities still. Nonetheless, I judge Edward's qualities with "universal intent" (to borrow a phrase from Polanyi).[82]

These reflections on "the reasoning of the heart" have an important bearing on individuation. Jung meant this term to name a process of differentiation and integration by which one's personal identity is kept responsive to the self in such a way that that identity is drawn beyond the one-sidedness of one's present conscious outlook, of one's upbringing, and of collective values unreflectingly assumed. This process may be said to have a logic, but its logic is emergent.[83] A precondition of its emergence is what Jung in his early psychiatric work—following upon investigations by the French psychiatrist Pierre Janet and others—called "the dissociability of the psyche," the tendency of the subjective sphere to disintegrate.[84] That is, just as logic entails the capacity for logical error, which may lead to new logical discovery, so the same principle applies to emotion and value—and to individuation. And just as emotion and value connect the person with others, so individuation is irreducibly a form of relationship with community. There is no subject that is not also a fellow-subject, no "I" that is not also "we."

The relations between individuation and community, and between psychic integration and disintegration—or deintegration—are complex. Though identification with collective values may tend to erase individual differences, without a deep sense of community, efforts to further individuation lead to self-deluded isolation from sources of vitality and of a more embracing order of meaning. Moreover, adequate integration requires the abandonment or destruction of meaning in its less adequate forms. Though enduring attitudes, sentiments, and beliefs are necessary, they are vital only in process. In process the ordering principle of the self that has formed and that re-forms and revitalizes them is felt. Access to that ordering entails, and has as its precondition, passionate crisis. Boehme's diagram could be taken as an emblem of the individual's relation, through passionate crisis, to the pathic ground and hence to the self.

A drawing of the mother and infant feeding one another (fig. 4) raises issues that complement those I have been discussing. What is here pictured is, in its larger implications, less a reciprocal exchange

Fig. 4. The mother-infant dyad: mother-as-infant and infant-as-mother. In the words of Winnicott, "Psychologically the infant takes from the breast that is part of the infant, and the mother gives milk to an infant that is part of herself."[85] This drawing suggests an emotional and preverbal counterpart of the *reaching* and "rounding out" in philosophical attempts to push verbal terms to their limits. The circle implied by the picture may thus be compared with that of fig. 3.

As a way of getting two people fed with oatmeal, the activity shown here has little to recommend it. Ostensibly a form of reciprocal exchange, it is more truly an experience of mutuality, reaching into and drawing upon a larger order of relatedness. This collaborative effort—under the aspect of community—accords on the feeling level with sympathy—or feeling-with—as distinct from more primitive forms of empathy (as when a mother, for example, automatically opens her own mouth as she spoons food into the mouth of her infant). Mother and infant here mirror one another, but they are also open to the mystery of one another's otherness. Therefore, their interaction is not fusion or symbiosis but a preform both of reality-based relationship and of contemplative, loving mutual regard.

What is depicted is partly, and importantly, the kind of reciprocity to be seen in the exchange of money for work or goods. It is also, and in some respects more importantly, the kind of mutuality that effects an opening to a larger life of mature experience and meaning (discussed in parts 5 and 6).

than an experience of the mutuality and abundance that are major themes of this book.

About the time of birth, the original self of the infant deintegrates. (See part 2.5.) In the mother's interaction with her infant, her well-developed ego functions on behalf of its incipient ego, but does so in ways implying the more comprehensive viewpoint and balancing propensities of the self. An ordinary real infant may also awaken in its mother, and in others, an imaginative resonance related to that which makes infant gods (such as the Christ Child) serve as symbols of the self.[86] Thus the drawing suggests ways (discussed in part 4.4) in which ego and self may function on behalf of one another.

One sees in the drawing, further, an emotional and preverbal counterpart of the reaching and rounding out accomplished by language and other human symbol systems as they push terms to their limits: symbolism even at its most abstract is ultimately rooted in the pathic ground. Thus the circle implied by the action depicted in the drawing may be compared with the outer circle in figure 3. When I spoke of the rounding out of philosophical discourse, I meant to allow for the possibility that such an outer circle may prove arbitrary or false, and may thus be dissolved, so that the meaning conveyed by such a diagram as a whole may disintegrate. (Thus religions and philosophical systems are replaced by others.) In an ultimately related way—though at a distance from such abstraction—the harmony of the implied circle of the mother's and infant's mutual feeding may at any moment disintegrate as the infant emotionally falls apart.

2.10 The Oedipus Complex in the Context of the Mother-Infant Relationship

In the mature life of the mind, dyads—in such forms as religious and philosophical dualisms—have sometimes been superseded by triads—in such forms as the Christian trinity and the dialectical procedures of Plato, Hegel, and other thinkers. And in the early emotional life of the individual, the dyadic relationship of mother and infant gives way to the triadic relationship of mother, infant, and father. Triads are generally dynamic, and this triadic personal relationship generates tensions demanding resolution. What concerns me now is the fate of the dyadic relationship under the stress of these tensions, and its role in an adequate resolution of them.

Being True to Oneself in Abundance and Limitation

Owing to the special circumstances of human life, including protracted infancy and childhood and the child's need to acquire a repertoire of cultural values, the triangular relationship of mother, father, and child becomes internalized in the form of the Oedipus complex described by Freud. But the Oedipus complex may be of varying degrees of importance in psychic life, may be to varying degrees "normal" or pathological, resolved or unresolved, and may to varying degrees impede continuing connection to still earlier development levels.

As the Oedipus complex is resolved, the developing person is thought to become able, on the one hand, to cope with the rough-and-tumble of reality while accepting the attendant frustration, conflict, and defeat of desires, and, on the other, to sacrifice the obstinate wish for what has been characterized as the "paradisal" tie of mother and infant. Adequate resolution of this important complex does indeed entail recognition of socially defined reality and the bearing of disappointment, but it is one-sided to think of this as the primary component of such a resolution. The mother-infant tie must be transformed in the process, but in a way that preserves and affirms it. This component is quite as basic to the resolution of the complex, since richness of experience within the mother-infant dyad establishes in the infant resources for dealing later with triadic tensions. Such transformation of the mother-infant tie—a transformation in which that tie is preserved and affirmed—has never been given the attention it deserves.

Much of being a baby is not "paradisal" but hard work, with myriad difficulties to be overcome as it achieves skills despite the recalcitrance of objects and of its own poorly coordinated body. And to describe the mother-infant tie as paradisal is also to blur an important distinction made in the psychological literature between fusion, in which boundaries are dissolved, and union, in which, though greatly relaxed or expanded, they are implicitly maintained, and with them at least a vestigial sense of separateness.

During the earliest days and weeks of the infant's life, experiences based on the distinction between "I" and "not-I," and between "inside the body" and "outside the body" are delayed, as though mother and infant are both intent on providing the infant with a form of pleasure, that of fusion, lying in states that approximate as closely as possible the intrauterine state: "no stimuli; no wants, no tensions; no sensations, no boundaries."[87] Then experiences of union gradually become

91

prominent, indeed making up a large part of the infant's play. Thus Winnicott speaks of "transitional objects," such as a bit of fluff, a blanket, a doll, to which the infant forms a special attachment, fascinating because it represents not fusion but the union of mother and infant, both of whom the infant is beginning to experience as separate beings.[88] The mutuality of which I am speaking in these pages, as the protoform of community and individuation, is based not on fusion but on union. Within the framework of mutuality, union might be thought to open out to experiences of fusion, which continue to be important, and to gather them back into a sense of separateness. Ego boundaries are in the process relaxed or expanded, and reaffirmed.

Personal development takes a bad turn when the mirroring of mother and infant depicted in the drawing (fig. 4) gives way to a mirroring between subject and rival, in such forms as father or sibling, with the result that the mother-infant bond is devalued and disowned. Then the mirroring between subject and rival amounts to a variant of what the psychologist Alfred Adler called the masculine protest,[89] repressing the mother-infant bond, with its implications of weakness and vulnerability. But this bond, alive in the psychic depths, remains the basis for further development along the lines of individuation, and repression of it results in armored pseudoindependence. When we reject dependency, and with it mutuality, in our determination to go our separate ways, we aggrandize ourselves while diminishing our relation to the sources of life and meaning.

The importance of continuing access to psychic regions reflecting the early mother-infant bond may be seen strikingly with regard to introjected notions of good and bad, and right and wrong. They are introjected as part of the process by which what Freud called the superego, or internal censuring authority, is constituted, its constitution being part of the resolution of the Oedipus complex. But this inner authority may become tyrannical and sadistic. And one's notions of value—indeed one's whole activity of valuing—may become envious, dependent on the authority of rivals following upon the prototypes of parents and siblings. In both cases the capacity for pliancy and yielding is sacrificed to conflict-creation and conflict-resolution, with conflict-resolution assuming forms that perpetuate conflict.

A baby must work so hard because life is difficult, and because in it conflict is inevitable. But it is a defensive oversimplification and a mistake to assume that life is basically the war of all against all, and that the most important way to cope with it, and to maintain one's personal integrity, is through vigilant striving. This mistake is not inevitable. But to avoid it one's values must not become petrified in a tyrannical specimen of the superego, and they must not be delivered up to "mimetic desire"—desiring what the other person desires because the other person desires it.[90] Rather, they must remain flexible and responsive to the personal core in its openness to the process of individuation and its aspiration to authentic community. This requires the ego to have continuing access to preoedipal psychic regions in which the rich interrelatedness of mother and infant is still alive. Continuing access to them is a requirement for the adequate resolution of the Oedipus complex and is essential to the self-validation that is a major concern of this book, and to the right loving and right hating based on that self-validation.

Indeed, in the course of several years of work as a psychotherapist in psychiatric clinics, I was often struck by the vast array of psychopathology in such forms as emotional aridity, rigidity, brittleness, and gray intellectualization that were clearly symptomatic of radical disconnection with the mother of one's early experience. All such forms of psychopathology amount to unrelatedness. One's first and usually most determining relationship is with one's mother, and the mother-infant bond is alive in whatever relatedness one does achieve throughout life. When there are deficits in that bond, it need not be the case that the person suffering from them has—fleeing the Oedipus complex—hastened into robust yet discriminating engagement in the Father World. More commonly, a bad relationship to Mother means a bad relationship to Father, so that for a great many purposes one could most accurately speak not of a mother complex or a father complex but of a parental complex.

A recent article largely about the Oedipus complex is instructive in its neglect of the kind of self-validation that most concerns me and in its one-sided treatment of the dyadic mother-infant relationship. In the article, Leila Tov-Ruach describes the mother's acceptance, security, and care of her infant son in a nonjudgmental relationship that comes to an end as he grows up to the point of entering the masculine world of relentless comparison, measurement, and placing in hierarchies. Judging and being judged is in the father-son relationship from the outset, as the father sets standards for the son but also fears being judged by him. (These complications become clear when, for example, the boy feels guilt for surpassing his father in some accomplishment.) As the boy comes to be delivered up to rigors of judgment, he feels betrayed by his mother, whom he discovers to have become one of the judges. The fate of the girl-child is different, as her relation to her father becomes important to her later than the son's does to him, and because he encourages her anyway to be non-judgmentally accepting toward him.[91]

This description assumes something like Freud's distinction between the pleasure principle and the reality principle, a false dichotomy, since the seeking of pleasure and the avoidance of pain are not motives in themselves but are constituents of complex, goal-directed developmental processes. (Thus the infant just learning to wave its hand in response to the waved hand of an adult takes pleasure in the waving, not because it feels good but because it represents an excitingly new and more complex form of interaction with others.)

Moreover, this description implies that judging and being judged start some years along into a person's life, whereas an infant's life is made of continual valuation—in forms that might be translated, "too cold," "wet," "hunger," "cozily secure," "Da-da come here," "fright!" "strained upsetting confusion," "pretty Christmas-tree lights," "drifting toward sleep."

This description implies, further, that judging, measuring, criticizing, placing in hierarchies begins with—is derived from—being judged, being measured, being criticized, being placed in hierarchies. On the contrary, becoming the object of such activities is a secondary development, albeit a greatly important one, based on the earlier kind of valuation I have just described. In the mother's "mirroring" of the infant, she supports and molds this unfolding pattern of activities, leading it in the direction of community. Rather than simply turning traitor and delivering the boy-child up to the judges "out there," the mother may also help the boy to maintain a relationship, in appropriately maturing form, to the self-validation—and the sense of the self as valuable—at the basis of his socialization.

Whether this development takes the form of the masculine protest against anything feminine, and whether the son comes to experience

94

his father as Saturn eating his children, depends partly on the kind of father the son has and the kind of male society he is being asked to join. But it also depends very significantly on his mother's sense of the value of her own femininity, and on her way of mediating the values of the Father World. If she is successful in supporting her son's self-validation, while encouraging respect and love for femininity, and tempering masculine drives to autonomy and competitiveness, she will help assure that *logos* for him remains grounded in eros, and she will make him aware of a form of community in which self-validation opens out in felt appreciation of mutuality and complex interconnectedness, including that of the natural world. In this sense cultural sanity is served by regarding Earth as Mother.

It is thus important to grant the fundamental cultural importance of the mother-infant bond. Indeed, it is worth bearing in mind that through such institutions as the festival, to be discussed in part 4, even highly patriarchal cultures offer means for their adult members to renew contact with the level of themselves suggested by the drawing of the mother and the baby feeding one another. As we will see, a festival is not simply a regression to instinctual gratification and celebration of the idols of the tribe: it also revivifies the sense of mutuality of which I have just spoken. This sense is essential to the education of the heart by which we may someday become decently human.

3 Abandonment, Wish, and Hope in the Blues

3.1 Triadic Tensions and the Mother-Infant Relationship in the Blues

Often deeply moving, subtle, complex, and mysteriously condensed and ambiguous, the blues is a form of musical folk poetry originating around the turn of this century and developing through various phases and styles to the present. Geographically, it encompasses the Mississippi Delta, the Texas Panhandle, Georgia, the Carolinas, Tennessee, New Orleans, Memphis, and Chicago. A performance art, its notable singers have included Skip James, Mississippi John Hurt, Charley Patton, Blind Lemon Jefferson, Blind Willie McTell, Ida Cox, Ma Rainey, Bessie Smith, Leroy Carr, Memphis Minnie, Robert Johnson, Joe Turner, Jimmy Rushing, Robert Pete Williams, Lightning Hopkins, Muddy Waters, and John Lee Hooker, each of whom has an instantly recognizable musical and poetic voice. This individuality is manifest for the most part in variants of a simple musical form. The lyrics of a blues performance may be drawn from a vast stock of traditional "floating" verses, may be improvised to fit the occasion, or may take the form of set compositions, usually reworking traditional materials. Highly formulaic in the manner of folk epics, the blues is itself a world patterned in accordance with characteristic themes, images, and symbols, a world familiar yet mysterious, public yet subjective and idiosyncratic, offering deep satisfactions to be had in no other way than through one's imaginative habitation of it.

In principle, blues lyrics can be about virtually any subject that strikes the interest of the blues singer or composer. Blues may celebrate good times, feeling good, partying, and sexual pleasure. But most blues

97

lyrics are about "troubles"—hardships of lower-class black Americans—in the forms of thwarted love, abandonment, infidelity, death, murder, poverty, hard work for little pay, homelessness, natural disasters, drunkenness, drug-taking, gambling, prostitution, and jail. There are overtly joyous blues, often boasting or reveling in grandiose fantasy or in prospects of sexual pleasure. There are no blues about wildflowers or beautiful sunsets. And though a few blues artists (such as J. B. Lenoir) have dealt with such subjects as racial violence, social protest is rare in the blues,[1] the many ironies of which have little to do with those of such "committed" writers as Bertolt Brecht. Indeed, the most characteristic attitude of the blues toward life is "noncommittal,"[2] which is far from meaning simply "hopeless." The broadest subject matter of the blues is *having* the blues, so that overtly joyous blues, too, usually refer at least indirectly to having the blues as a deplorable but probably inevitable condition.

Though noncommittal treatment of such themes as I have listed reflects a fatalism well justified by the real-life experience of many blues performers and much of the blues audience, I will focus on another reason for the inclination of the blues to leave problems unsolved or to offer solutions with at least a suggestion of further problems. Emotional life in general is predicated on the certainty of uncertainty—as we saw in the connection between the heart and "Flash" in the diagram illustrating Boehme (fig. 3). And feeling, as a special dimension of emotional life, is also so predicated. A mother must read and relate to the feeling-state of her infant, whom she must comfort even under adverse circumstances, and even in the certainty that circumstances now ameliorated will become adverse again. And the mother's feeling-relationship with her infant is the basis of further developments of feeling, which at the deepest level are concerned with survival. In its exploration of such themes as what it is like to be on the "killing floor," the blues draws us back to this level of feeling.[3]

In its concern with knowing what to feel and with feeling what is proper to be felt, the blues is an extraordinary development in the education of the heart. The blues shows with special clarity things of importance about the relationship between individuality and community; the need for the whole person to remain open to the world with its contingency and pain; the emotional force and restraint necessary to differentiated feeling; and the ways in which the mother-infant dyad may be potently implicit in the artistic—or, more broadly, the spiritual—transcendence of real-life frustrations and conflicts. Further, despite the frequent bleakness of its subject matter, the blues is a comic art celebrating the triumph of both individuality and community. The blues shows with special clarity important transformative workings of the imagination—imaginative transcendence—and the interrelations between imagination and feeling.[4]

A blues performer does not need to have the blues at the moment in order to sing the blues well, though deep feeling is one of the valued qualities of a blues performance. (Muddy Waters has been described as leaving the bandstand, after a strong performance, in a state of near-trance lasting about half an hour; another blues artist has been censured for "phoning in" his blues message as though it were an order to a business firm. And Texas barrelhouse and sawmill pianist Buster Pickens observes, "The only way anyone can ever play blues—he's got to have them. . . . [N]ach'al blues come directly from a person's heart: what he's experienced in life. . . . Whether he's been troubled, whether he's ridden freight trains, where he's been put in jail; been beaten up by railroad dicks and everythin' else you understand—pushed around in life. . . . You have a tough way in life—that makes you blue. That's when you start to sing the blues—when you've got the blues."[5]) Nor does the audience need to have the blues at the moment to appreciate a blues performance. But it is essential for performer and audience to know at least tacitly what it is to have the blues.

The relationship between having the blues and performing the blues is, however, more complex, subtle, and above all more indirect than Buster Pickens suggests. If blues performers and their audience were just sitting around having the blues, there would be no blues performance. This is because having the blues and not having the blues are essentially related to one another—most simply in that when one has the blues one hopes that one will find the path to not having them, and that when one does not have them one fears that one may already be on the path to having them. Having the blues and not having the blues exist, metaphorically speaking, at a distance from one another. And knowledge of both conditions is assumed and drawn upon in a blues performance. Basically, blues performers and their audience are not present at the performance because they now acutely have the blues. (Some may be present for this reason, but they do not supply the governing motive of the occasion.) Rather, they are present because they might come to have the blues, because the blues remains a potentiality, to be faced now in the hope that it will not be actualized in an incapacitating way but will instead be converted to something else, to self-enhancing feelings and states, beginning with the vital, bodily good times of the performance. Thus, the blues performance assumes the present or available reality of not having the blues. This is as much the point of departure of the blues experience as is knowledge of having them.

Still, knowledge of having the blues is what could be called the emotional frame of reference of the blues experience. In calling it this, I am pointing to its character as existing at a distance from not now having the blues, though the two conditions are interrelated. I have in mind the semanticist Alfred Korzybski's oft-repeated summary statement that map is not territory, and am thinking of the emotional frame of reference as such a map. According to Korzybski, the word *cat*, belonging to the figurative map, cannot scratch us, as it could if it were real as the territory is but as the map is not. Still, we must know something about the reality "cat" for the word *cat* to have meaning; some sort of knowledge of real cats provides a frame of reference for the word *cat*. The condition of having the blues is the territory—the emotional frame of reference—that the blues performance attempts to map—that is, to bring to imaginative awareness. Some sort of prior knowledge of the condition is necessary to evoke that awareness (though one need not have been beaten up by railroad dicks to possess it).

A territory can be—and in a strong blues performance is—mapped by feeling. But as one might begin sketching without having the intention of representing anything specific, making a map can be— and in a strong blues performance is—inseparable from discovering what is to be mapped. One's prior knowledge of the condition of having the blues need not be specific. Indeed, one function of the blues performance is to articulate the not-yet-articulated, even though

Abandonment, Wish, and Hope in the Blues

what is thus expressed is in some sense already tacitly known. What is it to have the blues? How do we know what it is to have the blues? And what does having the blues have to do, even if indirectly, with performing the blues? Whatever answers we can give to these questions will help to illumine the nature of feeling.

Though having the blues is in one sense the emotional frame of reference of a blues performance, having the blues is also an expression of the pathic ground and is thus inaccessible to consciousness. It can be only crudely translated by such words and phrases as "despondency" and "soul-loss." In a sense related to the philosopher Spinoza's contention that by knowing the causes of our emotions, we are freed from the passivity they entail, the blues as musical poetry is an ongoing process of trying to define what having the blues is.

Much of the blues is about "the blues," often, importantly, in such a way that it is not possible to draw a clear distinction in a blues text between the blues as "having the blues" and the blues as art form. The lack of distinction is important; the ambiguity is calculated and deliberate. Thus Otis Spann, the splendid pianist with the Muddy Waters blues band for many years, sings, "When you in trouble, blues is a man's best friend. . . . Blues ain't goin' to ask you where you goin', and blues don't care where you been," and later, "We can't let the blues die, the blues don't mean you no harm. . . . I'm goin' back to the lowlands, that's where the blues came from."[6] The blues that we can't let die is probably (mostly) the consoling, soul-strengthening music; going back to the lowlands implies a return to the poverty of lower-class southern farmers that Spann and countless other blacks had moved to Chicago and other northern cities to escape. The blues of the lowlands is perhaps partly the music but surely also the toil and pain out of which it was born. The line says ironically, "The blues as music and as an imaginative world-view makes having the blues harmless; so let us pay tribute to the music and the world-view by going back to the real misery, to the condition of having the blues, that made the music and the world-view necessary."

If we did not, at least tacitly, already know the unwilled condition of having the blues—if we did not already partly know the territory— the blues performance would not work in freeing us from the condition

101

by offering us a provisional definition of it. Although map is not territory, in lived experience the ambiguity between them is as important as the distinction between them, and the blues exploits this ambiguity in ways that have rich implications for the psychology of feeling and imagination.

A child partly regards a doll as a real person; we partly forget that the people on a stage are actors representing characters in a play; we are usually unaware that we have performed a leap as we mentally pass from the word *cat* to an image-idea of the real animal that may scratch. Indeed, in emotional life we map the territory in order to gain the distance from it that we have lost or feel ourselves in danger of losing. Maps must be replaced by other maps, as new emotional situations in need of being read take form. Feeling is never final; feeling is process; feeling always begins again. Even habitual and well-tested feeling-judgments must be continually enlivened by being experienced as part of feeling as process, if such judgments are to be validly binding and not lifeless things on a shelf. In its appreciation of the provisional nature of its products, feeling is essential to imagination, fraught as imagination is with ambiguities and tensions that link it to the pathic ground and that make any final map impossible. Spann knows much about this: if the best solution he can offer to the problem of having the blues is going back to where the blues was born, the problem is—subtly, indirectly—exposed as unsolved, and new imaginative maps will, as he knows, have to be devised to reveal the nature of the territory of having the blues. More blues will have to be played and sung; continuation and repetition are as necessary to the blues party as they are to solemn festivals.

By offering a specious solution to the problem, Spann is in a sense pushing his audience further in the direction of having the blues. But the nature of the emotional issue changes significantly in the process. The issue is no longer the direct danger of having the blues, though the audience is being vividly reminded of what it is to have them. Rather, the issue is the disintegration of the defense against having the blues as the implications of the specious argument come to awareness. Spann, that is to say, has convincingly presented himself as the blues expert. But what are we to do, after he has stirred our awareness of how bad it feels to have the blues, as it begins to dawn on us that his expertise may be inconsequential, or that he may be pulling our leg?

Let us assume in Spann's audience—in ourselves insofar as we have firsthand prior knowledge of the territory he is mapping—an ongoing, "normal" defense against having the blues, this defense being related to the mental set that enables us to ignore distractions. Though useful, such a defense may become too severe and thus result in an impoverishment of inner life and an increase in the danger that the defense will fail. In general in psychic life, letting in a defended-against force— any energy-charged psychic content—is a first step in arriving at a more adequate conscious attitude toward it. (For example, one must let oneself be depressed before one can find out what one is depressed about and then seek the most fitting perspective in which to regard the object of one's depression.)

The kind of defense I have in mind is well illustrated, along with its failure, in a film about the blues, *Bottle Up and Go,* in which a black hat salesman describes circumstances that make one have the blues. Grinning and laughing nervously, his hypomanic manner is a striking instance of what psychiatrists call "inappropriate affect," denying the pain of the familiar realities he is enumerating. But as his account proceeds, his jollity disappears and his eyes look troubled, as he allows himself to feel the import of what he is saying.

The letting in of such a force generates emotion which, if it is to remain ego-syntonic, demands a new distancing, in the form of a more alert and precise reading of the emotional situation—in our case, that described in the blues verses. Emotion thus motivates imaginative engagement in which distancing plays a necessary role. It is this distancing that allows the emotional situation to be read in the mode of feeling, and allows the literal to open out to the metaphorical, the symbolic, the ironic. The distance thus achieved is, however, variable, and the process by which it is increased or decreased is subtle.

Indeed, though the blues is concerned with issues of pathos, blues verses and the blues performance as a whole are ironic, in the sense that what is said is always at some distance from what is meant. Occasionally the irony is clear-cut, as when Howlin' Wolf ("three hundred pounds of comfort and joy") sings that he "ain't superstitious" and then lists his superstitions one by one.[7] Usually, though, the irony is more subtle, as in Spann's verses already considered, or in another piece in which he declares that he has a wonderful feeling everything is going to be all right, a feeling deep down in his soul, a feeling that he is going to love his woman every day and every night. The confidently loping melodic line and driving, charged rhythm totally fit this joyous and hopeful sentiment. Still, his declaration that she "done came back home" to him implies conflict and separation; and in admitting to being worried that she might leave again, he hardly offers cause for feeling all that wonderful.[8]

Sometimes the clues to *how* ironic the tone is are unspecifiable. For example, if a blues performer sings about leaving his present woes and going somewhere else to begin anew, his message and manner may partly inspire our confidence. And yet we might have reason to wonder whether he really does have any new place to go, or if he will do anything other than find himself in a new version of his old situation if he does go, or if, indeed, flight is not also a form of defeat. Such ambiguity, forcing one to reach *through* the semantic text to the expressive features of the overall performance, is fundamental to what could be called the blues esthetic.

Verses sung in 1983 by guitarist-singer Johnny Copeland offer a striking example of ironic distancing coupled with a breakdown between emotional map and territory. In high spirits he sings, at a brisk tempo:

> When the rain starts falling,
> My feet start to itching;
> I know that it's time to go.
> You know, I promised myself
> It ain't gonna rain in my life no mo'.
>
> When you all out of money,
> Things get funny;
> Look like everybody know.
> I'm gonna pack my bag, and down the road I go.
>
> Well, the rain keep a comin', and I keep a runnin';
> I'm movin' like the wind.
> You know, when the rain catch up,
> I'm on the move again.

Abandonment, Wish, and Hope in the Blues

When you hear from me again,
I'll be somewhere down the road.
I'm gonna ride that train
Just as far as my money goes.

When the rain starts falling,
My feet start to itching;
You know, I promised myself
It ain't gonna rain in my life no mo'.[9]

Having the blues is the rain the singer wants to escape. And his joyously imagined flight is predicated on certain defeat: if he is out of money, he cannot pay for a train ride. Moreover, as the clown Feste sings at the close of *Twelfth Night*, "For the rain it raineth every day," and as a once-popular song has it, "Into each life some rain must fall." Having the blues is ultimately no more controllable than the weather.

When a blues singer sings the traditional line, "The sun's going to shine in my back door someday," he is expressing hope that things will get better; and he knows, and we know, that he, like Feste, is speaking metaphorically when he sings with wistful resignation about the wind and the rain. Copeland's fantasy, in contrast, goes much further in the kind of concretization of metaphor we see when, in *A Midsummer Night's Dream*, the fairy Puck puts an ass's head on the fool Bottom and causes the fairy queen Titania foolishly to fall in love with him, or when in *King Lear* the distraught king exclaims, "I have full cause of weeping, but this heart / Shall break into a hundred thousand flaws / Or ere I'll weep. O Fool, I shall go mad!" (II. iv. 281–83) after the sound of "*Storm and tempest*," symbolizing emotional turmoil and madness. The expressive features of Copeland's voice and music, with their soaring, charging energy, their brash exuberance, convince us that he takes his fantasy literally. He sounds utterly delighted to be actively not understanding the implications of what he is saying.

Our pleasure in the singer's self-confident delight is derived from our tacit awareness of the condition of having the blues. That awareness is affirmed even while its tacit character is insisted upon. We know what we are looking away from even while we are looking away from it. The artistic persona of the singer denies painful reality; the performance as a whole does not. Its irony serves the interrelated functions of detaching us from that reality while keeping us in touch with it. In the imaginative world-view of the blues, joy is born of pain, and pain is not to be denied. Joy is not simply the denial of pain but represents an order of value in its own right. Irony assures that pain is not only not denied but is taken into account as the value of joy is affirmed. The view of reality I have just outlined is related to that discussed earlier (in part 2.7) of Chrysostom and Luther about sin and death, on the one hand, and abounding grace, on the other.

One could regard the fictional persona's swaggering denial of reality as a form of what psychoanalysts call manic defense—against depression and the rage that may be latent within it. But regarding it in this way still leaves questions about the relations among, first, the reality-denying verbal content; second, the hints of ironic distancing in the presentation; and third, the tumultuous energy of the performance as a whole. By "ironic distancing" I mean that, although the singer presents himself as not understanding the dissembling illogic of his own words, what we hear is precisely the self as thus presented, an artifact neither inviting nor allowing a response based primarily on identification with him. Rather, we are meant, and called upon, to register incongruities of which he, in the artifact of his self-presentation, is unaware. Is the energy of the performance simply that of wishful manic defense? Or is it rather the energy of a hopeful determination to survive and rejoice? Or does irony, in the performance, effect a transformation from the mode of wish to that of hope?

Schopenhauer's "Will," or fundamental life force, makes use of whatever illusions are available that will serve its purposes. We may imagine this life force as using the illusion of the blues singer's fictional persona to live itself out in the vigor of the music. His wish thus blindly serves the purpose of the deeper Will, while giving him access to its power. We feel the surge of that power but retain at least some awareness that he is its victim.

The kind of double perspective I am describing is characteristic of dramatic irony, which allows us to sense energy based on illusion as having a deeper purpose and meaning. In A Midsummer Night's Dream, as in others of Shakespeare's love comedies, love generates such energy, which we sense in such a way. (A production of the play

Abandonment, Wish, and Hope in the Blues

by the Royal Shakespeare Company, directed by Peter Brook some years ago, was introduced by rock drummers, and the energy of the lovers, who swung from trapezes, was accordingly frenetic, with the illusion of the lovers being highlighted by the stark black, white, and red of the set.) Still, though the judgment of the Athenian lovers is the product of the love magic in their eyes, their energy also, on another level, serves an ordering principle that leads the lovers to adulthood and regenerates society through their marriages. We, the audience, see this ordering principle in the formal, dancelike pattern of attractions and aversions among the lovers, so that the final outcome strikes us as necessary and destined, though from moment to moment blind chance seems to be governing the course of events. Thus, in the Shakespearean vision, nature and society make use of illusion and the energy generated by it in a way related to the use made of them by Schopenhauer's Will.

Ironic detachment can help one to participate in life—as Will, society, or nature—without being its mindless tool or victim. And this entails seeing illusion as illusion, as we do as we watch the Athenian lovers. Just as our knowledge that clowns are clowns—and will not seriously attack us, and will not kill one another with their sledgehammers—allows us to be enlivened by the high spirits of their knockabout, so our appreciation of Copeland's posture as posture, and as comic, gives us the proper form of access to his energy. This gift requires and demands of each of us a reorientation of the ego.

In some important respects, we always know too little, too late; and the ego continually needs to have its attitudes challenged. Partly, however, it is through the exercise and affirmation of its own discriminating powers that the ego is persuaded and enabled to open itself to contents, including emotional currents, varying from its prevailing set. To deal with irony, to recognize illusion as illusion, is to master ambiguity while opening oneself up to it. Discrimination—holding separate things apart—allows imaginative sympathy based on an awareness of levels. We feel with the Athenian lovers and the blues singer, while hearing as part of a larger artistic whole the details of their utterance that they offer as the expression of conscious intent, and while assessing that conscious intent as illusory. Thus, ironic detachment may allow the ego of the audience to enter into a fictional representation of wish-fulfillment in such a way as to find life-giving hope in it, through it, beyond it. The ego may use the detachment of its ironic stance to look through the level of ego defense to the deeper movements of the self to be discussed in part 3.3.

In general, the blues is radically committed to what has been called the blues ideology, which holds that real-life problems are not soluble in real-life terms, or that if such a problem is solved in such terms, it will immediately lead to further problems. Nor does religion offer an alternative. (Blues people may go to church; some have been preachers; but religion does not acquire the force of conviction within the specifically blues context.) One must remain open to the reality of human misery. This openness is the price and the precondition of the artistic transcendence of misery offered by the blues.

The verses of Spann that we began by considering invite a process of reasoning that serves to maintain emotional distance. Some of the rawer and more intense blues of the impassioned, short-lived genius Robert Johnson illumine another aspect of the emotional engagement fundamental to the blues. Johnson begins "Preaching Blues" (recorded in 1936) thusly:

> I was up this morning, I got blues walking like a man.
> I was up this morning, my blues walking like a man.
> Well, the blues—give me your right hand.

It is the singer, not the blues, that proffers his hand. The singer reaches out to grasp the hand of the blues, thus to feel the blues, in a tactile sense, and thereby to learn something of their character, as from a handshake one learns something about a person. He hurls himself into the encounter, continuing,

> And the blues fell, Mammachild, and they tore me all upside down.
> Blues fell, Mammachild, and they tore me all upside down.
> Travel on, poor Bob, just can't turn you round.[10]

No longer "walking like a man," the blues have become a diffuse, shapeless power falling, perhaps like rain—often symbolically linked, as in the piece by Copeland, with having the blues—their effects lacerating and bewildering. The last line (about traveling on) represents not flight, which would be futile, but rather the movement of someone who is underway because standing still is impossible, but who is inexorably doomed, as Johnson proclaims himself to be in another blues in which he is pursued by a hellhound on his trail.[11] So much is clear. But who or what is "Mammachild," and what is his, and what is our, relation to the thing thus addressed?

Mammachild names the whole mother-infant relationship: the infant needing and receiving its mother's care, the mother caring for her infant. Mammachild is addressed as being on the singer's mind and relevant to the situation he is exploring, because abandonment in the sense of loss of contact with Mammachild—abandonment of the child—is tantamount to exposure to the blues. (The Texas street singer Blind Lemon Jefferson sang in 1926, "Blues jumped a rabbit, run him one solid mile. . . . That rabbit sat down, cried like a natural child."[12])

We are in some sense *with* Johnson as he grasps the blues by the hand, with him as the blues fall on him, with him in having a relationship to "Mammachild." But the singer is not in any simple way drawing us into having the blues. He is singing *about* having the blues. He is at a remove from the blues he is singing about having, and we are at a remove from the dramatic episodes he is imagining. The term *identification* could be used to designate the process bringing the singer, us, the blues "walking like a man," the blues falling on him and tearing him "all upside down," and "Mammachild" into an imaginative relationship while keeping each separate. But it should be noted that to speak this way is to imply that identification has disidentification within it as a potentiality—for separation to be overcome, there must be separation—indeed, that identification and disidentification are complementary aspects of a complex process. That this is so can be seen frequently in psychotherapeutic practice.

I offer two brief vignettes based on observations made in psychotherapy, because the processes they illustrate—of identification and disidentification—are important in the blues and are basic to the larger concerns of this book.

For example, "Denise," who dislikes her businessman father, and who has shaped her life to honor values he does not appreciate, sometimes clearly exercises valuable traits she "has" from him when she is working at her best as the artistic director of a theater. Moreover, from time to time, usually unknown to herself, she overtly manifests in her behavior this or that of the traits for which she dislikes him, including his contentious willfulness. Or: "Charlotte," who had a dissolute, sadistic, neglectful mother, is an excellent psychotherapist in her work with disturbed children. The process by which she has become disidentified from her family background has given her a rich understanding of its psychodynamics, and this understanding enables her to identify with her young clients and to use that identification on their behalf. Occasionally, however, the image of her mother possesses her as she bursts out in rage at her husband or a female co-worker.

Denise's moments of willfulness and Charlotte's of rage raise an important point: just as for separation to be overcome there must be separation, so for identification—and, in turn, disidentification—to take place, there must be a prior knowledge of oneness. Identification and disidentification presuppose and work with vestiges of archaic identity.

In speaking of archaic identity, I am not assuming (as some have) that the original psychic state of the infant is one of nondifferentiation and nondiscrimination, and that this state is prominent in the psychic life of so-called primitive people. Rather, I find the phenomenological psychologist Stephan Strasser persuasive in remarking about interaction within the mother-infant dyad, "The most elementary of all human experience—we together in [the] surrounding world—is not at first perceived, thought or sought after; it is primarily lived, through feeling."[13] We are first—and always, though we forget this—"we together in the surrounding world."

Archaic identity is, then, the form of experience that prevails when the distinctions implicit in Strasser's phrase are annulled, for example, in sleep or in states of fusion. Though the capacity for union, in which boundaries are relaxed but preserved, is essential to psychic maturity and to mutuality, fusion, in which boundaries are negated, also plays an important role in psychic life.

Fusion is a process of dedifferentiation in which sameness is emphasized at the expense of difference, an emphasis that is basic to the identifications that make the human person a member of society, and to the workings of the imagination. The archaic identity resulting from this process is also a component of such feeling-toned complexes as those formed in Denise's relationship with her father and Charlotte's with her mother. And although *relationship* with emotional reality is possible—one can shake hands with the blues—the play of emotion, which can always assume unexpected and puzzling forms, is a constant reminder of unconscious regions of the psyche and of the subordination of the ego to the largely unknown self.

Denise may try, and may be right to try, not to be *like* her father, but map, in the larger whole of her life, inevitably gets lost for moments in territory: though she has extensively qualified and differentiated, and partly discarded, her identification with her father, on the level of archaic identity drawn upon in the long life of that identification, and still drawn upon in her efforts at disidentification, Denise effectively *is* her father. On the same level, and in the same way, Charlotte effectively *is* her mother. These identifications, insofar as the archaic identity upon which they draw is indissoluble, are patterns of fate. (Both women have done much of value about, and with, these patterns. The women exemplify an important part of individuation as I understand it. But they have done so, necessarily, within limits implied by Jung's view that psychic problems are dealt with not by solving them directly but rather through an expansion of consciousness modifying their role, function, and value within the psyche as a whole.)

This is to say with another emphasis that feeling has emotion as a concomitant, that feeling is always partly *about* emotion, though it is about many other things as well, and that emotion, and consequently feeling, is rooted in the regions of the person that are ultimately autonomous with respect to conscious purposes and values.

To one's felt sense of who and what one is, emotional currents arising from these regions of the person sometimes do, and sometimes do not—like the hellhound on one's trail—seem to belong to oneself. Such currents display in this sense the ambiguity we have noted in the identifications of Denise and Charlotte—indeed, such currents are at work in those identifications. Especially owing to the bodily immediacy of such currents—as close to me as my body is to myself— they can largely overwhelm all sense of "me" and "mine" as representing a secure center of appropriate and responsible action. Yet the ambiguity occasioned by this weakening of ego-reference can bring

111

with it a gain, since precisely in not knowing what I know in the way I usually know it, I may surmise the activity of the self, as it makes itself known in its own manner, like the wind that bloweth where it listeth. This experience may revitalize and modify in a clarifying way the ego's capacity for appraising value. And this brings us again to "Mammachild."

To speak of "secure" ego-functioning, as I did a moment ago, is to recall that the first security is that of "Mammachild." The archaic identity of Mammachild might well be thought to refer, on the one hand, to the security the loss of which has delivered the blues singer up to having the blues, and, on the other, to the emotional frame of reference offering him the hope that he will be able to maintain sufficient emotional distance to endure his present state.

The emotional territory must be mapped and remapped. Losing the map in the territory is an inevitably recurrent part of this mapping and remapping. In this sense blues music is itself dangerous, though one may yield to the danger much as one may yield to the bitter-sweetness of certain experiences of love. Thus, the blues artist John Lee Hooker speaks of "feelin' very normal, nothin' on your mind, period," but then hearing a blues record that so threatens you with "hurt" and "heartaches and things" that you take a walk or go for a ride in your car: "Because you'd rather *not* hear it than to hear it. Because there's some places in them records, there's somethin' sad in there that give you the blues; somethin' that reach back in your life or in some friend's life of yours, or that make you think of what have happened today and it is so true, that if it didn't happen to you, you still got a strong idea—you know those things is goin' on. So this is very touchable, and that develops into the blues."[14]

Still, though blues music may cause the condition it is supposed to relieve or cure, one can trust the blues—"The blues is man's best friend," as Spann sings. Blues music will sooner or later do its healing work.

In the blues as in life, feeling always begins again, regardless of how forbidding the emotional territory to be mapped. And so in his charged encounter with manlike blues, Robert Johnson displays and celebrates the courage to feel even the implications of a harrowing emotional plight.

112

Abandonment, Wish, and Hope in the Blues

Johnson names "Mammachild" as the frame of reference within which the individual contemplates the threat of annihilation and the possibility of survival. But the mother-infant dyad also opens out to community, of which it is the protoform. It is striking that in the blues the mother-infant dyad remains the frame of reference for further developments of relationship, especially those colored by sexual love (and hate). This is evident in the fact that the most common forms of address to a desirable woman are, interchangeably, *Mamma* and *Baby* (and for a man, interchangeably, *Pappa* or *Daddy* and *Baby*). This is not that the blues denies the triadic tensions touched upon earlier. On the contrary, in the blues love is very often thwarted by a rival. Thus, the powerful pioneer blues artist Charley Patton sang in 1929 about imagined instances of the dreaded "back-door man":

> I'm gonna buy me a banty [rooster], put him in my back do'.
> I'm gonna buy me a banty, put him in my back do',
> 'Cause he see a stranger comin', he'll flop his wings and crow.[15]

When Howlin' Wolf sings that "evil is goin' on," he specifies the evil by admonishing his hearers to guard against the back-door man. Yet in another blues, he moves from such warning to declaring "I am a back-door man," and detailing the advantages of that role.[16] In 1938 the trombonist Jack Teagarden presented a compelling blues statement consisting of two verses, "O Mammo, Mammo, Mammo, where did you stay last night?" (two times), "The last time I saw you your hat didn't look just right." Then: "I'm goin' to get myself some brick, Lawd, and build my chimney high-o" (two times), "To keep my neighbor's tomcat from puttin' out my h-o [fire]."[17] And New Orleans pianist Billie Pierce recalls the words to the first blues she learned, at about the age of seven: "I never loved but one man in my life" (two times), "He was a married man an' I stole him from his wife."[18]

Tensions about rivalry are also exploited powerfully by the contemporary singer-guitarist-composer Jimmy Johnson who, singing about his hopeless love for a woman who loves someone else, concludes by repeating three times, "I got nowhere to turn, so tired of being alone, I feel like breaking up somebody's home," making clear that the only way he can imagine getting out of the triangle he is in is to create a new triangle with someone else as a victim.[19]

113

Other blues singers have imagined ways of "making do" within triangles: "he may be your man, but he comes to see me sometimes"; and, in the same vein but limiting the proliferation of triangles, "you can have my husband, but don't mess with my outside man."

Triangles in the blues can also take other forms than that of the singer, the loved one, and the rival. Floyd Jones, a Chicago blues performer, sang in "Stockyard Blues," early in the 1950s, about the triangular situation of needing money and facing a picket line blocking him from earning it.[20] And another Chicago blues artist, pianist Sunnyland Slim, sings (following Doctor Clayton), "Woman, I ain't goin' to drink no more whiskey, because you and liquor take advantage of me. . . . You keep me blue and disgusted as any man can live and be," thus describing a triangle in which the woman and whiskey are allies in opposition to him. He goes on: "I'm goin' stop drinkin' before you and liquor ruin my life," but then concludes ironically, "I done lost my money, I believe I lost my wife," making clear that he, on the one hand, and the Other-Woman-and-Whiskey, on the other, have been two sides of a triangle including, further, his wife.[21] Rather than being resolved, the triangle is thus translated to a deeper level. Though some blues verses describe love as thwarted by death or abandonment, it is highly characteristic of the blues to find the cause of one's loss of love in a rival, and, for example, to contemplate the image of a stranger's muddy shoes next to the bed of one's woman.

Still, in the community of which the mother-infant dyad is the protoform, individuality must be affirmed in a cooperation with others that withstands and resolves rivalries. Speech among individuals— "talk"—facilitates such cooperation. "Talk," both as an activity and as a metaphor, is important in the experience of blues music. Various features of talk in blues performance provide a perspective on the ambiguities in the blues between twos and threes, and between the verbal and extraverbal, and on ways in which the mother-infant dyad is implicit in the transcendence the blues offers—also when the blues one has or might have as a soul-condition is caused by some form of triadic tension. Breaking down the distinction between twos and threes, the blues also breaks down the distinction between the verbal and the extraverbal. Ambiguities in the blues between twos and threes and between the verbal and the extraverbal are interrelated.

114

Abandonment, Wish, and Hope in the Blues

A recent study of blues in the Mississippi Delta includes a chapter on "Blues Talk" followed by a transcription of a blues party.[22] Such talk includes banter among members of the audience, between them and the performers, and among the performers. Rather than being extraneous to the performance, such talk is intrinsic to it, bringing the participants into a special form of relationship to one another — one very different from that which obtains in a classical concert hall, for example. Such talk gives the performers a means of gauging the mood of the audience, and of influencing that mood if need be— interaction to these ends being especially important when whiskey, sometimes homemade, is helping the good times roll. And the performers can incorporate such talk in their performance in various ways (for example, by elaborating on a comment from the audience in appropriate verses).

Exclamations of blues performers to one another, and of the audience to the performers, might include "Talk to me!" and those of the performers to the audience might include "Hear me talking to you!" To say that a blues musician makes his instrument "talk" is to bestow praise. Guitarist-singer B. B. King "talks" to (that is, sings to as he plays on) his guitar "Lucille," and as the title of one of his blues numbers declares, "Lucille Talks Back." In the African background of the blues are the "talking drums" that function as an equivalent of speech.

A subgenre of the blues is "talking blues," a blues monologue with musical accompaniment. And one blues scholar who conducted hundreds of interviews with blues performers was struck by how often the person interviewed would begin accompanying himself on an instrument such as guitar or piano, so that his verbal utterance was partly transformed into a blues performance.[23]

Generally, for talk (in the literal sense) to be possible, expressive sounds must have acquired semantic meaning within a framework of social conventions, thus becoming part of a field of discourse expanding and being rounded out in ways we have considered. This acquisition of meaning, making the difference between a sound and a word, is a form of transcendence. (My cat Lester would in important respects transcend his cat-condition if he could learn to talk.) But verbal meaning dies. (A month-old newspaper has lost much of its meaning. Sacred texts

115

become mumbo-jumbo. As is easy to prove experimentally, simple repetition of a word may render it meaningless. When Macbeth says, "Tomorrow and tomorrow and tomorrow," he is actively realizing the meaninglessness of his future.) Moreover, verbal meaning has its limits: painfully trapped within our words, we may find that music serves preciously to revive verbal meaning or to reach beyond it.

The verbal content of the blues is concerned with emotional situations implying stories that are usually not told explicitly. Rather, the personal, subjective reactions of the singer or fictional persona are made the center of attention. That is, the blues, unlike the ballad, is nonnarrative and often even antinarrative in its suppression of the story line. For example, Johnny Copeland, in another blues, sings about his daddy's telling him not to stop by the creek to swim on the way to school, advice which the singer had to ponder. The incident is treated in isolation from other incidents, and the significance that made the incident seem to the singer worth relating is left undeclared. One might imagine that the incident was fatal in the sense of initiating a process of dropping out of school, leading to other forms of dereliction that ended by shaping his life in a particular way. But no such story is told.[24]

Incidentally, the same blues by Copeland suggests something of the way in which the nonnarrative or even antinarrative tendency of the blues is sometimes clearly related to the nonspecifiable irony common in it. After singing, "Don't stop by the creek, Son, that's what my daddy said," the singer remarks that he "almost didn't obey"; but after elaborating on his daddy's advice, he admits that that was where he "went astray," only to fall back thereafter to claiming that he "almost didn't obey." The interest of the account centers in the fictional persona's wavering between maintaining and dismantling an edifice of lies about the course of his life and about the extent of his responsibility for it. Since it is essential in the blues, as an art of survival, not to sentimentalize and to see to it that false hopes are treated ironically, bravado and other forms of apparent wish-fulfillment are to be heard in a double perspective. Bravado in the blues often asks to be heard as, "This grandiose posture is fun and an ego-strengthening exercise in courage and in demanding what I want. It is nonetheless make-believe, a form of 'lying' (or tall-tale–telling)."

Abandonment, Wish, and Hope in the Blues

The antinarrative tendency of the blues is related to its tendency to develop its materials more in an associative than in a linear or logical fashion. Indeed, the verbal content of the blues and its development sometimes seem dreamlike. Thus, Howlin' Wolf sings, "Smokestack lightnin', shining just like gold," which is for Sam Chatmon "Smokestack lightning, bell what shine like gold," and for Lightning Hopkins, "Smokes like lightnin', velvet shines like gold."[25]

As one writer about blues lyrics comments, perhaps consoling himself for fruitless efforts at comprehension, "It's not that what [blues singers] sing is trivial exactly. It's just that it does not entirely reflect what they are singing about."[26] Indeed, often in the blues performance only snatches of the verbal content are intelligible. (Son House, a blues-artist contemporary of Charley Patton, confessed that he often could not understand the words of Patton's blues.) Often fragmented in our comprehension of them, blues verses give glimpses and clues inciting associative processes in the listener—much as one may make up a meaning for what one is hearing in an unknown language. Though it is a relief when one comes to understand blues verses that had baffled one, it is in keeping with many other elements of the blues aesthetic that a blues performance does not necessarily stand or fall on the basis of the intelligibility of the words. Just as the blues tends away from the linear, rational, explicit, toward the diffusely global, irrational, suggestive, so it tends to press through the semantic altogether toward extraverbal expressiveness.

In the blues, everyday speech is expressively altered in various ways. A syllable might be prolonged or divided, or be given a stress it would not have in conversation, or be rendered falsetto or as melisma (the ornamental elaboration of a syllable as a succession of notes). In the singing of blues verses, words may be replaced by expressive but nonsemantic sounds, such as moans, humming, and musical figures played by guitar or piano or harmonica. A special case is presented by such blues artists as Mississippi John Hurt and Fred McDowell when they sing only part of a verse line, or do not sing it at all when the singing of it is expected, so that the listener must "hear" the words in the guitar part—in a way related to B. B. King's making Lucille "talk." In this case it would not be quite true to say that words are being replaced by nonsemantic but expressive and communicative

117

sounds, since the listener does, in a subliminal way, "hear" the expected but unsung words. By such devices the blues performer blurs the distinction between the verbal and extraverbal or creates and explores ambiguities between them. Just as making expressive sounds into words is transcendence, so the decomposition of words into expressive sound may be transcendence of another kind.

In this extraverbal transcendence, words are reabsorbed into gestural, postural, proprioceptive, sensory, emotional currents of the body. These currents are basic to one's experience of oneself as having a personal vital core. And attending to these currents is a means both of acknowledging (from the side of the ego) the value of that core (as the self) and of making its vitality manifest.

Magical and religious ritual may, by drawing attention to such currents and to that core, revivify one's sense of self through procedures intended to help assure such boons as the vitality of cattle and crops. As I have said, the blues in its basic spirit, unlike such ritual, refuses to declare commitment to a belief that life will get better. (Many blues verses assert that life will get better, but they do so as a partly ironic strategy for fending off the danger of having the blues, and such utterances are no more to be taken at face value than are verses in which a rejected lover boasts of his irresistible charms.) Still, the blues generates vitality in the way that ritual does, and it is more than casual analogy to describe a blues performance as a ritual.[27] In its engagement of these deep bodily currents, blues ritual and blues "talk" activate the dyadic level of the psyche, in which residuals of the early mother-infant relationship constructively live on.

For activation of the dyadic level in later life to have salutary effects, I have been suggesting, feeling, in its concern with gradations, transitions, continuities, and coherence, must take up into itself, and must contain, potentialities for disruptive emotion. (For there to be such salutary effects, neither mother nor infant of this inner dyad can be falling apart, like an exasperated or exhausted real-life mother, or a real-life infant crying itself blue in the face.) The blues is especially knowledgeable about the matters I have been discussing, and demonstrates its knowledge of them in its interrelating of verbal and extraverbal expressiveness.

Though the real-life problems described in the blues are often triadic, dyadic elements juxtaposed with the triadic are essential to the larger artistic effect of the blues. As we have seen on the level of verbal content, the mother-infant relationship is suggested by the frequent epithets of "mamma" and "baby" as expressions of yearning for security and warmth, though the epithets are heard as highly metaphorical—and though the yearning is expressed in such a way as strongly to imply that it will not find concrete fulfillment. The double elements—the instances of "two"—do not themselves directly refer to the mother-infant relationship, but they do suggest the mirroring and the active mutuality characterizing that relationship. And it, in turn, is basic to the concern with individuality and community to which the blues gives expression by its relentlessly subjective orientation—its emphasis upon "I" and "mine"—its protestations against loneliness, and its assumption of an audience of kindred spirits.

Basic to the musical structure of the blues is the African call-and-response pattern characteristic of field and work songs sung by black Americans on southern plantations, and also characteristic of religious singing and preaching in black southern churches. In this pattern a lead singer sings a line to be followed by a choral response, or one group sings a line to be followed by the response of another group.

The most usual blues form consists of stanzas, each consisting of twelve measures (bars) of 4/4 time, based on a characteristic blues scale—most often thought to correspond to the Western major diatonic scale, with the difference that the third, seventh, and sometimes the fifth intervals are treated with considerable—and important—expressive ambiguity, so that it has been proposed that these intervals be called not tones but tonal areas. Each stanza repeats variants of simple harmonic progressions (e.g., I–IV–V–IV–I), and is divided into three sections, the first verbal line of which (A) is repeated, sometimes with a slight variation, the stanza closing with a different line (B) usually assonant or rhyming with the first.[28] Thus the AAB structure itself suggests the subsuming of the triple (the three lines of the stanza) to the double AB, with the B line being, in effect, the "response" to the "call" of the A line. Further, the words of each line fill slightly more than two bars and are followed by an instrumental response to the voice. Indeed, this instrumental answering to the voice is so important as a structural principle that it may override the convention of twelve bars, so that some performers may produce stanzas of thirteen or thirteen and a half bars. The instrumental line, too, amounts more to a second voice than to a musical accompaniment subservient to the verses. And some performers succeed by various devices in keeping multiple melodic lines going, either successively or simultaneously.

Answering is important in the blues in another way as well, deriving from its traditional, communal character. A grand current word for what I mean is *intertextuality*: the text of a blues verse is heard not only in itself but also in relation to other verses sung by the same and other performers. Thus, when the young Robert Cray sings, "I'm the causin' of it all"—that is, of his woman's buying a train ticket "long as my right arm" and leaving him—we recognize the older Howlin' Wolf's song and hear Cray's version as a variation on it, and in this sense an answer to it. Howlin' Wolf's authority is acknowledged in Cray's taking over of the odd word "causin,' " indeed in Cray's singing the song at all, but we also hear the verses rearranged, and we hear Howlin' Wolf's admission of penitence considerably developed. (Howlin' Wolf's penitence, in turn, gained part of its effect from its contrast with his usual bravado.) It is as though Cray is saying, "I am presenting what would for me be the most proper feeling response to the situation described by Howlin' Wolf."

I am partly describing what I think of as the "self-reference" of the blues: the blues has a body of characteristic themes, images, and attitudes, and—consciously, even self-consciously—perpetuates them and comments upon them. Cray (in his early thirties) has possibly never seen a train ticket long as his right arm; when he sings about it we are aware of him as wearing the bluesman's persona in a way that oddly lifts him out of time. And when Alberta Hunter (in her mid eighties at her death) sings that she will take "Amtrak" in pursuit of her errant man—to "crack his skull and drink his blood like wine"— we hear her presenting herself, against a background of innumerable railroad blues, as the ever up-to-date, stylish lady. These echoes among blues texts deepen one's satisfaction in a blues performance but are of secondary importance. Someone who does not know Howlin' Wolf's song but hears Cray's version of it can appreciate most of what Cray is expressing through it.

Though realistic problem-solving is foreign to the aesthetic and ideology of the blues, in the blues performance as a whole there is a great deal of answering. In the blues, complaints are stated and heard, and what is said is taken up in a deeply related response; whether accepting or rejecting, compassionate or mocking, the response interacts or even unites with the statement in a way that often suggests implications of which the fictional persona embodied by the singer was not aware at the outset. This answering, which is of more significance than any solution the blues verses propose or might propose to the problems as stated, is the transformation of energy effected by the blues performance. In the blues, as in life, problems are in important respects phenomena in the movement of energy. Just as there must *be* life in order for life to be impeded or endangered, so in these respects what is happening in the larger movement of energy is more important than the idiosyncratic features of one's problems.

The effect of personal problems on the movement of energy may be readily seen in such psychopathological symptoms as depression, emotional lability, and motoric excitement. In psychotherapy, energy in the form of conscious attention and concern may be brought directly to bear on one's personal problems to the end of releasing energy from them. But they may also be affected by energy brought to bear upon them more indirectly by such means as music, bodily movement, and modeling with clay. Whenever energy moves, no matter what makes it do so, the energy invested in one's personal problems has a different value in the psyche as a whole than when energy is dormant.

The name of the blind bluesman Sleepy John Estes, a highly distinctive rural singer-guitarist from Brownsville, Tennessee, is derived from his habit of unexpectedly falling asleep, presumably as a primitive reaction to stress. (One of his record albums is titled, alarmingly, *Electric Sleep*—perhaps because on it his singing and old-fashioned acoustic-guitar playing are accompanied by a more modern amplified guitar. Still, the phrase "electric sleep" aptly and graphically suggests charged stasis, a need for transforming outward expression and gaining access to community.) In Estes's case, singing the blues with the words inflected by his characteristic sob is an answer to listlessness and the condition of being a helpless victim. In general, the blues, employing a vast array of expressive means, activates emotional currents of the deep body, and guides them to be taken up by feeling. In this way it generates energy. In generating it, the blues performance answers in the broadest terms the having of the blues, while the content of the verses, concerned with problems, is placed in an embracing and liberating context.

In blues verses, personal problems are treated both pathetically and ironically in ways that neither deny the reality of such problems nor strive for realistic solutions to them: the verses raise no false hopes, though they may treat false hopes ironically. In the final stanzas of one recorded version of his "Wee Baby Blues," the Kansas City blues shouter Big Joe Turner buoyantly claims that his disaffected woman can't get away now, that all his troubles are gone, and that she will spend the night "rolling" in his arms, as the instrumental accompaniment concludes with a figure that can be heard as shrugging off the fantasy as dismal foolishness leading to an even worse state of having the blues.[29]

The bass guitarist of the Robert Cray band, Richard Cousins, plays the role of imp, sometimes making a series of jumps or pirouettes to express his own felt relation to the music being sung and played. Often his face is directed to Cray's, and his facial expression is in unsettlingly ambiguous response to what Cray is singing. Sometimes Cray will sing a verse infused with deep pathos, and Cousins will respond with an expression that mockingly exaggerates the pathos to absurdity. Or again, Cousins will seem to be responding to Cray's pathos with sly and detached bemusement. Always it is as though Cousins is listening hard and hearing something that we are not hearing. He performs the function of forcing the audience to ask itself again and again, "How, exactly, should we be taking what Cray is right now singing? Is it sad, funny, or both—or what?" This disorientation helps us to get beyond halfhearted taking for granted, and to find our own wholehearted felt relation to the music.

In the blues performance as a whole, the verses play an important role in maintaining an awareness of personal problems as the very stuff of life but one nonetheless subordinate to the more fundamental aim of generating the energy which having the blues depressively saps. Recovering it, the blues performance awakens the sense that, in Blake's words, "Energy is Eternal Delight."[30]

I have observed that the AAB verse structure most common in the blues creates an ambiguity between two and three, related to the ambiguity between the three verse units in the twelve-bar stanza and

122

the vocal part and instrumental answering within each unit. Further, I described the blues as basically in 4/4 time, but, owing to syncopation and the use of triplets, musicologists have often been puzzled as to when a blues performance should be notated as some version of modified 4/4 time, and when as some version of a triple rhythm. These ambiguities between two and three are related to those in the blues treatment of its verbal content. Often, as we have seen, conflicts described in the blues are triadic in character (the stranger's muddy shoes next to one's woman's bed). But the resolution of a conflict in this noncommittal art is through an opening to feeling, which tacitly draws on its model in the mother-infant relationship. This amounts to an affirmation of individuality, including the ability to be alone with oneself, and to commune with oneself. Thus, when the contemporary bluesman Albert King sings of the visit of Queen Elizabeth II to San Francisco, he treats in a jocular way a public, formal occasion (albeit to his imagination an aborted one). Yet in the course of the piece, his interacting guitar lines and moans, like a conversation of a person with himself, seem to celebrate his own robust personal joy in being alive.[31] The opening to feeling, even in solitude, implies an affirmation of community. Thus, an album of another contemporary bluesman, Albert Collins, is titled ironically *Love Can Be Found Anywhere (Even in a Guitar)*. Many a blues performer has used the interaction between voice and instrument as the means of recreating a world with others, at the verge of isolation and defeat.

The triadic world of mother, father, and child generates tensions that, both in themselves and in the strategies used to master them, have been actively present as motives in some of the highest human achievements. But the mother-infant relationship remains in a special way implicit in differentiated feeling, and in this sense that relationship may return in force on a level more embracing than the triadic.

There are certainly grounds for favoring another view of dyadic and triadic elements in the blues than the one I am proposing. In this alternative view, the blues could be regarded as the artistic product of a social group that is mother-centered and, in a certain construction of this fact, prepatriarchal, a group having a psychology that is, in psychoanalytic terms, preoedipal. And the dyadic elements of which I have spoken could be understood as offering a regressive consolation for rigors attendant upon the incipient patriarchal, or oedipal, stage. So, too, the triadic elements concerned with betrayal and envy could be regarded as fascinated glimpses of issues belonging to a developmental level not yet securely attained—glimpses, akin to the intimations of sex and violence related to what psychoanalysts call the primal scene. Such a view would call attention to anxieties that arise when the time comes for the mother-infant relationship to be transformed through a more realistic recognition of the complex and partly antagonistic reality of other persons. The regrettable price of this partly valid but too specialized focus is neglect of the intricate differentiation of feeling achieved by mother and infant in their interaction—and by the blues as it reflects and builds on that interaction. The differentiation of feeling in the blues is precisely an important means of maintaining a restoring coherence despite envy and thwarted desire.

Of course, it may in one sense seem odd to emphasize the differentiation of feeling in a music so long and strongly associated with social occasions notorious for their rowdiness and frequent violence. Though presenting no insuperable paradox, this convergence of opposites deserves a moment's attention.

We might recall the obscure relations between Bernard of Clairvaux's profound insight into the affectional basis of religious contemplation and his nefarious campaign to destroy his opponent Abelard. Or we might recall the self-contradictions of Dr. Smile. As Bernard and Dr. Smile demonstrate, one of the deepest and most perdurable human problems is that of finding and maintaining a superior felt and imaginative relation to one's inferiorities. Analysis offers an illustration of what I mean: analysis does not usually solve problems—refine inferiorities—directly; yet they must be engaged—their energy must be drawn upon—as attention is paid to matters indirectly related to them.

What I have called "inferiorities" belong to the psychic region that Jung calls the "shadow," consisting of elements and tendencies divergent from one's consciously held values. One does not deal with the shadow by seizing the solution to one's problems, the cure for one's disease—one does not deal with it by storming the kingdom of heaven (Matt. 11:12). One deals with it, rather, by meandering among ambiguities in a state of alert and receptive reverie. The progress of one's course is signaled less by the crunch of the object hit than by the balance and finesse of one's movements toward or away from it. Thus, it should not surprise us that in the blues, and in the mother-infant relationship, anxieties about abandonment and loss, and the thrill of peeking—looking and seeing the fascinatingly forbidden—should be ambiguously concomitant with the differentiation of feeling, indeed should play a role in that differentiation.

My mention of peeking should suggest something important about the ambiguities I have been discussing. The word *peeking* implies attraction to what is erotically and aggressively charged—implies attraction by virtue of that charge. But seeing is also, in a broader sense, knowledge offering its own rewards in relation to a wide range of objects, from the most bodily immediate to the most exaltedly spiritual. Peeking at erotic and aggressive objects and acts is not in any simple way the primitive form of more spiritual kinds of knowing into which it is later sublimated. "All men by nature desire to know," in the words of Aristotle, and such peeking is a special and delimited kind of knowing. And one would have to push a preconception very hard to relate the peekaboo of Baby to the sexually and aggressively forbidden.

Still, if feeling is to remain a vital, pliant, and differentiated mode of knowing, it must remain cognizant of emotion-inducing potential impediments to its own smooth functioning. Beethoven's song-flights coexist with his night terrors. The blues performer celebrates the "I" and "thou" implicit in true community, while keeping an ear open to the footsteps of the back-door man.

In sum, whatever Paul means by seeing face to face, it has its protoform in the mirroring of mother and infant that I have been discussing—in the mother who can see and feel as her infant does, but who can also respond to the infant in a reasoned way. In the world of disorder and trouble represented in the blues, proper modes of feeling are necessary to survival, and the art of the blues celebrates them. When the blues performer calls his "mamma" "Baby," or calls his "baby" "Mamma," he is acknowledging where proper modes of feeling begin. How ironically ambiguous the relations between "Mamma" and "Baby" can be in the blues, and how consciously so, is suggested by Valerie Wellington's "My Baby Treats Me Like a Stepchild."[32]

3.2 The Dyadic in Developed Ego-Functioning

A musical vignette may clarify the way in which the dyadic mode, far from simply offering a regressive relief from triadic tensions, may play a role in a proper transcendence of them, while helping to keep available to the ego certain important resources of personal integrity.

Competitions in the performance of classical music are in many ways a problematic institution, but many young performers regard doing well in them as a necessary part of establishing themselves in a professional career. These performers tend to emphasize bravura technique—they try to play hard, loud, and fast. They work up a repertoire that will allow them to display such technique, and with it they are more than moderately successful in winning the judges' favor. Though the pianist Natalie Rose (introduced in part 2.7) has entered such competitions, her teacher, in contrast to some others, is determined that she not become another "typewriter pianist," with much power and flash and little delicacy and musical substance. To this end he has her spend considerable time working not on blockbuster concerti but on very simple Schubert songs, which she indeed plays in such a way that the piano sings, intimately and with subtle, graceful inflections. Especially when she has had to learn a more imposing, more "masculine" piece, she turns again to work at the most musical playing of the Schubert songs of which she is capable. Many of her bravura-ambitious fellow pianists, like muscle-bound football players attempting to execute a pas de deux, are no longer able to make Schubert songs sing.

Part of mastering triadic tensions—one thinks of the competitiveness and envy fostered by the classical-music competitions—is claiming one's powers and using them, if need be, over and against others. Let us take playing the blockbuster concerto in a way that wins the competition as a model of such self-assertion. But this example, like others offered in this book, suggests the cost to feeling of this accomplishment. Let us, further, take the loving, melodic, and graceful playing of the Schubert songs as both a value in its own right and the measure of one's musicianship, which should be suspect if one can perform an imposing piece imposingly but cannot make a Schubert song sing. And let us take the proper performance of the Schubert song as rooted in the dyadic.

126

I would link Beethoven's night terrors with dark themes of triangular conflict in the blues. But it is important to remain aware that a very small infant may experience night terrors, and that the seeds of one's knowledge of separation, abandonment, and loss are germinating long before the conclusion that such conditions are felt *because* a rival has caused them. Open as Beethoven was to his own internal processes, his night terrors, as a mature man, were surely also those of himself as a very small infant. When things go wrong for such an infant in what it construes as its relationship with its mother—an adult observer might construe that relationship very differently—only the infant or its mother can make those things right again. At such a time no one is a substitute for Mamma. And, though Beethoven's imagination also concerned itself with revolutionary fervor and Napoleonic heroism, these offer nothing to assuage the night terrors of the infant. Blake's *Songs of Innocence* precede his *Songs of Experience;* the comfort of the fleecy lamb precedes contemplation of the fearful symmetry of the tiger. The "good enough mother" offers reserves of strength enabling the infant to deal with abandonment by the mother who, inopportunely having to leave the room, seems thoroughly bad. In its simplicity, the Schubert song comes first but is not for that reason left behind. Indeed, in darkest adversity, when there is openness to hope, "a little child shall lead them" (Isa. 11:6).

3.3 Mother, Abandonment, Self-Alienation, and the Blues

Roughly by the end of its first year, the infant may suffer agonies of feeling abandoned, as its mother seems to it to be disappearing forever when she steps into the next room. Fear of abandonment, along with envy, plays a role in the oedipal phase of development described by psychoanalysts, as it does in later significant times in a person's life. And as the growing child becomes increasingly independent, its mother in turn may feel abandoned. But the sense of abandonment may also be activated in the mother, and sometimes in the father, before it becomes crucial for the infant.

The mother of an infant is especially attuned to its needs, to what would be pleasing or harmful to it, to what would help it to thrive. And this attunement amounts to a characteristic differentiation of thought, feeling, and perception. In some ways mother truly knows best. She knows better than anyone the rhythms of the baby's activities, its moods, the emerging pattern of its development, the meaning of its efforts at communication. She may even seem clairvoyant in registering dangers the baby could ingeniously reach. And in various ways the singling out of this woman to be the mother of this baby may expose her, too, to experiences of abandonment. She may, for example, suffer the unshareable misery of lying in bed for hours while needing to go to the bathroom, as she chooses the discomfort that is keeping her awake over the prospect of a squalling baby. She may sometimes be overwhelmed, feeling completely alone in the face of unmasterable confusion. And if someone relieves her of her burden, giving her a chance to read a book, for example, she may find herself incapacitated from doing so by an overpowering desire to be with her baby. She may feel abandoned in the sense of having given up some highly satisfying employment to have the baby. Moreover, she may find herself unbearably the object of the baby's rejection—for example, if she cannot produce enough milk and must supplement it with a bottle that the baby refuses as an outrage. And even her confidence in her empathy and skill in dealing with the baby may isolate her, as she cannot keep from being aware that the quality of care offered by others helping her to care for the baby is inferior to her own, so that she cannot, as they resentfully sense, simply rely on them.

Thus, if her husband helps with the baby, and feels his help unnoticed or unappreciated—mother's knowing best is not always endearing—he may find himself driven into his favorite form of retreat—work, tavern, the sports pages—so that she is even more alone in caring for the baby. Moreover, her lack of appreciation for the helping hand he thought he so eagerly offered may remind him of the sternly judgmental—rejecting, hence abandoning—mother of his own early years. And so, Magna Mater moves through the suburbs, giving everyone—infant, mother, and father—ample chance to feel abandoned. Importantly, though, the mother's knowledge of abandonment, however acquired, helps shape her relationship with her infant: to know her infant is to know a creature that might be abandoned, that will, inevitably, know abandonment. Abandonment is the extreme form of separation; and to know that experiences of even that extreme form can be survived, as mother knows this, is to help the infant in the separation from mother necessary to the infant's autonomy.

It should not be surprising, however, that when early experiences of maternal abandonment are powerful and sustained, they may result in forms of self-alienation in which the ego does not feel securely grounded in the self. But it should also be realized that reparation may be possible, in the form of real-life experience, religion, psychotherapy and analysis, and art—including the blues.

In focusing on abandonment, the blues enhances the grounding of ego in self, since to focus on what is wrong, rather than to sense it dimly, is an important part of making it right. This is a matter of feeling. The kind of feeling cherished and cultivated in the blues is the product of emotional heightening: a focusing on issues of emotional import, especially abandonment, and an evocation of the emotional response appropriate to them. Feeling-judgments implicit in the prevailing ego attitude are modified as a result. The need for such a modification of feeling-judgments becomes clear when one considers feeling-judgments that are muddled because this emotional heightening and focusing is for some reason impeded. I will discuss some of the feeling-judgments of "Henry Newman" and, later, of "Darlene Baker," because, in different ways, they illustrate the processes with which I am concerned.

I call attention first to Mr. Newman because his life has been a victory of the human spirit, providing a striking further instance of the self that knows what is good for itself, coming to expression in ways that further life under daunting circumstances. (Of German-Irish extraction, he has little firsthand familiarity with the blues music I have been discussing, though he shares its joy in survival.) My discussion of these matters requires a brief sketch of his life.

Mr. Newman, now fifty-six years old, vaguely remembers his mother as sickly and noncoping. In his very early years, his father would return from lengthy binges of drunkenness, grovelingly penitent, as he sent Mr. Newman or one of his two older brothers to the drugstore to buy him paregoric. By the age of four, Mr. Newman and his brothers had been sent to the first of the charitable institutions in which they spent the next several years. He was early aware of the irony that he did not even qualify as a genuine orphan, as when he was allowed to make

129

some excursion outside the walls of the institution, it might happen that he would run into his staggering father. And Mr. Newman lived with the hope that his mother would take him home.

The food served by the institution repeatedly made Mr. Newman vomit in his plate. He was punished for such infractions by being made to kneel on wooden rods. He also accumulated demerits each of which was to earn a blow with a stick. One day he learned to his joy that a car would soon arrive to take him and his brothers home. Since he had accumulated twenty-seven demerits, he had to lower his trousers and receive that many blows in preparation for his departure. The car arrived, and he and his brothers were driven across town and through a gate on which a sign proclaimed, "County Asylum for Orphans"; there they spent the next years. During this period a re-tarded or deformed sister may have been born, though evidence for this he has only in patchy memories.

In the course of his childhood, Mr. Newman was frequently treated in hospitals for a succession of injuries and illnesses. It seems to him that he spent two successive birthdays, between the ages of four and seven, hospitalized with diphtheria, occasionally visited by an aunt, who peered at him through the glass of the room in which he was quarantined.

Mr. Newman spent his adolescence living with various relatives and attending a parochial high school, constantly dreading that his schoolmates would learn the shameful secret that he had been an orphan. He excelled at athletics, and also distinguished himself scho-lastically, being motivated in his school work not by grades but by a lively intellectual curiosity, undampened—remarkably—by his history of deprivation and abuse.

After high school, he entered the Marines, in which he served for some years, in the course of which he was awarded a Bronze Star for valor in combat. Upon his discharge he arranged to enter college, intending to study ethics in an attempt to make sense of his war experiences. His older brother "Tom" had plans for them to room together, but Mr. Newman, wanting to distance himself from his brother, moved to another city and attended college there, finally completing an M.A. degree in sociology by writing, in Latin, a re-search essay on alcoholism.

Abandonment, Wish, and Hope in the Blues

Mr. Newman has spent the last decades working at a succession of some eighty jobs. Usually menial, these have enabled him to develop an impressive array of skills but typically have offered him no opportunity for advancement. Often his employment has ended in a conflict with superiors about some issue of justice, for example, as when he tried to organize workers on behalf of a labor union. His wide reading in theology, philosophy, psychology, and history is certainly not drawn upon in his present work as a custodian for an athletic stadium. Once engaged, he has never married, though he sometimes thinks he may still do so.

Upon leaving the Marines, Mr. Newman had sought the help of a psychiatrist. When Mr. Newman was twelve, the orphanage, for reasons not explained to him, had sent him to a doctor to be circumcised. In an appointment after the operation, the doctor, not announcing what he was about to do, jerkily rammed an injector filled with lubricating jelly up the urethral canal of Mr. Newman's penis. Screaming with pain, Mr. Newman thought the doctor was trying to kill him. When Mr. Newman told the psychiatrist of this, the latter assured Mr. Newman that the event had not taken place—outside his imagination—as the procedure he described had been abandoned more than twenty years before the time of this supposed incident. Mr. Newman tried to convince the psychiatrist that orphans like him were sent to the cheapest, least competent doctors available, so that such an anachronism was easily possible, but the psychiatrist did not believe him. Mr. Newman therewith ceased seeing the psychiatrist. Years later he did, however, seek analytic help in trying to make sense of his life and to mark out a more promising course of action for the future.

One of Mr. Newman's striking qualities is his sense of responsibility, his correctness, even punctiliousness, in meeting obligations. Laudable as this may be, it must partly express his fear of indebtedness, and so reflect the problematic nature of the charity on which he was so long dependent. As Catholic theology taught Mr. Newman, there are no privileges without obligations, and such charity is a privilege, even if part of him regards the treatment he received as dreadful. Thus assured, he sometimes feels that he should express gratitude by sending money to the charitable institutions that cared for him, and he can feel this even while wincing at his painful recollections of the years spent in them. This is partly the psychology of someone who with part of himself assumes that he exists only by sufferance, that he does not have a secure right to the food he eats and the space he takes up. And it is related to the psychology of the despised nation within a nation that created the blues.

One might expect Mr. Newman to be depressed, but for the most part he is not in any overt way—indeed, he seems chipper and realistic—though he has shown slight signs of what might be called controlled depression when reviewing with his analyst some of the more painful parts of his past. After talking about one of them, Mr. Newman insisted that it would make no sense for him to feel sorry for himself. His analyst replied that, even so, it might be appropriate to *grieve* for some of his experiences of abandonment and loss. Alarmed, Mr. Newman countered that the thought of such grief was more than he could handle: "Hostility, maybe, but *grief*, no!"

Recently, Mr. Newman has dreamt several times of his brother Tom, who in the dreams, far from being a helpful ally, is a problematic encumbrance. One dream about Tom, along with Mr. Newman's response to it, brings us to one main point of this narrative with respect to the blues.

In the dream, Mr. Newman has just left the Marines and is beginning college. Ignoring his real-life decision to separate himself from Tom, the dream has Mr. Newman sharing quarters with him. Tom has decided (in the dream), however, that at age twenty-seven he is too old to be trying to complete his degree and will instead spend as much time as he can reading. Mr. Newman is confused by this, as he himself is twenty-five and is just starting college. Both men have jobs, and Tom wants them to trade jobs, as Mr. Newman's job would give more opportunity for reading. This makes sense to Mr. Newman, because he can appreciate his brother's desire to read. And so Mr. Newman is inclined to go along with the trade, but then he reflects that he, too, needs time to read, and wonders why he should give Tom this advantage of Mr. Newman's job.

Baffled by the dream, Mr. Newman felt that it was deliberately trying to confuse him, like a bad practical joke—that whatever part of himself had created the dream was treating him in the same crazy-making way he had been treated in the orphanage. To be puzzled or even alarmed by a dream is common, but it is a large step from such responses to Mr. Newman's impression that his dream was a new instance of the bewildering cruelty he had earlier experienced—it being all the more such a step since the dream was not a nightmare and did not have a hopeless outcome. (It might very well be true, however, that Mr. Newman feels a pressing need for clarity about Tom—indeed, that those relations contain a story of disappointment and even betrayal that Mr. Newman senses but has not yet clearly grasped.) In short, the mistrust that would have been appropriate with regard to figures in his past has—at least for moments—become distrust of the dream-making part of himself. And the abandonment represented by the orphanage has—at least for moments—become the self-alienation expressed in this distrust.

Actually, the dream would seem a positive product of the self, picturing a characteristic way in which Mr. Newman gives the other person the benefit of the doubt, hastens to assume responsibility himself, arrives at a waveringly uncertain feeling-judgment of the situation he is in, and as a result is used by the other person. By no means content with the role of victim, Mr. Newman in his waking life recognizes the injustice of being used, and acts to redress it. Still, this pattern often puts him in the reactive position of repairing damage to his self-esteem that could have been averted if he had not surrendered the initiative.

Mr. Newman's resourcefulness and sense of responsibility gave him an orientation in the midst of conflicting and self-contradictory values, and surely these qualities of character developed in him to that end. But he also internalized—as intimate personal knowledge and a store of potent memories—the disrespect with which he was treated. (We might think again of Denise's relation to the internalized image of her father and Charlotte's to that of her mother, discussed in part 3.1.) And both the strand of self-doubt in Mr. Newman and the correctness that compensates it, while also giving him an ethical orientation, sometimes impedes the kind of spontaneously assertive impulse required if he is to ask for, and claim, what he both wants and truly needs. The same sort of impulse would be required for him, before this, to know what he both wants and truly needs. And his dream is a helpful representation of the fruitless ambiguity that results when such an impulse is needed but does not arise.

Feeling, Imagination, and the Self

By "self-alienation" (in the title of this section) I mean distrust in the self that knows what is good for itself. Certainly the vital core of Mr. Newman has brought him through hardships that would have defeated many. And it would be remarkable if he did not have moments of distrust in the power that did so. (Jesus, too, knew such distrust.) My point is that distrust of the self that knows what is good for itself is on one level a reexperiencing of early abandonment, and that the self has capacities for making things right when Mother fails to do so. Indeed, as much of blues music demonstrates, knowledge of abandonment, when not overwhelmingly sustained and severe, may be an important part of trust as what Brentano calls right loving—a realistic opening to the good.

Mr. Newman's claiming of his aggressive energies—"hostility, maybe"—is surely important. But with his experiences of abandonment and loss in mind, one might think that a measure of *both* grief and hostility would be indicated as part of a clarification of the feeling issues that his life so far has left him to deal with. And hostility needs to be focused, in the sense that he needs to know what it is most truly about. May it not ultimately be about experiences to which grief would also be appropriate?

Whereas Mr. Newman finds the prospect of rage less disquieting than that of grief, the predilection of the blues—as the name *blues* implies—is for sorrow that might become grief. Still, in the blues rage sometimes comes to expression with a fine edge—for example, in blues lyrics depicting the vengeful actions of the spurned lover. (Alberta Hunter: "I'll crack his skull and drink his blood like wine.")

A song that the old-time bluesman James Butch Cage (born in 1894) learned from his mother, the daughter of a slave, expresses hostility as part of a clarification of a feeling issue bearing upon survival:

> Black nigger baby, black feet and shiny eyes,
> Black all over to the bone and india-rubber thighs,
>> Turn that nigger round and knock 'im in the haid,
>> Cause white folks say, "We're gonna kill that nigger dead."
>> The white folks eat the hog in the skillet,
>> Niggers was no-good, so very little in it,
>> Old Uncle Dicker-Dagger eat up the grease—say,
>> "Get up in the mawnin', I'll be free!"

134

Abandonment, Wish, and Hope in the Blues

Black nigger baby gonna take care of myself,
   Always carry a great big razor and a pistol in my vest,
   Turn that nigger round and knock 'im on the haid,
Cause white folks say, "We're gonna kill that nigger dead."[33]

This song is not in any simple way an expression of what psychoanalysts call identification with the aggressor. Such identification is assumed by the song—the song goes out from it—but it is in the song a matter of conscious role-playing, which is part of a process of ironic detachment, amounting to disidentification. As a result of this ironic detachment, the persistent pattern of injustice—creating new generations of victims despite the end of slavery—is described simply and clearly. Moreover, the very caricaturing of the baby as an inhuman thing makes it seem indestructible. And though there is no way to spare it the unjust situation into which it has been born, a strong ego is attributed to the baby, along with meanness and determination that will make it a dangerous victim.

Mr. Newman finds self-pity dangerous. Presumably for reasons similar to his, the irony of the song obviates self-pity, which would detract from a clear perception of the pattern of injustice and the baby's plight. Still, its irony serves a feeling-judgment that includes a tacit awareness of the grief—the cause for grieving—actively implicit in the story. It is possible to grieve not only in depression and convulsive sobs, it is also possible to grieve—to know grief—with a detachment that holds grief open to joy—joy that we, like the baby, are alive and intent on living. Irony allows this detachment.

Ironic detachment may be rejecting, even disdainful, as in much satire. But ironic detachment may also create the distance that allows measured engagement with issues of emotional import, including occasions for grief. That is, pathos and irony are interrelated in such a way that ironic detachment can offer the distance necessary for feeling, and can thus help to revivify feeling, both as process—the activity of feeling—and as feeling-judgment. And such revivifying of feeling is the restorative, life-affirming gift of the blues.

The heroic capacity for self-protection and self-restoration exemplified by Mr. Newman's largely successful efforts to assert his personhood in the face of the relentless abandonments and betrayals of

135

his youth is demonstrated more subtly in the dream of thirty-year-old "Darlene Baker." She dreamed this dream during a time of stress resulting from experiments, prompted by analysis, in new and less guarded ways of relating to the world. Her promiscuous maternal grandmother was schizophrenic. Her mother entices trust and answers it with attack and betrayal. It would be hard to guess whether her sister is a "good enough mother." Darlene Baker herself is childless.

She dreams:

> In a boat like a hydrofoil or ferry, moving from the sea into an inlet or river. [She later associates the boat with a salmon heading upstream.] Sensing that we are about to hit something, I shout to the man in charge [perhaps her father], but he does not respond. I then grab up a baby to protect it from the crash. The mother of the baby [perhaps the dreamer's sister] is sitting next to me. The baby is smart enough not to cry and to let me protect it. [She later associates this attitude of the baby with that of babies quietly accepting their mothers' comforting during bombing raids.] Frightening as the crash is, we survive it unharmed, and when it is past the baby makes a conscious decision to return to its mother. I feel a pang of regret that the baby isn't mine.

The apparently neglected baby is "smart enough"—knows well enough what is good for it—to inspire and accept the maternal protection it will need in the impending danger. It is also capable of making a "conscious decision" (a complex feeling-judgment of the kind discussed in part 6.9) to return to its real mother. It presumably does so because it has developed affectional bonds to her, and because these, whatever their character, are important, even if the baby's mother might be less capable than the dreamer of dealing with acute threats to it.

One might take the dream ego and the baby—but also the real mother in the dream—as representing various resources of the dreamer to cope with threats to ego and self. It seems impossible in any simple way, however, to assign either ego or self to either figure in the collaboration between the baby and the dream ego in its self-adopted maternal role. This is because in general the infantile self and ego are located nonspecifically and variably in the mother-infant dyad as a whole.

Abandonment, Wish, and Hope in the Blues

I do not mean that the infant is psychologically contained in its mother until it gradually over many months achieves what Margaret S. Mahler calls "psychological [as distinct from actual] birth."[34] I would stress instead the relatedness and "fit" between mother and infant present from birth in significant if rudimentary form. I also do not mean that the infant's psychic life is a chaotic *prima materia* of later development. I would stress instead the infant's ability, within the context of the mother-infant dyad, to muster integrative resources to counter, or to get it beyond, states of deintegration—symbolized, for example, by the boat crash in the dream.

Moreover, though I would locate the infantile self and ego in the dyad as a whole, I am impressed that the dream ego in this dream takes the kind of responsibility for the baby that Saint Christopher does for the Christ Child (in fig. 1). And though such responsibility implies a mature ego, I am impressed that in the dream this responsibility is shared by the dream ego and the baby. And I am further impressed that this shared responsibility is manifest in what could be called a completed act of community.

One might generalize that the mature ego represented by Saint Christopher bears the germ of self-realization achieved through the ego's interaction with the symbolic Christ Child. This describes one form individuation may take in a later phase. By the same token, as this dream suggests, the actual infant from strikingly early on—bears the germ of the mature ego represented by Saint Christopher that will later be capable of such self-realization. This describes an important aspect of individuation in an early phase.

Macroscopically regarded, individuation may accord with such successive phases, though developmental tasks do not all strictly accord with a fixed and simple sequence, so that in fact one observes various overall patterns. In all of them, individuation, microscopically regarded, consists of an ongoing flow of interactions between ego and self, drawing on various potentialities of each. It seems to me useful to assume that the early mother-infant relationship is dynamically implicit in all of these interactions, and I take Darlene Baker's dream as illustrating an important respect in which it is so. It also illustrates the capacity of the self to redress impairments in that relationship.

3.4 Wish and Hope in the Blues

After describing the poverty and hardship of his life, one black Mississippian remarked,

> . . . And you get to thinkin' about where can you go, or what can you do for to change. And there is no change. That's when the blues gets you. When there's nothin' else to do but what you doin' . . . and sing the blues:
> I know . . . I know . . . Yes, I know. . . .
> I hope one day my luck will change.
> I done had to work so hard,
> Nothin' still won't go right,
> I don't have no girl friend,
> The onliest one I had, she lef' me las' night.
> That can be bad, and the truth it's sad,
> Oh so sad, when you lose the best girl you ever had. . . .[35]

The most potent image of having the blues is that of being abandoned by one's woman or man. The cause of the condition is imagined as for now unchanging, and the single most dominant sentiment in the art of the blues is, "My luck is bad right now, but I hope one day it will change." What is the blues form of hope?

Let us begin with what the blues form of hope importantly is not: it is not wish. Wish makes up much of the content of the blues presentation. But it does not follow that the expression of wish in the blues amounts in any simple sense to wish fulfillment. Indeed, reflecting upon hope and wish in the blues must lead one to question the adequacy of Freud's understanding of the role of wish in imaginative products more generally.

It is useful to think of wish as the product of fantasy as a relatively passive process, expressing the feeling-toned complexes described by Jung in a way that is compatible with ego-defenses and other impedimenta to a more genuinely imaginative life. Thus a certain man has what he calls his "pornography complex." What he means by this is that when his conscious energy becomes depleted, certain sexual preoccupations emerge in a way that he pictures as an object exposed owing to the lowering of the level of sinking water. These preoccupations then get played out in stereotyped fantasies vivid enough to be distracting or pleasantly diverting but not forceful enough and not

Abandonment, Wish, and Hope in the Blues

of such a character as to engage him in a way that challenges or alters his workaday assumptions about what his life is about. Much popular fiction serves purposes related to this kind of private fantasy, and it may be fair enough to call this "wish fulfillment," provided that one does not assume too readily that one knows what constitutes this "fullfillment" and what it means to call the urge to this fulfillment "wish." Importantly, this kind of fantasy is partly continuous with, but also partly of another order than, imagination of a kind that does challenge ego assumptions and is transformative in a deeper way.

As an art of survival, the blues cannot afford the idle luxury of wish divorced from a deeper transformative process. In the context of the blues, a good name for wish so divorced would be "false hope." Denying that the blues-inducing circumstances can be changed, at least now; never proposing what are meant to be taken as realistic and adequate solutions to real-life problems; and always allowing that a problem solved may soon be replaced by a problem of at least the same magnitude, the blues plays with wish in a rich variety of ways, implicitly exposing it as false hope. The result is not hope as a plan of action, but it is hope as affirming and enhancing both the vital core of the individual and the community of the blues performance, and of the larger blues world of shared idiom and attitude. In the blues performance, hopelessness is sacrificed to such affirmation and enhancement.

Looking at the matter another way, one sees a natural link between false hope and despair. An illuminating perspective on the treatment of this link in the blues is offered by a passage in Shakespeare's *Richard II*, in which the sorrowing Queen Isabel is given the advice, "Despair not, madam," to which she replies:

> Who shall hinder me?
> I will despair and be at enmity
> With cozening hope: he is a flatterer,
> A parasite, a keeper-back of death,
> Who gently would dissolve the bands of life
> Which false hope lingers in extremity.
>
> [II.ii.67–72]

Thus, in the queen's view, to entertain false hope is to cling to life in an illusionary way, which invites despair and death, which she

139

welcomes as freeing her from her former illusion. The blues is thoroughly aware of this train of emotional logic—from false hope to despair and death—and rejects it, just as it rejects falsely hopeful solutions to possibly insoluble problems.

Important in the process whereby the blues affirms and enhances individuality and community, while denying false hope, despair, and death, is the proper form of detachment. The queen's hopes for death are a pseudoform of this detachment, the proper forms of which are imaginative. There are indeed blues about wanting to die and about plans for suicide, but they are, in effect, a rebuttal of the queen's position. The sentiments they imaginatively explore have their meaning not as literally presented intention or direct practical advice, but as elements of a blues performance in which they are contemplated in a way that allows both exploration of them and detachment from them. This contemplation no more encourages the audience to give way to them than an impending murder in a stage play incites the audience to try to stop the action.

Taking being abandoned by one's woman or man as the basic image of having the blues, one might say, with an oddness that may prove illuminating, that the blues detaches one from one's abandonment. My purpose in speaking in this odd way is to contrast the sort of detachment I have in mind with behavior to which John Bowlby applies the same term in his study, *Attachment and Loss* (1969). By *detachment* Bowlby means the kind of affectional distancing to be seen in children who react to their mother's prolonged absence by adapting dully to having a succession of caretakers, and by listlessly turning away from their mothers when they do return.[36] This affectional limbo is related to the pornography complex discussed above. In contrast, the blues would say, "Don't despair; don't be listless and numb. *Feel* your pain; *want* to reconnect." This pain and this want are hope and life, which must be served by various kinds of distancing, framing, and detachment that allow wish to be seen as false hope, and abandonment to be protested against. The pathos of the blues is characteristically treated ironically.

Let us take a simple example of blues wish. A familiar line has the singer boast, "Never had one gal at a time, always had six, seven, eight or nine." In one sense, this sounds like an insurance policy both against abandonment and the complications that come with trying to deal with a single woman. Of course, this is also sexual boasting, but how is it to be heard? In the culture reflected in the blues, women are for men a value, albeit often a problematic one. But only the right amount of a good thing adequately makes up for the lack of that thing, and in this line the right amount is lost in a wishful vision of plenty. Considering the misery of triangles, we are able to appreciate the jealousy, spite, confusion, and mayhem that would be unloosed by a man's attempts to deal with nine women at once: having nine women would surely leave a man justified in the worry, reiterated in the blues, about the iodine an irate woman might put in his coffee. His troubles would probably be mild, however, compared with those that could be predicted for Robert Pete Williams, who imagines buying his own railroad, insisting, "I wanna haul nothin' but women; / I don't want no men allowed."[37]

Similarly, the ironic perspective of Fred McDowell's "Good Morning Little School Girl" is apparent at the outset, as a clearly adult male presents himself as a schoolboy proposing that he walk a girl home. After talking about buying her a diamond ring, there is an enigmatic hint at an altercation. Then she is gone, apparently without a trace, and he is looking for her. He says that he will buy an airplane and fly from town to town, and that if he does not find her, he will not let his airplane down. Can a schoolboy or a black Mississippi farmer buy an airplane? Of what use is an airplane if one has no particular destination? What kind of looking for a woman can one do from an airplane? Presumably this perpetual-motion airplane is fueled by the same kind of magical power that operates the ever-ready sexual apparatus of the man with six, seven, eight, or nine women. Moreover, after describing the airplane trip, he again speaks of buying his woman a diamond ring, thus denying that she left him, and dealing with his sense of loss and injured self-esteem by reminding himself of his imagined wealth and, hence, power.[38]

Johnny Copeland assumes a similarly heroic and foredoomed stance when he pictures himself on an airplane to North Carolina, where he is sure that his woman is "somewhere." Airlines do not sell tickets to "North Carolina," though they do to Raleigh-Durham, Fayetteville, High Point, and Charlotte: practically, arriving in North Carolina

141

will have him no closer to the elusive woman than he was in New York City, where his imaginary trip started.[39]

In other ways, too, the ironic stance may offer means of making the best of a bad lot. Thus, Muddy Waters, abandoned, hears what "sounds like" his "little honey bee," who has been all around the world making honey and is now coming home to him: he expresses pleasure in the return, ending his abandonment, of a woman he shares with countless other men. Then again, the "lot of buzzin' " he hears is pretty indefinite; perhaps it is not his little honey bee after all.[40] His grandiose but feeble, because unspecific, attempt to locate his woman, incidentally, has ample precedent among blues performers. Thus Elmore James in his "Dust My Broom," for example, intends to "call up China" to see if his baby is there; if not, it seems to him a reasonable next guess that she is in the Philippine Islands.

Small children do not understand irony; the irony of the blues is pervasive, complex, and often highly ambiguous. Blues pathos draws upon experiences of attachment and separation within the mother-infant relationship. While insisting that we know the painful reality of abandonment, deprivation, and constriction, the blues ironically plays with wish, for the delight of play, and to the end of mocking the delusions to which wish may lead. By its beauty and generation of energy, the blues reawakens the joy in survival that is the basic form of hope—and draws one into the blues community of survivors.

4 Festival, Communion, and Mutuality

The words *communion, community,* and *communications* are inter-related in ways that tell us something important about the nature and purpose of feasts and feasting. Communion is a celebration of community—of participation in a social group whose members communicate with one another by means of shared images, words, and concepts. But *communion* can also name a mode of emotional interaction that is largely preverbal or subverbal in character, and such interaction, too, is communication. The chief characteristic of this second kind of communion—and communication—is mutuality. This mutuality is both presupposed and fostered by the giving and taking essential to festival.

Some striking comments by Winnicott about the relations between mother and infant bear directly and importantly on this nonverbal and emotional communion.

There are moments in which the infant is appreciatively aware of its own security. Such moments, according to Winnicott, "have no climax. This," he observes, "distinguishes them from phenomena that have instinctual backing, where the orgiastic element plays an essential part and where satisfactions are closely linked with climax." He criticizes psychoanalysts for neglecting "the tremendous intensity of these nonclimactic experiences of relating to objects." And in an earlier, larger version of the paper from which I have quoted he is said to have denied strongly that "the most intense experiences belong to instinctual and orgiastic events," since such a view "leaves out of account the function of the ego-organization. Only if someone is there adding up personal experience into a total that can become a self," according to Winnicott, "does instinctual satisfaction avoid becoming a disrupting factor, or have a meaning beyond its localized meaning as a

143

sample of physiology."[1] In other words, ego-organization and the sense of self-identity are largely built up through nonconsummatory experiences of mutuality, these being in important ways independent of physiological appetite.

Indeed, there is experimental evidence that even in small infants physiological appetite may be subordinated to nonappetitive aims easily brought under the headings of "communion," "community," and "communication." In one experiment, for example, infants were presented with problems of listening. When they solved a problem correctly they were rewarded with a feeding nipple, and when they failed they got a nonfeeding nipple. The three-month-old infants would then smile when, on the basis of a signal tone preceding it, they had predicted the appearance of the feeding nipple. They were not smiling at the prospect of food, because, even though they were hungry, they declined actually nursing at the nipple, instead turning to the researcher in delight at their success and wanting to play again.[2]

Another experimenter rigged up electronic nipples, measured the rate at which his infants sucked, then attached the nipple device to a movie screen on which a film was shown out of focus. If an infant hit a prescribed rate of sucking, the film came into focus. The infants quickly learned to focus the film and quickly adjusted their rate of sucking when the prescribed rate was changed. What is striking about this is that an infant cannot suck and focus at the same time since either entrainment takes up the whole brain attention. Yet, the infants managed to establish a balance resulting in maximum focus and minimum attention to sucking.[3]

In both sets of experiments the appetite of infants was accommodated to interpersonal interaction under the aspect of mutuality.

Festival not only affirms mutuality but may even elevate it to the status of an ultimate value. For example, Augustine did this, in effect, when he sought to express his vision of perpetual communion with God by asserting that in the House of the Lord festival is eternal.[4] Festival affirms mutuality in the special way of satiating appetite. In the following reflections I will be regarding appetitive behavior and experiences of mutuality as embodying distinct but interrelated and complementary principles. Even more broadly, mutuality enables the self to be what it is and become what it is becoming: it is essential to the process of individuation by which the self is manifested as personality.

Our lives are largely governed by what I will for the moment call emotional evaluation—that is, by psychic processes reflecting our self-esteem, trust, and hope—or lack of them—our loves and hates, our immediate feeling responses, and our more enduring attitudes. A sense of mutuality is crucial in bringing meaningful coherence into these processes. In festival appetite is made to subsume that coherence.

4.1 Festival and "The Natural Man"

In many places Shakespeare makes dramatic use of elements drawn from marriages, wassails, and pageants, and from such festivals as Shrove Tuesday, Midsummer Eve, and the twelve days of Christmas ending in Twelfth Night. As the literary critic C. L. Barber observes, Shakespeare's use of such elements brings about a surge of "the vitality normally locked up in awe and respect," and this results—for both the characters and the audience—in a clarification of perception. This Barber describes as "a heightened awareness of the relation between man and 'nature'—the nature celebrated on holiday. . . . The plays," he remarks, "present a mockery of what is unnatural . . . [as well as] of what is merely natural."[5]

Though leaving some important things unsaid, this account—based on Freud's analysis of wit—does call attention to an essential function of festival. As Barber observes, festival generates and channels energy partly to the end of modifying the forms of consciousness that govern ordinary life. It modifies them by enhancing our awareness of mutuality.

Mutuality, as I am using the word, is not primarily the result of making up a deficit. It rather entails at the outset a sense of abundance. It is very little like making sure that there is exactly enough money in one's account to cover all one's outstanding checks. It is very much more like investing money from one's savings account in a stock that will earn a higher yield, and then learning to one's surprise that the yield is even higher than one had expected. (The reader may recall Luther's story, related in part 2.7, about a person writing to ask for silver of a father disposed to give him a thousand pieces of gold.)

145

These reflections bear on the theme of festival in that a festival offers its participants more than enough. It is a celebration of abundance. But what, in a psychological sense, is the primary source and nature of the abundance experienced through festival? *How* does festival make us feel more fully alive?

Barber's answer, as we have seen, is that the psychic energy formerly "locked up in awe and respect" is, through festival, devoted to a renewed appreciation of nature and of that part of our makeup that Paul called "the natural man" (1 Cor. 2:14). And indeed, though words for "spirit"—such as the German *Geist*—are derived from words suggesting churning, spontaneous activity,[6] there are forms of "spirit" that are listless and deadening. We might think, for example, of the medieval ascetic whose spiritual exercises resulted in what he recognized as "spiritual dryness." And pondering the personality of an obsessively rigid bureaucrat, we might express some of the ironies of *spirit* by describing him as overly spiritual but spiritually constricted and inert. When spiritual salt loses its savor in such ways, the natural man may provide energies for a needed renewal of attitude.

It is wrong, however, to make too neat a distinction, as Barber perhaps does, between nature as the immediate satisfaction of appetite, on the one hand, and spirit—or culture—as the force impeding that satisfaction, on the other. In fact, one of the functions of festival is to soften the distinction between nature and spirit, so that nature becomes nature-as-spirit and spirit becomes spirit-as-nature. Festival does this by making the satisfaction of appetite a process of understanding. What is understood is in a broad sense spiritual: a festival is an occasion on which people celebrate something they deem larger and more significant than their individual lives, most usually something having connections with divinity.

As we know from psychosomatic illnesses, there is a "thinking of the body." Festival behavior—even in festivals of license—is highly coded, and the satisfaction of appetite in festival is a complex processing of information. The excellence of the dish, for example, tells the guest that his host is magnanimous, and that he himself is valued; its delicacy tells him that he is regarded as discriminating; its traditional character tells him he has ties with his ancestors and the gods. Festival includes such transpersonal elements as the configuration of the group and the occasion being celebrated. For example, a festival with the king present is different from one with the king absent; the joy of Easter is different from the riot of Carnival. Indeed, the festivals of Catherine de Médicis and other rulers in the sixteenth century were elaborate and sumptuous works of art.[7] Nonetheless, though rules, structure, and inhibition are necessary to the large meaning of festival, the experience it offers is one of abundance. More specifically, this experience of abundance is a quality of mutuality.

4.2 Festival and the Debasement of Mutuality

On the East Indian island of Alor, feasting amounts to a grim game in which one person tries to force a rival to sponsor a feast—for example, by shooting one of his pigs to make him have to offer a feast so that the animal will not go to waste.[8] And in many times and places a major purpose of feasting has been to impress the guests and enhance the host's prestige. Thus Catherine de Médicis consciously employed elaborate festivals as an instrument of political power to impress foreigners, arouse loyalty to the monarchy, and bring warring factions together in pleasant and harmless recreations.[9] Ingredients of festival are given a related emphasis in the Roman slogan, "bread and circuses." And the sinister side of festival as an instrument of power is suggested by the title of a recent book about the potlatch—complex feasting and gift-giving—ceremonies among American Indians of the Pacific Northwest: *Feasting with Mine Enemy.*[10] It is important to grant, however, that the potlatch, far from being entirely a form of compulsive and aggressive one-upmanship, accords with a principle affirmed by the teachings and institutions of many societies—and by this book—that gifts are meant not to be hoarded but to be used or given on. Thus, the potlatch symbolically attests to the truth expressed in Christ's parable of the talents (Matt. 25:14–30) and in Bernard of Clairvaux's admonition that "there is a great natural gift within us, and if it is not allowed full play the rest of our nature will go to ruin, as though it were being eaten away by the rust of decay," a development that "would be an insult to its Creator."[11] Surely, any halfway sensitive analyst must early learn what the potlatch in its way teaches, that unused gifts are a curse.

147

I have noted Augustine's idea that in the House of the Lord festival is eternal. Still, when earthly festival becomes perpetual, it loses its meaning, and it may even debase mutuality when feasting is made to serve crass purposes of power. Thus one historian has written that life in the baroque court was nothing but festival, that apart from festival there were no ordinary days and no work—nothing but empty time and boredom—and that a *horror vacui* endangered this condition of perpetual festival.[12] Shakespeare's Prince Hal reflects in this way on his wastrel life with Falstaff and his dissolute companions: "If all the year were playing holidays, / To sport would be as tedious as to work" (*Henry IV, Part I*, I.ii.201–2). The historian describing the baroque court does not focus on the implications of this condition for personal relations, but it is easy to surmise them. And the interaction between Prince Hal and Falstaff is in some ways—on both sides—a self-serving parody of mutuality.

Just as there are negative forms of mutuality—bonds of mutual hatred, and alliances based on deceit and self-deceit—so rather than the heightening of the sense of community, festival made grossly coercive or grown chronic may blunt and debase that sense. But such developments tell us nothing about community as a vital value or about festival as fostering it.

4.3 The Self That Knows What Is Good for Itself

Jung antedated by several decades the psychoanalytic writers currently concerned with a distinction between ego and self, and his concept of the self, manifold and paradoxical as it is, is dynamic in ways that recent psychoanalytic concepts of the self at their best scarcely approach. The self as he understands it is often symbolized by religious contents of various kinds, which he studied in his later writings. But one can find his concept of the self prefigured in his early work, "The Psychology of Dementia Praecox" (1907), and I will use that prefiguration as my point of departure in what I want to say now about personal self-identity.

In that extraordinary essay Jung focused on a "central psychological disturbance, a disturbance that sets in at the vital source of all the mental functions; that is, in the realm of apperception, feeling, and

148

appetition." He follows the early German physiologist and psychologist Wilhelm Wundt in calling this disturbance "apperceptive deterioration," apperception being in Wundt's words "the single process by which any psychic content is brought to clear comprehension." Pondering the problematic term *apperception*, Jung remarks that it "is volition, feeling, affectivity, suggestion, compulsion, etc., for these are all processes which 'bring a psychic content to clear comprehension.' "[13] Jung is here implicitly talking about the self as what Merleau-Ponty would later call the "body-subject." And it is as body-subjects that we participate in festival.

Schizophrenic disintegration results from what the analytical psychologist John Weir Perry has called a "central injury," an injury to this vital core of the personality, which has capacities for integration and disintegration ranging from the simplest appetitive behavior to the most refined complexities of language, art, and religious symbolism.[14]

There are vital needs on the level of physiology—the need for air, water, and a certain range of temperature, for example. But *vital* is also a term of value, as certain things may in a literal but also in an extended sense be "vitally important." Such physiological vital needs are finally inseparable from a vital need for self-esteem, which is found and given through mutuality. Mutuality is vitally important—in an extended but also in a literal sense—in that frustration of the need for it may result in a central injury manifest in the most varied domains of mind and body. And yet even in someone so afflicted there may be attempts—expressive of the vital core—to reconstitute the personality. Thus Jung regarded the sense of worthlessness of one of his patients as in part "the normal correction of her grotesque ideas of grandeur"[15]—such ideas themselves often representing attempts to compensate impaired self-esteem. A failure of mutuality surely contributed to the formation of this patient's psychopathology; an increase in *genuine* self-esteem—and the abandonment of her grandiosity—would be required for her to achieve a fuller participation in community. Still—precisely with regard to these issues—her psychopathology was partly the product of a failed attempt at self-healing; and such attempts must be regarded as expressions of the will to live.

I am talking about self-esteem in connection with the will to live on this fundamental level because the self as the vital core of the person has an evaluative aspect that has never been sufficiently stressed—and has never been made explicit enough—though Jung had it in mind when he regarded feeling and affectivity as essential qualities of the vital core. I would basically summarize the evaluative aspect of the vital core in this way: *somewhere in one's person, relatively distinct from the ego and supraordinate to it, is a self that knows what is good for itself. That good must be found in the world, but knowledge of what must be found is presupposed in the seeking.* Augustine expressed this in religious terms when he thanked God for giving him as an infant a care for his own well-being.[16] And two of Jung's patients expressed care for *their* well-being in the form of "teleological hallucinations," one as he tried to kill himself by jumping out of the window but was hurled back into the room by a tremendous light, the other as he tried to kill himself by inhaling gas but felt himself grasped by the throat and thrown to the floor by an enormous hand.[17]

In saying that self-esteem is found and given through mutuality, I have meant to give as much importance to the seeking and finding on the part of the infant as to the giving on the part of the mother. I would elaborate upon my description of the evaluative aspect of the vital core in this way: *to know what is good for oneself is to know oneself as good.* This knowledge can be amplified, attenuated, inhibited, or even largely destroyed through interaction with others, but it is not simply given by them. The expression "good enough mother" implies that no mother is perfect—indeed, it is important that any mother should not be—and that the infant has resources for finding what it needs, and for making do, in an imperfect environment.

As Jung realized, compensation is one of the fundamental principles of psychic life—at work, for example, when daydreaming offers relief from the rigors of directed thinking, or when a dream corrects one's conscious understanding of a situation, or when delusions of grandeur balance injured self-esteem. *Compensation actively expresses the evaluative aspect of the vital core as the self that knows what is good for itself.* Compensation embraces processes and contents of the most varied kinds, but its essential nature is evaluative—and emotional.

Cultural values are made part of the developing personality through introjection. Very important among these values are those proscribed by the injunction, "Thou shalt not." But before these cultural "Thou

150

shalt nots" are even intelligible to the infant, it evaluates on the basis of the self that knows what is good for itself. Thus, the infant may fall into a depression that amounts to a rejection of a mother the infant finds *not* good enough. The positive meaning of such a depression is an attempt to defend the vital core of the infant, even though the attempt is, in effect, suicidal.

4.4 Self, Not-Self, Ego, and Mutuality

In an important essay the analytical psychologist Leopold Stein discussed relations between self and not-self using as a model the workings of the immunological system of the human body.[18] Skin grafts, for example, succeed only under quite specific conditions; under others the body rejects the grafts as alien. This acceptance and non-acceptance on the bodily level suggests the way in which the self— long before the consolidation of the ego or despite its psychotic disintegration—may act purposively in the interests of its own well-being. What the self accepts is self-enhancing; ultimately, however, the self must not only be enhanced but also find an accommodation with a largely not-self world.

The term *accommodation* implies bringing separate things together. Separate as self and not-self may be, however, there are also ways in which they are from early on experienced as continuous with one another. And these experiences of continuity are also basic both to personal identity and to mutuality.

Research into the limbic system of the brain indicates that one of its functions is to register the world as an "aesthetic continuum" in which discrete objects are not discriminated and the distinction between subject and object is not sharply drawn.[19] The nature of this continuum is suggested by Chinese painting in which figure and ground fade into one another, thus reflecting the attitude of the artist, who has tried not to see the landscape in a focused way but to immerse himself in it and become one with it.[20] And indeed, if I gaze serenely into the clear blue of the sky, where do I experience myself as leaving off and where do I experience the sky as starting?

Similarly, various psychic agencies that are in some sense discrete—among them the ego—are in other senses continuous within the overall psychic organization. The infant may regard its mother as part of itself and feel that she "should" be there when wanted. And she may comply with this feeling and even encourage it, while sometimes needing to go about her own business that has little to do with the infant, with the result that the mother from the infant's point of view then becomes not-self. An important part of ego development is learning to tolerate ambiguities of self and not-self in their continuity with one another.

The hallucinatory hand tearing the man from the gas jet (in part 4.3) offers a striking example of such ambiguities. The hand was an expression of the self as the vital core. In acting on behalf of the ego—doing what the ego would have done if it had not been impaired—the self reveals its continuity with the ego (in the form of the "emergency ego" mentioned in part 2.5). Still, the self acts on behalf of the ego precisely by opposing the ego's purposes, and by seeming to be a horrifying instance of not-self from the ego's point of view—much as the disobliging mother becomes not-self to the yearning infant. Just as the self may act on behalf of the ego, the ego may act on behalf of the self. Indeed, Perry's observation about the inner psyche as a dynamic matrix intent on getting its contents into consciousness implies both that the self acts on behalf of the ego and that the ego acts on behalf of the self—relations that will be explored more fully in part 5.

The ego is largely, though not exclusively, concerned with accommodating new experiences to preexisting schemata in such forms as concepts, attitudes, and beliefs. Though the self as the vital core of the person is concerned with survival, it is also concerned with the growth and development of the personality as a whole, and what furthers immediate adaptation may not also further such growth and development. Indeed, much of what we call neurosis is—precisely—immediate adaptation: a low-grade, day-to-day getting by, while settling for too little in neglect of long-range purposes and larger frames of meaning.

This discrepancy gives rise to different ways of evaluating the world and ourselves, especially under the aspect of potentiality. The hand and light of Jung's suicidal patients in part 4.3 could be construed as saying, "You have lives to live, and you have not yet exhausted the possibilities of living them properly." Indeed, Jung's later distinction between the morality of the ego in its adaptation to conventional values, on the one hand, and an ethic of the self as the supraordinate principle of growth and development, on the other,[21] was prefigured in this early psychiatric work. The hallucinatory hand and light make clear that the self, knowing itself as good, and knowing what is good for itself, may act to force the individual to take account of this principle in his evaluations.

The continuum between self and not-self, on the one hand, and between self and ego, on the other, is the basis of important psychological processes. These include identification and disidentification, and inhibition as a component both of action and of emotional reflection. This continuum is also the basis of self-division, as I actively disown this or that, although I cannot disown what I do not implicitly own as part of myself. Such self-division is tantamount to inner conflict, whether or not the ego experiences it as such. And inner conflict may find a pseudoresolution in inauthenticity, as I deny what does not fit the specious unity I have thus created. But it is important also to remember that the capacity for self-division is inseparable from the psyche's capacity for rearranging and even recreating its contents to the end of more adapted functioning and increased authenticity— since integration and deintegration imply one another. The continuum between self and not-self also makes mutuality possible. I become identified with other people and things: I put myself into them, or they are taken into me. Thus the developing individual progresses from identification with his mother to identification with larger and often more abstract entities: the personal family, an age group, a nationality, a particular generation at a particular moment in history. Personal identity may also be maintained and even extended through disidentifications. ("I was a fool to have said that to her." After many years the American novelist Howard Fast resigned from the Communist Party.) Sometimes earlier identifications that are now seemingly unimportant must be reestablished and given new energy. (An English-speaking woman whose mother spoke French to her as a child finds herself speaking French on the occasions—and only those occasions—

on which she feels love or anger toward her small child. Often in analysis people must reestablish connection with their repressed childhood pasts.) Ego and self both serve in forming these identifications and disidentifications with people, things, and more abstract entities that on some level retain their character as not-self.

Much of what I have just said about identification and disidentification is well illustrated by a dream of Henry Newman, who, as the reader will recall (from part 3.3), spent years of his childhood in an orphanage, though he had a living, but dissolute, father. In the dream Mr. Newman is himself as a small boy in some sort of an institution with many beds. A red-haired man arrives and says that he is the boy's father, although his father did not have red hair, and although in the dream the boy knew that the arriving figure was named Sam Hawkins. As Hawkins, holding a hypodermic needle, grows menacing, Mr. Newman, now an adult, can see himself as a small boy lying in one of the beds. As the menace of the red-haired man increases, the bed is suddenly empty, and Mr. Newman begins to experience what is happening as he would as a small boy. As the menace increases still further, Mr. Newman can see his own mouth contorted in terror as he gasps for air. The dream closes as he pushes against the bars of a window, hoping he can throw himself out of it and kill himself, thus bringing this vision of hell to an end.

In the dream Mr. Newman's father and the red-haired Sam Hawkins are identified. Mr. Newman feels enough identity with the small boy to recognize him as a younger version of himself. When the bed is suddenly empty the identification is complete, and he *is* the small boy. As he sees his own contorted mouth a disidentification has taken place, though on the basis of an identity that allows him to recognize himself. Even the shift from life-affirming terror to suicidal despair represents a disidentification with one attitude and an identification with another. Mr. Newman felt curiously calm in the days after the dream, because the dream as a whole amounts to a disidentification that creates distance from his traumatic past while giving him a clear symbolic picture of it and thus making it available to be taken into account in conscious thought and action. This distancing—while staying in conscious connection with a psychic content of emotional import—is essential to art and is a major theme of this book.

Festival, Communion, and Mutuality

All purposive and coherent action entails an inhibition of alternative action. Inhibition is necessary to all forms of reflection, including that which makes possible a relatively detached reading of emotional expression (as distinct from emotional seizure). Inhibition may also, however, take the form of repression and the dissociation of parts of one's person from one's conscious personality. Though such dissociation often impairs conscious functioning, it also creates an energetic potential that can be used by the self to various purposes, including that of enabling the ego to achieve a wider and more adapted perspective. Though the self that knows what is good for itself may be manifest in such massive, unilateral, defensive actions as those that saved Jung's suicidal patients, the self has an inherent predisposition to mutuality. Indeed, mutuality is the optimal form of relationship between self and not-self, between ego and self, and between one person and the persons and objects of his world. The implications of this condensed formulation will become clear in the further course of this book. Now I want simply to remark briefly on the relevance of festival to the themes I have just touched on.

In its expansive life-affirmation, festival may activate the self that knows what is good for itself and may stir the individual to desire to take it into account in his evaluations. Festival entails identification—with the occasion celebrated, with the structure of values implicit in the occasion, and with other participants in the feast. This process entails disidentification—for example, with the person one is in workaday, nonfestive life. Festival entails inhibition—in the form of etiquette, for example—even if the satiation of appetite in festival is also a form of disinhibition. Disinhibition may help to create a holiday mood, but inhibition is essential to the reflective attitude of mind that allows that mood to be read as feeling.

I wish to note here that the view of the self I am now presenting is very different from that propounded by Edward F. Edinger in his book *Ego and Archetype*. Edinger's basic terms for describing the relations of the ego to the self are *inflation* and *alienation*, states inviting disaster, the prospect of which should inspire fear and trembling. Such states do occur, as does the disaster resulting from them. (I have spoken of self-alienation in part 3.3.) And, as Edinger argues, the oscillation between such states may be followed by something like a dialectic process between ego and self.[22] The self that knows what is good for itself may indeed be manifest in such dreadful forms as those experienced by Jung's patients. But more characteristically, the self that knows what is good for itself tells us that whatever is necessary and desirable for our truest well-being is available, accessible, indeed perhaps even already present. Our response to this knowledge is not fear and trembling, as we hover between inflation and alienation, but joyous calm.

As I have argued, mutuality is an experience of abundance. More specifically, it is an experience of the abundantly good. Festival is a reaching out to this good. There are, to be sure, festivals commemorating dismal shades of the dead, and there are festivals of mourning. But even a funeral banquet conveys an affirmative message: "Reduced as we are by this loss, we are and must remain part of life and open to its goodness." Indeed, one philosopher has regarded the essential nature of festival as the affirmation that *"everything that is, is good."*[23] The self that knows what is good for itself is at work in this affirmation.

Declaring everything good is obviously not a statement of literal fact. Taking it as such would be like jumping from one's seat in a theater to save the heroine from the villain. The assertion that everything is good is valid within the festive frame, as the dramatic performance is real within the dramatic frame. The point of the assertion becomes clear if one thinks of ways in which realistic common sense, with its recognition of evil, fails. It sometimes fails because it underestimates complexity and is naive. (That of many heroes of picaresque fiction fails through such underestimation.) But it also fails through a lack of trust and good will. (The United States and the Soviet Union distrust one another; in the absence of trust they are without the good will necessary for common efforts on behalf of their joint survival.) There are private and partisan interests. (Germany and France have both annexed Alsace by force.) But there is also the general good. (It is a desideratum of the general good that the world should not be destroyed by nuclear arms.) Festive celebration of everything as good is a way of symbolically affirming the common good and of revivifying our imaginative awareness of it.

4.5 Festival and Symbol

Much of the power of festival derives from its appeal to nonverbal levels of our being. Still, as we have seen, festival has symbolic content—in the form, for example, of the occasion being celebrated or the "higher power" being invoked. Thus there is a relation between festival and the kinds of overdetermined, complex, polyvalent symbols of special interest to depth psychologists, especially those in the tradition of Jung. I mean the kinds of symbols that give one the sense of not only stating and summarizing in an illuminating way but also of providing a momentary glimpse of something otherwise unknown, something that will fade again into its unknownness. It is a mistake to draw too pat a distinction between such symbols and the more prosaic "signs" employed in our practical work in the world. Still, *some* such distinction can validly be drawn and it will reflect divergent attitudes concerning our purposes and the nature of our actions.

We are creatures of language, which, through its resources of metaphor, extends the known into the unknown and makes the unknown known, and thus gives us mastery over the world. But utilitarian mastery is not the only form of relationship to the world. Indeed, it is in many respects a self-deceiving and self-destructive one. This may be seen if we contrast it with one that also can define purposes and actions: I mean the attitude expressed in the beliefs of various peoples that human life is some sort of partnership between man, animals, the elements, and spirits of various kinds. The attitude of utilitarian world mastery erodes the sense of mutuality I have been describing. But as such beliefs in man's partnership with elements of his world suggest, the mind also has resources to create symbols fostering the sense of mutuality. Their nature and function—and the process of their creation—have been well described by Dufrenne.

We may begin, Dufrenne proposes, by considering the perception of an ordinary object, which—even when singled out by perception—remains part of a larger world of objects, from which it cannot be completely separated. Thus, in a certain sense the perceived object may be said to reach beyond itself into the world against which it is silhouetted, or to draw upon that background as a guarantee of its

157

form and its reality. "It is by means of the world that the object is real," Dufrenne remarks, "not only because its profile stands out against it but because it is supported and nourished by that unfathomable reservoir of beings."[24]

Generally, ego-consciousness in its discriminating analytic mode—reflecting the utilitarian attitude of world-mastery—leads us to experience ourselves as self-encapsulated subjects, and to experience objects as isolated from the living context that is part of their reality and meaning. Poetic and mythic symbolism serves to complement this one-sided attitude. Thus Dufrenne observes that "most ancient religions call on us to perceive the world (as if it were an incomplete spatial totality and, perhaps, in order to compensate for what that totality lacks) as an elementary power—the Earth-Mother, the Ground—a fundamental force of which myth is the explanation."[25] In such a view the individual thing or event is experienced as integrated into the world by virtue of its participation in this fundamental force. Festival is one of the most ancient and widespread ways of being mindful of this participation. This is so because festive abundance corresponds on the level of appetite to what could be called the "fullness" of the mythic symbol—of the "fundamental force" described by Dufrenne—so that festival becomes the medium whereby such a symbol is apprehended by the "thinking of the body."

The most fitting response to this abundance—as well as to the magnitude of the divinity or other "fundamental force" invoked by the festive occasion—is gratitude. Thus festivals have as one of their primary aims the giving of thanks. To turn from festival to Winnicott's observations about the nonorgiastic mutuality of mother and infant, I find it not farfetched to imagine that such experiences are partly characterized by gratitude: for the otherness of each other, and for that otherness as ultimately unknown. Melanie Klein has convincingly maintained that the gratitude of the nursing infant is an important formative experience.[26] Conjectures about the infant's undifferentiated psychic unity with the mother surely need to be tempered by the reflection that mother and even a tiny infant may indeed be mutually grateful in such a way.

I have been considering festival as a vehicle of mythic symbolism. But as we have seen in Augustine's description of the House of the

Lord as a place of eternal festival, festival may itself become such a symbol. I wish to elaborate upon this point by means of observations about Shakespeare's *The Tempest.*

4.6 Festival, Communion, and Mutuality in *The Tempest*

In this play Prospero, the banished Duke of Milan, lives on an enchanted island with his daughter Miranda. A shipwreck brings to the island his evil brother, along with the King of Naples (his brother's accomplice in treachery), Ferdinand (the King of Naples's noble son, whom the king believes drowned), and various others. Miranda and Ferdinand fall in love, and Prospero blesses their intention to marry. Toward the close of the play Prospero stage-manages three spectacles bearing on the themes I have been discussing.

The first of these is a banquet magically prepared for three of the shipwrecked "men of sin," who reach for the food, only to have it vanish. In this brief action we see food, the material for the satisfaction of appetite, divorced from mutuality and from the broader meaning of festival. The vanishing of the food is a judgment on the men intent upon simply eating it.

The second spectacle is an entertainment of songs and dances presenting to Miranda and Ferdinand the goddesses Iris, Juno, and Ceres. (Juno and Ceres are patronesses of the fidelity and fruitfulness that should prevail in the coming marriage; Iris is the intermediary between the divine and the human worlds.) Such an invocation of "higher powers" is a common ingredient of festival, which brings us into communion with them. This second spectacle, too, is broken off, as though the festival of the wedding must take place within a larger community fit to celebrate it, and, with the evil characters still unrepentant, this community has not yet been achieved.

The third spectacle is remarkable in its brevity and pointedness. The time has come for Prospero to reveal to his evil brother and the King of Naples that Ferdinand is alive and will marry Miranda. Prospero does this by drawing back a curtain to disclose the two lovers playing chess. Miranda is overheard saying, "Sweet lord, you play me false," to which Ferdinand replies: "No, my dearest love, / I would not for the world." And Miranda protests: "Yes, for a score of kingdoms you should wrangle, / And I would call it fair play" (V.i.172–75).

Chess employs the discriminating, analytic intellect to the final end of winning. It thus reflects a world in which wars are fought, dukes banished, and dukedoms usurped. But the game, with its elaborate rules guaranteeing mutuality, is being played by lovers whose love is the ultimate value in their lives. And if the permutations of chess moves are abstract and "spiritual," the love—and the mutuality—of which the chess game here becomes the expression is bodily and erotic.

As we have seen, mutuality is not a matter of starting from a deficit that somehow needs to be made up. Thus if Ferdinand wishes to "wrangle," Miranda will "call it fair play," as she is unconcerned with the sort of deficit that would be represented by losing a game. She is concerned, rather, with a sense of abundance that would magnify the kingdom of the chessboard into a "score of kingdoms," which she would happily let Ferdinand have.

In these three scenes Shakespeare has, in effect, analyzed festival into its components. The last component presented—the sense of mutuality—is the most basic. Without it we are at best fragments of ourselves. Mutuality is, as I have argued, a vital need. The trust and hope that this vital need will indeed be fulfilled is itself cause for celebration. All festivals are on some level celebrations of this trust and hope.

4.7 Postscript

When I presented a shorter version of the foregoing material as a paper at the Eighth International Congress for Analytical Psychology (in San Francisco in 1980), I found that I had offended some of the audience by not having preached about Original Sin. (Here I reflect on some psychological implications of the doctrine in part 5.11.) When that paper was published in the *Journal of Analytical Psychology*, appended to it was a "Comment" from a reader representing the same misunderstanding of what I had said, and raising issues of general psychological importance. Since the reflections in this book touch upon these issues at various points, I close this chapter with the body of my reply to that comment:[27]

Festival, Communion, and Mutuality

Since the issues have been presented with a theological cast, let me sketch a theological position to which—when understood psychologically—I can subscribe: "faith, hope, charity, these three; but the greatest of these is charity" (1 Cor. 13:13)—for which I would substitute the plainer and broader word "love." If faith, hope, and love are to foster realistic knowing (rather than illusion) they must be tempered by an alert awareness that evil is real, that our lot is imperfection, and that we must take fair responsibility for what we imperfectly do. The doctrine of original sin is one way of construing this state of affairs. It is not the only way, and there are profound reasons for preferring others.

Saint Paul begins his list with "faith," which I will here translate as "trust." The world's evils, commencing with the infant's pangs of hunger, could not be endured without it and the courage generated by it. My paper is not about evil but about trust.

Trust is, on the one hand, an achievement. It persists and consolidates despite threats and frustrations. Before it is an achievement trust is, on the other hand, "given," as potentiality, as active predisposition, as a vital and indispensable part of the "fit" between person and world. Festivals affirm and generate trust.

Some festivals affirm trust as an achievement, doing this by acknowledging the reality of what Joseph Conrad called the "destructive element" and celebrating deliverance from it. Festivals need not do this; many do not.

Many festivals rather affirm trust as "given," affirm the condition of well-being largely in disregard of forces that might pervert or diminish it. They are basic in the way that experiences of justified trust are basic to the courage necessary to deal with frustration.

Even festivals that acknowledge the destructive element effect a disjunction between awareness of it and awareness of whatever is to be celebrated as good. If this disjunction were not necessary Hamlet would have been content rather than outraged to see the baked meats from his father's funeral coldly furnish forth the table of his mother's marriage feast. The aim of this disjunction is the full appreciation of the good as "given," reliable, and abundant. More immediately, the good is that of the festive occasion. Though that occasion begins and ends, it is experienced as granting access to a greater good that is self-sufficient and an inexhaustible source. (A saint's feast day may come once a year, but the saint lives on in heaven, replete with his characteristic potency.)

Some festivals include thanks for the "*promise* of abundance" and the hope of deliverance from various evils. Our relation to abundance may be construed in this way, but need not be. Indeed, many festivals celebrate abundance not as promised and not as the result of deliverance but as present and actual. To regard Holy Communion, a festival of deliverance, as the model of all festivals is parochial special pleading.

An essential *content* of trust is mutuality. To repeat: abundance is a component of mutuality "from the outset." The point is crucial—and its force is undiminished by our recognition that mutuality is also an achievement and that actual experiences of abundance are inevitably intermittent. (In the words of Shakespeare's Prince Hal, cited earlier, "If all the year were playing holidays, / To sport would be as tedious as to work.")

As I said earlier, "Mutuality . . . is not primarily the result of making up a deficit . . . [but] rather entails at the outset a sense of abundance." That is, mutuality is a matter of breaking even *only secondarily*. If we live at all it is because we have been given an abundance and therewith the *capacity* for breaking even. For example, I know of paraplegics who concentrate not on their limitations but on newly developing abilities, realizing potentialities they did not know they had. That one's resources may become depleted—that one may go mad or die, for example—says nothing against this. (One's finances may be ruined by a rash bet or a fall in the stock market; this says nothing against one's having had money in the bank.) Festive abundance awakens a sense of abundance more generally. This more general abundance includes resources of many kinds to deal with evils of many kinds.

I have years of acquaintance with the horrors to be seen in the locked wards of psychiatric clinics, and I know how important to psychological development states of depression can be. Though I have dealt briefly with the destructive element under the heading "Festival and the Debasement of Mutuality," I have placed my main emphasis on what I regard as basic: trust, mutuality, and our rituals for strengthening them. To paint a picture using the colors of spring is not to deny the existence of the black and white of winter.

Psychologically important as the "tension of opposites" is, emphasis on polarities—so characteristic of Jung's thought (as I will stress in part 6.6)—may lead one to neglect the gradations, transitions, continuity, and coherence that are essential qualities of differentiated feeling. And Jung's one-sided emphasis on awe and numinosity as the basic form of religious experience may encourage the same neglect. Festivals may or may not generate awe; more basically, they cultivate feeling values.

I did not say that I regard the self "as more often than not expressing itself in a positive way," since I am in no position to measure. I did insist that the benign workings of the self I described occur and have a fundamental bearing on the issues treated in my paper.

Anyone who finds the viewpoint I have been expressing unappealingly "tender-minded" (in William James's phrase) would do well to consider the ways in which tough-mindedness may falsify perception. The tough-minded person may declare, in effect, "Self-aware and courageous as I am, I can see life as it truly is: nasty, brutish, and short. Strong as I am, I can stand up to its drabness and senselessness by being dour, rigid, and snide." This reductive way of having got to the supposed bottom of things gives one a privileged—and defended—position ironically akin to that of having got to the supposed top of them through metaphysical speculation. The inflated pseudoheroism of the narrowly tough-minded is dearly bought by warding off and thwarting the tender and expansive emotional qualities essential to the development of feeling. (To speak of these is not to deny that right hating is as important as right loving.) Feeling provides realistic knowledge of the world.

The scene of the lovers playing chess in *The Tempest* (see part 4.6) is, in an important way, about feeling. Ferdinand is about to enter the world of politics and war in which he will *have* to "wrangle"—to make uncertain decisions and dubious compromises, distributing rewards and imprisoning people, and perhaps even putting them to death—in ways that may require a statecraft not entirely distinguishable from cheating. In her response Miranda is implicitly saying that she knows he must succeed in being "male" in this way but that his doing so is in the larger view less important than relationship, intimacy, love. The interaction of the lovers hardly "reduce[s] separation or difference to a minimum," and to regard the mutuality expressed in the scene as "recalling a state of paradisal beatitude or blissful mirroring," as the commentator put it, would be to reduce the play to nonsense.

The realism of the play includes Miranda's trust in mutuality and the abundance of the good. The wonder she manifests, based on this trust, is not religious awe. It is rather the hopeful, faithful, loving openness essential to the differentiation of feeling.

5 Magic and Participating Consciousness

5.1 Love and Magic

Jung, criticizing Freud's theory of the death instinct, observed that the opposite of love is not death but power.[1] In the broader view the relations between love and power are more subtle and complex than this polarity suggests. There is, for example, "nutrient power,"[2] and one can "empower"—give power to another or enhance another's own. But the forces resulting in the segregation and opposition of love and power are strong and perdurable—Jung has accurately described a state of affairs prevailing in much of life as everyone is fated to know it.

Many chapters in the history of religion are concerned with looking beyond surfaces to the intricacies of love and power. Other chapters, but sometimes also the same ones, are concerned with capitalizing on the crude opposition between love and power that persists despite the exploration of these intricacies. I am now concerned with some of the resulting ambiguities.

Love is compelling—a "mighty daimon," in the words of Socrates—but I doubt that it can be compelled. The Judeo-Christian commandment to love (God and other people), a central tenet of a broad and powerful tradition, is a paradox. Raising the religious problems of grace and free will, this paradox calls attention, more generally, to the respects in which we are bound and limited but also free and potentially open to plenitude (discussed in part 2.7) and to the larger life (discussed in parts 5.8 and 6.12). The finesse of imagination and feeling required to deal with this paradox in anything like an adequate way we have already seen in Bernard's attempts (discussed in part 2.6) to describe the nature of affection in relation to God. Such finesse is rare, and the paradox presents other psychological difficulties as well.

165

Feeling, Imagination, and the Self

The Judeo-Christian commandment to love raises issues requiring an appreciation of the now-you-see-it-now-you-don't quality that, as I have said, characterizes everything psychic. One cannot do justice to this quality without sometimes having to say, "Now I don't see it," while refraining from trying to secure it in the form of an illusion of its fixed and abiding presence. (A religious term for such illusion is idolatry, which sustains the false hope discussed in part 3.) More specifically, the issues raised by the commandment require that the ego refrain from appropriating the prerogatives of the self.

To say, "I will myself to love God and other people because that is what I am supposed to do" is to say something that may in one sense be true enough. But in putting it—and feeling and imagining it—in this way one may be assuming a kind of responsibility that implicitly amounts to an attempt on the part of the ego to control a "mighty daimon." By way of analogy, a certain violinist sometimes gets into trouble in making herself practice. If she tells herself in one way that she should practice, she feels possessed and driven and plays badly. If she tells herself in another way that she should practice, she plays well, drawing on parts of herself that enable and encourage her to do so. In both cases she is responding to versions of the command, "You should practice."

Hypocrisy, sentimentality, pride, and self-deceit have proved highly compatible with conscious allegiance to the Judeo-Christian commandment to love. And the absurdity of this state of affairs might be thought to speak against such allegiance. On the other hand, one might do more justice to the complexities and ambiguities involved if one regarded this absurdity as comparable to that of the violinist practicing in a self-hindering way. In any case, there is much to recommend caution about construing the commandment to love as a manifestation of imposed will and power within a field of the dehumanizing "force" discussed in part 5.12. Such caution is consistent with doubt that I can be compelled to love what I do not love, and with "right loving" and "right hating" regarded as activities of differentiated feeling expressive of the self discussed in these pages. Such right loving and right hating may be understood to imply a more open process of learning what things are to be valued and in what way than that expressed as obeying a commandment.

166

Magic and Participating Consciousness

I take a similar satisfaction in Kent's admonition to King Lear, near the beginning of Shakespeare's play, that he must "see better." I take Kent to mean what all of the good characters in the play understand—that the right perception of value entails the right form of relationship to the thing valued, with no special need for one to be told, or to tell oneself, that it must be valued. If I need to be told, or to tell myself, I "ought" to love something, it must not, in fact, deserve my love, or else I must misunderstand it in such a way that I am right not to love it as it exists in my understanding of it. Misunderstanding can be corrected—one can come to "see better"—and the correction sets the object free to flourish in the plenitude of its own being as one remains in relation to it. Or if it deserves to be rightly hated, one may oppose it or remove oneself from it with a decency to which one "ought" to aspire. But love moves of itself.

Love implies trust, respect, openness, and mutuality. Allowing whatever is loved to be itself also implies detachment; love moves toward contemplation. Indeed, love begins in a preform of contemplation. At least, that is how I understand Winnicott's description (discussed in part 4) of important moments of emotional communion between mother and infant.[3] Nonetheless, I recently read a report of a lecture about contemplation in which the author warned that we "either contemplate or we exploit," and I was struck by the exaggerated simplicity of his slogan. For to begin with our relation to the world is not and cannot be made disinterested. Detachment is a movement *within* passionate participation rather than in opposition to it. Moreover, we must live with the opposites of love and power—rather than detaching ourselves, as we cannot, either from power or from the opposition between them. And power presents unavoidable ambiguities. Though the will to power may kill love, the openness of love demands strength. And power—much of the time—inevitably reflects narrow self-interest. We exploit; and if we do not, someone else does so to our harm, so that we inevitably have to deal with exploitation—with the base use of power. We "ought" to "see better" than we do, and within a larger frame of reference. Yet sometimes the more unreflective act is the more appropriate one. (If I encounter a burglar outside the door of my sleeping child I will not contemplate him.) Still, love gives us the courage to deal with such ambiguities, as it gives us the faith and hope to try rightly to see what only it discloses.

Given the ambiguities I have been discussing—between love and will, and between commandment and compulsion—what, to begin with, are we to make of the charms and spells of love magic, known in all the times and places in which love has been recognized as a force in human affairs? And beyond these, what are we to make of the relations between magic and religion, and between either magic or religion or both as pathogenic and as curative? With these relations in mind I will now proceed to reflect on various aspects of magic as a manifestation of culture. As I go on, I will spell out some psychological implications of issues I have so far raised.

5.2 Successive Ages of Magic, Religion, and Science?

The early ethnologists E. B. Tylor and Sir James G. Frazer envisioned a presumably universal sequence of cultural stages, with an age of magic being followed by an age of religion, which is in turn followed by an age of science. Thus the amoral operations of magic give way to a religious appeal to higher powers within a framework of ethical obligation, and the intellectual errors of magic and religion come to be corrected by scientific observation and reasoning. Though this program assumed the certainty of progress, ambiguities sometimes appeared in the exposition of it, since the magician and the scientist could be thought near-allies in their concern with the regularities of nature, and since the relations of science to religion were finally no less equivocal to these writers than they were to many of their thoughtful post-Darwinian contemporaries.

The positivist scheme I have been describing partly represented an attempt of these investigators to secure a detached position with respect to the "primitive" mind and soul. Their difficulties—and those of many later scholars—in defining the relations among magic, religion, and science show how complex those relations are, while also casting doubt on the detachment to which these writers aspired. I will examine some of these difficulties briefly to see what they may tell us about the psychology of both detachment and engagement, and about the fate of what Jung has called "the living symbol" when it is subjected to self-aggrandizing manipulation.[4] My reflections will also be about social and economic power and will aim at bringing Jung's and Freud's ostensibly opposing views of religion into a single perspective.

The distinction between coercive and noncoercive qualities of mind and action has recurred again and again in the theorizing about magic and religion initiated by Tylor and Frazer. What I have already said about power and love suggests that some such distinction must be important in the broad field of magical and religious phenomena, even if the distinction is sometimes relative, and even if there are many fixed and borderline cases. Indeed, what I have said about ambiguities of love and power in ordinary human life should suggest that related ambiguities—of letting happen and making happen—must appear abundantly in religious and magical dealings with extraordinary reality.

When Hopi Indians in their rain dance draw raining clouds on the ground with cornmeal, then swing bullroarers to make a sound like thunder, they would seem to present an instance of the imitative magic described by Frazer in which like compels like.[5] Yet the meaning of this act is supplied by a cosmology expressing veneration of divine powers. Similarly, the Catholic eucharist is cognate with many magical procedures creating miracles—and compelling love—in part by ingesting the body of a god.[6] Indeed, Catholicism in the late Middle Ages was a vast cultural edifice in which magical and religious elements were inseparable and often indistinguishable. Thus the consecrated host could be used profanely "to put out fires, to cure swine fever, to fertilise the fields and to encourage bees to make honey"; it could also be used as a love charm and could protect a criminal from discovery.[7] And though these practices were folk elaborations of churchly elements, the Church itself gave its approval to relics, indulgences, Saint Christopher's medals, and other devices similar to those used by non-Christian sorcerers.

One difficulty with the evolutionary scheme of magic-religion-science is precisely that religion in at least some of its phases often exhibits tendencies to become increasingly magical. Thus the reformist ethical teachings of early Buddhism were assimilated to a religion sanctioning prayer wheels, and the radical monotheism of Islam is propounded in a mosque in which the pious may venerate a footprint

169

formed when marble melted owing to the fervor of the Prophet's devotions. Similarly, the magical Catholicism to which I have alluded represented in part a coarsening of religious awareness as symbols lost their transcendent quality and became concretized in mechanical operations.

It has been claimed that the primitive Church in its own intent and practice brought magical religion to a close,[8] even if time and time again magic would again exert its sway—just as time and time again the Israelites turned from the Lord to the Canaanite baals. This kind of reversion to magic is my main concern; but in order to pursue it without losing sight of important complexities inseparable from it, I will comment on the origins of Christianity and then on an important theory of magic.

It was earlier widely thought that the historical Jesus had been secondarily mythologized and now needed to be recovered through a process of "demythologizing" that would remove the magical elements from his story. But Jesus-the-magician appears in very early records by both proponents and antagonists of Christianity; indeed, Jesus comes to figure very early in both Christian and non-Christian magical spells.[9] What needs to be realized is that myth is the natural language in which to make statements about religious life, and myth describes magical occurrences. Parts of human experience are ordinary in the sense of confirming the ego in its habitual assumptions. Other parts are extraordinary in defying or altering those assumptions. The magic of myth and fairy tale is part of the imaginative language natural in talking about extraordinary reality. But it is possible to try in various ways to appropriate this magic to ego purposes. For example, one may use magic propagandistically to appeal to people's urge to gain practical mastery over their lives by magical means. Thus the story of Jesus walking on the water may be taken, on the one hand, as a statement about the nature of the symbolic god-man, the *Anthropos*, as an imaginative form of the self as the transcendent core of the person. Or it may be taken, on the other, as an illustration of the slogan, "My magician (Jesus) is stronger than yours."

The theory of magic to which I want to turn is that of Daniel Lawrence O'Keefe, presented in his monumental recent study, *Stolen Lightning: The Social Theory of Magic.*[10] O'Keefe follows various psychoanalysts (including Freud at certain moments) in regarding the conscious ego as developing secondarily on the basis of the superego as an authoritative internalization of social values. Just as society, in this view, has evolved institutions that employ the superego to hamper and crush individuality, so it has evolved other institutions that strengthen individuality and the conscious ego. Magic can serve both kinds of institutions.

To begin to see how this may be so, it is important to grant a measure of truth to the contention of such sociologists as Emile Durkheim and Max Weber that religion is a cosmic projection of the social system. Thus the potlatch of the Tsimshian Indians of the Pacific Northwest employs "every mode of symbolic expression in Tsimshian culture to make statements about the panoply of social relationships and statuses in that culture, including the changes in status as individuals go through the life cycle, the ordered relationships between kin groups, and the system of rank difference in and between groups." Generally, among Pacific Northwest Indians the ritual celebration of the gods is intended also to demonstrate the social and economic power of individuals, who may buy, inherit, or otherwise come to own the right to perform a certain song or dance.[11]

As I have noted, in an important way the potlatch illustrates the potentiality of the social and economic order to create victims. The most striking example of how magic may accord with religiously projected social values to the end of victimage—and the destruction of individuality—is the "voodoo death" reported from many parts of the world—when, for example, one person points a bone at another and the other takes to his bed and dies. Yet when religion becomes oppressive of individuality, the individual may employ magic to fight back—in an operation a little like using voodoo against the voodoo doctor.

Individuality is in an important sense a cultural achievement in which magic has played a highly positive role.[12] This may be seen strikingly with regard to individual scientific exploration in seventeenth-century England, an example I offer because it shows interesting further complexities that appear when one tries to apply the evolutionary scheme of magic-religion-science, and because it shows how all three elements of that scheme can serve power politics.

The occultism flourishing in several forms in early seventeenth-century England was interwoven with antiauthoritarian political tendencies in opposition to the Church of England. With the restoration of the monarchy following the Puritan revolution and the end of the Commonwealth, occultism was strongly denigrated owing to its political implications. Accordingly, Sir Isaac Newton, who had long engaged in alchemical experimentation, was careful to state the principle of gravitation in a way that avoided reference to such occult principles as the theory of correspondences between microcosm and macrocosm. Since magic was regarded as a threat to the new political-religious-scientific orthodoxy, he stated it instead in a way that accorded with the mechanical philosophy now dominating the Royal Society.[13]

Power has been regarded as the most fundamental category of religious experience.[14] But such power can hardly be just that of the spirit that bloweth where it listeth, unbound by narrowly egoistic conceptions of human self-interest. Rather, as my examples of Tsimshian ceremonialism and seventeenth-century science suggest, the urge to venerate and contemplate such power is often indistinguishable from the urge to manipulate it opportunistically. In this regard magic is sometimes more honest about its aims than is religion, and such honesty may after all further human right loving of the spirit that does what it will.

My reflections till now should show that attempts to arrive at a satisfactory account of magic—or even a definition of the term—must be beset with difficulties. In many ways O'Keefe has succeeded remarkably in making sense of the subject. But the clarity of his view is achieved by his accepting the positivist program of cultural evolution beyond magic and religion through a cultivation of the rational ego informed by the world-view of modern science. The clarity of O'Keefe's view is also achieved by virtue of its radical antipsychologism, its attempt to circumvent psychological explanation, as (in the company of such psychoanalysts as Géza Roheim) he envisages a direct grafting of social values onto the physiological substrate of the human person—in a way that does not require "psyche" as a medium. "Voodoo death" offers the clearest instance of what he has in mind.

Magic and Participating Consciousness

This view preserves the value of the clear and distinct ideas that the empiricist tradition has regarded as the surest guide to truth. And such rational cognition is a large part of the Freudian program of making the unconscious conscious. But what, one may ask, of the formative, creative, synthetic powers of the unconscious, the unconscious structuring principles that do their work silently and invisibly, indeed that cannot in any direct way be made conscious? To grant the reality of these is to grant the reality of "psyche" or "soul" as the domain in which these principles may be imaginatively manifest and their values made known, for example, in dreams. Dreams may be reactive in ways Freud has described, but they may also serve a prospective function requiring a conscious relation to them that is more imaginative than interpretive, that lets their poetry live and breathe without being translated into clear and distinct ideas. In any case, in dreams such ideas lose their power to render extraordinary reality ordinary, as things, living beings, words, and fantasy images interpenetrate in unaccustomed ways.

O'Keefe is especially persuasive in his account of magic as it tries to counteract religion. Indeed, this function of magic is especially striking when one considers the characteristically great reliance of magic on religious paraphernalia and scripts—for example, in the magical use of the host and in the black mass. Still, it is useful to relate this function of magic to an observation of the object-relations theorist W. Ronald D. Fairbairn about certain forms of neurotic behavior involving guilt. Which would one prefer, he asks, to be a sinner in a world governed by God or to be sinless in a world governed by the devil? One would surely rather be a sinner in a world governed by God, since it would presumably have some kind of coherent structure and would offer some means of mitigating one's plight.[15] The magic-ridden society of Dobu also offers means of mitigating the plights of its members, but the Dobuans live a nightmare of reciprocal sorcery. If we were to imagine a divine creator of their terrifyingly bizarre reality he would be hard to distinguish from our devil.

I have spoken of unconscious structuring principles of the psyche; I wish to return to them to make one further comment on the relations between religion and science. Polanyi was concerned with some of these principles and argued that we know them tacitly rather than focally, much as we rely on bodily processes that create our knowledge of the world without our being aware of them. This tacit understanding plays an important role in the activity of science, as does trust in the community of scientists. For Polanyi all knowledge, including science, is personal; and science is motivated by intellectual passions and sustained by commitment, which is ultimately related to the commitment cultivated by religion.[16]

Finally, I would like to comment briefly on how—in the context of these reflections—I understand the term *magic*.

I regard magic basically as a subcategory of religion, and assume that there is magical religion and nonmagical religion. To speak of magic and religion as I have been doing—and as I will do again—is simply to press the distinction between magical and nonmagical religion very far, for the most part without breaking it down: " 'Magic' and 'religion' constitute in most cases the two sides of one and the same rite."[17]

Magic, unlike science as it is most commonly understood, takes place within an animated world. The difference between magic and religion in this regard is "an ideal typical dichotomy between the magical attitude with a dominant compulsive [or coercive] conduct and the religious attitude with a dominant dependent conduct towards the object of belief."[18]

That such a definition does not amount to a rousing slogan I readily grant. But I would ask the reader to imagine a situation in which there are many herds of sheep mixed with goats but no herds of sheep alone or goats alone. To describe the actual herds it is important to know what sheep and goats are. Knowing this, one may then try to devise a language for talking about herds of more sheep than goats or more goats than sheep. In discussions of magic, as of related subjects such as myth, many theorists make falsely exclusive definitions and false dichotomies, as though they would reduce sheep mixed with goats to goats or sheep alone. The muddled discussion resulting illustrates the way in which thinking-based theory defeats itself, and defeats the principle of thinking, when it radically denies the claims of feeling, with its concern for gradations, transitions, continuity, and coherence.

Magic and Participating Consciousness

Magical elements may, however, free themselves from the official religious structure. The magician may then use them—in their relative independence of it—to circumvent, subvert, or oppose it. In this way magic may serve secularization—may help to deanimate the world—and thus further the development of certain kinds of ego strength.

With an important qualification, magic can be said to be concerned with issues of emotional import and to engage and reflect primitive levels of the human person. This qualification is provided by the analogy between magic and language, the emotional and primitive resources of which may or may not be drawn on—indeed, they may be suppressed—in a particular utterance, though they are fundamental to what language is. Magic is at least implicitly—tactily—concerned with issues of emotional import. Magic at least implicitly—tacitly—engages and reflects primitive levels of the human person. (My use of the word *primitive* follows, with qualifications, that of the developmental psychologist Heinz Werner.[19])

Since it is the crux of what I am talking about, I want to qualify my assertion that magic is coercive. I mean by this actions intended to induce animating powers to a narrowly preconceived end. When in earlier times someone had a chantry built and endowed a benefice so that a priest would say daily masses to shorten the stay of himself or someone else in purgatory, he was, in the view I am proposing, engaging in magic, albeit within a total setting of belief and action that is perhaps more nonmagically religious than magically religious. The same person might pray, saying, "Thy will be done," which I take to express a very different attitude—depending on what he took the words to mean.

The distinction I have in mind is related to Jung's distinction between ego and the self, and to that between curing and healing. (I understand curing to aim at a specific outcome that the ego recognizes as desirable, and healing to aim at a much more indefinite one with a greater concern for the larger context of one's life and with a greater hope for a deepening of it that may not be to the ego's immediate and wholehearted liking.[20])

What is especially important about magic—in the context of these reflections—is that it occurs at the juncture between what has been called "participating consciousness,"[21] on the one hand, and willed action, on the other. Such consciousness, which I will characterize further, is relatively open to the structuring principles at work in the background of consciousness. It is thus a basic ingredient of imagination. Much perturbation of the human spirit occurs at precisely the juncture between such consciousness and willed action, and magic has an important and illuminating bearing on it.

5.3 Magic and Emotional Import

Much magic is devoted to such emotion-engendering matters as childbirth, disease, death, weather, the growth of crops, hunting, and warfare—which are also matters of nonmagical religion. And some magical acts are carried out in a highly emotional state. But many are carried out dispassionately, thoughtlessly, mechanically, as one knocks on wood to avert bad luck. This distinction should present no insuperable problem, however, since "emotional import" may be experienced emotionally or unemotionally, or not experienced at all. (A murderer, for example, may be overwhelmed with fear and remorse, may coolly consider his act and its consequences, or may have no awareness of the murder.)

Experiencing emotional import is feeling—one definition of which might be "emotional intelligence." Many forms of psychopathology entail experiencing emotional import inappropriately.

Much magic creates emotional distance in ways that employ the mechanisms of ego defense described by Sigmund Freud, Anna Freud, and others. But such magic may also help to free the ego for more flexible and adapted action—as when a jilted lover performs the magical rite of burning old letters and photographs as a step in putting an obsession to rest.

5.4 Magic and the Conviviality of the Native Mind

One early theory of magic regarded it as originating in a level of psychic functioning on which presemantic gestures expressive of a wish are indistinguishable from the fulfillment of the wish—for example, the follow-through movements of a bowler who, after he has thrown the ball, keeps his hand in the air and slowly gyrates it to try to influence the ball's course, or the person waiting for a train who leans in the direction from which it will come, as though his leaning will speed its approach.[22] Though unconsciously intentional, such gestures are automatic in a way suggesting some of the mechanical and wishful symbolic actions of magic.

This level is presumably closely related to that of the "diffuse emotional conviviality" described by Polanyi, to be seen, for example, when a baby is frightened by a frowning face without any experience of the dispositions corresponding to the frown, or when experienced doctors faint at the sight of a deep incision in the eye of a patient.[23] This level is surely the basis of sympathy and imitation but is partly anterior to both. When a whole group of so-called primitive people have fallen into states in which they begin undulating at the edge of the sea, they are perhaps imitating both the waves and one another. But it is likely that their movements also express the quality of archaic will seen in the follow-through movements of the bowler. We thus arrive at the juncture between participation (in such forms as sympathy), on the one hand, and will, on the other. (See fig. 5.)

The psychiatrist Sylvano Arieti has proposed terms to describe some principles operative in such primitive experience. He speaks of "exocepts," by which he means primitive action tendencies—to be seen, for example, when a dog recognizes the footsteps of his master and jumps up to greet him. Among humans exoceptual activity is prominent during early years and remains important in such activities as manual work and sports, which only very indirectly make use of high levels of symbolization.[24] He also speaks of "endocepts," by which he means qualities of atmosphere or intention that are global and diffuse and do not in themselves amount to representations, though they may become represented by borrowing words and other products of higher psychic levels. For example, someone undergoing psychoanalytic treatment described a red living room reserved for big occasions. His memory of it, which was from ages two to four, he portrayed in sentences employing such words as *aura, sacred, solemnity,* which he acquired much later in life. Yet he remembered *something,* however diffuse, and his abstract language represented an attempt to translate it and make it communicable.[25]

Fig. 5. Photograph of bowler and spectators at the All-Ireland road-bowls championship. The bowler's stance—which the spectators emphatically mimic—is presumably intended to influence the course of the ball he has thrown (in the manner of "follow-through" movements). The "conviviality of the native mind," or primitive sympathy and empathy, is thus expressed in processes of the deep body. These processes underlie, and are tacitly known in, conscious feeling and imagination. The psychic regions active in such empathy are prominently accessible to both partners in the early mother-infant relationship—as when Mother feeding Baby opens her own mouth to "make" Baby open hers. Higher forms of sympathy—and feeling—presuppose and differentiate this kind of interconnectedness.

Magic and Participating Consciousness

In speaking of forms of cognition arising from this level, Arieti uses the term *paleologic*, in which identity is accepted on the basis of identical predicates rather than being limited to identical subjects. An example of such "paleologic" would be the syllogism, "I am a virgin; the Virgin Mary was a virgin; I am the Virgin Mary."[26] Such thinking is apparent when patients with organic brain damage are asked, "What city is the capital of France?" and answer, "London," an answer which shows that they have in a diffuse way constructed the concept of "capitals," but have not analyzed its contents further to select the right one.[27] All of these principles are characteristic of many magical acts. And these principles, too, belong to the juncture between participation and will.

It seems to me likely that activation of these primitive levels of psychic functioning has played an important role in creating magical practices and concepts—without for that reason being their sufficient cause. (In a similar way, sports may entail skilled motor functioning shaped by cultural patterns and motives that cannot be reduced to the motor level.)

At first sight there would seem to be a great gulf between the spontaneous and deeply bodily qualities of gestural expression, and the fixed, rigidly formulaic quality of magical spells and incantations. Still, the same form of relation may well obtain between gestural expression and rote recitation of a magical spell that obtains between emotional and nonemotional ways of experiencing matters of emotional import. Indeed, the main topic of these reflections is precisely the apparently antithetical relation between feeling with its relation to these primitive levels, on the one hand, and will, on the other.

To help put the relation between feeling and will into perspective, I would observe that before they come to seem antithetical they are profoundly interrelated in ways that accord with some of the principles I have been discussing. And it is important to realize that this profound interrelation subsists in the workings of our purportedly Aristotelian minds. When I go into a store full of books and phonograph records and come out with one, I may say that I picked it out and bought it. But in an important sense it would be truer to say that when I surveyed them in the store they emitted various and shifting qualities of coolness until one of them became hot, agitated, and insistent, and finally shouted, "Buy me! Take me home with you!" and I submitted to its will. Who and what feels and who and what wills in such a subjectively experienced transaction, and where is the line to be drawn between feeling and willing?

5.5 Participating Consciousness and Application

O'Keefe offers a telling account of the way in which the law of noncontradiction has come to be built into our hard-edged logical concepts.[28] (To illustrate this law: " 'Snow is white' and 'snow is not white' cannot both be true.") Such concepts are less characteristic of primitive thought, which the ethnologist Lucien Lévy-Bruhl regards as obeying the law of participation rather than that of noncontradiction.[29]

To begin to see what Lévy-Bruhl means by this, we may reflect that in modern Western thought concepts are presumed to exist in their own domain—except in their reference to sensory qualities. There are things, there are ideas, and there are ideas about ideas, but in fact this presumption serves to hide the ways in which our concepts inform our sensory experience without our being aware of the process. This occurs tacitly, to use Polanyi's term. Thus, someone adept at certain kinds of medical diagnosis may come to "see" a certain disease without being able to specify either conceptually or in any of the physical evidence what makes him know he is seeing the disease.[30] Arieti's term *endocept*—to describe the global quality of a red room remembered from early childhood, for example—also describes an experienced something that is neither concept nor sensation.

The so-called primitive, unlike the modern Westerner, has a more plastic sense of the intermediary realm in which his immediate experience participates in representations—in such forms as spirits, totem, and ancestors. His participation opens him up to them while also making them subject to his manipulation—to his magic, which may be derived from their power.

Several important thinkers—among them Owen Barfield, Jung, and Polanyi—have argued persuasively that the positivist program I have discussed must give way to a view of the world based on a new sense of participation,[31] a new awareness of the representations that (in Jung's view) are forms of interaction between consciousness and the unconscious. This participation entails activation of the primitive psychic regions discussed in my account of magic. It is important to realize that they are reflected in the myths from which we derive the larger meaning of our lives, and in such great art and poetry as that of Shakespeare. These psychic regions are richly alive in imagination as a world-shaping, reality-revealing, truth-telling power.

Another ethnologist, Adolf Jensen, distinguishes between a creative phase of culture and a later phase of what he called "application." The creative phase is "purposeless," the product of extraordinary individuals imaginatively charting man's place in the world. The phase of application consists of the working out of that vision in practical terms, often on behalf of what individuals or groups regard as their self-interest. Thus religion gives way to magic, or nonmagical religion gives way to magical religion.[32] Since (as I have maintained in part 5.1) our relation to the world cannot be made disinterested—however contemplative we become—man's practical life surely cannot in any clear-cut way be secondary to his imaginative grasp of an autonomous spiritual reality. And yet imaginative vision does tend to die in being willfully put to use. Thus, for example, a ritual may gradually become so senseless to the people performing it that a new myth must be invented to reinvest it with meaning. This amounts to a rebirth of imagination.

Our workaday lives continually need to be imaginatively revivified; thus we have holidays as festive celebrations of myth, and thus we dream every night. Do we dream at night after working all day, or do we work all day after dreaming at night? Do holidays follow workdays, or do workdays follow holidays? It is clear to me that consciousness is most authentic and adapted when it is imaginative, and that when it is not imaginative it becomes afflicted with the sterility and loss of meaning characteristic of Jensen's cultural phase of "application."

This brings me again to feeling, and again to Lévy-Bruhl and Polanyi. In a late work Lévy-Bruhl proposed that so-called primitives, rather than being "prelogical," as he had once contended, thought systematically but did so on the basis of affective categories such as friendliness, enmity, and luck.[33] "Prelogical" thinking would presumably correspond to thinking according to the "paleologic" described by Arieti. ("I am a virgin; I am the Virgin Mary.") Under the stress

181

of emotion, logic often becomes condensed and elliptical in such ways—for example, when consciousness falls under the sway of the feeling-toned complexes described by Jung. And what is in principle true of Lévy-Bruhl's earlier view is that primitive people do think about matters of emotional import and may do so emotionally and without the benefit of the logical clarity built into the concepts of modern Western people. But Lévy-Bruhl's later emphasis on affective categories would say that primitive people know what we must discover anew and in a way appropriate for us, that mind does not exist in any authenticity without heart, that will can only be exploitative in the absence of feeling. In agreement with this view, Polanyi argues that when we attribute truth to any methodology, including that of modern science, we perform an act of faith that cannot be analyzed in non-commital terms.[34] Our complex task is to doubt and have faith and be open. This, too, could serve as a description of differentiated feeling in one of its dimensions. Such feeling is an important quality of the ego strength and resilience that affords us a viable form of relationship not only to the outer world but also the feeling-toned complexes of the psychic background. When they are constellated, logic may deteriorate, but trying to iron out the resulting logical confusion often does little to push them away. Feeling, though, may help to diminish their magically compelling power.

The differing approaches of Freud and Jung to religion also bear upon the issues I have been discussing. For Freud religion is the obsessional neurosis of mankind, coercive in a magical way. For Jung, in contrast, religion canalizes psychic energy and creates consciousness, which it keeps related to the structuring principles of its unconscious matrix. Jung regarded numinosity as the most important component of religious experience, and numinosity is also in its way coercive.

What is true about Jung's emphasis on numinosity is that the ego does not freely dispose of its own energy and freely choose the objects of its interest, but is rather acted upon by what have been imagined as higher and lower powers. Images of these may help to place personal concerns within a larger and more meaningful context; in such ways as this religion may serve contemplative detachment.

The same images may, however, serve the ego in its narrow conception of its interests and in its reliance on mechanisms of defense.

Magic and Participating Consciousness

Mighty gods have been invoked to bless paltry and thieving schemes. The ambiguity I have in mind may be made clear by comparison with feeling-toned complexes, our relation to which may be conscious or unconscious, pathological or benign. In a similar way the mythic content of religion may give the ego a proper grounding with respect to the psychic reality that transcends it, but may also reflect and further psychopathology, as Freud and O'Keefe contend. As I have maintained (in part 4.4), it is precisely "problems" symptomatic of self-division and inner conflict that are the precondition of higher forms of consciousness.[35] Religion may provide material either for the symptomatic expression of such problems or for a deepening of one's experience of their meaning.

For higher forms of consciousness to develop, magical compulsiveness and coercion must yield to contemplative detachment, and the self-aggrandizement of the ego must yield to imaginative participation. Jung's emphasis on numinosity as the most important component of religious experience needs to be tempered by an appreciation of the great importance of religion in cultivating feeling values. Emotion-engendering mythic contents must be taken up and comprehended by feeling as a mode of ego-awareness. When religion furthers this process it may indeed cure souls. That it helped to define or even create the sickness it is curing says nothing against this.

We begin our lives strongly dominated by the bodily urgency of "drives." But very early we also experience the nonconsummatory mutuality of which I have spoken. It is the basis of the detachment-in-participation realized in love, contemplation, and art. Magic and religion constrain our imaginative capacities by dictating the contents that should occupy them. (In this they are different from the free play of fantasy.) Magic and religion may free such capacities. (They may help people to imagine.) And magic and religion may sometimes free such capacities from one another. (Magic may transform religious images, as in the profane use of the cross as a talisman, and religion may put magical procedures to its own use, as in the eucharist.) When magic binds our imaginative capacities, it does so by being coercive in ways related to bodily drives. When religion frees them it does so by fostering participating consciousness and detachment, often by the intermediary step of rituals that induce magical compulsiveness while having a strongly contemplative cast. That these may degenerate into coercive hocus-pocus does not lessen their importance in differentiating feeling.

We act, and the vast complexity of our symbolism—in language, mythology, and mathematical formulae—may be conceived as a species of action, with each act and agent having a purpose within a scene that partly defines them.[36] But the actor is always also acted upon. He may seek to seize means to act into his own hands, or he may open himself more contemplatively to the larger context of the action, a context potent with forces shaping the scene in ways that he is compelled to admit he cannot now understand. Glimpses of extraordinary power are sometimes the only clues he can have of their nature. They are important contents of the symbolic attitude—I have been calling it imagination—essential to our full humanity.

5.6 Magical Contemplation

When O'Keefe argues convincingly that magic helps give individuals the courage to speak, to act, and to think, he is basically describing the kind of ego strength necessary for instrumental action in practical projects.[37] Magic serving this function might seem to have little directly to do with contemplation, which I have so far aligned with nonmagical religion. This broadly valid alignment needs, however, to be qualified.

Though magic largely belongs in the domain of Jensen's "application," it may, paradoxically, further participating consciousness of a more contemplative kind, and may do so precisely owing to its preoccupation with real-life problems demanding practical solutions. Many such problems require imagination, which magic may provide with rich and fruitful images.

Whatever meaningful order there is in human life is shot through with contingency, the fortuitous, randomness, often challenging ego assumptions. ("That *should not* have happened to me.") Magic often challenges them by invoking signs, and does this—through such devices as tossing coins—by opening itself to the fortuitous in an attempt to find meaning in it or ascribe meaning to it. These signs are then interpreted in accordance with symbolic languages for talking about patterns of fate—including such things as plenty, deprivation, freak occurrences, births, and deaths—and about qualitative aspects of time—including such things as propitiousness or the need for retreat or dogged persistence. In lived experience, patterns of fate and qualitative aspects of time are inescapably real and important but also irreducibly irrational, and they will surely continue to be this no matter what scientific principles are devised to account for paranormal phenomena. Science may obscure or impoverish participating consciousness but not dissolve or replace it. Though symbols expressing patterns of fate and qualitative aspects of time may serve rationalization—as the cards tell me what I want to hear—they may also challenge ego assumptions in ways that heighten awareness of the supraordinate self.

Whereas magic often seeks such signs, religion more typically attends to them as already part of a fixed structure—for example, by acknowledging them only as part of an exclusive and already complete revelation or as miracles that have been tested for authenticity. Magic characteristically reads such signs in relation to a language made up of symbolic material that has been freed from the broadly communal purposes of religious cult and ritual, that has been scrambled, combined with heterodox elements, rearranged according to different principles, and put at the service of subgroups (often peripheral) and of individuals. When magic becomes dissociated from the canon of dominant cultural values, it often provides a cogent means for imaginatively exploring perturbations unacknowledged by the official culture.

Magical appropriation of religious symbolism entails something like the shuffling of a pack of cards, a shuffling repeated when the fortuitous is casuistically invoked—for example, when the diviner shuffles magical cards. Thus, despite the rigidity of many of its procedures, magic often engages fantasy and psychic processes leading to individual symbol formation more strongly and immediately than does religion. (If I go to church I encounter *our* shared and generally valid symbols in the temporal context of the mythic and historical past and the cycle of the church year. A gypsy fortune-teller, on the other hand, offers me what are in a different sense *my* symbols *now,* related more or less specifically to my chancing upon an old friend, to the death of a relative, to the commencement of an enterprise. Ecstatic religion is

185

no real exception to this distinction, since seizure and trance can be as socially coded—as profoundly communal—as liturgy.)

The signs of which I have been speaking are of dispositions in what could be called the magical field. These dispositions are manifestations of an agent or a network of agents that challenge habitual ego assumptions, including those defining the distinction between subject and object, and that reveal the fortuitous as the mode in which a new and more viable order emerges. (The fortuitous proves to be such a mode in a variety of ways: the mythical hero is born "magically," in fortuitous and miraculous circumstances. In the words of information-theorist Gregory Bateson, fortuitous noise is "the only possible source of new patterns,"[38] an observation applicable to the randomizing that plays a role in natural selection. Dreams presume a weakening of association that allows ostensibly trivial—fortuitous— elements to become potent terms in a novel statement. New theories have their inception in seemingly fortuitous hunches.)

Jung speaks of "psychoid" processes, in which psyche and matter seem mysteriously to interpenetrate in meaningful patterns that do not accord with our empirical assumptions about causality. What I have called the magical field often appears to be a manifestation of the psychoid as magically perceived and understood.

Magic—in the form of tarot-card images, for example—may deepen meaning much as may a dream, or as may elaborating upon a dream by bringing associations and relevant symbolic material to bear upon it. But many missteps are made in the further, more discursive interpretation of magical signs—as they are in such interpretation of dream images—especially as one tries to use them as guides to practical life. Magic may thus lead one out of perplexity either into a truer grasp of one's situation or into a new form of banal error—just as analysis may further either an enrichment of the personality or a stronger entrenchment in one's pathogenic complexes. (A card reader turns up the card of Vengeance, and her client assumes that it refers to his ex-wife, whereas unknown to him it may with equal justice refer to his daughter, his present woman friend, and her friend the card reader: he is as in need of enlightenment as before, and his ego would need to contribute more imaginatively to the process. Macbeth's messages from the witches, too, needed more imaginative ego-processing than he gave them.

Granted, he is in some ways highly imaginative, but not in those that help the ego to deal with witches. Despite the stirring power of its images, magic does not lessen the need for imagination as partly an ego function.)

Belief in the reality of the occult powers has the justification that our conscious viewpoint is always distorted and partial, that we are in countless ways implicated in a world that transcends it, and that these ways are largely undecipherable. Causal understanding diminishes the unknown, but causation is many-layered and complex, a matter of manifold endless chains. Tracing such chains may bring the mind to the limit of the complexity it can master, while giving little satisfaction to the evaluating heart. And the heart, drawing upon primitive levels of psychic functioning, is central to the experience of personal meaning. Tracing such chains may, especially, do little justice to one's felt sense of *this* event *here* and *now*. (What "caused" the Second World War? How did John Smith understand whatever "caused" him to lie dying in it?)

The stable structures of religious cult, myth, and ritual help to make us at home in the world by granting imaginative access to the transcendent dimension of which I have been speaking. Magic in its more contemplative manifestations also grants access to it, often in ways that emphasize its fleeting, here-and-now yet marginal nature. Such glimpses are of value because access to the transcendent dimension cannot be reduced to a steady state. (Magic may, of course, try to reduce it to this by nervously tapping into it every few minutes with its equivalent of gauges and pumps. But such attempts are as self-defeating as attempts to force one's way into heaven by ever more strangling self-control.)

Since we are imperfect creatures in an imperfect and imperfectly understood world, whatever agent or agents we imagine as animating the transcendent dimension must finally insist on its or their freedom. This insistence amounts to its or their being known, if at all, in contingency, the fortuitous, randomness. The magical reading of such glimpses as signs is of value because patterns of fate and qualitative aspects of time are inescapably real and important and because some magic offers a differentiated language for talking about them. That egocentricity, prejudice, and insensitive willfulness often skew the reading says little more than that there is much prejudice and insensitive willfulness in the world. Neither religion nor science has been able to eliminate them.

Proper qualities of feeling and imagination need continually to be cultivated and revivified. Magic may assist or thwart this process. Contemplation is, however, not well served when magic is trivialized to an applied technology supporting mental laziness; this happens easily. (I will ask the *I Ching* whether to have my egg boiled or scrambled.) Myth may serve contemplation better by holding to the magical field within the forms of its narrative and by identifying the agents of that field as divine—as not here and now—and not "me" but other, though partly in my likeness.

5.7 Magical Timelessness and Egolessness?

Concerned with issues related to some I have been discussing, the analytical psychologist Edward C. Whitmont has spoken of a "magic layer of the unconscious." In his view this "layer," dominated by the archetypal Great Mother, came to cultural expression in a "phase"— or age—of prehistory, and it is prominent in individual development from birth to the age of three or four, as it is in collective regression in the form of such ideologies as Nazism. Experience of this layer, phase, or condition is spaceless, timeless, and egoless. The magical phase is superseded by a mythological phase—lasting in individual development from three or four through puberty—and then a "mental" phase—beginning after puberty.[39] Sketching some of my reservations about such a formulation should help further to elucidate my view of magic.

It is true that what has been called the "Civilization of Old Europe" (ca. 6500–3500 B.C.) was dominated by forms of the mother goddess,[40] that the supersession of this civilization by one elevating the Indo-European thunder god was of great cultural and psychological significance, that the mother is the most important figure in the life of the infant and small child, and that regression in various forms may entail a powerful activation of the mother image. Still, cultures have also shifted from father-centered models of social organization to mother-

188

centered models, and male divinities have been pushed into the background by female divinities (as in the cult of the Virgin Mary).

There is no good reason to assume that matriarchy universally precedes patriarchy or that individual psychological development repeats cultural history thus schematized. The notion that it does so rests partly on an analogizing extension into cultural history and individual psychology of the biological doctrine that ontogeny (or the development of the individual organism) recapitulates phylogeny (or the development of the species). This biological doctrine has been strongly challenged,[41] and there are in any case serious objections to the analogizing extension of it into cultural history and individual psychology.[42]

Surely, too, it is an oversimplification to think, as Jung did, that the psychic life of infants and small children is in a relatively simple way contained in that of the mother, a view criticized cogently by Fordham in his book appropriately entitled *Children as Individuals* (cited in part 2.5, n. 16). And though it makes sense—along lines pursued by Werner—to describe some mentation of children as "primitive" and magical, their psychic lives are also realistic. (There is reason to think Freud wrong in conjecturing that infants magically hallucinate the absent breast; surely they realistically know that it is absent. Moreover, it is hard to see why the mother-goddess civilization, with its surely rich—if now largely unknown—mythology, should be pre-"mythological," and why the religious life basic to it should simply be called "magic."[43])

Further, it seems an ethnocentric presumption to suppose that the experience of people who celebrate the great periodicities of nature is timeless and that they live their egoless lives in the Round of the Great Mother. Indeed, it is a sign of impoverished consciousness that we no longer celebrate these periodicities with much vigor. It is true that the language of the "primitive" Trobriand Islanders can present action in a timeless mode,[44] but this no more shows them to be unaware of time than our calling European people "white" shows us to be unaware of the color of their skin. And while "primitive" societies often (though by no means always) emphasize communal values and action more than individual values and action, to regard their members as egoless is to obscure such questions as the following: What kind or kinds of egos do they have? What institutions—including magic, religion, technology, and law—assist their egos to function? And how do such institutions do this?

As I have suggested in my remarks on Arieti's concepts, under certain conditions primitive modes of psychic functioning become operative, and these have played a role in the creation and continuing existence of magic. In speaking of dispositions in the magical field (in part 5.6) I have referred to a quality and an orientation of consciousness reflecting these modes of psychic functioning and to characteristic products of such consciousness. When these products prevail, the ego may be diffuse or may be not yet strong or may have become weakened, but it is still the seat and organ of whatever conscious experience is taking place. To speak of a basic "magic layer" of the psyche could misleadingly suggest that it, of itself, creates the kinds of experience with which I am now concerned. I prefer to take the ego-reference of magical perception and action explicitly into account. Magic happens to the ego, but magic is also a mode of the ego, as it seeks to deal with its own stresses, to maintain its strength, and to revivify itself. Asserting oneself may be an expression of ego strength; so may surrendering oneself. Magic may facilitate both such assertion and such surrender. Magic may be the mode of a primitive "emergency ego," but it may also be that of a self-aware and reflective participating consciousness—as will become clear when I further discuss *The Tempest* (in part 5.14). Linking magic with the unconscious and regression does away with these complexities.

5.8 Magical Power and Death

In a refined version of the magic-religion-science evolutionary sequence, the philosopher Susanne K. Langer regards magic as an instrument of "The Dream of Power" ignoring the reality of death.[45] She contrasts the magical mentality with the form of consciousness that obtains when the inevitability of individual death has been faced and magic has given way to a religious celebration not of power but of life. This contrast she persuasively illustrates with photographs of, on the one hand, an Egyptian pyramid, its rigidly geometric form in defiant opposition to the surrounding desert (the caption reads, "the stark lines of the monument declare nothing but royal power") and, on the other hand, a Buddhist stupa rooted in the earth out of which it rises, and Hindu temples symbolizing life and the profusion of its manifestations.[46]

This view, too, needs to be qualified in ways that require me to elaborate on my earlier remarks about the ambiguities of love and power. To begin with, despite the remarkable contrast between the pyramid and the stupa and temple, power and life are by no means mutually exclusive categories. Rather, they are continuous with one another, shade off into one another, are sometimes aspects of one another, and are sometimes indistinguishable. Life may be subsumed in a coercive assertion of power: the mummified pharaoh's implication in a rich symbolism of continuing life demonstrates his power to defy death. Power may also be manifest in the profusion of life: power may be manifest *as* life.

These reflections provide a useful perspective within which to ask a question the answer to which is often—and mistakenly—thought to be self-evident: How magical are the ancient and widespread funerary practices of arranging the corpse in the fetal position, painting its bones with ochre symbolic of blood, and furnishing the grave with food, weapons, and other appurtenances of continuing life? The answer depends on how literal-minded the people engaging in such practices are about their symbolism. Though the capacity to regard symbols under the aspect of "as if" is essential to the higher forms of imagination, it is also true that symbolism that completely loses its concrete character loses its contact with concerns of emotional import. Thus, if in the Eleusynian mysteries a sheaf of wheat was held up in a gesture intended as an epiphany, this was not because the officiant in the rite lacked the superior mental gifts necessary to deliver a sermon or a philosophical disquisition instead. The poet Marianne Moore speaks of "literalists of the imagination":[47] we must think about being imaginative in a literal-minded and bodily way.

Langer rightly observes that the creative function at work in such fantasy creations as dreams and the gods, ghosts, and demons of waking life is always far below what she calls the "psychical limen." They are products of symbolic activity rooted in such rudimentary bodily processes as the sense of balance, which we experience in projected form when we visually judge physical forms to be balanced or unbalanced. As soon as such creatures of the spirit world have been conjured up there is a need for defense against them, and magic serves this need. Consequently, the mainspring of magical thinking is as deeply buried as that of symbol-making. Magical action has its origin in "the feeling of mental activity—of an invisible doing—that underlies the notion of exerting a non-mechanical influence on the course of events, without contact, without physical push or pull on the external objects and persons involved."[48] Thus magic harnesses the spontaneous activity of the psyche and protects the nascent ego, giving it the courage to speak, act, and think. And since it arises from the basis of the psyche in pre- or subpsychic bodily life it seems thoroughly "natural," and hence has impressive success in eluding conscious criticism.

It does seem to me that linking magic with the illusory, ego-defensive denial of death blurs a distinction of great importance, however hard it is to draw. This may be seen with regard to the funerary customs already mentioned, especially if these are considered in relation to the Christian doctrines of the resurrection of Christ and the resurrection of the body of the believer. Pondering these doctrines critically, one quickly arrives at such questions as, How are the various parts of dismembered corpses to be reassembled? What will the biological age of the reassembled body be—six months, six, twenty-six, or seventy-six years? What kind of physical habitation would be required for all the risen individuals of so many generations and centuries? Do dogs and cats have souls, and will they go to heaven? Will they be judged first? Will elephants also go? And centipedes? It is not, I believe, simply the magical denial of death that keeps such questions from arising or, when they do, keeps people from remarking how fanciful their imaginative speculations in answer to them are.

To draw the distinction I have in mind, we must return to nonconsummatory mutuality in its relation to appetitive behavior, to being imaginative in a literal-minded and bodily way, and to the relations between ego and self.

If appetitive behavior, with its stressful desire and fulfilling satiation, belongs to the realm of action, nonconsummatory mutuality belongs to that of essence. If our actions earn us heaven, there we will see face to face in a receptive—as distinct from active—form of contemplation. Not seeing through a glass darkly but knowing also as I am known will surely be different from a subject's knowing of an object as that subject carries out empirical projects in the world. "Even as I am known" implies mutuality, with its abundance, rather than reciprocal exchange, with its implication of limitation and closure. And yet action and essence are and were and cannot cease to be profoundly interrelated.

According to Langer, the prescientific "natural" view of events construed them as acts, these being "based on the feeling of organic processes, i.e., in the pattern of impulse, effort, and realization." She illustrates this attitude, which minimizes the causal intention of the individual subject, with a revealing story about an Eskimo in the act of carving. Asking the ivory what form is hiding in it, he might carve aimlessly until he sees the form. "Then he brings it out: seal, hidden, emerges. It was always there: he didn't create it, he helped it step forth."[49] Her illustration shows that in this "natural" attitude, action is inseparable from the contemplation of essence, a point already suggested by my remarks about magical contemplation.

Nonconsummatory mutuality and the contemplation of essence are supported by a fundamental fact about our world: in it life survives death. This does not necessarily mean that the conscious life of the individual human person survives his death. But the fact that I am here, now, writing this means that I somehow participate in the life that has survived the death of everyone who has died, for generations, centuries, millennia. If I try to imagine the *agent* of this surviving life, I think of the phyletic strains of the individuals and species now extant. If I try to elaborate this thought in a way intended to define this agent more specifically, I run into difficulties that are partly those of knowing where my person starts and leaves off, where its boundaries are. This is a puzzle in many ways.

My Swiss Army pocketknife is intimately familiar, "mine"; I have somehow invested myself in it. It is a memento of important years I spent in Switzerland. Is it part of who "I" am? Not essentially, I would hazard, but where and when does who I "essentially" am start and leave off? Such an object *may* represent an essential part of who one is, as is clear when the protagonist of Orson Welles's film *Citizen Kane*

193

on his deathbed utters the word "Rosebud," naming a sled he had as a child. If I were a hunter thousands of years ago my equivalent of this pocketknife might have been put into the grave with me. Would it have been put there as an instrument for use in the afterlife, or as a statement—on the level of magical contemplation—about who I most essentially was?

A priest of my acquaintance reports that one of the few things that still vitally interests him about the Christian religion is the eucharist, and that it does so precisely because of its primitivity, its links with cannibal feasts and other rituals of archaic magic and religion. These links thrill him to an awareness of what his highly educated intellect and imagination take to be the spiritual meaning of the sacrament, while somehow revivifying that meaning in a way that reveals new aspects of it. Was that meaning at some point grafted onto the primitive ritual, much as commemoration, thanksgiving have been grafted onto the perdurable custom of having a feast at a certain time of the year? To put these questions in either-or form immediately makes clear that there is something wrong with their formulation.

Surely the spiritual meaning of the sacrament cannot be equated with the most theologically satisfying statement of that meaning that the priest could find in his library. Indeed, his shocked sense of the primitivity of the ritual is surely, he would agree, an important part of his knowing what it means. And though he might try to state that meaning theologically, he might also—with respect to that meaning— appreciate the force of Polanyi's summary of his theory of tacit knowing: "we can know more than we can tell."[50] But perhaps participants in pre-Christian prototypes of the eucharist also knew more than they could tell, and perhaps what they knew was also what Christians knew and know.

With regard to such symbols I do not wish to ignore the shifts of levels of meaning effected by succeeding stages of civilization—for example, when the Hebrews took over the myth-and-ritual pattern of the ancient Near East and put it to their purposes of celebrating not a dying and reviving god but an ever-living God of justice. But the Hebrews could not have made this pattern say what they made it say if it did not already in good part say it. Similarly, "mother" could not be made into the symbol "Mother Church" if "mother" did not already mean, implicitly, much of what "church" means, including protection, love, compassion, propriety, concern with community and tradition, physical and spiritual nourishment, and connection with the great periodicities of nature. My point is to emphasize continuities, the ways in which a common symbolic core can be given very different readings that nonetheless remain related—much as radically different productions of *Macbeth* are still *Macbeth*.

Bateson uses the term *context* in a special way that has a bearing on the question of where and when who I "essentially" am starts and leaves off. The context necessary to the meaning of human words and actions is a *"pattern through time,"* and the "mind" utilized and expressed in this pattern is continuous with the "mind" of genetic communication that tells the sea anemone how to grow. He thus draws an analogy between context in human relations and context in the deep and archaic processes of embryology and homology, insisting that the term *context* be applied to both.[51] To say this is to say nothing about the survival of individuality (in whatever form) after death; it is to say that individuality is a nexus in further and further-reaching levels of a context that has evolved over millennia. Bateson is thus concerned with the meaning of the life that—however it is defined as an agent—has survived death. I will call this the larger life. (This topic will be discussed in more personal terms in part 6.12.)

A closely related point is made philosophically by O. S. Wauchope, who points out that *life* and *death* are not simply correlative terms like *rich* and *poor*. In the case of the latter, he points out, to understand one is to understand the other, and one understands both words or neither. This is not true of life and death, since the latter "is deviation from life; but life is not deviation from death. Life is the unity, and death is the difference in that unity"; life is positive, and death negative—and not because we would prefer to be alive than to be dead, but rather, simply because we are alive and not dead yet. "A living thing is alive-but-mortal, not mortal-but-alive." "Just as, logically, an open door is a not-shut one, and a shut door a not-open one," so is "a living thing . . . a not-dead one, and a dead thing a not-living one." But trying to understand *alive* as meaning "not-dead" cannot be made to work, except logically. This is so because *life* names a form of spontaneous activity that we take to have intrinsic value that cannot be reduced to death-avoiding, as though life were simply a defensive activity against "not-life." Our nature as living subjects forces us to understand life in this nonlogical way.[52]

Such an argument translates into logical terms an awareness expressed more fully in mythic forms and images that reach beyond logic to activate archaic levels of feeling, imagination, and the self. In my concern with power *as* life, especially as manifest in what we may apprehend as the larger life, I will briefly call attention to a few of the more immediately telling of these mythic forms and images.

The first thoughts leading to C. Kerényi's *Dionysos: Archetypal Image of Indestructible Life* came to the Romanian classicist in a vineyard, as it occurred to him that any account of the religion of this god "must put the main accent not on intoxication but on the quiet, powerful, vegetative element which ultimately engulfed even the ancient theaters. . . ." This element is in Greek *zoë,* "life in general, without further characterization," in contrast to *bios,* which implies "the contours . . . the characteristic traits of a specified life, the outlines that distinguish one living thing from another." Lacking contours, *zoë* nonetheless contrasts sharply with *thanatos,* or death. As non-death, *zoë* "does not even let death approach it." Further, *zoë* is (in Plato as in Homer) equated with *psyche.* "It is our simplest, most intimate and self-evident experience." But it specifically "does not admit of the experience of its own destruction: it is experienced without end, as infinite life"—inexhaustible and indestructible, surviving all individual carriers of it, as the vine survives the ruined theater and temple.[53]

The life that cannot be equated with not-death is, then, unfathomably abundant and a gift. Further, the ecstatic, dying-and-reborn god Dionysos should remind us that the more measured life of feeling retains its ties to the pathic ground, and that the openness requisite for the enhancement of relationship and the articulation of values is also openness to the dissolution of ego-attitudes—and sometimes the ego itself—in passionate crisis.

Transcendent life is also expressed in the male and female symbols of generative power—phalli and vulvae—known from many times and places, and in symbols of the Great Mother. In keeping with my emphasis on the mother-infant relationship, it is striking that in the

196

religion of prehistoric Malta a sexual entering of the Great Mother leads to rebirth in a new relation to the supremacy of life, a rebirth which, despite differences, is related to the resurrection of Christ and other resurrected—and in this sense ever-living—gods. For the ancient Maltese, in the classics scholar Günther Zuntz's account, the Great Mother "is the deep Earth receiving in her womb the bodies of the dead; she is the power of birth which renews all life; she is the force of sex through which, miraculously and unceasingly, this renewal is brought about and, therewith, the eternity of all life, in plant, animal, and man. The dead entering her womb are themselves the seed of renewed life. . . ." The worshipper entering her sanctuary "had gone 'the way of all flesh' and had mystically experienced death; at the same time, having passed through the divine vulva, he had, in a realistic symbolism, become the mate of the goddess. . . . He that so entered died, and begat—himself; when . . . he went out where he had entered, he had become the newly-born child of the goddess."[54]

But in what sense, we may ask, did the Maltese worshipper *have* the larger life he had helped to symbolize through his ritual actions?

So far as I am able to determine, we may not *have* the larger life as our egoistic possession. But we may participate in it by knowing it contemplatively. Still, to picture having it may be a way of knowing it. And thus what at first sight looks like magical coercion and ego-reference implicitly may have a broader and deeper religious value.

In earlier times the king, for example, was regarded as embodying the larger life or at least providing access to it. At the same time he represented a preform—maintained by projection—of a certain kind of autonomy that would in time be introjected as part of the responsible individuality of nonroyal people. In the course of this process the symbol of the king was transvalued and depotentiated: it was democratized in the sense that kingly functions became the prerogatives of a large number of individuals.

The king and related symbols—like the symbol of the resurrection—thus have both ego-reference and self-reference. By self-reference I mean significance related to the totality of the psyche in its participation in the larger life. It will be clear that the boundaries of the self in this sense cannot be drawn and that its nature can only be approximated in symbols the content of which must remain

197

indefinite—that it can only be seen through a glass darkly. It cannot be simply assumed that the funerary customs and other life-affirming symbols I have been discussing—including Dionysos, certain forms of gift-giving, and ancient Maltese rituals of devotion to the Great Mother—are limited to ego-reference.

The state of affairs I have been describing entails ironies and complexities that should not be smoothed away by oversimplification. The kinds of symbols I have been considering, for example, must in some way appeal to the ego, must invite the ego to put itself into them if the symbols are to open the ego to wider ranges of context and are to help the ego to apprehend the larger life. But symbols of this kind do not come labeled with instructions as to how they are to be taken. Indeed, there have been religious wars arising, in effect, from conflicting attempts to apply labels supplying such instructions. Thus the ego may construe the invitation to enter the symbol as an opportunity for coercive possession of its power—as when the consecrated host is used as a love charm.

Also, however, the symbol that itself seems to express a coercive expression of power may, in turn, have an important self-reference as well. This might even be true of the pyramid discussed by Langer, guarded and hoarding as it seems to be. Rather than simply being an egoistic assertion, it should perhaps also be regarded as a self symbol in the double sense of pointing to the larger life, and—as an expression of the kingship—of being a bearer, by proxy, of a meaning that would gradually be incorporated into the ego structure of nonroyal individuals. (This does not mean that the pharaoh had an ego whereas the common people did not. It means that the person of the pharaoh was invested with values that would, when introjected by his nonroyal subjects, transform their values and the structure of their egos.)

In the preceding paragraphs I have spoken of ways in which symbols of the self may anticipate future forms and directions of the ego. This implies that the self—with its greater comprehensiveness, its homeostatic propensities, and its own intentionality—may serve as the agent of the ego. Indeed, that the self does so can be seen in a great many dreams. In them the conscious attitude and situation of the dreamer may be reflected in a drama in which the dream-ego (the person of the dreamer as represented in the dream) acts in a discernible relation to the waking ego of the dreamer. Yet in its creation of the dream, the self is in a sense serving as the agent of the dreamer's ego by making available to the ego insights reflecting its own greater wisdom.

The ego may also, however, serve as the agent of the self. Inducing the ego to do so is indeed one of the functions of religion insofar as it furthers individuation. Indeed, the condition of having the ego serve as the agent of the self is one important aim of individuation, however it is achieved. In the image of Saint Christopher (the ego) bearing the Christ Child (the self) on his shoulders, the Christ Child, further, represents a potential attitude of the ego, while also being the child form of the mythical hero who will triumph over death. And so we are brought again to the relations of the individual to the larger life that has survived death, and to the question of the way in which the individual may be said to participate in it.

Jung has on various occasions pondered the remarkable fact that the dreams of many dying people seem to disregard the imminence of death, as though their psyches expect them to go on living. One may think about this that everything that lives wants to live forever, and one may regard it as a manifestation of wish-fulfilling ego-defense. But one may also relate this fact to prophetic intuitions, clairvoyance, and other unusual but real phenomena suggesting that the empirical world is in a sense appearance and that below it or behind it there is another order of things in which there is no distinction between "here" and "there" and no extension in time. This may lead us to the conclusion that "something of our psychic existence is outside space and time."[55]

Such reasoning is related to that which convinced Indian metaphysicians that *something* of the subjective reality of the individual got handed on beyond death, though they disagreed as to whether it was personal or impersonal. The Lord Buddha accepted the handing on but regarded the issue of its personality or impersonality as fruitless. His agnosticism is true to the unlikelihood that there can ever be empirical certainty about such matters. (For example, as Jung observes—touching on a problem Hamlet was up against—suppose one encounters a ghost: how can one know whether it is identical with the person it seems to be the ghost of?)

Still, if dreams—including those of dying people—are in an important measure truth-telling and reality-revealing, the afterlife symbolism of archaic and "primitive" peoples may partly express an awareness of their participation in a dimension of reality in which time and space are relativized in ways I have described—and an awareness of the value of that participation. Perhaps such symbolism expresses a conviction that something, namely life, survives death; that life is therefore the more embracing symbolic term; that in an imaginative understanding of the total world—in the mythic apprehension of reality—the life that survives death must be given the strongest accent of value; and that death has its meaning in the more embracing term of surviving life. Perhaps for many such people the question of whether they are magically denying death or expressing such an awareness is unanswerable because for them magical action and magical contemplation were or are largely undifferentiated. But even if this is so, their magical action *can also be* a form of contemplation. In particular cases we are left with ambiguities and shades of emphasis related to those that led me to draw Freud's and Jung's views of religion into a single perspective and to find each applicable to some phenomena—and both to some.

I take the fundamental concept of the Judeo-Christian tradition to be that we are not self-created (as what are currently called "narcissistic personalities" assume) but are creatures. Our creatureliness is primarily a matter of relationship, to what that tradition calls God and to one another. We are in relationship with the larger life, as I have described it, and we are what Aristotle called *zoon politikon,* man as the social and political animal; as subjects we are also irreducibly fellow-subjects; "we are members one of another" (Eph. 4:25).

The concept of creatureliness is compatible with refined scientific understanding. Thus Bateson is drawn to two basic and contrasting terms used by Jung in his visionary, pseudo-Gnostic fiction *Septem Sermones ad Mortuos* (Seven Sermons to the Dead). These are *pleroma,* the nonliving world of billiard ball-like cause and effect, and *creatura,* the living world of what Bateson understands as "mind," entailing the registering and exchange of information on many levels—including the genetic, the sensory, the intellectual, and—to use another term of which he is fond—the sacramental. The chief characteristic of this living world is relationship, and an adequate understanding of it includes a proper appreciation of dependence and interdependence.[56]

Independence is illusory unless the person feeling it admits dependence and interdependence and can not only abide but even take

pleasure in them. Though the willfulness of Freud's infantile omnipotence of thought is real, to bring all of Baby's psychic life under that
rubric would be to overemphasize her drivenness by appetite and its
domination of her reality sense, and to underestimate her capacity for
nonconsummatory mutuality.

The ego has its crises, aberrations, deaths, and rebirths. In relation to these the ego may be said to be related to the self as the
crises, aberrations, lives, and deaths of individuals are to the larger
life. This is meant not as a metaphysical assertion but as a description
of lived experience as it conforms to mythic forms and images, asserting or implying that the larger life is the most embracing symbolic
term—the ultimate characteristic of the mythically apprehended total
world.

After symbols of self-reference, creatureliness, and mutuality have
been delineated and used to guide contemplative devotion, they may
be aggrandized, subverted, and used for egoistic coercion. (Luther
regarded Roman Catholic ritual as magical in this sense. In fighting
to reaffirm human creatureliness he created a religious movement
furthering the vested interests of certain social and political groups.)
The ego may use self symbols to maintain a defended, inert form of
pseudowholeness. (A Christian name for this is self-righteousness,
which Christianity has often vigorously generated in the very process
of condemning it.) But all knowledge strongly assuming the autonomy
of the ego is provisional (seeing through a glass darkly), and our
knowledge of predictable order cannot render it a certain possession.
Our emotionality rises in a rush to meet the unexpected—and itself
assumes unexpected, never-to-be-taken-for-granted forms and colors.
Passionate crisis may revivify the ego and help to bring it to proper
modes of feeling. I have said that the ego may serve as the agent of
the self: feeling, as a potential activity of the ego, may redeem self
symbols by acknowledging them as expressive of the larger life and of
our participation in it.

To restate a main theme of this section—and to illustrate the
persistence, indeed inevitability, of archaic patterns of thought and
feeling described in it—I will conclude it by calling attention to the
climactic word in a twentieth-century poem, "To Waken an Old Lady,"
by the American poet William Carlos Williams (1883–1963). The
poem is about the relation of the often-beleaguered ego to the larger

life. Its final word, *plenty*, powerfully implies the abundant ongoing of
life despite the inescapable "dark wind" of mortality:

> Old age is
> a flight of small
> cheeping birds
> skimming
> bare trees
> above a snow glaze.
> Gaining and failing
> they are buffeted
> by a dark wind—
> But what?
> On harsh weedstalks
> the flock has rested,
> the snow
> is covered with broken
> seedhusks
> and the wind tempered
> by a shrill
> piping of plenty. [57]

5.9 Open-minded Skepticism about Magic

According to the Marxist social theorist Theodor Adorno, "Occultism is the metaphysics of the dopes."[58] The clarity and conclu-
siveness of this pronouncement are appealing, but it goes counter to
the more complex view of magic implicit in impressive works of imaginative literature. I will comment briefly on two such works, which
are both skeptical and open-minded about magic.

In the fourteenth-century romance *Sir Gawain and the Green Knight*,
Gawain accepts the challenge of the mysterious green figure who comes
unannounced to King Arthur's court. Gawain is to use the Green
Knight's ax to chop off his head; in a year's time Gawain is to go to
the Green Knight's chapel and receive an ax-blow in turn. When
Gawain has chopped off the Green Knight's head, the Green Knight
simply picks it up and departs.

As the time for the second part of the agreement to be kept
approaches, Gawain sets out to find the chapel of the Green Knight.

202

Magic and Participating Consciousness

Happening upon a castle inhabited by a sinister knight and his beautiful wife, he stays three days as their guest. The knight, who goes hunting every day, makes a pleasant wager with Gawain that the knight will give him his quarry for the day if Gawain gives him in exchange whatever he receives while staying in the castle. While the knight is hunting, his wife comes to Gawain's bed intent on seducing him. But Gawain is steadfast, and she must settle for a kiss, which Gawain dutifully gives in turn to the knight. The second day the lady gives Gawain two kisses and on the third three. On the third day she tries to give him a ring, which he declines. She also offers him a magical green girdle that will protect him from harm, and he accepts it. The second and third days, too, he gives her kisses in turn to the knight. But to avoid compromising the lady and to save his life he conceals the girdle.

Directed to the chapel of the Green Knight, he arrives there to hear the Green Knight sharpening his ax in preparation for the blow. Twice the Green Knight begins to swing the ax down but interrupts himself. The third time he carries through with a blow that just nicks Gawain's neck. He then explains that he is the knight whose guest Gawain had been, that he interrupted the first two blows because the first two days Gawain had kept the terms of their agreement, and that he had nicked Gawain's neck because he had not disclosed the gift of the girdle. He also explains that his wife's attempts at seduction were at his request, and that if Gawain had given him the girdle he would have also been spared the third blow.

The Green Knight, a magician, thus argues on behalf of the code of chivalry, maintaining that Gawain's loyalty to the code had saved his life and that his infringement of it had earned him the nick on his neck. If Gawain had not been wearing the girdle and had escaped with his life there would be strong evidence in favor of the Green Knight's interpretation of the events. But Gawain was, in fact, wearing the girdle, which both he and the reader have accepted as magical. The reader is thus put in the thoroughly ambiguous position of being asked to accept the argument of a magician—whose magical power has been awesomely demonstrated—that magic is irrelevant and that it is one's honoring or infringement of an ethical code that determines one's fate.

Feeling, Imagination, and the Self

A similar ambiguity is presented early in Shakespeare's *King Lear*, as the old Earl of Gloucester and his villainous bastard son express opinions about the influence of the stars on human affairs. Edmund's reflections on the subject end:

> An admirable evasion of whoremaster man, to lay his goatish disposition on the charge of a star. My father compounded with my mother under the Dragon's Tail, and my nativity was under Ursa Major, so that it follows I am rough and lecherous. Fut! I should have been that I am, had the maidenliest star in the firmament twinkled on my bastardizing.
> [I.ii.129–36]

In fact, however, Edmund's father and mother mated not under the maidenliest star in the firmament but under the Dragon's Tail; moreover, his birthday is under Ursa Major, and he is as rough and lecherous as an astrologer would accordingly expect him to be. These facts do not confirm astrology, but they certainly also do not disconfirm it. And when Edmund claims superiority over his legitimate brother Edgar he does so on the basis of the "fierce quality" of his character owing to the vigor of the sexual act by which he was conceived "in the lusty stealth of nature" (I.ii.11–12), an argument resting on assumptions as magical as those of astrology.

I cited (in part 4.5) Dufrenne's assertion that the objects of our experience are supported by an "unfathomable reservoir of beings": the objects of ordinary experience are supported even in their ordinariness by a reservoir of beings that refuse to be made ordinary. These may be known as what (in part 5.6) I have called dispositions in the magical field manifested as qualitative aspects of time and patterns of fate. Many stories, including those of Gawain and King Lear, are about such qualitative aspects of time and patterns of fate. And magical power in such stories may serve to create an awareness of the dimension of extraordinary beings. It may do this because magic, utilitarian as much of it is, can never be made exclusively into an applied art. Though it may serve reason—as Adorno's phrase "the metaphysics of dopes" unenthusiastically grants—it finally defies rational understanding and always may elude conscious control.

In the texts on which I am commenting, the Gawain poet and Shakespeare refer to magical beliefs. Our acquaintance with these beliefs and our emotional response to them allow them to awaken in us an imaginative sense of the reality of magical power. The stories, however, are ambiguous in ways that do not allow the reality of that power to be proved or disproved, or its nature defined. Proof or disproof and definition would allow us to convert our imaginative sense of its reality into rational understanding, and thus to contain it within our ordinary assumptions. We are left with the impression of magical power lurking in undefined and perhaps undefinable relation to ordinary reality—of magical power as one symbolic form providing us imaginative access to the reservoir of beings of which Dufrenne speaks.

When the Green Knight picks up his cutoff head, his action is *unheimlich,* compellingly weird; and our emotional reaction is one of fascinated dread, the response demanded of us when the familiar becomes strangely unfamiliar. Of course, what he does is familiar in the sense that he belongs to a class of beings whom we know to do such things. Still, its familiarity in this sense is not sufficient to annul its unfamiliarity, opening into the extraordinary in which our empirical grasp of reality is threateningly loosened. This is a model instance of the way in which received meaning in many forms—ideas, opinions, conventions of action—is again and again dissolved through the activation of the pathic ground, as what is known becomes once again unexpected and inexplicable. I have spoken of the way in which parts of the perceptual field must be sacrificed if we are to attend to new objects: the passionate crisis that is analogous to this state of affairs on the emotional level revivifies consciousness by calling the total frame of meaning into question. Magical power, defying proof, disproof, and definition, may function in symbolic utterances serving that revivification.

5.10 Magical Barter and the Price of Self-Transformation

Though dependence and interdependence figure importantly in our roles as fellow-subjects in relation to one another and to the larger life, there are debilitating forms of both qualities, and ego-autonomy of a flexible and adapted kind is necessary to the integrity of the ego's relation to the self. Concerned with such ego-autonomy, Jung describes how the unconscious compulsion resulting from family fixations and uncontrolled infantility results in one's recreating the same dependence and lack of freedom that formerly characterized one's relations with one's parents. In *Symbols of Transformation,* he notes, "The Stoics called this condition *Heimarmene,* compulsion by the stars, to which every 'unredeemed' soul is subject."[59]

In its compulsiveness, neurotic behavior often defends the ego against the influence of these metaphorical "stars" by various kinds of reciprocal exchanges having a magical character. Sometimes such exchanges comprise an arrangement adumbrating—often in caricature—the self-transformation that would be required to free the person from this unfree condition. Such arrangements accord with Jung's realization early in his psychiatric career that neurosis and even more extreme forms of psychopathology represent failed attempts at self-healing.

By such reciprocal exchanges I mean[2] a kind of barter that—in another metaphor—gives the devil his due so as to placate him and at the same time win a simulacrum of whatever would genuinely satisfy the vital needs of the self. If this simulacrum were reality, the problem implied by it would be solved. But the self-transformation necessary to its solution entails participation in the larger life, and this has another kind of price. It is symbolically proper that the priest should receive the offering before the ritual transformative act.

Two fairy tales, "The Doctor and His Pupil" (from France) and "East o' the Sun and West o' the Moon" (from Norway)[60] have a bearing on these considerations, as have the psychodynamics of two contemporary people whom I will describe in brief vignettes.

The twelve-year-old hero of the first of these tales is striking from the outset as he passes by the castle of a doctor first wearing a jacket that is red in front and white behind and then wearing the same jacket backwards. The doctor asks him whether he can read; he says he can, and for this reason the doctor refuses to give him the work he is seeking. The boy returns a few days later, and when the doctor again asks him whether he can read, he says he cannot, and the doctor gives him a curious job that consists solely of dusting the doctor's book of magic while he makes a succession of long trips, in the course of which his pupil memorizes the book's contents. The pupil then performs various magical feats—for example, magically producing a horse to be sold at the fair—that allow him to give money to his poor parents. The doctor reacts to the pupil's disobedience with magic—for example, transforming him into a horse. The main part of the story is devoted to a magic contest between the doctor and the pupil, as (in one set of exchanges) the pupil as horse transforms itself into a hare, whereupon the doctor transforms six boys into hunting dogs that chase the hare to a reservoir into which it jumps, transforming itself into a carp. When the doctor drains the reservoir and tries to grab the carp it turns into a lark, which the doctor pursues in the form of an eagle. The lark escapes the eagle by falling down the chimney of a castle, where the pupil becomes a grain of wheat under the table in the bedroom of the girl of the castle.

The girl ends by "acceding" sexually to his seduction or force, but the relationship is by no means elaborated upon, and she remains a pawn in the power struggle between the pupil and her father (who has become sick after the pupil's arrival at the castle) on the one hand, and the doctor who is summoned to cure the father, on the other. (Earlier in the story the pupil's father is made his son's bungling helper in magic tricks, but his mother is not explicitly mentioned; the girl has "parents," but only the father is described in action.)

The story closes when the girl's father, now cured, tells the daughter to take off her engagement ring, which is the daytime form of the pupil, and give it to the doctor. "She took it off and let it fall; the ring turned into grains of wheat, which scattered on the floor. The doctor turned into a rooster to pick them up. The young man turned into a fox and ate the rooster."

It is significant that the story ends not with the pupil's return to his bride but with his killing of the doctor. Surely the doctor is a father figure, and the whole story is about a young man's attempts to achieve some kind of accommodation with the world of the fathers, who in this story are sinister and trickster-like (the doctor); poor, bungling, and succumbing to drink (the pupil's own father); and suspicious, unbelieving, and sick (the girl's father). Rather than modifying the egoistic intentions of the two principals, their magic serves those intentions. It is curious that the doctor asks to be duped (by putting the pupil in charge of the magic book and then absenting himself). But sometimes a father (or father-figure) wants contact with a son (or son-figure) and knows no way to get it but through conflict—and in this way feeds the son's inclination to gain autonomy through force. Sometimes the older man is even willing to risk defeat as the price of this interaction. Perhaps their conflict is a just-so story in the sense of distantly echoing the ritual combat between the old king and the challenging hero in the ancient ritual pattern: the challenger wins because he is young, and the prevailing authority knows that the test must take place, even if he is foredoomed to defeat. Even if this pattern underlies the action, the contest is one of ego-wills, and magic is the instrumentality of it.

"East o' the Sun and West o' the Moon" is much more complex and engages many more psychic levels. In this variant of the Amor and Psyche story (recounted in Apuleius's *The Golden Ass*), a girl helps her impoverished family by agreeing to marry a white bear, really a prince enchanted by a troll (with a nose three ells long) whom he is doomed to marry if his marriage to the girl does not continue without problems for a year. The bear-prince's castle is magical—his bride can have anything she wants by ringing a bell—and he is himself magical—he is a bear by day and a man in bed with her at night. Soon the satisfactions of this magical world wear off for her, and she asks to visit her family. Failing to heed the bear's warning not to talk to her mother alone, she yields to her mother's insinuation that her husband might be a troll and that she should light a candle and see who is with her in their bed. Returning to the castle, she follows her mother's advice and thus loses the prince.

The main part of the story describes her attempts to find him "in the castle that lay East o' the Sun and West o' the Moon," to thwart his marriage with the troll, and to redeem him. In her quest she is provided with help by various magical helpers—first, old hags who give her a golden ball, a golden carding comb, a golden spinning wheel, and the use of magical horses; and then, the East Wind, West Wind, South Wind, and North Wind. Finally she succeeds in her task.

The magic in this story belongs to the symbolism of self-reference. It brings the girl into contact with the larger life in the form of her marriage with the prince and her journey borne by the four winds of the cardinal directions of a mythic world. The girl has had to break her tie of obedience to her mother, while being in a position to appreciate the paradox that by obeying her mother she produced a crisis that led to an extraordinary consciousness-expanding development that would not have taken place if she had obediently remained in the bear-prince's castle. She has come into relationship with the wise and powerful old hags (who might be vestiges of the mother-goddess world), and she has used wiles to defeat the evil troll. Again and again in the story, the ego of the heroine (as of the hero) must modify its intentions to accommodate them to the larger context being revealed. We might say that she (and the prince) are working on family fixations—outmoded patterns of behavior—and that the magic in the story is instrumental in freeing them from the compulsivity of those patterns and in enabling them to make meaningful use of this freedom.

Natalie Rose (discussed in part 2.7) provides a good example of magical barter, as she pays for her musical accomplishment by suffering fantasies of disaster and the phone calls of presumed friends who "dump" on her at length by telling her their sordid woes and "weirdnesses" on the pretext of asking for advice. But some further implications of such barter may be even more clearly seen in the life of forty-year-old "Genevieve Collins."

When Mrs. Collins drinks too much, as she periodically does, she takes it as a sign that something in her life is out of control. This "something" may be a variety of things, including her relationship with her children or her man friend, and various aspects of her work as an interior decorator. For her to feel in control she needs everything in her life to be perfect—this is a highly significant word in her vocabulary—with her work going well, her house well cared-for, and proper progress being made on various projects such as landscaping her lawn. She is an ardent list-maker, and if some things in her life are not perfect she at least has made lists of what is to be done about them. On the other hand, she hates her perfectionism and says she would like to "blast it out of my life."

When her analyst asks her to think about the history of her perfectionism, what comes to her mind is her wedding, which she wanted to be perfect. (After their marriage her husband gradually developed various kinds of bizarre behavior and finally killed himself.) She especially did not want her alcoholic uncle to come to the wedding and had a heated argument about this with her mother, though in retrospect Mrs. Collins finds this absurd. Surely she did not want her alcoholic uncle to spoil her perfect marriage for the same reason that she does not want her excessive drinking to spoil the perfection of her life. Still, she recognizes not only her drinking but also her perfectionism as the enemy. And in this regard her drinking could be said to serve the laudable purpose of subverting her perfectionism.

However the links between magical practices and psychopathological compulsivity should best be drawn, they are strong and real enough that "magical compulsivity" is more than a loose metaphor. Two magical powers—Mrs. Collins's perfectionism and her drive to drink—are pitted against one another. She is partly the agent of both—she does the list-writing and the drinking—but they are also largely autonomous, as are the magical powers summoned and coerced by a magician. She hopes for a magical barter: to use some of the power of her perfectionism to limit her drinking, so that she drinks just enough to compromise her perfectionism slightly and to get a bit of relief from its tyranny. But the opposing powers are entrenched in their own forms of relationship to one another.

Mrs. Collins moralistically condemns drinking, but her moralism is entirely compatible with the larger arrangement of driving powers in the sense that her moralistic efforts cannot protect her against them, and that they can use those efforts to initiate their own forms of interaction. She says that she would like to be able to drink occasionally and moderately. Alcoholics Anonymous would call this rationalization, but symbolically her desire represents the true solution to the problem of being free of the kind of moralism that would banish drinking from her life entirely, being free of compulsion, and being responsible and accepting of her imperfections, including those of being inclined both to drink too much and to be moralistic about it. This would mean giving up her moralism in favor of a more broadly ethical outlook. And it would require a more thoroughgoing self-transformation than she has so far imagined—much more like the one depicted in "East o' the Sun and West o' the Moon" than the one depicted in "The Doctor and His Pupil."

5.11 Original Sin, Transference, and Relationship

I close my discussion of Mrs. Collins by pondering the possibility that the doctrine of Original Sin might figure in an expanded conscious viewpoint that would help free her from her cramped willfulness. I do so in part because Original Sin wavers with such rich ambiguity between religious conception and the immediate subjective experience of being immersed in a field of magical powers.

Certainly the doctrine of Original Sin, owing to her strict Baptist upbringing, contributed to the etiology of her present condition. But the doctrine might also, at least in principle, be part of an emotional vocabulary that could be used to illumine her condition. After all, why not use the emotional vocabulary that is already there, if it can be made to serve? And in any case, Original Sin is one way of describing powerlessness, the admission of which is so important in the program of Alcoholics Anonymous. But to appeal to the doctrine of Original Sin, in this connection, would be to walk a very fine line, partly because one of the functions of magic—including magic in the extended sense of neurotic compulsivity—is to fight Original Sin when other psychological means have failed, and partly because (as we saw in part 5.5) when magic binds our imaginative capacities it does so by being coercive in ways related to bodily drives. One cannot break the compelling pattern by trying harder. One is not strong enough to try that hard.

Perhaps the doctrine, one might imagine, would provide a frame of reference within which to modify Mrs. Collins's perfectionism, since it might be thought that our native sinfulness dooms us to an imperfection needing to be thoroughly acknowledged and accepted before religiously sanctioned strategies for getting beyond it can be embarked upon. But even within this larger plan of action, the practical effects of the doctrine are almost unavoidably paradoxical—in ways suggested by the story of the charlatan who sold a peasant an alchemical recipe for making gold, adding, after taking the yokel's money, that the recipe would only work if he did not think of a brown goat standing on his hut and eating the straw thatches of its roof. Thwarting the psyche's propensity for self-validation—and provoking the gluey emotions appropriate as a response to this thwarting—Original Sin becomes the

211

brown goat that the imagination finds it impossible to get beyond. Trying hard not to try harder, the will tries harder.

Incidentally, the crossing of purposes expressed in the story of the charlatan has an ancient religious prototype in Yahweh's injunction to Moses, after the defeat of Amalek by the Israelites: "Write this action down in a book to keep the memory of it, and say in Joshua's hearing that I shall wipe out the memory of Amalek from under heaven." The Israelites, Yahweh declares, "are to blot out the memory of Amalek from under heaven. Do not forget" (Exod. 17:14; Deut. 25:19 [Jerusalem Bible]). Thus they are to make a memorial of what they are to forget—they are to try hard to forget what their trying hard to forget can only make unforgettable. The commentaries I have consulted neglect to say anything about these dark and pregnant utterances of the Lord.[61]

It can, of course, be objected that the doctrine of Original Sin is intended not so much to make people try harder as to make them aware of God's forgiveness, predicated on a fundamental need for it. If in this view we may already be trying too hard, we can instead try hard to try less hard. But we will very likely find ourselves left with the problem of remembering to forget Amalek—and the brown goat.

It is a notorious fact that the bad guys in stories are often more interesting than the good guys, and many people who read the "Inferno" of Dante do not get as far as the "Paradiso." In addition to interest, manifold psychic processes, including the complex play of identification and disidentification, shape our aesthetic response to a story and to a villain in it. It is thus one thing to interact imaginatively with such a villain—even if it is the devil of the Christian myth. It is another and very different thing to believe that one is oneself the villain from the outset, or from before the outset. In the latter case there is no story and hence no distancing; there is not the frame that a story provides, and hence villainy cannot be contained "out there" and related to. In the absence of this distancing and this frame, the condition of being a villain is meaningless.

Of course, as the argument of Fairbairn suggests, the doctrine of Original Sin may hold out at least a distant hope that some accommodation with the prevailing structure of values may be found. In this it serves something of the function of the hallucinatory light and hand mentioned earlier in connection with Jung's psychotic patients. (One might wonder, though, in what sense these patients, given the disintegration of their egos, could be said to have found their hallucinatory experiences meaningful.)

Readers of Dante's "Inferno" know that the sinfulness of the sinners portrayed in it was not bestowed upon them but was actively achieved as the result of choice. One may choose to sin, but one does not choose to be born in original sin. One may, of course, argue that original sin does not obviate free choice, that it indeed makes choice precious and imperative and leaves it free. Mrs. Collins, however, partly believes that she is free to drink too much or not, whereas for all practical purposes she is not. I grant that if Mrs. Collins were to think about original sin in a way that brought her to the conclusions of Alcoholics Anonymous, she might avail herself of their form of help—for AA does help many people. Yet her aim is not abstinence but flexible self-control, and to bring Original Sin into her attempts to attain this would be, as I have said, to walk a very fine line having implications with regard to major themes of this book.

Original Sin takes our defective creatureliness, which is relative, and makes an absolute of it, even while offering hope for a reprieve from it. Though presenting itself as starting out from a lack that can be made up, the doctrine rather, in effect, starts out from a lack that can never be made up. This is owing to the self-reinforcing perturbations of the spirit attendant upon conceiving of life under the aspect of deficit. (As we saw in part 5.8, "alive" cannot, except logically, be made to mean "not-dead.") In this way Original Sin readily has the practical result of minimizing our participation in abundance and undermining the basis for mutuality. Though the task is in principle possible, the charlatan alchemist has yet to find a peasant capable of not thinking of the goat he has been induced to imagine as on his roof.

The doctrine of Original Sin may be felt to loom just over the horizon from what analysts call an idealizing transference. The analysand in such a transference might feel, "I have a connection with this glorious person, my analyst; therefore, although I am a miserable wretch, and although my life is drab and constricted, and although my relationship with my spouse is boring beyond belief, everything is basically fine with me." There is justification by faith; there is justification by works; and there is justification by idealizing transference. Of course, for the analysand to think well of the analyst is necessary to their joint undertaking, and even idealization may for a time serve what is in the larger view a positive purpose. But its usefulness is limited, and beyond those limits it is sterile and stultifying. Mutuality and a sense of abundance are not idealization.

Some analysts who know the dangers of idealization also think, on the other hand, that the most promising precondition for progress in analysis is a so-called negative transference: the analysand's sustained projection of threatening psychic contents onto the analyst. This process may allow the analysand to learn useful things; but in years of concern with such matters—during which I have heard and read many case presentations extolling the therapeutic wonders wrought through negative transferences—I have seen no convincing evidence that such a transference provides a basis for the kind of transformation that Jung would consider part of individuation. That many analysts remain deceived about this may be owing to the pleasure they take in being brought into contact with their own disowned but fascinating aggressiveness. Some people enjoy being idealized; others enjoy being regarded as nasty—and being permitted to be nasty in the form of talking about nastiness.

Many analysts implicitly denigrate feeling by conflating transference and reality-based relationship in such a way that the latter is hidden from view. If an analysand comes to his appointment late, this may be a function of something in the transference. If he comes on time—indeed, if he comes at all—he is honoring a commitment to a reality-based relationship. Sometimes what may be regarded as negative transference is at the same time, and on a deeper level, a shrinking from such relationship. Mrs. Collins went to an analyst for a few sessions, then stopped, in part because to continue would be to concede that for her, too, mutuality might be possible, and because conceding this would jeopardize the whole arrangement of psychic forces and counterforces upon which she relies to cope with life as well as she does—an arrangement presupposing massive frustration to be defended against, and thus restricting the openness that mutuality would entail. To be open, she fears, would be to be defenseless.

Original sin and the various kinds of justification I have mentioned earlier are reminiscent of the donkey Eeyore (in *Winnie the Pooh*) and the justification of the existence of his tail. When offered the cheering explanation that he has a tail in order to whisk away flies, he replies that he would rather not have the tail and not have flies. He does, however, have both. Two thousand years of idealizing transference—and the self-abasement sustained by it—are an important part of the history that made most of us, in our part of the world, what we are. Their products are part of the reality of the psyche. But within these constraints we are free to search for better ways of understanding the human condition.

5.12 Religious Power and Magical Force

In 1940, amid the horrors of the Second World War, Simone Weil wrote an essay, "L'Iliade *ou le poème de la force*" ("The Iliad, or, The Poem of Force").[62] Her use of the French word *force*, as distinct from *puissance* and *pouvoir*, which have related meanings, is striking. Especially, she makes "force" mean something clearly different from "power" as (according to Gerardus van der Leeuw) the fundamental religious category. Some of her reflections making use of the term force have a bearing on issues treated in this section—and on power as a psychological reality.

Maintaining that force is the true hero, subject, and center of the *Iliad*, Weil defines force as "that x that turns anybody who is subjected to it into a *thing*." It does this by making a corpse out of him, but it also has the ability to turn him into a thing while he is still alive.[63] "Force is as pitiless to the man who possesses it, or thinks he does, as it is to its victims; the second it crushes, the first it intoxicates. The truth is, nobody really possesses it." In the poem the human race is not divided up into conquerors and the conquered; rather, every character is described as at some time bowing to force.[64]

It inevitably "happens that those who have force on loan from fate count on it too much and are destroyed," since they are unable to see that their relations with others amount to a balance of "unequal amounts of force." Those wielding force always "exceed the measure of [it] that is actually at their disposal." And then they are delivered up to chance and to Nemesis.[65] Force achieves its maximum effect when the tide of the day has turned and everything in the battle is rushing toward a decision. The battle is not decided by the man of strategy, it is decided by "men who have undergone a transformation, who have dropped either to the level of inert matter, which is pure passivity, or to the level of blind force, which is pure momentum." Hence the warriors are likened "either to fire, flood, wind, wild beasts, or God knows what blind cause of disaster, or else to frightened animals, trees, water, sand, to anything in nature that is set into motion by the violence of external forces."[66]

The poem is saved from monotonous desolation by scattered moments in which the human person possesses his or her soul in inner deliberation, courage, love.[67] In part owing to these moments, Weil sees a direct line from the *Iliad* through Greek tragedy to the Gospels: "He who does not realize to what extent shifting fortune and necessity hold in subjection every human spirit, cannot regard as fellow-creatures nor love as he loves himself those whom chance separated from him by an abyss. . . . Only he who has measured the dominion of force, and knows how not to respect it, is capable of love and justice."[68]

Striking in Weil's account of force is the impersonality of its field and its ambivalent character, sustaining life for a moment but being always lethal to its object as well as to the person wielding it.

We participate in what Bateson calls the "context" of the larger ecology within which we live our lives—a complex suprapersonal form of interrelatedness. And this interrelatedness is in important respects impersonal. (It may be more self-deluding than not to seek first and foremost for a personal meaning in having one's car stolen—"Why mine?"—in a city where cars are stolen every hour.) Yet this interrelatedness is personal, too, in the sense that all human knowledge is personal. And it may be necessary to give importance to that personal quality, even if doing so means thinking "magically." ("I was bullied into buying the car by a salesman who managed to get at the father complex that has stood in my way in living my life. Losing the car represents one further step in becoming my own person.") What Weil calls "force" is one aspect of this interrelatedness. And though force is impersonal, our relationship to it is also personal. But it tends to be personal in the wrong way, and here lies the crux.

Magic and Participating Consciousness

The warrior hopes to gain personal control over force, so that he can make others into things and thereby enable himself to remain a person. Many a magician has a similar hope—on behalf of himself or of his clients—even if it is expressed in the vocabulary of a highly textured and articulated world of spirits. Indeed, the warrior of the *Iliad*, too, inhabits a spirit-world, in which the ultimate actors, the precipitating causes, are the gods and goddesses. Though these are divine persons, the actions they initiate are worked out in the impersonal field of force, in which qualities of personhood are lost. Weil, in effect, attributes to both the wielders and victims of force a failure of imagination and feeling, and with that failure—to translate her terms into those of this book—an isolation of the ego from the self and from the principle of mutuality.

To acknowledge one's participation in the larger interrelatedness is to admit dependence. Moreover, it is to admit dependence within the field of force described by Weil. The price of admission into real life—as distinct from the half-life of the living dead—is high. Part of the price is recognition of one's implication in the lethal field of force. Weil writes, "Those who believe that God himself, once he became man, could not face the harshness of destiny without a long tremor of anguish, should have understood that the only people who can give the impression of having risen to a higher plane, who seem superior to ordinary human misery, are the people who resort to the aids of illusion, exaltation, fanaticism, to conceal the harshness of destiny from their own eyes."

Without the armor of the lie, the experience of force touches one to the very soul. "Grace can prevent this touch from corrupting him," Weil continues, "but it cannot spare him the wound."[69] We live, inescapably, in divided and distinguished worlds.

The mother of sixteen-month-old Amanda has learned much from her about force. Mother now knows that to encounter force head on by saying "no," like the Mosaic God, is to invite, and therefore to encounter, force as it issues from the depths of the human subject, contributing to that impersonal field. Relationship to that field—on the evidence of the *Iliad*—takes the form of self-deceiving will or ignominious submission, and relationship of one person to another within that field is constantly threatened by its encroachment. Amanda in her frailty succumbs to it and goes far toward overwhelming Mamma with it.

Amanda's refusal to engage anything other than Mamma—this refusal embraces Papa, Cat, Toy, and Storybook—is as uncompromising as the Mosaic God's refusal to countenance what he accounts as sin. Evil exists: Mamma does not do Amanda's will. Something must be done about evil—Mother knows that Amanda must be got interested in something other than her immediate misery. This could be called distracting Baby. But it also means reminding Baby that there is a larger world of interrelatedness that has aspects other than those of force—that her misery has a context in which personhood is, in principle, possible.

In praying that the cup pass from him, but then in bending his egoistic will to the will of God the Father, Jesus moves from a magical relation to force to a religious relation to power. In cultivating feeling and imagination in Amanda, Mother is helping to make her capable of related acts of self-transformation.

5.13 Higher Powers, Habituation, and the Unmasterability of Passionate Crisis

"Kate Madison" tries to deal with her binge-eating by joining a weight-reduction organization, but then shirks its meetings out of a fear of deprivation. She complains that her emotions, feelings, moods, are determined too much by things outside herself—the weather, how early dusk comes, a momentary success or failure in her work as a solicitor of funds for a charity. She would like to be more "in control" in having her emotional life determined more by things inside her. She would like to have a good day because she has planned to have one. After all, there is much truth to "as if": if one behaves as if one is going to have a good day, the chances are good that one will. And rather than simply be the victim of the things outside herself that determine her emotions, feelings, moods, she would like to interact with those things—accommodate herself to them, take the initiative in dealing with them, modify them when they can be modified.

Yet at other times she also complains of being too much in control. Primarily she means being too much in control of herself with regard to such things as tears, anger, and the sexual concerns about which she is prudish. She fears being out of control, which to her means looking ridiculous and having to feel ashamed. She sometimes controls other people, but when she does so it is because she is so afraid of losing control over herself that she reaches out to seize *anything* she can control. Her binge-eating would seem in part a strategy precisely for sabotaging her control, much as with the drinking of Genevieve Collins (discussed in parts 5.10 and 5.11).

When Mrs. Madison says that she wants to be more in control with respect to the things that affect her emotions, feelings, moods, her analyst reminds her of her earlier insistence that she already controls herself and others too much. She replies that one of the tenets of her weight-loss group is that one cannot by oneself control one's excessive eating, so that one's only hope lies in invoking a higher power. But then, the analyst thinks to himself, if this power—imagined as outside her—were to shift its locus so that it were inside her and in her control, it would no longer be "higher" in being a manifestation of the transcendent function, linking the ego to the self.

This is neither the first nor the last instance of such a crux to be discussed in these pages. I glance at this one as a prelude to reflecting about ambiguities characterizing our relations to higher powers, about feeling and passionate crisis, about emotion and symbol, and about the experience of consciousness when it is irradiated by an awareness of the self as supraordinate to the ego. I will be concerned with the bearing of the early mother-infant relationship on these topics.

Nat Pierce, a jazz pianist, tells a story about another jazz pianist he highly admired, Erroll Garner. At a recording session Garner continued improvising long after he had obviously flubbed something. Asked why he did not stop, Garner replied that he "just wanted to see how it would come out." About this Pierce remarks that "it's like he had no control. Like something was telling him he's got to figure this out. It was something higher up; it makes you want to believe in God because of this talent he had. He wanted to see how it would come out, not how he could make *it* come out; how *it* was going to come out by itself anyway, but he just wanted to be along with *it*."[70]

It is easy to want to be along with such an "*it*," such a clearly creative manifestation of the self. But what about the experience of

219

deintegration as also a manifestation of the self? When Mrs. Madison thinks of forgoing Hostess cupcakes and jelly doughnuts, she feels waves of impending panic—she succumbs to passionate crisis. The kind of control for which she longs—the assurance that her emotional life is being largely determined by things inside herself—might seem to accord with my description of feeling as expressive of the self that knows what is good for itself. But what she longs for is really a semblance of such feeling. And this semblance is in one sense at a further remove from the reality it mimics than it is from a good many other realities.

There can be no greater disappointment to the lover than to realize that what he has been revering in his beloved is the insubstantial semblance of his true heart's desire: Mrs. Madison's longing for control, and for having her emotional life dictated by things inside herself, is like the delusion still entertained by the soon-to-be disappointed lover. The relation of such a semblance to the reality to which it deludingly refers accords with a thesis maintained by Andras Angyal, a psychologist whose views deserve wider attention than they currently receive. Angyal contends that neurosis and psychic health may coexist in the same person, in such a way that the neurosis is a certain organization of the same elements that, differently organized, constitute the healthy personality.[71] Thus neurosis is a caricature of psychic health, and the autonomy that Mrs. Madison longs to have with respect to matters of emotional import is a caricature of differentiated feeling.

These considerations help to make clear why the emotional substrate of the personality—the pathic ground—must remain relatively autonomous with respect to the ego, why the ego must remain subject to passionate crisis, and why they must do so precisely to the end of individuation. They must do so because passionate crisis is the emotional aspect of the deintegration that benignly hinders the self-dystonic ego in its attempts to secure a hegemony for its one-sided attitude. Awe has been regarded as the primary religious emotion. It seems to me truer to say that the play of emotional life in its unmasterability grants—insists upon—access to the realm of higher powers, and that these, in turn, demand the cultivation of feeling.

Magic and Participating Consciousness

A recent moment in the life of "Maureen Evans" illustrates Angyal's view of neurosis and psychic health as different organizations of the same elements, while also showing something further about the interrelations of feeling, emotion, and higher powers.

Having taught for two years in the special education program of an elementary school, Mrs. Evans has resigned her position in order to complete a doctoral degree. She will support herself by tutoring children with learning disabilities. In her last day at school her heart began to race, and she felt a wrenching spasm in her back. Earlier, in moments of stress, she had had experiences of "flying away"—of seeming to leave her body—and of becoming rigid in her posture and facial expression. She could recognize these experiences as symptomatic but was powerless to do anything about them. In contrast, she knew that her racing heart and her back pain were *about* something, that they had a meaning, and that she needed to show them the respect of becoming clear as to what they meant. This brings us again to Spinoza's view that understanding the object of an emotion frees one from being its passive victim. But it is worthwhile to think more carefully about what *kind* of meaning her symptoms have.

Her back pain seemed to her quite clearly to have some such meaning as, "I have just got off my back a burden that ought to be off it, but my new freedom brings with it the insecurity of being without a regular paycheck, and is thus another back-straining burden." This kind of meaning is like an entry in a lexicon: back pain = burden of responsibility. But the pain in her back was not simply a wordless version of the kind of utterance made in ordinary language. Her pain was rather more closely related to the transformative symbols of such interest to Jung and so prominent in the writing about Jungian analysis.

Some dreams are clearly more about a whole stage of life, a needed major change of conscious direction, a pattern of fate, than about a momentary problem of adjustment. And such "big" dreams often include emotion-stirring symbols that resist reduction to the kind of meaning expressed by an entry in a lexicon. (The distinction I am making is relative, but its relativity does not make it any less practically real and important.) Such symbols conceal while also revealing. Rather than surrendering themselves to understanding in accordance with

221

one's prevailing conscious viewpoint, they retain their unmasterable otherness. Mrs. Evans's back pain has its meaning precisely because it hurt enough to provoke emotion relatively autonomous with respect to the ego. (Some physical symptoms such as mild headaches may acquire signal quality, may warn a person of a needed change of attitude, while inducing less intense emotion than Mrs. Evans's back pain. The degree of "loudness" required to get a message heard is relative. Mrs. Evans presumably needed a "loud" one.)

Emotion is symbolic in referring to an as yet undisclosed movement of the self. Given the relation of feeling to emotion that I have been proposing, to regard emotion as "symbolic" in this sense is further to link feeling with imagination.

Angyal compares the neurotic with a medieval knight so loaded down with armor that when he is knocked from his horse he is unable to get up from the ground by himself.[72] Accordingly, Mrs. Evans's back pain is neurotic in being symptomatic of her desire for a degree of autonomy—of independence—that is not realistic in view of the calculated risk she has reasonably decided to take in giving up her job. But her back pain is also a statement of her healthy self *about* the burden with which her neurotic self afflicts her. And it is the relative autonomy of emotion with respect to the ego that makes it symbolic. Thus her back pain, and the emotion engendered by it, expresses a movement of the largely unknowable self as the deeper center of the personality—bearing intimations of the self that knows what is good for itself.

Let us imagine that someone were to move through time and space to the premises of the Delphic Oracle when it was still a living cult, and were there to set up a vending machine dispensing copies of a book entitled "The Delphic Oracle Decoded." Such a book would presumably be based on an analysis of all known utterances of the Oracle, which it would analyze with respect to the rhetorical and psychological strategies manifest in them. The point of the book would be to translate oracular utterance into more rational and linear discourse, and to provide a means whereby any future utterances of the kind could be immediately "deconstructed." With its wisdom thus assimilated to the book in the vending machine, the Oracle would be reduced to one stage in a two-stage game of posing a partly predictable riddle and looking up its already clearly articulated solution.[73]

One of the most striking characteristics of religion is its tendency to petrification. One way in which it petrifies, and loses its capacity for effecting transcendence, is very much like reducing the Delphic Oracle by frequent application of "The Delphic Oracle Decoded," as living experience is attenuated in the course of being defined, pre-scribed, and surrounded by prohibitions. But the self, wiser than creeds and theologies, would keep the higher powers higher, would insist that the ego remain responsive to "the burst / And the ear-deaf'ning voice o' th' oracle, / Kin to Jove's thunder" (*The Winter's Tale*, III.i.8–10). It would do this out of its awareness that the ego is endemically more encapsulated and more confident in the adequacy of its assump-tions than it should be to serve the interests of the self.

To say the same thing another way: feeling issues are always emo-tional—rooted in the pathic ground, which occasions passionate crisis. And that they are this assures that we are referred again and again to higher powers, and that—by the appropriate activity of feeling—we recognize them as higher.

In speaking of "higher powers," I am assuming a fundamental connection between feeling and imagination, and am assuming that imagination recognizes the world as animated, full of powers, and that feeling evaluates them, recognizing some of them as "higher," to the end of drawing us into an appropriate form of relationship to them (or causing us to turn away from them). And I am assuming that imagination is itself a shaping power, in being both productive and selective. To need to select is to admit that there is too much. And this too-muchness brings us again to the unfathomable reservoir of beings in the background of perception, and the "fullness" of the mythic symbol (discussed in part 4.5), to the pathic ground (discussed in part 2.5), and to nonconsummatory mutuality as the experience of more than enough (discussed in part 4.1). And nonconsummatory mutuality brings us again to Mother and Baby. As I speak of Mother and Baby in this connection, I will have in mind the view elaborated by James J. Gibson that in perception the senses function in important respects as information-reducing systems—systems of selection—and

I will be concerned with the nature of independence and dependence within the mother-infant partnership of shared roles.[74]

Much of what I have said about the decoding of the Delphic Oracle, and have implied about the resulting increase of boredom, accords with what is known about habituation, which plays an important part in the interaction between the infant and its mother.[75]

The psychologist Daniel Stern has studied how the infant actively seeks stimulation, to which it attends. For the infant to attend to it, it must reach a hypothetical lower limit of intensity—a sound, for example, must have a certain degree of loudness. If the stimulation reaches a hypothetical upper level of intensity, the infant becomes excited—it reacts to the loud sound with aversive behavior. Within these limits an increase in stimulation typically results in an increase in attention—the infant gazes deeply at its mother's look of mock surprise. But within the mother-infant interaction, both the stimulating behavior of the mother and the attention of the infant tend to follow a curve of rising and falling intensity. And repetition of a stimulus tends to result in decreasing attention. (Thus, if in an experimental situation an infant is shown a bull's-eye pattern for thirty seconds, followed by thirty seconds in which the pattern is absent, and if this sequence is repeated a number of times, the infant will respond with decreasing attention, which will revive, however, if a new stimulus—say, a checkerboard pattern—is introduced.) This waning of attention is part of habituation.[76]

Habituation is important in freeing attention from such "background" phenomena as the ticking of a clock and sounds of passing automobiles. But habituation is important in another fundamental way as well. At first, the stimulation is for the infant primarily sensory, but by its third month, cognitive stimulation has become increasingly important. (If in a succession of tones of a certain loudness a softer tone is introduced, the softer tone will offer less sensory stimulation, but it will stimulate cognitively by offering a mismatch with the other tones.) Cognition entails awareness of a relation between a stimulus and a referent. This may be seen in rudimentary form in the infant's decreasing attention to repetitions of the bull's-eye pattern—the response of "Oh, that again." Habituation represents a midway point between sensory and cognitive stimulation, and is part of the process

224

by which internal schemata are built up, so that the infant can, for example, refer the appearance of its mother's face, now, to a mental representation of the mother's face in the past.[77]

I have mostly been talking about how the infant strives actively to assimilate information in such a way that it has a reliable measure of consistency. The mother greatly facilitates the process; and while she willingly introduces surprises into her play with her infant, she is also aware of the infant's need for consistency, and so tries to provide it. But in her relationship with her infant there are also what Stern has called "the virtues of 'messing up' "; these have a bearing on what I have said in this section about the positive aspects of passionate crisis.

As mother and infant attempt constantly to adjust their behavior to one another, they are in continual flux. Both the stimuli provided by the mother and the infant's attention repeatedly fall below an optimal level where interest is lost, and climb above an optimal level where aversion sets in. Then both mother and infant can bring their behavior back within the optimal range, where it fluctuates until the boundaries are again exceeded. Much of their play is spent crossing and recrossing the upper and lower boundaries.

By "messing up" Stern means that the mother, "more consistently than usual," crosses the infant's upper or lower tolerance boundaries; the "virtues" of such messing up are clear. Only when these boundaries are crossed must the infant execute some coping or adaptive action to change or avoid the situation or signal to the mother that something needs to be done. If the infant's behaviors are to develop fully, they require constant practice under varying conditions. And unless the mother risks exceeding a boundary, inadvertently or intentionally, she will be unable to expand the infant's range of tolerance for stimulation. "From this point of view," Stern writes, "the mixture of off days, good days, bad moods, high moods, going through the motions, faking it, and overcompensating is all part of the necessary panorama of real events that help the infant acquire the interpersonal skills of coping with social interactions."[78]

In other words, it is important for the unpredictable to remain partly unpredictable, and for the unmasterable to remain partly unmasterable; it is important for the "good enough mother" to remain

225

"bad" enough to violate many of her infant's expectations. And since social skills develop concomitantly with affective expression and understanding, it is important for the structures of affective life to retain the capacity for dissolution that helps them—and the ego—to keep in touch with the unpredictability and unmasterability of so much of experience. As the psychologist Carroll E. Izard remarks, "Whenever a particular emotion feeling does exit consciousness, one or more of those waiting in the wings immediately enters."[79] But for this to happen appropriately, the affective configuration that has occupied the stage must dissolve in the interest of the continuing drama.

To speak of higher powers is to allude to the principle of hierarchy so prominently at work in social relations and in our language and other forms of symbolism. What is higher is often in important respects independent of what is lower; an abstract legal principle, for example, is independent of the specific case to which it may be applied. But in another sense this independence may be tempered by interdependence; the American legal system, for example, is a modified version of Anglo-Saxon case law, in which the principles enunciated in the Constitution have ultimate authority, though what those principles really are and mean must be worked out with reference to specific cases taken to be representative. This example should suggest that the relations between higher and lower may be complex and ambiguous; indeed, they are sometimes paradoxical.

The independence of the higher—for example, as a certain natural law—from the lower—for example, as the physical manifestation of that law—and yet the interdependence of lower and higher: these relations are evident in a number of issues arising in science and the philosophy of science. (Of the thinkers concerned with them, Samuel Taylor Coleridge [1772–1834] is perhaps especially helpful in conveying a sense of such issues.[80]) The one that concerns me here is that of consciousness and its relation to the physical and psychic processes that support it. One could call these "lower" and it "higher," but doing so quickly becomes problematic. For example, one may conceive of "inspiration," entailing relative unconsciousness, as coming up from below or down from above, mediated by a messenger from the underworld or a heavenly Muse. The ambiguity of lower and higher in this instance suggests how elusive some of these issues are.

In this connection it is useful to consider the ways in which some thinkers—Angelus Silesius, Coleridge, Jung, and Sir Thomas Browne (1605–82)—have described the relation of consciousness to God and nature.

Angelus Silesius (alias Johann Scheffler, 1624–77) remarks, "I know that without me / God can no moment live; / Were I to die, then He / No longer could survive."[81]

Of Coleridge, Owen Barfield writes that there are plenty of people today "who can conceive of God in man, but very few to whom it means anything to speak of man in God. Yet Coleridge held that the one is correlative to the other; and that, unless we realise that, it is simply not meaningful to speak of 'God' in man at all."[82] God and man thus constitute a polarity for Coleridge.

Accordingly, man has been regarded as a necessary agent in "the becoming of God," as a complex of ideas widespread in the age of Goethe has been called. Indeed, the interrelated notions of the evolution of God and the dependency of God on human consciousness belong to a tradition of thought reaching from Meister Eckhart (ca. 1260–ca. 1329) through Angelus Silesius, Coleridge, Hegel, Schelling, and Franz von Baader to Jung, Max Scheler, and others in the twentieth century.[83]

Moreover, according to Barfield, just as Coleridge saw God and man as constituting a polarity, he also saw man and nature as constituting a related polarity, since "for him nature and the human soul were not two separate entities. Not only was their creation not two consecutive processes; it was not even two simultaneous ones; it was one and the same—nature being 'in' man no less than man is 'in' nature."[84]

These reflections provide a useful background against which to consider a personal experience that Jung recounts as "a confession of faith." His description of it conveys why he conceives of a self that is not identical with the ego (or, along psychoanalytic lines, with self-feeling or a particular "self-concept"), a self that is not simply subjective here, set over against an objective world there. Rather, for Jung the self implies and (as one might say) "asks for" consciousness, which is indispensable to the individuation in which the *telos* of the self is fulfilled. And self in this sense presupposes world and a

227

meaningful connection with it. Angelus Silesius and Coleridge conclude that God needs man in a way parallel to that in which man needs God; and Jung in this passage joins Coleridge in concluding that, to come fully into being, nature needs human consciousness. The passage implies a kind of conscious openness to the world that contrasts starkly with the instrumental intelligence Mrs. Madison often puts in the service of her self-manipulation and self-sabotage. Jung writes,

> I believe that, after thousands and millions of years, someone had to realize that this wonderful world of mountains and oceans, suns and moons, galaxies and nebulae, plants and animals, *exists*. From a low hill in the Athi plains of East Africa I once watched the vast herds of wild animals grazing in soundless stillness, as they had done from time immemorial, touched only by the breath of a primeval world. I felt then as if I were the first man, the first creature, to know that all this *is*. The entire world round me was still in its primeval state; it did not know that it *was*. And then, in that one moment in which I came to know, the world sprang into being; without that moment it would never have been. All Nature seeks this goal and finds it fulfilled in man, but only in the most highly developed and most fully conscious man. Every advance, even the smallest, along this path of conscious realization adds that much to the world.[85]

It is significant that the notion of higher powers insinuated itself into Jung's description, though now they move through "the most highly developed and most fully conscious man." I take Jung to be saying not that he himself is such a man, but rather that at this moment he had a powerful intuitive grasp of the purpose of consciousness in bringing the world fully into being. As the analytical psychologist Roger Brooke comments on this passage, "What is going on here is not to be found in Jung's 'psyche' but in the relationship between him and the world, that is, in existence itself. This is not to deny that the experience is made possible by an integration (momentary perhaps) of his psychological functions, or that it is incompatible with repressive, dissociative, or splitting tendencies. The experience is not, for example, sentimental or nostalgic. It is also true that the experience seems to be as humbling as exhilarating, in other words, it does not reflect an inflation"—an identification of the ego with psychic contents that improperly enlarge it.[86]

This reflection by Jung in the twentieth century was strikingly prefigured by one by Browne in the seventeenth: "The world was made to be inhabited by beasts but studied and contemplated by man: 'tis the debt of our reason we owe unto God, and the homage we pay for not being beasts. Without this, the world is still as though it had not been, or as it was before the sixth day, when as yet there was not a creature that could conceive or say there was a world."[87]

Jung's description of his experience in East Africa is striking in how personally he regards the relation between objective nature and the consciousness necessary to realize its existence and thus, as Brooke puts it, "to bring the world into being . . . in that individual and irreplaceable way that is one's personal destiny."[88] But there are many other accounts of an elementary relationship between nature and con-sciousness that, while presenting themselves as more impersonal, still imply the personal knowledge that Polanyi regards as irreducible. I wish to comment very briefly on three of them—the beginnings of Genesis and the Fourth Gospel, and a poem by Robert Frost.

The same God who in Genesis called light into being, divided it from darkness, and called it good—thus affirming the value of con-sciousness—first created the Earth as without form and void, and allowed darkness to be on the face of the deep. God's consciousness was implicitly at work in his creation of the prestage of the ordered world; and the intention of the narrator to praise a deliberate and conscious creation is implicit in the chapter as a whole, from the first verse. The Fourth Gospel puts the principle of conscious order at the very beginning of the account. Though the *logos* that was there at the beginning may have impersonal meanings, the term can also readily be used to refer to the sphere of personal and concrete words and actions. And however much drawing upon traditions of thought, the Gospel clearly expresses a personal vision—to be seen, for example, in its characteristic shaping of its narrative materials in accordance with certain interests.

The personal quality of Frost's "A Never Naught Song"[89] is evident in its whimsical title. It begins,

> There never was naught,
> There was always thought.
> But when noticed first
> It was fairly burst
> Into having weight.
> It was in a state
> Of atomic One.
> Matter was begun—
> And in fact complete. . . .

The "it" in the fourth line must be "thought," but if it was "fairly burst / Into having weight," it already has physical qualities, and is the object of some sort of physical process. "But when noticed first" raises the question of who or what noticed it: was there some sort of thinker somehow independent of the thought present at the beginning? The poem goes on to evoke a microworld "so infra-small / As to blind our eyes / To its every guise," and concludes by summing up the operation of the poem as a whole:

> So the picture's caught
> Almost next to naught
> But the force of thought.

It can only have been some equivalent of a person that "noticed first" this picture of a world "next to naught," but already complete, its creation inseparable from its coming into consciousness.

The humbling and exhilarating—and personal—qualities of such an experience as Jung's in East Africa relate to—draw upon residuals of—the mother-infant relationship. And I take the same thing to be in varying degrees true with regard to the other texts that I have related to the passage from Jung.

A moment ago I remarked that the self in the sense I have been elaborating presupposes a meaningful connection with the world. This connection is mediated by mothers, most of whom, according to T. Berry Brazelton and his collaborators, "are unwilling or unable to deal with neonatal behaviors as though they are meaningless or unintentional. Instead, they endow the smallest movements with highly personal meaning and react to them affectively. They insist on joining in and enlarging on even the least possible interactive behaviors,

230

through imitation. And they perform *as if* highly significant interaction has taken place when there has been no action at all."[90] I would comment only that, even when on the infant's part "there has been no action at all" corresponding to the mother's interpretation of its behavior, the mother's act of interpretation is meaningful in guiding the infant toward a form of affective understanding that implies intention, interaction, and mutuality.

To recognize higher powers as higher entails acknowledgment of the dependence that in various ways characterizes the relationship of mother and infant. The infant, of course, relies on its mother for the provision of its needs, and is in that sense dependent. But also, to be a "good enough mother," a woman must actively, if tacitly, know what it is to be an infant—must know an infant's dependence. Moreover, mother and infant together constitute a partnership of shared roles. In sharing these roles, mother and infant are interdependent, and to be interdependent is to be dependent. That interdependence implies dependence will be clear if one reflects that interdependence—mutuality—is annulled by the pseudoindependence expressed in Kate Madison's drive to control herself and others, and implied in Maureen Evans's back pain. It will also be clear if one considers our current mutually self-destructive depredation of the ecosystem on which human life depends.

If the infant may be presumed to experience nonconsummatory mutuality not as the reward of work but rather as a gift, so the mother may be presumed to experience it as such a gift. If the mother gives, so does her infant. Ethologists have described the physiological changes, including dilated pupils, induced in many women by the sight of an infant.[91] These changes amount to an opening, a reaching out. Opening and reaching out to Baby is paradigmatic of opening and reaching out to the world. Of course, Mother's opening and reaching out to Baby is finally inseparable from Baby's opening and reaching out to Mother. As Winnicott observes, *"There is no such thing as a baby"*; what one sees is "a 'nursing couple.' "[92] To open and reach out to the world in this way is to have it as a gift.

Mother is—imaginatively—a ground and a source (as may be inferred from the mother goddesses considered in part 5.8). But the infant, too, is a ground and source, symbolic of potentiality, futurity, hope.[93] That is, the infant, like the mother, may assume the form of a higher power. At moments it may not be hyperbole to say that an ordinary mother adores her ordinary baby. And certainly one of the dominant mythic images of Western civilization is that of a divinely chosen mother adoringly holding her divine child. (See fig. 6.) If we imaginatively make ourselves devotees of Mary, we are drawn into an act of adoration, that of mother and infant in their mutuality. And that adoration, activating our awareness of their deep intimacy, is an opening and reaching out to a free gift. The most common religious term for this free gift is grace, but whatever we call it, feeling must be activated if we are to apprehend it.

Differentiated feeling is concerned with qualities of gradations, transitions, continuity, and coherence. Just as Pascal could speak of a "logic of the heart," one could speak of a structure of feeling values. But feeling is concerned with these qualities and structures as affective currents bear upon them. Mother and infant in their mutual attunement and interdependence display the sensitive openness necessary to the proper development of such qualities and structures. But their relationship is also the space in which the full range of emotional reality gets played out. Such qualities and structures are subject to deintegration.

More generally, all of psychic reality, including feeling, is subject to the form of deintegration I have been calling passionate crisis. The infant falls apart, and its mother "messes up." Still, the falling-apart infant becomes recomposed, and in the larger picture, the "messing-up" mother copes well enough with Baby. Feeling recovers from passionate crisis. And feeling plays a special role in assuring that other forms of psychic functioning also do so. It plays this role owing to the tendency of feeling to value affective coherence and, generally, the more embracing view of things made possible by a recognition of interdependence.

5.14 Magic in *The Tempest*

Having discussed the close of *The Tempest* (in part 4.6), I will now turn to some aspects of magic in the play by way of illustrating issues I have just been discussing.

Fig. 6. Mary holding Christ Child. Mother and infant as the ground of transcendence in one of the dominant transformative symbols of Western civilization—Mary holding the Christ Child. Interdependence—suggested by the positioning of arms and hands—implies dependence—suggested by the Christ Child being held. The facial expressions of both figures are reflective—suggesting the receptivity of mother and infant to one another as a source and component of mature contemplation.

Feeling, Imagination, and the Self

First, a reminder of the basic situation: the dukedom of Prospero has been usurped, apparently because he spent too much time in his library and gave too little attention to state business, including intrigues. He has subsequently spent years on an island that he is able to control owing to magical lore recorded in a book he has brought from Milan, as well as to magical appurtenances of a mantle and staff. But the island also has its own magic. The creatures there when Prospero arrived—the bestial Caliban and the spiritual Ariel—had had intimate connections with a magic-wielding witch—Caliban as her son, Ariel as her slave. Prospero undertook to educate Caliban but ended by simply using him as a menial servant; he has freed Ariel but has made him the instrument of his magic. Both Caliban and Ariel want to be delivered from their servitude to him. Although Caliban is base, the audience feels at least some sympathy with him in his contention that Prospero is, in effect, a protoimperialist.

When a ship carrying his old enemies comes near, Prospero uses his magic to create a shipwreck that brings them to the island and puts them in his power. The island offers them the possibility of beginning anew, but most of them quickly demonstrate that they are imprisoned in their habitual ways as they devise nefarious plots. Prospero is in the position of the Revenger, a favorite figure on the Elizabethan and Jacobean stage, but he uses his power to reform all the bad characters except his own brother. At the close of the play they are all ready to return to Italy, with Prospero's daughter Miranda betrothed to the King of Naples's son—one of the good characters on the ship—and with Prospero contemplating a retirement in which "every third thought shall be [his] grave" (V.i.312).

Prospero's magic is complex, as we see in the opening scene. The storm is the product of a magical spell; yet it is a natural event. (There is the same kind of ambiguity in the Hopi rain dance, for example: do the Hopis "make" rain, or do they perform their ceremony when the rain is naturally going to come?) The storm is also a piece of stage magic calculated to impress its audience (the characters thrown into the sea) with the reality of powers beyond conscious control. Other pieces of stage magic occur later on, as spirits present playlets (discussed in part 4.6) that Prospero has devised for the edification of the characters from the ship. This seems the manifestation of his art that he values most highly, but he becomes so engrossed in his dramatic production that he almost forgets a conspiracy of the bad characters against him. That is, through his own fault he almost calls upon himself a repetition of the fate that befell him in Milan. In this we see again the same kind of ambiguity that I have been concerned with: the bad characters are bad partly because of a sluggishness of imagination from which Prospero tries to wake them, but to get too caught up in trying to deal with the world's dirty business in this particular way is to invite disaster. We are back again with the opposites of love and power.

I have said that the higher forms of imagination make use of primitive modes of psychic functioning. Thus Caliban can declare, even while showing the perversion of his will by taking part in the vicious plot,

> Be not afeard; the isle is full of noises,
> Sounds and sweet airs that give delight and hurt not.
> Sometimes a thousand twangling instruments
> Will hum about mine ears; and sometimes voices
> That, if I had then waked after long sleep,
> Will make me sleep again; and then, in dreaming,
> The clouds methought would open and show riches
> Ready to drop upon me, that, when I waked,
> I cried to dream again.

[III.ii.138–46]

There is surely a connection between these words and those of Prospero, shortly before he abjures magic, about spirits, towers, palaces, temples, even the globe itself, dissolving into air—words ending, "We are such stuff / As dreams are made on, and our little life / Is rounded with a sleep" (IV.i.156–58).

It is an important sign of Prospero's own development that as the action comes to a close he can admit of Caliban, "this thing of darkness I / Acknowledge mine" (V.i.275–76).

Miranda's relation to magic seems to me extremely important. Since infancy her only companions have been her magician father and the spirit-creatures of the island. She has participated in its magic without "doing" it—being simply a natural, though noble-born girl. Her most remarkable qualities are her capacity for wonder and her

235

expectation of goodness. This is not naiveté. It is rather a special form of right loving. (The task of right hating has been left to her father.) This special quality of Miranda is clear when she describes the sinking ship as "A brave vessel / (Who had no doubt some noble creature in her)" (I.ii.6–7). We have already been introduced to the swearing seaman and the cynical noblemen on board. What she knows intuitively is that the company includes the "noble creature," her future husband. In the language of Melanie Klein, Miranda represents the conviction that good objects will outweigh the bad. Other names for this are trust and hope. And right loving is impossible without it.

As the title of Jung's book *Modern Man in Search of a Soul* should remind us, to live in a deanimated world is sterile and meaningless. But when the world is overly animated, its animation must be lessened or controlled. Magic may play an important role both in the animation of the world and in its deanimation in the interests of certain kinds of ego strength. The attempt to control the animation entails all the ambiguities of power we have seen in Prospero's complicated use of magic. In any case, a time may come when the animated world has to be left, as we see Prospero leave it for the ordinary reality of Italy.

There is marvelous ambiguity in the last moments of the play. When Prospero has returned to ordinary reality his every third thought, as he puts it, will be his grave (V.i.312). But Miranda, too, leaves the island to be married. Thus a part of ordinary reality—with all its means and sometimes sinister preoccupations with power—will gain a new queen capable of wonder and love.

6 Receptivity, Commitment, and Detachment

6.1 The African Ideal of the Cool Heart

I now want to explore qualities of feeling, emotion, and interest that have been expressed by the metaphors of "hot" and "cool." I will be concerned with "cool" as a quality experienced in itself—the telephone directory is now "cool" for me, in that I am not now interested in it. But I will distinguish between this "cool" and "cool" in a felt relation to "hot"—some matters of interest are manifest in a cool-hot way, marked by a heightening of engagement and detachment. I will be concerned with forms of interest belonging less to the ego than to the self, and I will regard interest expressive of the self as independent of emotion but as registered by the ego in felt relation to emotion. By way of background, I will discuss sixteen-month-old Amanda's use of the "cool" word *bye-bye* in relation to the "hot" word *Mamma!* and then I will consider William James's "hot parts" of the field of consciousness, a traditional African conception of the "cooling of the heart," and Jung's view of psychic intentionality, especially as expressed in interest.

For Baby Amanda *bye-bye* first meant separation, which she often experienced as abandonment, when Mother left her with a babysitter, as she did regularly. The word then came to mean "separation, departure" more generally and more neutrally, for example as she said "bye-bye" not about anything clearly happening but apparently to signal stirrings of a sense of emotional import, including that of her own fantasies and thoughts. Thus *bye-bye* with connotations of abandonment by Mother now could also mean, "Something emotionally important might happen." Her little playmate Jeanine, whom she

237

called "Nina," suddenly disappeared from Amanda's life when Jeanine's family moved away. Amanda then came to use *Nina* in much the way she uses *bye-bye* as though pondering abandonment as an important prototype of emotional life in general.

Bye-bye as "something emotionally important might happen" would seem to retain its links with *bye-bye* as "abandonment by Mother," but when the prospect of abandonment by Mother seems to Amanda actual, the only word adequate to her incipient falling apart is *Mamma!* Thus, Father, Mother, some of their friends, and Amanda make a weekend trip to a strange town, and Amanda reacts anxiously to the strangeness by repeatedly crying "Mamma!" when Mother steps out of her sight, and also when in near-panic Amanda rejects the attentions of others trying to comfort her. Incidentally, the most intense of such moments occur when Mother goes alone to the bathroom: does she imagine that Mother might disappear with the water Amanda has often contentedly said "bye-bye" to as it has gone down the drain? She can, however, continue to say "bye-bye" matter-of-factly, for example, as a comment on preparations of the party to take a walk.

Moreover, Amanda's "Mamma-crises" (of crying "Mamma! Mamma! Mamma!" as she weeps large wet tears about the absence of her mother) can also have a primarily ritual character. Thus, with the weekend excursion over and Amanda at home again, she is quite content for Father to put her to bed for the night after Mother has left the house on an errand. But as Father is putting her to bed, she produces a loud but quickly ended Mamma-crisis, as though this is a formal part of the occasion of going to bed.

Though *bye-bye* retains for Amanda its implication of impending abandonment, she can use it, as I have said, in a more abstractly descriptive fashion (for example, about bathwater and preparations for a walk). But her use of the word—importantly but subtly—still implies a readiness for emotional immediacy even if that immediacy is at the moment only potential, as she maintains a detachment and an integrated ego state, while scanning emotional clues: it is not far from *bye-bye* to *Mamma!* Thus, her experience of emotion—now, or earlier, or as an imagined future possibility—is continuous with her reading of her present situation. And she reserves the right to a Mamma-crisis if matters of emotional import seem to her to be treated too matter-of-factly.

It would be one-sided and hence misleading to imagine that for Amanda a "cool" word such as *bye-bye* about a potentially "hot" emotional situation primarily serves the purpose precisely of cooling it and thus allowing it to be mastered defensively, with the cool word serving as a derivative and muted token of something hot in lived experience. And it would be one-sided and misleading to exaggerate this function of words more generally. It is true that words can be used coolly to such a defensive end—the word *peace* may be used calmingly in describing preparations for war, and such a use of words serves the ideal of scientific objectivity—but Amanda's use of *bye-bye* in relation to *Mamma!* suggests a more complex state of affairs.

Amanda's use of *Mamma!* in a brief ritual Mamma-crisis as Father puts her to bed is very much like a hot punctuation mark in a basically cool reading of her situation at the moment. The hot punctuation mark of Amanda's wailing cry of "Mamma" functions in the creation of a message saying something like, "I don't want Father to forget, and I don't want to forget myself, that the despair at the prospect of abandonment I am now demonstrating is an emotionally important possible implication of my going to bed." Demonstrating this implication means making sure that it has been registered and is, since just now asserted so dramatically, close at hand, available for speedy recall. More specifically, it is now part of an emotional frame of reference for a cooler reading of matters of more moderate interest that may or may not turn out to demand reference to that part—depending on whether the cool object of attention remains cool or suddenly blazes up. (I have discussed this kind of emotional frame of reference in part 3.1).

It is not just that—partly to repeat—the cool use of a word to defensive ends allows some kinds of mental operations, such as those of much science, to remain cool. Nor is it just that the cool use of a word, as a derivative and muted token of something hot in lived experience, makes exploration of the emotionally hot possible. (To be sure, words do serve this purpose. The drab and unwieldy language of psychoanalysis, for example, with its "mechanisms," "cathexes," and the rest, partly facilitates discourse by dulling interest in things that in lived experience or in another sort of description might prove distractingly exciting.) It is also that the hot use of a word may make exploration of the emotionally cool possible. (The emotionally vivid inflection of a blues singer awakens the interest necessary to an engaged yet detached exploration of matters that without that inflection might not command our attention. Waking up in the morning or walking down a road might seem commonplace. A blues singer may make them seem emotionally important even before his intent in mentioning them is clear. Advertising seeks to awaken enough emotional interest to get one to register what are essentially platitudes.)

Something may be interesting for many reasons, not simply actual or potential emotional heat. Still, *hot* and *cool*, as I have used these terms in my account of Amanda, have a bearing on interest, which plays an important role in the interrelations of ego and self and in the activities of each. This will become clearer as we briefly consider remarks by William James about "hot" and "cold."

James observes, "Things hot and vital to us to-day are cold to-morrow. It is as if seen from the hot parts of the field [of consciousness] that the other parts appear to us, and from these hot parts personal desire and volition make their sallies. They are in short the centers of our dynamic energy, whereas the cold parts leave us indifferent and passive in proportion to their coldness."[1]

Indeed, James's concern with the close connections among emotion, interest, and value leads him to a depressing view of experience from which they have been erased: "Conceive yourself, if possible, suddenly stripped of all the emotion with which your world now inspires you, and try to imagine it *as it exists,* purely by itself, without your favorable or unfavorable, hopeful or apprehensive comment. It will be almost impossible for you to realize such a condition of negativity and deadness. No one portion of the universe would then have importance beyond another; and the whole collection of its things and series of its events would be without significance, character, expression, or perspective."[2]

We have considered (in part 2.5) Jung's use of the term *affectivity* to describe the basis of psychic life, and (in part 2.6) Bernard of Clairvaux's special use of *affectus*, which stresses feeling as partly corresponding to affectivity, on the level of the self, but also as capable of development into feeling as a mode of the ego. James's "hot parts" of ego consciousness would seem to make these in part the expression of deeper psychic regions, since he surely does not mean that the heat of which he is speaking is created by the ego out of its own resources. He relates this heat to attention, which is in important respects ego-transcending, as anyone knows who has when tired tried to concentrate on a difficult book. Jung agrees with Eugen Bleuler that "attention is an aspect of affectivity, and does nothing more than what we know affectivity does, i.e., it facilitates certain associations and inhibits others."[3] Though attention and interest are partly different kinds of processes—I may be interested in something without attending to it now—what we mean by the two terms partly overlaps; in the condition of nonemotional negativity and deadness described by James, both attention and interest would be absent.

One must distinguish not only degrees but also levels of feeling, and to do so allows one to align interest with feeling, both in relation to the ego and, on a deeper level, to the self.

The qualities of experience represented by the compound term "interest-excitement" have been thought to constitute "the most frequently experienced positive emotion, providing much of the motivation for learning, the development of skills and competencies, and for creative endeavor."[4] It has also been maintained, persuasively, that "the characteristic mark of interest seems to be a desire to *know* rather than to have or possess," and that "the first movement of the desire to know seems to be attention."[5] Still, one may be just interested enough in the ads that line the bus for one to glance idly at one or another before turning to one's newspaper. But there are much deeper levels of interest.

The ability to work and to love—which Freud thought it the aim of analysis to enhance—is subject to vicissitudes that imply interest or disinterest not so much on the level of the ego as on that of the self. And although the two levels are interrelated, it is on that of the self that the psychic intentionality I will discuss more explicitly in a moment is located. Thus, "Jean Calhoun," who has been the most successful salesperson in her business firm, finds herself unable to go on with her work. All reasoning about the necessity of getting a grip on herself is to no avail, and she faces the prospect of having to move to a nonselling job in her firm at half her present salary. Her prudent ego tells her to try harder. Her total inability to do so will tell her, when she is ready to listen, that interest has disappeared from her work as into a black hole. And thus, a psychotherapist might try to get clues as to Mrs. Calhoun's interest on the level of the self by asking, "If you are not interested in your work, what *are* you interested in? What can you imagine doing right now instead, and what can you imagine doing ten years from now? Have you had dreams and fantasies that might say something about where your true interest lies?"

And thus, "Professor Roderick," having spent a sabbatical in Denmark, and being given another opportunity to spend a year away from his American university, arranged to return to Denmark. Later judging the year as largely wasted, he realized that his decision to return to Denmark had been largely automatic—as though he had thought, "Being in Denmark was interesting once and so must be interesting now"—and that if he had put aside his preconceptions, or had examined them, he would have spent the year in Chicago. He had not given voice to his deepest interests as he planned the year.

Thus, further, "Robert Wilkins," who has consulted a psychotherapist about his eroded marriage, with uncontrollable distaste breaks off even trying to talk about "working on the relationship," and hears himself declaring emphatically that he is devoid of the slightest interest in his marriage, that he profoundly, from the bottom of his soul, does not care, that all he wants is *out.*

Thus, Amanda's Mamma-crises are expressions of deep and intense interest in Mamma, and of Amanda's awareness that the indispensable unfolding and articulation of the ego in relation to the self are taking place primarily between her and her mother and only very secondarily in her relations with others. When Amanda refuses to let her father put her shoe on because she wants Mamma to do it, or when she refuses to tolerate a grown-up conversation between her parents, one may rightly say that she is enviously trying to possess and control her mother. To say this is to see her behavior under the aspect of her avariciously willful incipient ego, little capable of dealing with restraint and frustration. But one might also see her behavior under the aspect of the self that knows what is good for itself (discussed in part 4.3), intent on securing the conditions most essential to her development. It is from this deep level that her intense interest in Mamma arises.

And thus, finally, "Samuel Todd" turns his life upside down and courts obloquy and ruin by insisting on being with a woman seemingly meant to be his companion by the interest-guiding self. To say that his interest in her draws on the same psychic levels as Amanda's in her mother is to say nothing against the wisdom of his actions.

Hot can express aggressiveness—*hot-headed, hot under the collar*—or sexual urgency—one Shakespearean character (Leontes) exclaims, "Too hot, too hot!" about his wife's imagined lewdness, while another (Prince Hal) pictures the sun as "a fair hot wench in a flame-colored taffeta." As Jung observes, heat can represent one's "inner affectivity" in general, fire being "the symbolical equivalent of a very strong emotion or affect."[6] Since one is subject to such emotion —is compelled by it—it seems fitting to Jung that the Stoics should link heat, to them (with light) the basic expression of life, with *Heimarmene*, or fate, as the compulsion of the stars.[7] As Jung observes, "When the libido [or psychic energy in general] . . . remains fixed in its most primitive form it keeps men on a correspondingly low level where they have no control over themselves and are at the mercy of their affects," precisely as the " 'unredeemed' soul" is subject to planetary influences.[8]

Thus heat is often symbolically linked with psychic forces having a measure of automatism with respect to the ego. Surely when James speaks of "hot parts" of the field of consciousness, he is assuming that they are directly or indirectly related to important functional elements that are unconscious and automatic.

Automatisms of heat, light, and flame are important in religious symbolism in such forms as the burning bush and the countenance of Moses, the fiery tongues descending from heaven at Pentecost, and auras and halos—all expressive not of the "unredeemed soul" but of an afflux of some sort of "higher" power. And so heat can play an important constructive role in relations between ego and self. Accordingly, Jung writes about Chinese alchemical instructions for creating the "diamond body" symbolic of the self under the aspect of integration: " 'Heating' is necessary; that is, there must be an intensification of consciousness in order that light may be kindled in the dwelling place of the true self," an intensification that is also that of life, since conscious life is the goal of the process.[9]

James's "hot parts" of the field of consciousness can now be seen to have a significant role to play in the ego's awareness of its important, indeed necessary, but also subordinate position within a larger psychic reality. This larger psychic reality includes constraints comparable to planetary influences; but supraordinate to these, as also to the ego, is the self as the deepest level of one's fate. As Jung remarks, "The power of fate makes itself felt unpleasantly only when . . . we are no longer in harmony with ourselves," that is, when the ego is no longer responsive to the integrative workings of the self.[10]

Yet it is entirely possible to live an illusion of being in harmony with oneself—the psyche has resources enabling the ego evasively to disown conflict and legitimate responsibility. And in this light, the ego-dystonic qualities of affectivity may maintain pressure on the ego to remain alert to its own potentiality for complacency. But just as favorable relations between ego and self cannot be reduced to a steady state, so passionate crisis cannot be entirely appropriated to the ego and made a reliable instrument of comprehensible and clearly helpful advice—although ignoring emotion often enough invites disaster. The energy value of emotion—and with it the capacity of emotion to challenge assumptions, to enliven, to motivate, and to be registered in suitable forms of feeling—is proportionate to its capacity for potentially destructive upheaval. The life of feeling and emotion is a game played for large stakes, and not with matchsticks but with real money.

The field of consciousness, with its "hot spots," may blaze into ego-dystonic passion needing to be cooled—as was the case with Leontes when he cried out, "Too hot, too hot!" Fortunately, *cool* need not imply lack of interest. Indeed, there are kinds of cooling that lead not toward valueless negativity and deadness but toward the differentiation of feeling. In parts of Africa such cooling and the resulting coolness are carefully articulated conscious values.

Among the Yoruba of Nigeria, "coolness" (*itutu*) is an important aesthetic and ethical quality, manifest in artistic execution and in religion—for example, in conciliatory words to angered deities—but finally inseparable from personal character, in which it may appear as

244

gentle generosity.[11] Indeed, "the semantic range of the concept 'cool' in thirty-five Niger-Zaire languages" includes the meanings "calm, beauty, tranquility of mind, peace, verdancy, reconciliation, social purification, purification of the self, moderation of strength, gentleness, healing, softness (compared to cushions, silk, even the feel of a brand-new mattress), silence, discretion, wetness, rawness, newness, greenness, freshness, proximity to the gods." The concept "is a matrix from which stem ideas about being generous, clear, percussively patterned, harmonized with others, balanced, finished, socially perfected, worthy of destiny." Robert Farris Thompson offers this summary under the heading, "Coolness: Truth and Generosity Regained."[12]

The importance of this African ideal of coolness can be seen with special clarity in drumming. Inferior African drummers play "by heart," the Dagbani word for this being *yirin,* meaning such things as "unnecessary, rude, rough, meaningless." Thus drumming "by heart" can be energetic and forceful but graceless. The contrary of this quality is *baalim,* which means "cool," not as water is cool, but rather slow or gentle. This word can be applied widely, so that someone may be said to walk *baalim,* and if an electric fan is running too fast, one may make it *baalim,* may slow it.

Someone playing the drums *baalim* may use much less force than someone playing "by heart," and the former will not grow tired as will the latter. One African drummer comments, "The one who has learned well, he plays with understanding, and he has added his sense and cooled his heart; if he is beating hard, it will be more than the one who is using only force to play."[13]

According to one African people, "music cools the heart," and the coolness thus attained entails an awareness of ethical and spiritual principles. "Without balance and coolness," a Western specialist in African drumming writes, "the African musician loses aesthetic command, and the music abdicates its social authority, becoming hot, intense, limited, pretentious, overly personal, boring, irrelevant, and ultimately alienating." Coolness is manifest as "collectedness of mind rather than self-abandonment," and "dialogue is essential for the [cool] avoidance of overstatement and isolation."[14] Though with a very different emphasis, this cooling of the heart is surely related to Bernard of Clairvaux's ordering of the affections.

The African notion of coolness as an aesthetic and ethical category qualifies James's use of *hot* with its implications of impending emotional urgency. And this qualification is helpful with respect to interest, which may be experienced in relation to emotional heat—"a burning passion for books"—or coolness—"a cool regard," "a dispassionate weighing of evidence." These examples should remind us that there can be no hot without the potentiality for cool, and no cool without the potentiality for hot, and indeed that hot and cool may describe different aspects of the same phenomenon of interest: a burning passion for books may be cool; a cool regard may imply the heat of anger; a dispassionate weighing of evidence may be impassioned.

Interest as an expression of the self is, I propose, experienced in implicit relation to the hot and cool of emotion and feeling, but is independent of them. Jung's view of psychic intentionality helps to clarify the distinction I have in mind.

In *Symbols of Transformation* Jung proposes a view of psychic energy, or libido, as "intentionality" (in the German original, *Intendieren*), "an energy-value which is able to communicate itself to any field of activity whatsoever, be it power, hunger, hatred, sexuality, or religion, without ever being itself a specific instinct." Insisting that "the concept of libido as desire or appetite is an *interpretation* of the process of psychic energy, which we experience precisely in the form of an appetite," Jung compares psychic energy with Schopenhauer's "Will as a thing-in-itself," knowable only in its phenomenal manifestations—in what it does. The transcendent character of the creative force known only by subjective experience is for Jung also borne out by the mythic forms and images used to symbolize this force—among them the cosmogonic Eros of Hesiod, the Orphic Phanes ("the Shining One, the First-Created, the 'Father of Eros' "), and the Indian god of love, Kama.[15]

In his reflections on the nature of libido, Jung quotes a long passage by Freud in which Freud wonders whether libido might not coincide with interest in general, a conjecture that Freud rejects in favor of his previously enunciated theory of the sexual nature of libido.[16] Jung clearly means to imply that Freud was on a more promising track in this conjecture than in his rejection of it. And the interpretation of psychic energy as being basically manifest as interest implies a link

Receptivity, Commitment, and Detachment

between the psychic intentionality described by Jung and what I have called interest expressive of the self—and have illustrated by vignettes of Jean Calhoun's problems about work, Professor Roderick's wasted year in Denmark, Amanda's Mamma-crises, Robert Wilkins's apathy about his wife, and Samuel Todd's commitment to the woman he deems meant for him.

Since interest cannot for the most part be created by the ego—as Jean Calhoun and the others I have described are in an excellent position to attest—the question of where interest as expressive of the self is going, where it *wants* to go, is important and often urgent. The direction and objects of one's truest interest are largely determined by unconscious psychic contents and processes, and in any case, the question of where my interest is going is inseparable from the ultimately unanswerable question of who I am. And so it is by being interested that I know what my interest is, but to know where my interest is going, and where it ought to go, is for me to face the unfathomability of both ego and self. Still, the play of feeling and emotion, with its hot and cool, gives approximate knowledge of the direction of interest as expressive of the self. The unpredictability of passionate crisis may help the ego to avoid the mistake of thinking that the direction necessarily accords with the ego's settled assumptions, and may help the ego to remain responsive to the self.

In my use of the terms *hot* and *cool* I am assuming a link between James's "hot parts" of the field of consciousness, in which value is experienced as interest, and the self as the deeper source of interest, but also of deintegration and passionate crisis. And I am assuming *cool* primarily to mean the result of the cooling of the heart, the ordering of the affections, the differentiation of feeling. Hot and cool in these senses are intimately related: coolness is cooled heat—just as the cooled Yoruba god is the angry god conciliated.

In this connection it is notable that jazz music was for decades "hot," until the extraordinary tenor saxophonist Lester Young replaced the term *hot* by *cool* as the expression of an aesthetic ideal and a term of approbation. The marvelous lyricism of his best playing was certainly not simply "cool," but "cool" in felt relation to "hot," like a cool breeze on a hot day. His use of *cool* spread in jazz parlance and from thence to the slang of teenagers, who used the term to call attention

247

to something of momentarily intense, though perhaps in the larger view quite mild, interest. Still—despite some erosion of meaning through this particular kind of popularization—metaphors of heated cold and cooled heat, cognate with that of the African cooling of the heart, retain their potency in jazz and the blues. (See figs. 7 and 8.)

There are, as well, ego-defensive forms of cooling and coolness sustained by such means as abstraction. These are no longer intimately related to heat, and they amount to an attenuation of feeling and of the ego's relation to interest expressive of the self. The specter of James's negativity and deadness hovers over these forms of cooling, as they hover over a crumpled bus transfer on the sidewalk. Individuation—the optimal development of the personality—demands that they as much as possible be sacrificed in the recovery or discovery of proper modes of feeling.

To speak as I have been doing of emotional hot and cool is to be highly metaphorical but also to approach baby language. (Baby understands *hot.*) My reason for speaking this way is related to Jung's in using such terms as *shadow* (as a name for certain kinds of ego-alien psychic tendencies) in order to avoid pretending to be more abstractly scientific than one can be and still be true to important qualities of lived experience. Indeed, it is striking that many people find it easy to believe, mistakenly, that a term such as, say, *ideo-affective structure* is less metaphorical than emotionally *hot* and *cool,* and closer to objective reality—presumably because closer to the condition of valueless negativity and deadness James asks us to try to imagine. In any case, one could bring emotionally *hot* and *cool* into relation with terms I have been using by saying that *hot* and *cool* in their interrelatedness are accents of value communicated (at least at first) affectively. They are especially important in granting approximate knowledge of interest expressive of the self.

It is true, of course, that a great many capacities may be brought to bear on the question of where psychic energy is going, and where it ought to be going. Thus, whatever the emotionally hot and cool is about may turn out to be describable in nonaffective terms, including those of intellect. (Analysis may sometimes, but then may also sometimes not, disclose an intellectually statable cause of someone's depression.) But Bernard was, I believe, right to imply—in my psychological

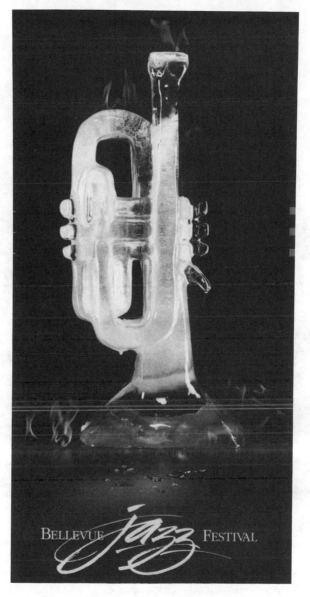

Fig. 7. Jazz trumpet of burning ice. This image suggests passion, control, and freedom—and form existing in tension with the force of its own dissolution. And so the image could be taken as that of an act of feeling within the more general context of emotional life. (Such acts of feeling are discussed in part 6.8).

249

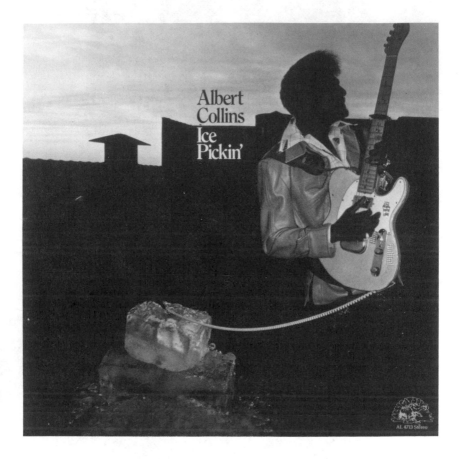

Fig. 8. Blues artist Albert Collins, with his amplified guitar represented as plugged into a block of frozen fire. His band is called "The Icebreakers," and titles of his record albums and tunes often play upon notions of ice and cold and coolness (*Ice Pickin'*, *Ice Cold Blues*, *Cold Snap*, "Frosty," "Sno-Cone," "Cold, Cold Feeling," "Frost Bite," "Icy Blue," and "Deep Freeze"—but also "Hot 'n Cold," "Melt-Down," and "Thaw-Out"). Ice should (symbolically) be picked, broken, melted, or thawed, but it retains the positive value of its capacity for cooling. Toward the end of a searingly impassioned performance, Collins sometimes touches the hands of members of his audience. His hand at such moments feels remarkably dry and cool.

250

translation of him—that affection has the potentiality of providing the best possible reading of the intentionality of the psyche. Affection—or feeling—does not share this distinction with intellect. To understand why this is so, we should recall that affective communication between mother and infant is the basis of their relationship, and that the self, as manifest in that relationship, "knows" more immediately and accurately things of great import than do some more clearly ego-based functions that develop later. (Think, say, of the scientist absorbed in his work who does not know whether or not he has eaten lunch and is unaware of stresses and strains deep within him, and is thus ignorant of conditions to which Mother and Baby would be highly attentive.) And what is true of the knowing that is responsive to the self in the mother-infant relationship continues to be true of feeling.

6.2 Interest and Archetype, and the Voice of the Self

I have spoken (in part 6.1) about the mythic forms and images that Jung took to be symbolic of the fundamental life-force or libido. These have an important and complex bearing on interest and affective accents of value. Such mythic forms and images he came to call "archetypes," a term calling attention to important qualities of lived experience but also raising problems. I will briefly discuss some of these qualities and problems—also problems posed by the use of the term *archetypal* by other writers—in relation to feeling, emotion, and interest, and to issues discussed earlier in this book.

Archetypes I take to be mythic forms and images structuring relations between ego and self and between individuals and their world. Archetypes can perform this structuring because they have the potentiality of touching the affective level of the self that is also the level of deep interest.

One can be emotionally seized (in German, *ergriffen*) by archetypal images, and Jung often emphasizes this form of relation to them. But emotional seizure is often at the expense of feeling, concerned with gradations, transitions, continuity, and coherence. And saying this brings me to an ambiguity especially common in the history of religion.

251

Feeling, Imagination, and the Self

Religion is often characterized by states of emotional seizure (*Ergrif-fenheit*)—the ecstasies of shamans and mystics, the striking down of Saul on the road to Damascus—but religion is also a fundamental force for the cultivation of feeling. (The shadow side of religion—its brutalities, indecencies, and idiocies—says nothing more against this than that everything human has its shadow side.) The ambiguity of which I just spoke arises owing to the necessity on the one hand for psychic energy to be directed and redirected by images strong enough to direct it and redirect it—archetypal images—and on the other for feeling to live in accordance with its own principle, enlivened by those images, which can also, however, obstruct it as they become tyrannically compelling or as they petrify. Archetypes are like magical and religious powers in being capable of weal or woe.

In agreement with Fordham, I take the self to be supraordinate to archetypes. (See part 2.5, n. 16.) They serve as something like strong signals within a communications network based on the affective level of the self and on the interest expressive of the self, as that interest is manifested within the domain of the ego.

In calling archetypal images "mythic," I mean to say that they are of more than personal significance, that they ground such significance in a world shared with other persons. Still, they have no significance at all—except, say, as matter for a dull textbook—unless personal significance is brought to them and invested in them. That is, much of the significance they have for me they have because I bring it to them; and their significance is relative to my interests, my desires, my condition. That is, the self, supraordinate to the ego, is also supraordinate to archetypes. And the ego and the self in their interrelations determine which archetypes are to be constellated—which are to be invested with emotion and made interesting. But archetypes do not of themselves generate interest, a point to which I will return.

Archetypes are pictures of situations, implicitly including two or more persons or part-persons—they are bipolar—and they are patterns for the canalization of emotion. The bipolar nature of the archetype is well illustrated by "Jack Wolfstone," who was in his view the rebel in his family, especially in relation to his wealthy, dour father. After completing college, in which he majored in sociology and economics, he adopted a philosophy of "voluntary poverty," while working in

252

various organizations for social reform, in one of which he managed to depose the director, and in all of which he fought vigorously to maintain his views and even force them on others. Later, entering the world of government and business, he resented the meagerness of his salary, much as he did his father's failure to show him any signs of love. In what he recognizes as his refusal to accept the world as it is, and in his striving to bend others to his will, Mr. Wolfstone is what could be called a "rebel-tyrant." Has not history been greatly shaped by such archetypal rebel-tyrants as Napoleon?

The way in which archetypes canalize emotion can be seen in the declaration of Indian prime minister Indira Gandhi shortly before her assassination, "If I die, my blood will invigorate the nation." During the student protest demonstrations of the late 1960s, one protestor at the University of Washington employed the same figure of speech: "I can see that some of you hate me; some of you would probably even like to kill me. Even if you kill all of us, you cannot stop us, as our blood will nourish the Revolution." And one of the postage stamps issued by the Iranian government to commemorate the Islamic Revolution of 1979 depicts drops of blood falling to nourish a red tulip with a green stem and leaves—red standing generally in these stamps for blood and sacrifice and green for Islam. [17] Indira Gandhi, the student orator, and the Iranian graphic artist thus made persuasive use of a transformative image, allaying potential fear and replacing it with hope of participation in a superpersonal force and of membership in a community informed with that image. This blood symbolism is related to that of the Christian eucharist, which (with the necessary qualifications) is in turn related to human sacrifice among the Aztecs; and the thought pattern expressed in these various ways is present in some forms of altruism and in some delusions of the insane. As structuring principles, archetypes can serve a broad range of cultural and personal ends.

I have two main reasons for emphasizing the bipolarity of archetypes and their participation in the principle of hierarchy. First, bipolarity and hierarchy are of fundamental importance in the domain of language and reason. And second, they are of fundamental importance in emotional life, especially in differentiated feeling, with its capacity for making complex feeling-judgments. That these two domains are to a significant degree potentially compatible is suggested by the compound word *mythology* (from *mythos* plus *logos*) and by my discussion (in part 2.9) of the logical and alogical halves of the soul. Assertions about their compatibility need to be qualified by a recollection of what I have said (in part 2.5) about the pathic ground and (in part 2.7) about the unfathomability of the heart, as well as (in part 2.5) about the impossibility of reaching by any means, including language and reason, whatever the world *is* beyond our emotional and interested involvement in it. ("It will be almost impossible for you to realize such a condition of negativity and deadness" as the world would present without such involvement; and what would prompt us to try?[18])

The illusory forms of oneness of which I have spoken (and which I will explore further in part 6.6) are well demonstrated, as is one important source of archetypes, by the views of the utilitarian philosopher Jeremy Bentham (1748–1832) about certain qualities of language that are created by "archetypation." An example is *Church*, when it is used as a general term subsuming subclasses and obscuring the fact that it is doing this. *Church* functions in this way when it names both the subject many and the ruling few. "When," as Bentham observes with crabbed eloquence, "for the purpose of securing in favour of both parties, and especially of the ruling few, the affections of respect and fear, then would the import of the word open itself, and to such an extent as to include under one denomination the two parties whose situations and interests were thus opposite."[19] Just as it would be important for Jack Wolfstone to understand that "rebel-tyrant" is psychologically a single thing having two distinct if interrelated aspects, so for some purposes it would be important to recognize that laity and clergy have some quite distinct interests within the church.

It is true that language develops on the basis of prelinguistic psychic processes, that images precede words and retain a special potency in psychic life, and that some mythic images activate prelinguistic psychic levels—so transcending rational discourse. This does not mean, however, that such mythic images are "archetypal" in the sense of constituting an exclusive class divorced from language, with its arbitrary and idiosyncratic features, and with such interwoven functions as demonstrating, defining, evoking, persuading, emotion-expressing, emotion-inducing, and lying. Language places us in the world while

254

separating us from it. Archetypes (as we will see) in some measure do overcome that separation, but also in large measure do not. (Mr. Wolfstone's rebel-tyrant pattern places him in the world while separating him from it.) With and despite archetypes, we live in uncertainty, the precondition of passionate crisis, our potentiality for which is an inescapable part of our openness to the world.

The way in which archetypes do ground us in the world—ground us in a larger context, to use Bateson's term—may be seen in our relation to what could be called strong forms of nature, such as the proportions of the so-called golden section. Such forms appear again and again in countless variations, owing to the inherent qualities that make them "strong." Since we find some of the same forms aesthetically pleasing, they also appear again and again in countless variations in works of art.[20] I understand archetypes to include such strong forms and our inclination to respond to them in certain ways. To say this is to imply that our affective natures presuppose a significant degree of "fit" between the human organism and the environment, and that the subject-object dichotomy of our instrumental intelligence develops on the basis of our potentiality for feeling, with its concern for gradations, transitions, continuity, and coherence. But our instrumental intelligence must and *does* develop; there is no way out of participation in divided and distinguished worlds. *Homo religiosus*, religious man, may seek the One, but *homo homini lupus*, man is a wolf to man. The same Hamlet who invokes grace and ministering angels could drink hot blood; at least these two Hamlets occupy the same person. If such self-division is our fallen state, it is thoroughly presupposed in any attempts to imagine or otherwise gain access to whatever unity and coherence there might have been or might be before or beyond that state—much as the description of the Creation in the first verses of Genesis presents a human, "factual," "historical" account of what happened before anyone was there to see it, so that the narrator's vantage point before the Fall is thoroughly paradoxical or fantastic. (And duality follows him even there: "In the beginning God created" two things, "the heaven and the earth.")

Though further reservations about the term *archetype* are still to come, it does—with its implications of primacy and priority (Gr. *archē*)—have the advantage of implying that such forms may in some sense be regarded as generative, as belonging to the order of final causes that have, since Aristotle, again and again figured in accounts of human motivation—and that, I believe, stand no chance of being banished by the various forms of behavioristic psychology.[21] (The wide appeal of Jung is to a large extent owing to his concern with psychic purposiveness.) One could speak of a disposition of this or that archetype to be embodied—for example, when the prevailing worldview of a person or group is being replaced by another, compensatory to it and based on different principles, as when a church-educated "good boy" becomes as an adolescent a sex-obsessed rogue-criminal, or when the pagan pantheon succumbed to Christianity. To speak of archetypes as dynamic forms in this way is not, because of their "firstness," to assign them to a supercelestial place in which they mediate between this divided world and the One—the problematic unity I have been discussing. Rather, archetypes are what they are, and are constellated or not, and have whatever character and effects they have, in relation to the particularities of concrete human existence. To say the same thing the other way around, we are what we are, our lives have whatever content they happen to have, and archetypes are actual only within that content. This leads me to the main point I want now to make about archetypes. They may be latent or irrelevant. (What Dante saw in Beatrice may be of little concern· to a four-year-old boy.) When they do structure experience, they do so by being given an accent of value deriving from interest expressive of the self and engaging deep emotional and affective currents. As structuring principles, they transmit that value in turn.

Years ago I discovered this about concrete human existence, archetypes, and interest in the course of my work as leader of a group psychotherapy program in a psychiatric clinic. Since this point is important to me, I will elaborate on what I am saying now by including (as part 6.3) a description of some of my findings in that work. But first, with feeling, emotion, and interest in mind, I wish to comment on thoughts by others about the terms *archetype* and *archetypal*.

In an article titled "Dethroning the Self," about trends in Jungian psychology since Jung, the analyst Andrew Samuels (of London) speaks of a psychic condition "with no preexisting focus or locus of interest or attention. That," he remarks, "is elected by the individual, or by the context, or by the field of reference—or simply elects itself," rather than being elected by an archetype as some independent entity. To clarify what he has in mind, he describes a discussion group of analysts "in which one participant told of a patient who had been caught in bombing raids" and since then has "had numerous terrifying dreams about being bombed." Samuels then recalls, "There was a more or less predictable discussion" of all this, after which the same participant called the group "wordy," and said "that she had always had trouble with words as a child and had only recently overcome" it. The effect of her remarks was dramatic. Some participants felt attacked, others identified with her, still others attacked back, saying she had not overcome her trouble with words. "Wordy" clearly touched the interest of the group at a much deeper level than "being bombed." As Samuels puts it, "At that particular moment and in that context, whatever was involved in 'bombing' was not archetypal in terms of depth or grippingness. Whereas what was involved in 'wordy' and a woman's struggle with words certainly was." Samuels asks, "What causes such shifts of attention to take place?" Taking the foregoing example as typical, he answers that "attention was generated by depth of emotion and, above all, by *a shift of emotion*," adding that "the interaction between attention and emotion is a central [psychological] concern."[22]

In using the term *archetypal* in this way, Samuels is following James Hillman, who has elaborated what he calls "archetypal psychology" as a revisionist version of Jung's thinking about archetypal images. Denying that an image is made "archetypal" by "dramatic structure, symbolic universality, strong emotion," Hillman maintains that the archetypal quality of an image arises out of portraying the image precisely, staying with the image while responding to it as metaphor, coming to see the necessity of the image, experiencing its analogical richness. In this view the term *archetypal* has no descriptive function; hence any image can be called archetypal. "Rather than pointing *at* something," Hillman writes, " 'archetypal' points *to* something, and this is *value*. By attaching 'archetypal' to an image, we ennoble or empower the image with the widest, richest, and deepest possible significance." Thus, *archetypal*, now divorced from dramatic structures having symbolic universality and engendering strong emotion, "is a word of importance"—it is "a word that values." He insists that what he is proposing is not "only a psychology of archetypes. 'Only a psychology of archetypes' would mean one that takes archetypal as an adjective derived from a noun," to which "we must address any question about 'archetypal.' " Instead, *archetypal* should be taken to name "a move one makes rather than a thing that is."[23] Note this use of the expression "a move."

It is true that to convey the idea of the archetypal, classical philosophers used the adjectival *archetypos* rather than a substantive. And so, though some adjectives openly derive their force from nouns—as *elephantine* does from *elephant*—*archetypal* is not entirely such an adjective. Still, just as one may reify—may artificially convert qualities into substances—one may also artificially exaggerate the differences between adjectives and nouns. (Which condition sounds more promising: "He is dying"; "He is almost dead"; "He is near death"?) Employing the term *archetype* need not mean regarding it as a thing or as a static pattern in the "supercelestial place" to which Plato metaphorically assigned his ideal forms. And therefore it is not necessary to retire *archetype* and elevate *archetypal* (transforming it in the process) to avoid this error.

In subsuming *archetypal* under *archetype* in the heading "archetype(s)/archetypal," the general index of Jung's *Collected Works* (CW 20) grants a fluid relationship between the two terms that is also characteristic of them in more general modern usage, and is implied by historical instances of them cited in the *Oxford English Dictionary.* A moment ago I spoke of "the idea of the archetypal": would not this fall somewhere quite indefinite between *archetypal* and *archetype?* And so there seems reason to doubt the need for a "move" to dispel an embarrassment presumed to exist by virtue of the fluidity of terms I have been describing. To declare that henceforth *archetypal* shall have a new meaning, linked with interest, is, I conclude, to pass a wand over an empty hat and produce no rabbit. It is also, I conclude further—another matter—to dress a child-term in the garb of the parent-term it has disavowed. And this further conclusion reflects my emphasis on creatureliness—and on being, and remaining in proper ways, a child. (While deserving of note, Jung's own occasional neglect to acknowledge influences on himself, and the tendency of some of his proponents to regard him as self-createdly original, are not now my concern.)

Indeed, if one were of such a mind, one could understand this revision of the terms *archetype* and *archetypal* as expressing the parricidal thrust of the Oedipus complex, with "archetype" equaling Jung, equaling father, and the newly created "archetypalists" equaling usurping sons. One gloss on the text read in this way might be Freud's *Totem and Taboo*, describing the primal horde in which the sons kill the loved and hated father and eat his flesh. An even more fitting gloss, compatible with Freud's, might be Harold Bloom's *The Anxiety of Influence*, describing a strategy employed by numerous poets of recent centuries, that of denying the influence of their predecessors—thus killing the father—while rewriting their predecessors' poems. Along with poetic evidence, Bloom illustrates his point by citing a letter by the American poet Wallace Stevens, in which Stevens claims, "I am not conscious of having been influenced by anybody and have purposely held off from reading highly mannered people like Eliot and Pound so that I should not absorb anything, even unconsciously." The passage closes, "As for W. Blake, I think that this means Wilhelm Blake."[24]

In other words, Stevens finds insufficient distance between himself and Blake, although they belong to different countries and different periods. After all, the United States was once part of the British Empire and hence child to the British parent. Moreover, Stevens and his forebear Blake share a common language. By making *William* into "Wilhelm," Stevens dissolves that linguistic commonality and transposes Blake to a country even more remote. (Incidentally, placing Blake there calls attention to Germany and distracts it from France, the source of some of the major influences on Stevens.) This parricidal banishing of an illustrious poetic forebear shows how great the anxiety of influence can be even in a poet as extraordinarily fine as Stevens at his best is.

As for the term *archetypal* in this regard, it is striking that the subtitle of the journal *Spring,* in which the articles I have been discussing appeared, is *An Annual of Archetypal Psychology and Jungian Thought.* In this subtitle, Jung is divested of his term *archetype,* and it is appropriated as "archetypal"; in the process he is deprived of his status as "psychologist" and reduced to that of "thinker." At least,

259

people welcoming the appellation *archetypal* would surely be reluctant to see the terms *psychology* and *thought* exchanged, so that Jung is made the progenitor of "Jungian Psychology" and they are made agents of "Archetypal Thought," with its connotations of a prepsychological—and hence weaker—age.

The corruption of Rousseau's noble savages (their sacrifice of self-validation to public opinion), the instrumental intelligence that makes the world into an object, the defeat of love by power, the perturbations of the Oedipus complex—these are all in some measure inevitable. Still, we can manage either more or less well with them. If our gratitude and sense of creatureliness is lost to them, we have managed less well. We are creatures of God, who is not simply "father." Thus denial of creatureliness cannot be reduced to the denial of the father in some forms of the Oedipus complex, but the denial of one is entirely compatible with denial of the other. Jung (as I have argued in part 2.4) dealt with the oedipal issues posed in the early history of depth psychology, and in his interactions with Freud, in part by exploring the preoedipal levels of the mother-infant relationship. He was right in doing this, as an adequate resolution of the Oedipus complex entails carrying important preoedipal qualities *through* both the formation of the complex and its resolution. These qualities include gratitude for more than enough, openness, and a sense of mutuality, essential if the ego, with its infant qualities alive and intact, is to be well related to the unconscious as the matrix—the mother—of consciousness, and thus well related to the self.

Dethroning the self—as (paternal) king—entails diminishing the power of the ego—as hero, and hence king-to-be. The program further entails abandoning the idea that the integration of the personality should be the aim of individuation. In Samuels's statement of this last point, "if the part self or psychic fragment is lived out fully, then wholeness will take care of itself."[25] Against this program one can maintain that the primary manifestations of both self and ego occur within the early mother-infant relationship, that if access to this early psychic level is kept alive the ego has resources to temper its illusory heroism, and that the thought of living out the part self or psychic fragment fully would be a consolation one might be reluctant to offer to Dr. Smile (described in part 1). (It should be recalled, however, that we considered Dr. Smile and Art Pepper together because their psychologies are related, if in important ways distinct, and that Pepper had lived his fragmented and tangled life fully—that he had been truer to himself than many people ostensibly more balanced and "whole.")

Certainly, most analysts assume that for most purposes it is better than not for the right hand to know what the left hand is doing, and that consciousness is a value for the most part worth the considerable pain of achieving and maintaining it. Though integration has sometimes been idealized; though deintegrative states, too, may have positive value; and though unconsciousness (as in sleep and dreams) may help to renew conscious life, these are hardly reasons for devaluing psychic coherence and consciousness. "Let it all hang out," a byword of the late 1960s, is too one-sided to be of use as a guide to individuation and analytic work.

To play down the role of the ego may, indeed, have the paradoxical effect of playing it up, precisely in its illusory and inflationary forms. To see how this may be so, we need only to think of the sometimes paradoxical effects (discussed in part 5.11) of a preoccupation with Original Sin as a way of reminding the ego of its limited powers. But limited powers are powers, and the ego's powers (and not only its powers to err) need to be subject to accounting. If psychic health consists in important measure of remaining mindfully aware of one's inferiorities and problems, this must mean bringing them again and again into conscious relation with the ego as the organ of personal responsibility. The attempt to diminish the power of the ego assumes that the ego finds its appropriate symbolic expression in the figure of the hero. But the primary model of the ego in relation to the self is, I would maintain to the contrary, the mutual receptivity of mother and infant, informed with the felt sense of "we together in the surrounding world." Acting and being acted upon are indeed important in the life of the infant, but they take place within the context of this receptivity, which is of fundamental importance in the optimal development of the ego. Thus receptive, the ego may be open to the self as "the inner voice which tells me frequently and precisely how I am to live."[26]

The integration of the personality is a desideratum, and an important one, though the statement that it is this requires qualification.

As I have argued (in part 3.1), the capacity for union, as distinct from fusion, is also a desideratum—the capacity for union is the capacity for love—yet states of fusion may play a positively valuable role in the development of the personality. So, too, while the integration of psychic elements in a coherent whole is a desideratum, deintegrative states may play a positively valuable role in the development of the personality, and may, further, prove essential to heightened creativity. But it is in the tension of their interaction with integrative forces that deintegrative ones are creative. Thus, in the paintings of Jackson Pollock, one is struck by the dynamism of order-in-chaos or chaos-in-order.

To insist too much upon the desideratum of integration invites results related to those that come from insisting too much upon being free of sin and error. In this, and in other points, I agree with Hillman, who is surely right in thinking that much else than archetypes can be interesting. Yet with the self dethroned and the power of the ego diminished, the integrative forces necessary to coherent and adapted personal identity are largely removed from the psychological picture. Neither archetypes nor the "archetypal" can legitimately function on their behalf. And it is difficult to see that the problems I have been sketching are solved by saying that *archetypal* means something like "extremely interesting," while retaining the connotations of universality, necessity, and emotional import carried by the term *archetype*— as the discussion does while pretending not to do so.

It does seem to me to make sense to distinguish not only degrees but also levels of interest, and to allow that what is more archetypal and what is less so may be either more or less interesting. Indeed, mythological patterns may positively kill interest. (Thus, a recent film, *Starman,* received an approving review, explicitly despite its "Christ-allegory pattern," in accordance with which the main character performs resurrections and forecasts his own death, to be followed by an ascension into the heavens within three days. Wondering whether there is willing suspension of déjà vu, the reviewer concludes by proposing that—to appreciate what the film has to recommend it—the reader forget having seen the story before.) What is not overtly archetypal (as is the strong form of the golden section) may be intensely interesting (clouds, rain, expanding gases, for example). And what is highly archetypal may be intensely interesting or scarcely interesting at all. (The same Mass that is for one person a transformative experience may for another be a boring exercise accomplishing little except enhancing his self-congratulation.) In sum, ego and self in their interrelations are the primary sources of interest. Archetypes may structure those interrelations, but interest may also move independently of them.

Since the most personally precious manifestations of the self include those of the voice of the self telling me frequently and precisely how to live, I will conclude this section by elaborating on this metaphor of the self as having a voice, and by considering the margin of freedom it affords the ego.

Attributing a metaphorical voice to the self does not amount to a magical recipe assuring possession of the True and Good. Rather, one might compare following this voice with the activity of an artist who in an attitude of serious play follows seemingly random hunches in choosing his subject matter, physical means, and scale, and who thus over the years creates a body of work having both variety and overall coherence.

Relating the self to the voice of conscience assumes a level of conscience that is not primarily made up of introjected social values. When the true nature of the relationship between Héloise and Abelard was revealed—as that of lovers as well as pupil and tutor—Héloise sought to avoid the marriage urged upon her, thus choosing to bring shame upon her family and herself. Doing this seemed to her preferable to diverting Abelard from what she considered his true calling as theologian and teacher. Indeed, while demanding that one be true to it, the self often engenders conflicts among tendencies within oneself and between the most authentic portions of oneself and social values. The self engenders them because problems, and consequently self-division, are essential to the creation of consciousness, which is a value of the self.[27]

One often hears the voice of the self *in* his problems and conflicts, not beyond them or around them. Thus the artist alluded to a moment ago may feel that the hunches showing him ways of dealing with artistic problems are *in* his engagement with those problems, not outside it, and that his artistic hunches are also the expression of

263

extraartistic conflicts the hunches are indirectly seeking to resolve. Thus, in speaking of the voice of the self, one must bear in mind that working *at* problems may transform psychic energy in the interests of the self, and hence that both the problems and one's working at them have a value independent of any direct movement toward their solution. [28]

The margin of freedom afforded the ego by the self in this view is both crucial and subtle, as may be seen from an analytic hour of "Sabina Cochran," a young cellist who supports herself modestly by giving cello lessons to children in small towns at a distance from her home. These lessons are based on a special method of instruction she is learning through paid lessons from Mrs. Black, whom she admires and fears. Learning to her chagrin that one whole group of children have decided to discontinue their lessons, Sabina, whose self-esteem is generally less than heroic, informs Mrs. Black of this. Mrs. Black responds with concern about the children, who she hopes will be able to find another teacher without too much trouble. At her analytic hour the next day, Sabina denigrates herself for her supposed incompetence and describes her interaction with Mrs. Black. Her analyst's response includes pointing out some of the things Mrs. Black did not say to Sabina: how unfortunate it was that Sabina should be deprived of income and forced to deal with further financial worries, that there must soon be some more adequate solution to her problems in making a career, that her setback is a blow to her self-esteem, and that the grounds for the setback need to be realistically assessed. He wonders aloud, further, whether Sabina simply does not expect the support of people whom she admires, and whether this negative expectation does not partly provoke the kind of response she got from Mrs. Black.

Sabina then feels herself reminded of her difficulties in learning to roller-skate and ride a bicycle when she was a child, difficulties with which neither her mother nor her father offered any help. She would, for example, fall off her bicycle, and, discouraged, would simply give up trying to ride it. About this defeat her mother would resignedly remark, "Sabina just doesn't seem to want to ride her bike yet." (In reporting this, Sabina inflects her mother's "just" as though that word were loaded with unspoken, and rankling, meaning.) After asking herself and her analyst how she will ever be able to pull the missing support out of herself when she has never been given it in the first place, Sabina recounts a dream.

In Sabina's dream she is in a lodge presided over by a Native American spiritual teacher named Sun Bear. In it are mattresses and various cats. As Sabina and her analyst discuss the dream, he points out that Sun Bear's calling himself by this name is itself a robust and forthright owning of power. Asked what she thinks about cats, Sabina replies, "They clamor for what they want, and get it, and make everyone love them for it." Her analyst's "interpretation" of the dream consists simply of insisting that it was *hers,* created by *her own* resources for knowing and making known what she wants and needs.

To assert (in the manner of the Gestalt psychotherapist Fritz Perls) that Sabina *is* herself Sun Bear and the cats would be to make the word *is* do some partly obscure work. Still, it is to the end of giving her a felt and imaginative connection with qualities lacking in herself that the dream pictures them. Indeed, they are pictured not as lacking but as present, and she (as dream ego) is pictured as interacting with them. That interaction continues in her conscious life as part of the margin of her ego's freedom. However nonsupportive Sabina's mother may have been in Sabina's early years, her mother was "good enough" to mediate to Sabina a precious degree of access to the self that knows what is good for itself—and that knows how to give voice to that knowledge.

Incidentally, though Sabina complained that the conversation she was leading with her analyst was wandering boringly—another demonstration of her supposed inadequacy—in retrospect it could be seen to have a pattern as clear as if its topics had been set down in advance in an agenda. (Such patterns will be discussed in part 6.3.). Indeed there is a sense in which the hour could be said to have *had* an agenda, unknown in advance to the egos of Sabina and her analyst, a pattern in which the integrative workings of the self would become manifest to the ego—as they did in her dream. But to say this about the analytic interaction is to recognize that the self can be operative in an interpersonal field (in ways also illustrated in part 6.3). And it is to recognize, in turn, that the mother-infant relationship remains implicit in interactions between ego and self.

6.3 Fantasy, Imagination, and Symbol Formation

The Zurichberg Clinic, a psychiatric clinic with a psychotherapeutic—and, more specifically, a Jungian—orientation, was opened in Zurich, Switzerland, in 1964. For the first few years of its operation I was in charge of group psychotherapy meetings, which I tried to conduct in a way that was in keeping with the special character of the clinic. In so doing, I noticed certain phenomena having a bearing on the topics just treated (in parts 6.1 and 6.2), and on the kind of shift that may sometimes occur from fantasy to imagination. In making this distinction I mean to align fantasy with the ego, often influenced by its shadow inferiorities, and imagination with the integrative workings of the self.

Though this distinction seems to me valid for important purposes, it needs at the outset to be qualified by two considerations implied or stated in earlier pages. First, "shadow inferiorities" may in certain respects be superior—as is the case with the vulnerability of Mr. Newman (described in part 3.3), since it is essential to his spontaneous response to life, though a good part of the time he would rather be regarded as tough than as vulnerable. This qualification does not mean that there is no difference between inferior and superior and that one should thus "let it all hang out." It means that the difference is relative and needs to be considered from multiple viewpoints in a way that engages differentiated feeling. And second, the integrative workings of the self are dynamically related to its deintegrative workings. To give special value to its integrative working is to value coherence. Still, coherence is not always a simple and clear-cut matter, any more than is the value to be placed on such qualities as Mr. Newman's vulnerability. Indeed, coherence may be intricate and complex, may partly be the result of trial and error, and may include elements of randomness. A mandala is coherent; so is a painting by Pollock; so may be the meandering course that gets one successfully through a labyrinth.

In my work in the clinic I ignored some widely accepted tenets of group psychotherapy (for example, that the membership of the group must be fixed). If it is possible to ignore them and, as I believe, still achieve valuable results, then my observations have notable methodological implications, even for group psychotherapy in contexts different from that of the Zurichberg Clinic in those years. And, as I imply, a rigorous preoccupation with method may inhibit the group leader's perception of the phenomena with which I am concerned and his capacity for responding adequately to them. This is especially true when the aim of objectivity on the part of the therapist is too narrowly defined. Thus, in describing and estimating the importance of these phenomena I stress the group leader's subjective as well as objective involvement in the group and in the levels of experience from which the phenomena arise.

The phenomena I wish to describe may be seen as expressive of the complementary relationship that, in Jung's view, exists between conscious and unconscious processes. Certain characteristics of this relationship, as it is manifest in group psychotherapy, have been well described by the Jungian analyst Robert F. Hobson, who regards the members of a psychotherapeutic group as neither subjects nor objects, "but as contingent parts in a dynamic whole." The group, in turn, he sees "as a system with self-regulatory homeostatic mechanisms which, by a process involving splitting and recombination, can develop towards a state of integration." The task of analysis, he maintains, is "the recognition and solution of resistances to the . . . integrating processes occurring in the group as a whole."[29]

I now want to concentrate on another dimension of the process described by Hobson, another attitude that the group leader may have toward it, and another kind of role that he can assume within the group. I will try to convey something of the form and content of group meetings in the clinic in those years, and in doing so I will outline some problems that arose, both practical and theoretical—including those that can be summed up as resistance—and my attempts to solve them.

My comments on the dynamics of the meetings will be focused upon the analogy that may sometimes be drawn between the content of the group discussion and that of a dream; the analogy between the form sometimes discernible in that content and the structure of a dream; the nature of the process implied by the phenomena that accord with this analogy; the relationship of the group members to this process and its effects upon the group as a whole; and the awareness demanded of the group leader by this process. The nature of this awareness I will describe by means of a concept enunciated by the jazz musician Ornette Coleman, the dominant ear of the moment, to describe an important way musical imagination may work in group improvising.

My emphasis will be not so much upon the analysis of resistance to the integrating process within the group as upon the spontaneous emergence of a symbolic content that expresses that process and has its own power to overcome resistances. Symbol formation is a property of what Jung has called the "transcendent function," supraordinate to the ego.[30] The process by which symbols arise in the kind of group discussion I will describe is, by implication, supraordinate to the egos of the group members (including that of the group leader) and to the shared consciousness insofar as that may be conceived (if only by way of analogy) as a kind of ego-consciousness. The process requires the kind of reverie that we call fantasy, but as deeper psychic levels are activated fantasy becomes imaginative—becomes imagination—in the sense of manifesting the constructive integrative working of the self. The fact that the phenomena with which I am concerned arise at all in group psychotherapy meetings of whatever kind implies something of interest about the nature of processes that may be at work, even if invisibly, in any group psychotherapy meeting and in many other kinds of human interaction.

Before proceeding further with this program, however, I wish to glance briefly at W. R. Bion's influential study of group therapy in the hope that doing so will clarify my assumptions in this section and their relevance to my larger argument.[31]

In his work with therapeutic groups, Bion came to distinguish between work groups and basic-assumption groups, by which he means different modes that can be assumed at different moments by the same group of individuals. In the work mode, the group is trying to deal with problems realistically, and to keep this kind of mental functioning from being subverted by the less conscious tendencies of the basic-assumption mode. One basic assumption that may govern the group is that the purpose of the group is to enact the dependency of the other members on a leader, either the nominal leader of the group (such as a participating psychiatrist) or, significantly, the psychologically least well member (often someone with paranoid trends). This dependency is infantile and magical, and the "culture" of the group thus constituted is like a religion, religions often having highly psychopathological leaders. Analysis in such a group serves the purpose of exposing the basic assumption of dependency so that the work group can again emerge. The work group is analogous to the conscious ego, and its activity is a rudimentary form of science.

The phenomena with which Bion is concerned are observable and important. Adults are, for example, capable of infantile dependency, which life in groups often fosters to everyone's detriment. And yet group life also includes phenomena to which he does not attend. My chief purpose in this section is to convey a sense of some of these in their bearing on my larger concerns. At the moment I will pursue this purpose by commenting briefly on ways in which, in earlier sections of this book, Bion's assumptions have implicitly been criticized as incomplete, and on the nature and goals of individual analysis.

Some of Bion's assumptions accord with a version of the positivist scheme of cultural evolution (discussed in part 5.2), religion for him amounting to systematized magic, suffused with illusions dispelled only by science. But this view leaves insufficient scope for the constructive workings of feeling and imagination as they are rooted in deep regions of the psyche. Further, the inner child implied by his account is helplessly dependent and wishful, whereas the more complex inner child of this book has a wealth of positive value. And dependency, far from being limited to infantile helplessness, is, I would contend, part of the inescapable dimension of our reality that one kind of religious language calls our creatureliness. When it serves social and individual transformation, and is not simply a collective neurosis, religion invests dependence with the meaning of mutuality and interdependence, thus increasing access to the mythic Child in a way that does not increase childishness but reduces it.

The main achievement of Bion's work group would seem to be the kind of rational insight hoped for in individual analysis. But by itself rational insight rarely effects growth and change. These require emotional engagement, as Bion would surely agree, but also the activation of deep symbolic processes—through dreams and other imaginative activity—that are largely irrational and that the subject feels to be manifestations of the self.

269

Feeling, Imagination, and the Self

I assume that the self (Fordham's "original self") precedes the ego, and that the self remains supraordinate to the ego throughout development. This section describes symbolic processes members of the group would seem to experience as manifestations of the self, and as synthetic in ways that reach beyond the synthetic powers of the group members' egos. Such phenomena are, I believe, significant in and of themselves. Of course, it matters greatly what the egos of the group members do or do not do with them—just as in individual analysis it matters greatly what the ego of the analysand does or does not do with, say, a potentially helpful dream. But with respect to my intentions in this section, such requirements of the ego are of secondary interest. By analogy, when studying a two-year-old, one might focus on elements of its behavior that indicate weakness or increasing stability of ego-functioning. But one might, instead, focus on moments of coherence it is able to achieve—alone, with its mother, or with the larger world—not so much through the workings of its ego as through its sense of a supporting and ordering self. My concern here is more like the latter.

Though my intentions cause me to discuss some topics (such as resistance) differently than Bion or many other group therapists, I readily grant that the phenomena they are concerned with are real and that their ways of dealing with them have their justification. My way of discussing such topics is dictated by the matters of greatest interest to me. I am aware that my account deserves to be criticized for incompleteness, as I have criticized Bion's, but I am consoled that I am calling attention to phenomena deserving it.

What now follows is a description of group meetings during the first years of the Zurichberg Clinic.

Form of the meetings. The clinic is small and has a large staff in relation to the number of patients, usually in the first years of the clinic numbering fewer than 25. The psychotherapeutic orientation and the physical arrangement of the two houses discourage the admission of primarily custodial cases and of patients who may be expected to be extremely violent or suicidal for long periods of time.

Several patients have keys and are free to come and go during the day, according to whatever rules have been laid down for each of them, and some of the younger of these attend educational institutions.

270

Rules that have developed governing group meetings are rules in the sense that they are generally understood and abided by, and while a few of them have been laid down by the staff, others, unstated, belong to the customs that have developed within the house.

Meetings, which are held twice a week, usually last a few minutes under an hour. Those patients who feel like coming do so—as do less enthusiastic patients who have been individually induced to come by a member of the staff. (There is, in fact, a rule that patients *must* attend if they are able to do so. Very rarely it is invoked as though it were a military command, though strict application of the rule is an exception to house custom.) The number of patients attending varies from three to over twenty, with an average per meeting of eleven or twelve. At least one member of the medical or psychotherapeutic staff is generally present in addition to the group leader; others come when they feel inclined and are able to do so. (Psychotherapists attend according to their feelings about their psychotherapeutic relationships with patients in the group.)

Nurses and, more rarely, members of the household staff come sporadically, and occasionally a visiting doctor or psychotherapist or a member of a patient's family may be present. Attendance, then, is not usually compulsory for the patients, and the composition of the group from meeting to meeting is somewhat fluid, with varying degrees of participation by the staff and visitors.

There are some immediate practical reasons for this fluidity. Patients attending school may be unable to come because of their classes; others may occasionally have medical or psychotherapeutic appointments that conflict with the group meetings; some patients who have been in the habit of coming enter a phase in which they must be confined to their rooms or to bed; the population of the clinic is shifting—new patients are admitted and old ones released or granted leave, and members of the staff have vacations. Patients are also more or less free to refuse to attend the meetings on grounds that may be interpreted as rationalizations of resistance.

Ruled out, then, is the kind of analytic psychotherapy possible with a closed group the members of which are committed to attending meetings regularly over a longer period of time. Nor do the meetings have the character of a compulsory house meeting (not primarily psychotherapeutic in intent) of all patients and all members of the staff.

Meetings are held in a large room with chairs arranged roughly in a circle. There is no fixed seating order. Occasionally patients will remove their chairs from the group—absentmindedly, shyly, self-protectively, or belligerently. Though most people attending a meeting are on time, some come late, occasionally or habitually. Sometimes one comes in the middle or at the end. One or another may leave early, either excusing himself and giving a convincing practical reason or clearly expressing agitation, anger, or contempt. Discussions usually proceed with one person speaking at a time to the group, but occasionally there is private whispering among members. A member may declare that the discussion is nonsense, stand up and turn the phonograph on very loud. All these deviations from the basic pattern of a one-hour meeting with all persons present for the full hour and attentive to the group are dealt with (or sometimes not dealt with) as they arise, by one or more members of the group or by the group leader. There are no rules governing these deviations. The patient community is polylingual, but most discussions proceed in German and English with a good deal of translation back and forth, either by the group leader or another member of the group.

As group leader I am usually quite active in the sense that I enter freely into the discussion. In certain circumstances, even when there are several people present, I am willing to let the discussion narrow for minutes at a time to a dialogue between myself and one other person, who may be a member of the staff. On the other hand, I do not generally propose themes for discussion, though I may formulate or reformulate as themes topics that have arisen and not received attention. I sometimes actively try to hold the discussion to the theme that has emerged; at other times I let the discussion move freely.

Content of the meetings. One cannot make a hard and fast distinction either between the content and form or between the content and dynamics of the group meetings. The object of discussion may, for example, be the fact that a member has stood up to leave the group— and his doing so belongs both to the form and to the dynamics of what is happening in the group. Nonetheless, much of the material of the discussions could be itemized as topics. These are of great

importance, because they express the conscious intention of the group—
"topic x is what we are now trying to talk about"—and the unconscious
content of the discussion (those things that are expressed but felt to
be extraneous and those things that are thought and felt but not
expressed) often has an important dynamic bearing on that intention.
It is, of course, possible to reduce nearly all content of the discussion
to the form and dynamics of the group. This is often felt to be the
principal task of group psychotherapy—but, as the preceding discussion of interest (in parts 6.1 and 6.2) should have made clear, there
are also excellent reasons for granting priority to this momentary topic
x and to its development. Often the group is brought to life by interest
in such a topic which not only frees energies but is an important point
in the dynamic field of the integrating process which it serves. Thus
movements toward integration may be registered in the treatment of
the topic, and the most dramatic of such movements may express
themselves in a transformation of it. Here are examples of the topics
we have discussed:

Arrangements for hikes or trips to the theatre. Proposals for new
house rules or objections to those in force. Whether or not the clinic
should have a television set. How to behave with a feeble-minded
member of the staff who has tantrums. That members of the staff should
do more for the patients (for example, by giving lectures to them).
That members of the staff abuse their power (for example, by moving
patients from bed to bed and room to room against their wills). Failure
of the staff to understand patients (owing to the fact that no one who
is psychically well can understand anyone who is psychically ill). Specific conflicts between patients or between patients and members of
the staff. That such conflicts in general can only mean a paralyzing
deadlock in which one is victimized.

Toilets and washing facilities that are busy when patients want to
use them. Neuroleptics. That when the regular cook is away the meals
become very strange. Whether or not patients should be allowed to be
alone in their rooms. The paucity of light bulbs. Whether letters written
by patients are really sent. The laziness and meddlesomeness of nurses.
The eerie impersonality of life in the clinic, that no one knows anyone
else.

Specific hallucinations and illusions. The way, for example, that
water basins inside various pyramids, some in Egypt, some in Germany,

273

control weather and through the weather the processes of nature and of human history. The snoring of a woman patient, caused, in her opinion, by the fact that her upper lip is too short. Falling hair among women patients: is it caused by emotional disturbance or by the medicine? Suicidal feelings and attempts at suicide. Whether or not psychic disturbances are the same as physical diseases or similar to them. Positive and negative feelings and how to conquer negative feelings through the power of the "mind." That women patients are supposed to fall in love with their doctors: what if they do not want to? The fallibility or infallibility of doctors. What psychotherapy is and how long it is supposed to take. Depression. Aggression.

That life is meaningless and should be regarded as a stupid game. Homelessness, the state of being in exile. Family problems: lying among family members, severe and weak parents, divorce, family myths. Education. Tolerance. Conscience. Shame. Selfishness. The persona: what it is and whether or not one should try to live without one. Growing old. Death: a terrifying reality, a source of value, a matter of indifference. Religion: ritual, confession, the religious element in psychic problems. Miracles: the miracle of getting well. Suffering: standing it in oneself and facing it in others. The necessity of sacrifice if one is to come to a new situation in life. The cold war. The war in Viet Nam. Great men in political history: what kind of people they are and whether they are necessary or desirable.

Crowded highways. Specific films and the problems they deal with. The difficulties of a person who has left a psychiatric clinic (for example, when he looks for new employment). The jargon-word *creativity* and the pressures it induces among research workers in certain industries. The value of exploring outer space (as contrasted with that of putting large amounts of money into medical research). Air pollution. The kind of person that Jean-Paul Sartre describes as "viscous." Boredom. Waiting. What constitutes a waste of time.

These topics could be brought roughly under the headings, "The Clinical Situation and How to Deal with It," "Odd Ideas and Experiences—the Factors Constituting the Eccentric Position of the Patient in the Clinic and in the World," "General Life Problems." What has struck me about the topics discussed at our group meetings is that on the whole the discussions are liveliest—there is the widest partici-

pation and the greatest expression of personal feeling in the group—
when topics discussed are of general interest and not overtly focused
upon the clinical situation or the reasons the patients have for being
in it.

The fact that the discussion proceeds on this level may sometimes
be interpreted as resistance, an expression of the same inclination
that, for example, leads a woman patient to sneak away and spend
half a day looking at shop windows because she feels it silly for her
to be cut off from life as she is in the clinic. But concern with the
generally human, rather than with the specifically personal, may also
be understood as a valid attempt to reach the world of others and to
achieve a transformation of the patient's adaptation to it.

One of the most devoted members of the group usually notices
and remembers little of what happens around him, yet in the group
meetings he concentrates on what is talked about and is able and
often eager to make a summary of it at the beginning of the following
meeting. He feels that he gets "new ideas" from the meetings and
that these help him, between meetings, to break out of the vicious
circle of his inner life for a time. It is also obvious during the meetings
that he takes the general theme as a challenge for some kind of personal
response and that through this response, when he can make it, he
comes much closer than usual to other people.

Another group member expressed the value of generality very
nicely: "I am always happy to talk about God. God is a subject which
is very important, about which no one knows anything and about
which one can discuss endlessly and pleasantly, elaborating it however
one will." Of course, the topic of God can also be of tremendous
personal concern, and that concern may be expressed in a discussion
of it. This is true of many other general topics which are impersonal
in the sense that they lie outside the immediate field of the complexes
and automatisms of the group members, but which may at the same
time be personal in the sense that they have a resonance within that
field.

In a discussion about the Berlin wall, for example, the increased
flow of connection between the group members could be strongly felt.
The theme itself is a matter of concern in the larger world beyond

the clinic, but it is also a possible symbol of the splitting from which the patients suffer, that within themselves and that which divides them from any community.

Compare this discussion with another in which a woman patient spent a large part of an hour sobbing, moaning, and howling about the fact that her roommate, having taken the three best drawers of the six in the dresser, was persecuting her. Various responses were elicited by her complaints, but it was evident that neither the topic nor her performance moved the other members of the group very deeply. That is to say, in the discussion that emerged, no relatively impersonal focus that would allow a kind of bridge between her and the other group members could be found. One may imagine that she wanted to draw them into her personal and self-destructive storm and that they resisted her attempts to do so.

If the discussion moved to the general problems of personal justice and injustice and of getting along with people very different from oneself, she succeeded in dragging it back to herself. An attempt to analyze what was happening within the group failed. It may happen, then, that the group is confronted with delusional material which is too potent and too personal to be dealt with directly and which may overwhelm attempts to deal with it directly.

However, I have been surprised by the capacity of the group to deal with exceptionally eccentric and affect-laden material if a relatively impersonal focus for the discussion has been established. This focus often serves as a formal counterpole to the most threatening sources of affective eruption in the group. In this sense it may be said to neutralize affect by granting the group members a standpoint at a distance from its most threatening source. But in another sense, by giving the group members this standpoint—and thus relieving them of the necessity to withdraw into their complexes and automatisms—this focus frees them to express personal emotion, the field of which may expand to touch what are felt to be sources of threatening affect.

An example of how a relatively impersonal thematic focus may work is provided by a discussion about suicide. It was initiated (by a patient) with the proposition, "Suicide should not be considered a crime or a sin, since so many people are intent upon destroying themselves through constant self-violation of various kinds." The young woman who introduced the topic had tried to kill herself, as had other members of the group. The general impression of the meeting, expressed by patients afterward, was that the discussion had been extremely lively and that something worthwhile had occurred in it, though no one had felt called upon to admit that the problem being discussed concerned him personally. During the discussion one did not feel that the group members most immediately concerned with suicide were holding back some personal confession demanded of them by the fact that this topic was being discussed.

I am not suggesting that group discussions in the clinic are like a debate or round table discussion about a set theme. If the topic at the center of attention assumes that character, group members begin to feel their inadequacies and withdraw into themselves. I emphasize the importance of relatively general topics because as a matter of principle I do not draw a rigid line between what seems to be happening in the meeting and what is *really* happening, between what the group members think they are saying and doing and what they are *really* saying and doing. Practically speaking, there is a difference of levels—of relative consciousness or unconsciousness—in what is happening, and sometimes there are deep and important splits between these levels. The task is, of course, to bridge them. I believe that the charge of energy in the topic at the forefront of discussion, the interest invested in it, is an important element of the integrating process, and that the continuity and development of that topic (or nexus of topics) is an important expression of that process.

Resistances. I have spoken, following Hobson, of the group as a "dynamic whole" and of "resistances to the integrating process" of the group. The impression that may have emerged most clearly from my brief description of the form of group meetings in the clinic is that of the free rein given to the disintegrating tendencies that the group should, ideally, serve to overcome.

This impression will, I hope, have been partly qualified by my emphasis upon the value, continuity, and development of the topic or topics at the forefront of the group discussion. But the problem of resistance deserves separate discussion and I will now present a brief survey of my own attitude toward it, beginning with my experience of individual psychotherapy. I will then turn to resistances within the group as a fluid subcommunity within the clinic, and finally to some of the ways in which resistance is dealt with in the group.

The resistance to be encountered in individual psychotherapy I regard as representing, very roughly, a self-protective tendency of certain dominant nonego complexes in the face of the ego; at the same time it represents a self-protective tendency of the ego in the face of these nonego complexes. The psychotherapist must, first, try to recognize such resistance.

Both the ego and these nonego complexes have value within the psychic field of the individual. This value (which the individual feels to be that of himself as a person) must be respected by the psychotherapist; so he must, secondly, respect the resistance. Overcoming resistance is, on the other hand, one of the aims of psychotherapy.

This aim may be achieved in one of two ways. First, through analysis, and here an important ingredient is tact: resistance can only be reduced at the right moment by the right person in the right way. If a crude attempt to analyze resistance is made in the wrong moment— or even worse, at the wrong moment by the wrong person in the wrong way—the patient will feel that his integrity is being violated. It may, in fact, be the integrity of an important nonego complex that is being violated; but owing to the nature of the relations that obtain between the ego and such a complex, the person experiences it as a violation of himself; the result is an increase in resistance.

Second, resistance can be overcome without analysis, by a spontaneous movement within the psychic constellation of the person and of the psychotherapeutic relationship. The therapist may, for example, talk for considerable time with someone who has a slightly crippled limb; they may talk about many things but not about the limb, though the disfigurement is obvious, as are the facts that the therapist has noticed it and that the patient is reluctant to talk about it. Discussion of other matters may form various lines of connection between the therapist and the patient and some of these may bring to light important values of the patient other than that of the disfigurement.

The disfigurement remains important to the patient but it is no longer as important to their relationship as it was when they first encountered one another as strangers. A moment may finally come when they can talk about the disfigurement and the complex it represents. On the face of it there seems to be no pressing reason to describe either the conversations about such other matters as resistance or that about the limb as "analysis of resistance," but in fact the former resistance, as reflected in the relationship, has diminished. The psychotherapist should, of course, understand what has happened as well as he can, and sooner or later he and the patient may be inclined to discuss this movement. It may seem advisable for that discussion to focus overtly upon the transference relationship; it may also seem advisable for it to focus upon material less immediately expressive of that relationship. The criterion, crudely expressed, is again a matter of tact.

Resistance within the psychotherapeutic group is, as Hobson indicates, different from that apparent in individual psychotherapy. It is also evident that the resistances on what Hobson calls the "group level" reflect in various ways the complexes of the individual group members. That is to say, there are lines of continuity between the resistances on the two levels, group and individual.

The reductive analysis of resistance in such group meetings as ours requires even more of the reserve that is essential to tact than does such analysis within an individual psychotherapy. This is because of the relatively uncontained character of the group—the fluidity of its constitution and the lack of a clear focus of transference—compared with that of individual psychotherapy. It is relatively more difficult for the group leader to know how the participants are reacting to what is happening than it is for a psychotherapist in individual psychotherapy. It may, for example, turn out that a group member has taken a remark about the weather as being a condemnation of him or as an assessment of the state of his soul. This reaction may come to no clear expression within the group.

It has occasionally happened that I or one of my colleagues has crudely attempted a reductive analysis of some expression of a personal complex. The results may be expressed by a punning slogan of my invention that I also find applicable to personal psychotherapy: "Boring is boring"—gouging and needling is insulting and tiresome. The lines of connection that have been established during the group meeting have thinned or been broken. These practical reservations about reductive analysis of resistance within the group give, for the purpose

279

of the clinic, increased importance to other ways of dealing with resistance.

There are, I believe (following Hobson), self-regulatory homeostatic mechanisms operating within the psychotherapeutic group. Such mechanisms also influence the behavior of each individual within the group or outside it and, very importantly, serve to link the group and its members to the larger community of the clinic. Resistances on the "group level," that is to say, are not confined to the group. They may come to expression in the individual outside the group and through him become part of the interpersonal life of the clinic. Patients in the clinic may express resistance in ways well described by Hobson; they may express it by avoiding the meetings for a shorter or longer time, and they may, further, express it by critical comments, delivered outside the group meetings, about the group meetings in general or about this or that aspect of them or this or that occurrence at a specific meeting. Many of these critical comments often find their way back into the group meetings and are discussed; others do not. Here is a brief summary of typical comments of this kind:

> The meetings are boring, a waste of time (for which no more specific reason can be elicited). They are too much concerned with unimportant household matters. The meetings stir me up too much, touching upon important themes that are not dealt with conclusively enough in the course of the discussion; the meetings confuse me. The group leader is too active; the meetings in the clinic are not like the real group psychotherapy I used to have. The group leader is too passive; the discussion reaches heights of great importance and is allowed to descend to the level of personal banter.

> Undesirable people attend the meetings (an expression of the clique mentality that blooms from time to time in the clinic). Not enough doctors attend the meetings. There is no point in discussing the themes that arise except in personal consultation with a specialist in whom one has complete trust. Not every word is translated from language to language; thus the meetings are not for a conscientious person who wants to know exactly what is going on. Undesirable topics (such as death) are discussed. The purpose of the meetings is for the doctors to observe the patients and assess their conditions: it may be best for me to stay out of view until I am certain that I can show myself in a good light.

Receptivity, Commitment, and Detachment

The meetings are scheduled at inconvenient times. I forget the times. My life is so full of important things to do that I do not have surplus energy for the meetings. My life is so empty and meaningless, and I am so depressed, that I cannot muster up enough energy to attend the meetings. I am so preoccupied with my problems that I cannot concentrate upon the discussions well enough to follow them.

If a patient who could come to the group meetings does not do so, this fact is generally known by his individual psychotherapist. The patient's refusal to attend and his justification of it may then be material for discussion between them. Different patients, too, adopt different patterns of attendance which express various attitudes of the patients toward themselves, the group, the clinic, and the world at large. This expression of attitudes may be an important means in a patient's attempt to make known and to claim for himself the position that he wants to occupy, or to avoid the position he feels is being forced upon him, in the clinic.

Since I am not only the group leader but also an individual psychotherapist in the clinic and thus a member of the larger community, I find the question of how I deal with patients in rebellion against the group meetings very important. They usually feel vaguely that they "should" attend, though they are also usually not quite certain whether attendance is compulsory or not. When I meet them, they are often coy, apologetic, evasive. Sometimes we discuss their absence. I sometimes show that I respect their reasons for staying away, but I do so without implying that there is now a new rule giving them the right to do so. I am friendly without yielding to the persuasive techniques of the rebels—without letting them off the hook they feel themselves to be on. Thus these brief discussions relieve anxiety while preserving the lines of connection, of attraction and repulsion, between the rebels and the group and are themselves a way of dealing with resistance.

Within the group meeting resistance is sometimes analyzed. If the group is buried under a heavy silence, I may just sit the silence out, waiting to see what happens. I may also try to initiate a discussion of *this* silence, of what it feels like, of the possible reasons why we are behaving as we are. If this is unavailing, I may feel called upon to try to exercise an actively protective attitude toward the group. By this protection I do not mean mothering one member or another, trying to see that he or she does not have too bad a fright. Nor do I mean avoiding the issue at hand, the painful silence. I mean, rather, that I may act to salvage and reaffirm the principle that on one level we are always concerned with relatively impersonal things, which remain impersonal even though each group member has personal association with them.

This may require me to reestablish a less personal focus outside the present silence but bearing upon it. It may be possible, for example, for me to elicit memories of painful silences that group members have suffered individually in the past—this theme reflecting the momentary isolation of the group members—or of silence in general, the various kinds of it and what meanings these might have.

If I am to act in this way, it must be very clear to me that the more general topic with all its potential value may, for me as for the other group members, provide an arid refuge from immediate personal issues. In proposing such a topic—and even in responding to it if someone else has proposed it—I must ask myself if I am being seduced by resistance in the group or if I am giving myself, another member, or the group as a whole a means of evading those issues. So long as I feel the force of the question, I have certain freedom of action; if I no longer feel it, I will probably discover later that I have myself succumbed to the forces of disintegration.

Dynamics of the meetings. It is (I feel with Hobson) accurate to speak of the integrating process of a psychotherapeutic group, even when, as at the clinic, the composition of the group is relatively fluid. This process may be considered to have two main aspects. The first can be summarized generally as *making connections.* In fact, various kinds of connections are made. Most of the patients in the clinic are intensely occupied with their personal problems or may even be living almost completely in private worlds, and though they may complain of self-isolation, they are generally guarded and distrustful of contact. It often happens in the group meetings that people who are usually taciturn come to speak and that people who generally avoid one another join in discussions. The most overt kind of connection brought about by the group meeting is on this level. Some kind of human presence is communicated between people who would otherwise ignore one another. This contact often continues beyond the group meeting—a heated discussion is, for example, continued at the dinner table—which means at least a momentary decrease in the self-isolation that envelops most patients in the clinic.

Another kind of connection sometimes made at the group meeting is between the patients and some problematic content of the collective awareness of the group, that content arising from some event within the house or outside the house in the experience of one of the patients. Something "bad" happens, but for various reasons, primarily because of the poverty of contact that characterizes many of the patients, the event cannot be talked about. They behave stiffly, and the house is filled with waves of more or less subterranean agitation. The event and the agitation may come out in the group meeting and be assimilated to consciousness in ways and with results familiar from individual psychotherapy.

Dramatic examples of this process are provided by two such events: a violent outburst by a woman patient who tried, screaming, to throw herself out of the window and had to be forcibly restrained; and an episode in which two young women disappeared from the clinic and, as the other patients became fragmentarily aware, spent the night in town pursuing lurid adventures.

The outburst of the suicidal woman, when brought up in the group meeting, released a tremendous wealth of responses in the participants: shock and anger that a fellow patient had been indelicately handled, horror that anyone could lose control to the extent that she had, guilt that none of the patients had tried to help her during the outburst or before.

The night in the town of the young women led to a meeting in which one of them, sobbing, construed herself as being under attack by the staff and by the group. Patients and members of the staff tried in various ways to make her feel that this was not so and that she continued to belong to the group. In the course of these attempts the escapade of the young women ceased to be a glaring pseudosecret; the other patients were freed of the strenuous pretense of not knowing what they knew, however inaccurately, and were brought into various kinds of connections with one another.

This making of connections between the group and a disturbing and frightening event in the life of the clinic—and at the edge of the patients' awareness—suggests the activity of the individual ego. This analogy is also borne out by other functions of the group, among them the making of practical decisions and the exchange of opinions in an attempt to arrive at a coherent and adequate viewpoint toward some general life problem. But other kinds of connections are sometimes made by the group.

These seem the expression of the second aspect of the integrating process of the group, that of *the play of fantasy and the emergence of a structure within it.* The analogy suggested by this second kind of connection-making is not the operation of the ego: it is the participation of the ego in the symbolic process. I shall illustrate this second aspect of the integrating process with two examples to be taken up in some detail and with two others to be glanced at briefly.

1. Patient A is a stiff and phlegmatic young American professional man who sometimes seems on the verge of exploding but almost invariably maintains a good-natured and reasonable manner. (Some months ago he made a pasty and lifeless oil painting of a woman, the top half of her on one canvas, the bottom half on another.) A belongs to the American Episcopalian Church and reports to the group about his attendance of the Church of England in Zurich. One thing that he finds odd, as an American, is praying for the British Queen. But in a way it pleases him to do this: he has thought a lot about the Queen and sees her as a "unifying symbol" for the whole world.

There is then a long discussion of the British royal family. A group member from a Latin-American country tells of a tea party he attended at which the Queen Mother was present. He describes the way in which she spoke briefly to people from many countries, always had something fitting to say to them, and in general showed herself to be socially very adept. The discussion then turns to kingship in general: it seems, with the single exception of the British monarchy, a dying institution. It was once a unifying force. Is there any equivalent of that power today? Someone remarks that the office of the presidency of the United States has something of the royal magic.

In an attempt to make a connection with patient A, I tell a story about the riots of blacks in Los Angeles. One rioting young man said that he had no intention of stopping what he was doing, that the only person in the world who could get him to stop was the President of the United States, who had better be half black! Various remarks are made about the problems of blacks in the United States; then the discussion shifts to blacks in Africa. Patient B (a depressive-compulsive young Swiss woman, brought up as a member of a rigidly puritanical sect) says that blacks are black because there is so much sun in Africa. Patient C says that if B were to marry a white man and to move to blackest Africa, their children would be white, and if these children again married white people, B's grandchildren would also be white.

Differences between whites and blacks and the difficulties of being a white settler in Africa are considered. The last part of the meeting is taken up with a joking collective fantasy about the fortunes and family line in Africa of B, who is finally the revered cofounder of a flourishing dynasty.

Overtly, this meeting was a rational discussion about certain topics of general interest, but at the same time it was a fantasy with both the structure and the imagistic content of a familiar kind of dream. As in many dreams there is an overall movement from light to dark, from more superficial to deeper and more problematic content. And also as in many dreams, that movement includes a decisive moment or turning, the *peripeteia* (according to the dramatic model that Jung applied to dreams).[32]

In this group fantasy there is a transposition of scene (from predominantly white England and America to predominantly black Africa) and of the central actor (from Queen Elizabeth to patient B). This transposition of the central actor is also a shifting of levels, from the collective to the personal. (Queen Elizabeth is a "unifying symbol" on the level of collective consciousness; patient B, in the group fantasy, makes personal decisions—to marry and to go to Africa—and is then faced with personal difficulties in preserving her white identity and that of her family in Africa.) And through Queen Elizabeth there is a connection between patients A and B. Patient A's concern with the queen may be interpreted as an expression of his hope that some force will counteract the disintegrating tendencies within himself and in his relationship to the world.

On the "group level" described by Hobson, A is also calling attention to the disintegrating tendencies within the group. In the group fantasy about patient B, this splitting tendency (the great number of

285

distinct races, peoples, and nationalities praying for the queen) is replaced by a simple opposition beween "I" and "not-I," between patient B (and her family) and the black Africans. This amounts in part to an affirmation of the strength and continuity of the ego. For the group as a whole the movement is symbolically one of penetrating the instinctual and affective levels of the psyche (Africa as contrasted with Europe, England, and America). Further, the fantasy carries a passive and inhibited member of the group (B) out of her isolation into a life of decision, action, and love and of suffering that would be bearable because, unlike that which she is living now, it would have a point. She was flushed with pleasure at her role in this piece of fantasy, and it is not difficult to see why. The fantasy played with possibilities of her future life. (For the depressive young woman this meant an affirmation of the fact that she had a future and that it would bring her choices both possible to make and worth making.) Moreover, she was brought into connection with the other people taking part in the fantasy.

The tone of feeling that prevailed at the close of the meeting and subsequent reactions of the participants suggested that something important had happened. It may be described as a change in the entire system of energetic connections within the group and within each member of it. Of course, this puts the matter in a highly abstract and hypothetical way, but then we are dealing with highly elusive phenomena. In any case, what Jung writes in many places about the symbol as a transformer of energy clearly has a bearing upon them.

2. I enter the clinic a few days after Christmas. Many patients have gone home for the holiday and most of the ones in the clinic have collapsed and are in bed. A few are drifting lugubriously around the halls. There are only a few people at the group meeting.

Group member D begins talking about how horrible Christmas is. In his family the holiday is a tremendous success when it has not ended in some rather major disaster. This idea is developed in various ways. Christmas is a time for regression; yet when one is in this regressed state one finds that other people, similarly regressed, are placing overwhelming demands upon one. It is no wonder that most patients in the clinic have collapsed; they will get better as soon as those who have gone away come back in worse states than the ones who have stayed.

Receptivity, Commitment, and Detachment

A has reported good-naturedly about his Christmas; others express admiration for the calm with which he seems to have taken the psychic carnage of the holidays. D observes that A "still has his head above water," that he is "still swimming." A then says that he had been to the swimming pool that day. I ask him how it was; he replies, "A madhouse!" Boys had been roughhousing dangerously at the side of the pool. Returning to the theme of his success in holding up, A admits that it has not been easy for him, but somehow he felt that he must not give way and collapse like the others.

We talk more about Christmas, then about Christmas presents. A then says that he decided to send only one present to his entire family, a present that the adults and the children could enjoy on different levels. He had gone to a Swiss handicraft shop and had bought a hand-carved model of Noah's ark and all the animals on it. He says that the ark is for him a symbol of Christmas. I tell him that by coincidence I have given a picture book of the story of Noah's ark to the daughter of a colleague on the staff of the clinic. I say that the pictures had been painted by "Alain le Fol." (A understands French and recognizes *fol* as "fool" or "madman.").

The discussion turns to the differences between American and European attitudes toward children, Europeans generally giving more value to maturity than Americans do, Americans making a cult of childhood.

This discussion, too, has the character of a collective fantasy with the structure and imagistic content of a dream. A problem is stated (that Christmas, which is supposed to be a time of joy and hope, actually fosters regression and disintegration). There is a *peripeteia* in which the problem is transposed from the collective to the personal level (the swimming pool emerging as the "madhouse" that threatens A from within), and there is a *lysis*, or resolution, with the emergence of a different symbol of Christmas, the ark which arises as a container of consciousness and personal identity while the scarcely bearable "madhouse" of the swimming pool yields to the unbounded waters of the deeper unconscious.

Identity is posited between the group leader (who gave the picture book of the ark story to the little girl) and A. This identity, incidentally, came to expression in an apparently fortuitous but nonetheless meaningful event of a kind that led Jung to speak of "synchronicity,"

287

or a subjectively meaningful but improbable coincidence: the combination of diverse elements (of the ark, the book, patient A, the child, and me) seemed to me to make an irrational sense.[33]

Other energetic lines lead from the crazy person that A is afraid of becoming (again) to Alain le Fol, who represents the creative force, managed by the ego, that makes an imaginative relationship to the ark possible. The ark is linked with the child (the little girl to whom I gave the book); that connection is preserved and affirmed, but the direction of the ark is toward maturity and away from infantile fixations that are played upon by the conventional celebration of Christmas.

The group, then, encouraged A in the intention expressed in his present. In giving the present to both the adults and the children he tried symbolically to maintain some kind of living link between the adult and the child in himself. The saving ark is symbolically a container that could withstand the splitting tendencies that beset him and endanger that link. But for A the meeting was more than a demonstration of moral support; a community was called into being based upon the value that he had been trying to maintain alone. (It was later reported that the meeting had been profoundly important to him.) A was the group member most immediately threatened by the general problem under discussion, but everyone else present admitted being concerned with it, and the symbolic resolution of it affected them, too.

In the fantasy content of the group meetings such moments of *peripeteia* and *lysis* arise in various ways and in various forms. Two further examples may help to convey something of this variety.

3. A discussion of death and modern funeral customs, funerals now being vaguely religious, the fact of death being skirted around or bathed in sentimentality: indirect lighting, indirect music, indirect death. The custom of the eulogy is described as a way of politely summing up the dead person's life and disposing of the fact of his death, rather in the way that primitive peoples try to drive the soul of the dead person away from the community of the living.

The Spanish attitude toward death is described, a publicly expressed concern with death being (in some Spanish circles) a sign of good taste and nobility. I say that the other side of the modern Northern sentimentality about death is the status of death as a kind of indecency; I compare this with the split between sentimental and obscene treatments of eros.

The discussion turns to pornography and then to eros and death in primitive religion. A group member describes a fourteenth-century Spanish book about love in which eros is dealt with in a way that avoids this split (obscenity-sentimentality); in the book death is also faced openly and frankly in a way that avoids this split.

Here, too, there is a general movement from the dim light of collective-conscious attitudes toward death in northern Europe and America to a more primitive level of feeling: the initial problem is transposed to the Spanish setting, much closer to blood and fire. The problem of an adequate relationship to the fact of death becomes (at the *peripeteia*) that of an adequate relationship to eros: thematically, life has come out of death. In the *lysis* the two themes of death and eros are brought together in the Spanish book; the possibility is suggested of a wise connection with the reality of each of them and of both of them at once.

4. The group is first concerned with a patient (absent) who smashed a window and a radio the night before. We talk about how unpleasant it is to have demands put upon one that have nothing to do with one's own feelings of who and how one is. (Before the absent patient's explosion another patient had made fun of her way of silently gaping at everyone and had invited her to enter a discussion that was in progress.)

The theme of breathing is then taken up, part of the interest in it coming from the gymnastic exercises of the patients: breathing and yoga. One member comments that the body is not really treated seriously and in the right way in modern psychology: there is talk about sexual organs and the body parts, but they remain parts—the talk is not really expressive of the way that he experiences his body. Pills and injections are discussed and the way they mysteriously work inside one. Someone says that the old baths and massages in a way made more sense as means of treating emotional disturbances.

A woman patient tells of dancing alone in her room. There is some comment about the film *Zorba the Greek*, in which the hero expresses his emotions through dancing, even those about the death of his son. Attention then turns to the queer relations that people in the clinic have to their bodies. The stiffest member of the group, A, has been rocking in a rocking chair. With no explanation, he begins rocking forward across the room. Everyone laughs uncontrollably.

The discussion is first about emotional explosion based upon one's feeling of being isolated and misunderstood. At the *peripeteia* the problem is transposed so as to become that of a person's relationship to his body. The *lysis* is provided by the sudden progress of A across the floor in his rocking chair. (His bit of play had something very dreamlike about it, as though we had suddenly become part of a semisurrealistic film by René Clair.) It was clear to everyone that his rocking had not only put an end to the meeting but brought a satisfactory resolution to the discussion. A possible translation of his action would be, "We talk and think about moving our bodies; instead, we should move them. Otherwise, the potentially explosive split between mind and body—like that between isolated people—remains. The body should be allowed to talk and think: the *whole* person should move, even if that movement is at first irrational."

The dominant ear of the moment. The rocking progress of patient A across the room struck the other group members as making sense and not making sense at the same time. In general, the integrating process seems to be at work both in the center of attention, in the topic under discussion, and in what could be called the level of disintegration, the irrational dynamism expressed in apparently senseless remarks and actions and in unexpected occurrences such as the intrusion of a nurse looking for someone or the passing of a very loud truck.

The fact of disintegration provokes anxiety in everyone present, including the group leader. That anxiety might be formulated in such statements as "What is happening now should not happen. I am guilty for the fact that there is not more coherence, that a containing totality is so far away." It sometimes happens that this disintegration seems the manifestation of a force hindering or breaking connections; it may be possible to map the movement of this force within the group. The disintegration may, that is, be understood and treated as an expression of resistance. The attribution of the scattered and apparently senseless phenomena to such a force brings coherence into them—or into one's attitude toward them.

Receptivity, Commitment, and Detachment

More often, however, disintegration is simply *there* as scattered content, apparently divorced from meaningful dynamic lines. This content has value for the group—if, at the outset, its value seems negative, that of leaden lumps that interfere in the making of connections. This scattered content places special demands upon the group leader. He must *recognize* and *respect* such disturbing and apparently meaningless occurrences as the intrusion of a nurse or a fit of sneezing in the same way that he does obvious expressions of resistance, as when a patient angrily leaves the room.

This respect requires the group leader to stand up under the anxiety and guilt that a person often feels when order goes to pieces. It requires him to refrain from the kind of analytic busyness that would amount to sliding out from under his own discomfort and pushing the responsibility for it onto the other members of the group. (This respect qualifies his respect for general topics of discussion. Though he is aware of the value such topics may have, he does not encourage generality as a refuge from the scattered material.)

If the group leader can bear the tension, he holds open the possibility that there may be a *spontaneous movement within the whole constellation* (such as the movement that came to expression in the turning of attention from the British royal family to blacks, in the concern with the ark, in the description of the Spanish book about love and death, and in the rocking advance of patient A).

In retrospect it is easy to speak of a spontaneous movement in the whole constellation, but it is much more difficult to recognize such a movement when it occurs. At the time one encounters instead, at least at first, what seem to be phenomena of disintegration having their own life. These phenomena may suddenly gain meaning. It then seems that the integrating process has begun to be effective on the level at which disintegration has till now been manifest.

Let us take the example of a group meeting that has already been interrupted several times. A patient has come late, wandered around, and, while another patient tries to find a chair for her, decided to leave. A door slams somewhere in the house. Quite apart from these disturbances the discussion is heavy, slow, and dull. Then a loud truck goes by, causing a window of the room to rattle. People laugh and talk nervously to one another. In the hubbub someone makes a remark such as "Something like that always happens when we seem to be getting down to the point," or "Things like that have been happening to me all day," or "That is the way things are in this house." A remark of this kind is, on the one hand, an expression of the general confusion: a tape recorder would perhaps not even render it as an intelligible statement. On the other hand, it may bring meaning into the disturbances and interruptions that had until then seemed meaningless. It has now become possible to discuss whether or not it really *is* "one of those days" when such things happen or whether or not the house really is that kind of house.

Such larger topics are often very eagerly taken up. They effect a release of energy in the whole group, and in the shift of attention to them the apparently meaningless disturbances are placed in a larger frame. This can only happen if a remark of the kind, "Things like that have been happening to me all day," has been granted a certain kind of interest. And the person (most often the group leader) who gives it that interest can do so only if he has already been bringing the same kind of interest to the apparently meaningless disturbances. That interest is grounded in the hope that some meaningful movement will take place within the whole constellation. When this happens, it often seems to him that the movement is emerging *from* the scattered material.

Thus the interest of the group leader is divided between, on the one hand, the theme of the discussion and its development, and on the other the level on which the disintegrating phenomena threaten the focus of overt interest. I believe that his paying attention to both levels at once furthers the integrating process, but it requires that focus as well. In my experience the process emerges most clearly when at least some of the group members are very much caught up in the discussion, when their interest is greatly engaged by the theme in the foreground and what is happening to it.

Sometimes (as in the slow-beginning meeting disturbed by the truck) this is not the case at the outset. At such times the process is served by the fact that several of the patients present have found other meetings to be highly worthwhile—not as bitter pills of "therapy" but as parts of a process in which connections have been made on any of the levels I have described.

Receptivity, Commitment, and Detachment

The interest awakened in such meetings is like money in the bank; in difficult times many of the patients draw upon it in the form of trust that the group will find its way. The degree of this trust shown by otherwise highly distrustful people has astonished me. It does not eliminate the momentary discomfort—even the suffering of anxiety and guilt—but it does sustain the whole enterprise, and it certainly helps to sustain the group leader in the division of his attention.

What I mean by the divided attention of the group leader may be made clearer by means of an analogy drawn from recent jazz music, one important stream of which, since about 1960, has been occupied with what the musicians playing it call "freedom."[34] The freedom they are thinking of entails a deliberate, sometimes even strained, denial of the formal conventions that governed the music earlier on. There is an attempt, for example, to break free from the set patterns—melodic, harmonic, rhythmic—that have in the past been used as the basis of one kind of development or another, especially that effected through improvisation.

In this music, there is much improvisation, both individual and collective, that is unrelated to structures other than those that emerge in the course of the improvisation. As might be expected, both the "freedom" and the expressive statement achieved in this way are severely limited by what the musicians themselves often feel to be chaos: nagging, boring, and sometimes terrible.

But, unexpectedly perhaps, out of the droning and twitching chaos emerge clear patterns, emotionally charged, and having their own kind of beauty. The conscious problem of the musicians is finding these patterns or allowing them to emerge, developing them in ways that will allow other such patterns to emerge and making links of form and feeling among them. It is easy to deny the wisdom of this self-restriction to musical materials that emerge in this way; it is difficult to deny the best musicians exploring this area a substantial measure of success in making—simply and surprisingly—music.

One of the most accomplished of these musicians, Ornette Coleman, has tried to describe what he is doing by means of the phrase "the dominant ear." He may be improvising and feel that what he is playing has lost the point that he and the rest of his group were trying to get at; that he has worked his way into a wasteland. He may then

293

feel that one of the other musicians, also improvising, is closer to the point than he is: the other musician has the dominant ear of the moment, and what is being heard with this dominant ear must be allowed a governing position in the further development.

The dominant ear hears what the group-spirit (or whatever else one wants to call the specific intelligence that the musicians feel in touch with) is trying to say, and the contents expressed by the person who has the dominant ear serve the principle of integration. Who has the dominant ear is not of primary importance, but it is essential that the principle be given value, that attention be paid to its workings. The musicians' task is to try to locate it and gain access to it as it moves, hiding and revealing itself, through the music and through the group.

Part of the function of the group leader in the kind of meeting I have described is that of listening for what the dominant ear hears; he tries to be aware of those movements that pull things together or mean changes of direction, and that make clear shapes to which various kinds—and often various levels—of relationship can be found.

In example 1, I expressed what the dominant ear was hearing with my remark about blacks in Los Angeles. But it is quite inessential for the group leader himself to express what has been striving for expression. If someone else has heard the thing that is to be heard (as when the group member thought of the Spanish book in example 3), I hope to realize that he has heard it. In my experience, the crucial moments—those that (again to compare the group discussion with a dream) provide the basic statement or the *peripeteia* or *lysis*—come through the participants with the greatest dedication to the meetings. This dedication is, of course, born of the hope of getting something out of them.

This leads me to a few final remarks about the position of the leader in this kind of group. By his own active participation in the material of the discussion he works to avoid confusion between the contained transference relationship of individual psychotherapy and the formally more diffuse relationships within such an open group.

My position in the group is, first, that of a group member. I participate actively and do not in the least confine my activity to that of analysis. I feel quite free to express my opinions about, say, General de Gaulle, my doing so being a way of insisting upon my parity (on an essential level) with the other group members.

Insofar as I have another status than that of the other group members, it is an expression of the depth and breadth of my *interest* in the group. I bear the tensions that they bear and I give expression to my own ideas and feelings and—surely—complexes. But I am concerned in a way different from theirs with the formal and dynamic content of the discussion. I reflect about the meetings in a different way than the patients do, and I am concerned with such things as the continuity between meetings, the relationship of a thematic development to the whole life of the house.

All this gives me the subjective attitude that makes the broadest and deepest sense of my participation as a member of the group. I may be thrilled in a different way than the other group members are when a highly threatened member breaks out of his isolation through an imaginative concern, shared by others, with the saving ark. But it is also an ark for me and means a resolution of the anxiety and sense of guilt attendant upon my connection with the level of disintegration within the group. With the emergence of such a symbol, fantasy has given imaginative expression not to one-sided ego attitudes and narrowly obsessing complexes but to the integrative self.

Patients deal with issues of the Father World, as it is expressed in regulations of the clinic, bus schedules, school, police, and sometimes court. Such issues prove to be the locus of the disintegrative tendencies of which I have been speaking. But these tendencies have their prototype in the infant's early experiences of falling apart emotionally and of being abandoned by its mother. When disintegrative tendencies are dealt with positively, the process of doing so may be like solving a Father World problem by imaginatively exploring, in ways using extensions of its own resources, issues confronting the ego. But such a positive outcome may also be a gift of the Mother World in the sense that a symbol such as the ark of the group's collective fantasy is a product of increased relatedness, mutuality, intimacy—of the interaction of ego and self as elaborated and differentiated in the mother-infant relationship.

In emphasizing the mother-infant relationship in this connection, I do not wish to oversimplify. I especially do not wish to do so by

295

linking rules of "ought" and "ought not" exclusively or even primarily with paternal authority. ("Mother always says 'yes'; Father always says 'no'," remarks a psychoanalyst of my acquaintance—thus summarizing a common way of construing experience, while also caricaturing the psychoanalytic preoccupation with the central role of Father.) After all, many months before Baby Amanda seemed very aware of Father as a distinct person—indeed, shortly after birth—she was interacting with Mother in the patterned activity of nursing, implying rules analogous to those of verbal communication.[35] Rules and incipient ego functions are, in short, implicit in the ways in which Mother and Baby give to one another.

These qualifications—granting importance to the levels both of ego and of self—are important to an understanding of fantasy and imagination as in various ways bridging ego-consciousness and the unconscious.

The unconscious is, as Jung many times insists, the "matrix" of consciousness. This emphasizes the prospective character of the unconscious and its capacity to give valuable products, as Mother gives birth, and as Mother and Baby give to one another. Such an image as that of the ark in the group fantasy is a gift to be understood in the context of this early giving, of which the adult retains an attenuated awareness. Much of the music of Mozart and some passages in the poetry of Rainer Maria Rilke (1875–1926) are clearly gifts in the sense of having been created apparently without the agency of the ego. Indeed, the figure of the Muse is a reminder of the secondary role that the ego often seems to play in artistic creation. Yet we speak of "works" of art. And we might contrast Mozart's and Rilke's revelations with William Butler Yeats's endless revisions of his poems in the hope of imparting to them the kind of inevitable-seeming rightness that cannot be created by the ego alone.

There is, however, no essential contradiction between gifts and work: gifts bring obligations, sometimes strenuous, with them. Though Mother and Baby give to one another, being a baby is, as I have remarked, hard work; if there is any doubt that being a mother is hard work, ask Mother at the end of the day. Such a symbol as the ark in the group fantasy is a gift of the imagination drawing on resources of the deep unconscious. Though it would be proper to call such a symbol "archetypal," doing so carries with it the danger of making the symbol seem too exclusively a gift—an image "made" by an archetype—thus one-sidedly devaluing the ego-consciousness of the group members trying to relate to one another and trying to talk about what they think they are talking about.

But there is also a danger in focusing on these attempts and the difficulties besetting them—on the "group dynamics" of egos under the sway of shadow inferiorities—since focusing on them might easily lead one to fail to appreciate the rich and deep meaning of the symbolic ark. This would be to close oneself to Mother and Baby, to imagination, and to an impressive particular one of its gifts. One fundamental obligation attendant upon a gift is that of recognizing that it has been given. Mother and Baby live in the awareness of giving to one another.

Giving does not, however, take place like manna falling from heaven but rather entails judgment—Who is to give what to whom?—which can take the form of blame. In their intimacy and mutuality, Mother and Baby affect one another, and sometimes blame one another for feeling states that each has induced in the other. Thus, Mother, anxious and irritable as she prepares for university examinations, affects Baby with her anxiety and irritability and then scolds Baby for Baby's unreasonable crankiness. Or Baby, frustrated by a cold, may cling to Mother and cry, as though Mother is the cause of Baby's frustration. This failure of empathy is a failure of imagination. When Mother and Baby are more adequately related to one another each has a felt sense of being "we together in the surrounding world," of being partners in a shared enterprise. Having intimations of oneness, they still retain an awareness of living in divided and distinguished worlds.

For imagination to produce a unifying symbol such as the ark in the group fantasy, there must be division. Feeling and imagination both require a measure of detachment. Reaching toward their object as Mother and Baby reach toward one another, feeling and imagination are nonetheless contemplative, as are Mother and Baby in the blissful nonconsummatory mutuality of gazing into one another's eyes. I have spoken (in part 4.5) of the "fullness" of such mythic symbols as the ark: Baby's experience of nonconsummatory mutuality is the primary precondition of her later capacity for apprehending such symbols in their richness and depth. The gratitude of the nursing infant is the protoform of the gratitude that is part of the mature person's recognition that such a symbol is a gift.

6.4 Mythic Forms and Images

Having spoken of mythic forms and images as archetypal, structuring our experience in ways that endow it with certain kinds of meaning, I wish now to offer a brief defense of this way of speaking, as well as a further note of caution.

Kerényi raises the issue of whether similar myths in different cultures are related through transmission or as diverse expressions of an archetypal foundation. Regarding the distinction as misstated, he remarks, "The question is, rather: spontaneous acquisition on an archetypal foundation or transmission on the same foundation. The term 'archetypal' seems to contain implications which compel one to accept it but which, for that very reason, make it a commonplace that arouses no particular interest. We must take care not to attach too much importance to the *word.*"[36] He nonetheless continues to employ the term in his later works, presumably because the mythical materials with which he is concerned in important respects accord with "types," and they have been imagined as—or imagined in relation to—beginnings or first principles, *archai*. But he also offers another reason when he speaks "of *archetypal facts of human existence.*"[37]

An example that occurs to me of an "archetypal fact of human existence" is birth. Over the earth as a whole, human births take place at the rate of a large number per minute; women have been giving birth as long as the human race has existed, and births are recorded as statistics of various kinds. In this sense the archetypal fact of birth is a commonplace. But a particular birth may be fraught with the profoundest personal meaning, may indeed seem a miracle, and birth as a fact of human existence has been elevated to the status of a mythic form or image in countless rituals and birth-stories of gods or heroes. Similarly, falling in love is a commonplace of much kitschy song and fiction, but may also be experienced as a fateful gift from another world and has been so elevated in myths and great works of literature.

Receptivity, Commitment, and Detachment

When I speak of mythic forms and images, I have in mind certain ways in which what Kerényi called archetypal facts of human experience have been apprehended and expressed. Indeed, I assume that in calling such facts archetypal, Kerényi means, in part, that they are significant in such ways as to lend themselves to embodiment in mythic forms and images.

In speaking of mythic forms and images, I have in mind such statements of Jung as these: "The collective unconscious . . . appears to consist of mythological motifs or primordial images, for which reason the myths of all nations are its real exponents. In fact, the whole of mythology could be taken as a sort of projection of the collective unconscious."[38] And " 'myth-forming' structural elements must be present in the unconscious psyche," producing not "myths with a definite form, but rather mythological components which, because of their typical nature, we can call 'motifs,' 'primordial images,' types or—as I have named them—*archetypes.*"[39] Thus, "mythic forms and images" basically translates *archetypes* in light of such definitions.

By "mythic" I mean pertaining to the kinds of elements to be found in myths. From a psychological point of view there are various reasons for using the term "mythic," and for using it in an open and partly figurative way. First, the foremost students of myths do not agree on a several-point definition of myth that cannot be contested on the basis of counterexamples, whereas a minimal definition such as "traditional tales" ignores essential characteristics of a great many myths—such as their sacredness, their concern with divine beings, and their association with cult.[40] Second, myths in the sense of traditional tales are not the only imaginative products containing mythic or mythlike elements. Thus in *Symbols of Transformation* Jung justifiably brought together mythical religious texts, passages from such poets as Goethe, dreams, and psychotic delusions. Third, it sometimes makes sense to allow *mythic* also to refer to cultic and ritual elements associated with myths but also distinguishable from them. (For example, one might have reason to call the eucharist "mythic.") And fourth, though myths have their context in a community, one may also have reason to speak of a life-shaping "personal myth," which may or may not be drawn from living religious tradition.

Feeling, Imagination, and the Self

The "forms" of myths include such aspects of mythic "logic" as the binary oppositions studied by the structural anthropologist Claude Lévi-Strauss.[41] To speak of mythic "images" is implicitly—and rightly—to link them with imagination. Another advantage of the term mythic *image* is, as Kerényi points out, that it suggests the question of what the mythic image is an image *of*, as such a term as *figure* does not.[42] This question may not be in any simple way answerable, as mythic images are often symbols in the sense of referring ultimately to something unknown, of which the symbol is the best possible but only approximate expression. (If it could be simply said what the Christian eucharist refers to, millions of words would not have been uttered in trying to explain it.) To have such a mercurial question in mind is to remain aware that mythic experience is transcendent as a reaching toward a certain psychic content, a reaching toward that is also, through imagination, a way of already gaining and having contact with it.

This transcendent quality of a myth is what gives it its capacity to transform psychic energy and to structure consciousness in accordance with the myth. (This may be seen, for example, in the myth of the mother-daughter pair Demeter and Persephone as celebrated in the Eleusinian mysteries, one aim of which was clearly to bring about a certain state of mind in the participants.) This quality is experienced as revelation, the content of which functions on the order of a formal and final cause. In saying this I am assuming that mythic forms and images are important in the reality of the psyche, and that they have a bearing on unconscious and conscious processes in their interrelations, which have both personal and collective aspects. That these interrelations are hard to trace and talk about does not make them unreal or unimportant.

One danger constantly attendant upon attempts to express these interrelations must, however, be admitted. It is to forget that conscious and unconscious systems are ultimately complementary, are a polarity within an overall whole, so that there is continuous feedback between the two. To forget this is to invite the reifying of archetypes in such a way that they are aligned with the unconscious and made causative, to the neglect of conscious action and knowledge. The result is a covert idealism (or even solipsism) to be seen, for example, in the implications of an oversimplifying diagram by the analytical psychologist Erich Neumann. It shows nuclei-like "archetypes" situated in the collective unconscious, whence they are constellated as contents of collective consciousness, a role that gradually depotentiates them; leaving husks behind, they then sink back into the collective unconscious.[43] It is surely this sort of danger that leads Kerényi to qualify his reference to archetypal facts of human existence by saying that they "cannot be mere realities of the psyche."[44] Of course, for Jung—as my discussion of participating consciousness in part 5 should have demonstrated—the reality of the psyche is anything but "mere." Yet once it is recognized, attention subtle enough to befit the enterprise is needed to explore the openness of psyche to the world. This issue I have already raised in my reflections (in part 5.13) on the polarities of God and man, and of man and nature.

My account of mythic forms and images needs to be further qualified by the admonition that the many things that have been called "myth" make up a sprawling variety difficult to classify. Thus G. S. Kirk maintains "that there are *myths*, which are traditional tales of many different kinds and functions, but no such things as 'myth.' "[45] It is surely true that some earlier students of Greek and other myths generalized too broadly, for example, in describing the relations of "myth" to "cult" as though these relations were fixed rather than variable or sometimes even nonexistent. And there are, as Kirk avers, problems about making a category of "mythical thinking."[46] But when Kirk also sees "no reason to suppose that most myths are especially symbolic," we may surmise that his clean-up operation on earlier thinking about myth has been at a high price, that he has clarified some issues by ignoring the intuitive grasp—shared, with differences, by Jung, Kerényi, Walter F. Otto, and others—of certain important things. These concern the nature of imaginative symbols as apprehended especially in the mode of feeling.

Otto might seem to fall into the kind of one-sidedness I noted in Neumann when Otto speaks of *"der ursprüngliche Mythos"*—original, primitive, initial myth—in contrast to secondary (and partly debased) versions of it.[47] This is related to the distinction (discussed in part 5.5) that Jensen has drawn between a creative phase of culture and its secondary "application." And the justification I adduced for Jensen, that he is saying something true about the bearing of religion (as distinct from magic) on feeling and imagination, I would also adduce for Otto. That is, I propose granting that a human urge to find and create meaning is not derivative but primary, and that feeling and imagination are necessary to some of the deepest kinds of meaning, which find their fullest expression in some myths—in mythic forms and images. If, then, we make an ideal type of such myths, as Otto does, we are regarding them as realizations of a formal and final cause inherent in man's capacity and propensity for myth-making. This view seems to me in principle compatible with also granting that myths draw upon the most diverse psychic functions and embody the most diverse concerns.

If it troubles us that such an ideal type cannot be neatly demarcated—not as neatly, at least, as Otto seems to assume—we should recall that where feeling and imagination are alive, boundaries are typically fluid. ("These things seem small and undistinguishable, / Like far-off mountains turnèd into clouds"; "Methinks I see these things with parted eye, / When everything seems double" [A Midsummer Night's Dream, IV. i. 188–91].) This fluidity—the reader may recall references earlier to deintegration—is a necessary concomitant of the quality of revelation Otto finds characteristic of the myths with which he is chiefly concerned. Whatever historical issues he oversimplifies, his view is in keeping with what I have maintained about the role of mythic forms and images in the transformation of psychic energy and the creation of consciousness.

The full title of Otto's essay is "Primitive Myth in Light of the Sympathy of Man and World"; this implies the polarities of man and God and of man and nature (discussed in part 5.13). I take this sympathy to be real. "*Lebt' nicht in uns des Gottes eigne Kraft, / Wie könnt' uns Göttliches entzücken?*" Goethe asks: "If the god's own power did not live in us, / How could the divine enrapture us?" Goethe also observes that only because the eye is sunlike can it see the light of the sun.[48] And I take this sympathy to be as fundamental in the reality of the psyche as are the workings of our instrumental intelligence.

That synthetic imagination is continuous with more prosaic forms of fantasy I have already maintained (in part 5.5) as I have (in part 5.6) that utilitarian and more contemplative concerns are often densely interwoven. Though giving mythic forms and images an important kind of primacy, I would also propose that imagination and feeling live in the real world of nature and other people and their God or gods. As the phenomenological philosopher Max Scheler (1874–1928) usefully reminds us, "We live with the *entire fullness of our spirit* chiefly among *things;* we live in the *world.* "[49] To call mythic forms and images "archetypal" is to emphasize the causative power they may sometimes have in the reality of the psyche. But, as we saw in the preceding section, this power is a function of interest—in nature, other people, and their God or gods.

The mother-infant relationship bears on these matters, since to be born is to enter a world of community, an animated world, perceived by a creature disposed to be interested in its animation. To see links between mythic animation more generally and the infant's interest in animate objects and, early in its second year, in fantasy stories is not to reduce gods to infantile projections. It is simply to affirm that imaginative apprehension of the gods draws on psychic capacities at work very early in the life of the individual. Further, Otto cites the philosopher Schelling as saying (in *The Ages of the World*) that each thing is more than its appearance, more than the eyes see and the hands can grasp, something that is true of every event and every condition of existence. As Otto remarks, this "more" is not something additional, that could also be lacking; rather, without this aura-like "more" the thing would have no existence. Otto is thus talking about what Goethe called *Urphänomene,* primordial phenomena, behind which, in Goethe's view, stands divinity.[50]

In talking about this "more" (in part 4.1), I have related it to nonconsummatory mutuality and the infant's sense of more than enough. Surely the mythic "more" rests and draws upon the infant's knowledge of plenty.

6.5 Myth As Formal and Final Cause

If abstract concepts (such as "atoms" and "particles") are fictions of one kind, mythic forms and images are fictions of another. The two kinds may be interrelated, but each has its own distinct and apparently necessary kinds of truth. Thus, the "soul" of the systematic theologian

303

and the "soul" of the shaman might both be treated in the same encyclopedia article but in different sections of it.

"Soul" belongs to the order of cause. (It is an ancient idea, for example, that the body lives *because* the soul inhabits it.) In its less abstract and theological manifestations "soul" belongs among the mythic forms and images that fictionally represent causation.

We may try to understand "cause" by translating it with such terms as "meaning construct."[51] In so doing we usefully remind ourselves that we are talking not about the Real but about models of our experience. As models of our experience, mythic forms and images especially accord with formal and final causes—among Aristotle's four kinds of causation (material, efficient, formal, and final). This is to say, mythic forms and images are expressive of the broad patterning and goal-directedness of psychic life. We use them, as we use abstract concepts, to live our lives meaningfully. Yet to say that we "use" mythic forms and images is to make them products of our instrumental intelligence, and is thus to oversimplify.

The view that our fictions are instrumental assumes that something is using them to some purpose. Partly this something is the knowing, acting subject that we call "I." But this something may also, on a deeper level, be the unknowable x that Schopenhauer has called Will and Bergson the Life Force (or *élan vital*). Whether our fictions are not only instrumental but also true we cannot in the larger view know, since—as Nietzsche has argued—there is no way to be certain that whatever agent and organizing principle is at work in the ongoing of life cherishes truth more than deception, no way to be certain that deception serves its purposes less effectively than truth. (A man and woman fall in love and marry; their union produces children. Is their falling in love deception or truth?) We may prefer truth, make of it an ultimate term, and persuade ourselves that it will prevail. To assume such an affirmation is to exceed rational and empirical knowledge, though we normally remain unaware of this. More cautiously, and at the price of greater ambiguity, we may say with Jung that even in our scientific constructions we are living the myth, some myth, onward. I will return in a moment to what it means to live a myth—and to live it onward.

If, then, I say that "I" live my life, I must be fully aware that this "I" is by no means identical with the conscious ego, and that the x that lives in and through my life also lives in and through the kinds of nonego psychic components that we have explored in various personal vignettes. Moreover, this x also lives in and through my life in my encounters with the world as the world corresponds to my inner dispositions. I mean by this, among other things, that I meet images of my problems, my aversions, my inclinations, in outer objects, people, and events. (Thus, for example, exactly Hamlet, with his capacity for "thinking too precisely on the event," is given a chance to kill Claudius exactly when Claudius is trying to pray.)

We may assume or conclude that there is some form of correspondence or even identity between the x I am describing now and the still larger x that causes there to be something and not nothing, and causes that something to have whatever character it has with and despite my limited participation in it. But one cannot be rationally and empirically certain that one knows what one thus assumes or concludes. Nor can one call the larger x "God"—a concept—and then say that one knows this concept in experience. One can do neither of these things because the qualification "as if" must always be part of the ultimate rounding out of our conception—since we can at best "stammer about Being," to quote von Weizsäcker—and because in important respects conceptual and nonconceptual experience so radically transcend one another. (If I talk about the nature of pain, I am not talking about my pain now.)

Mythic forms and images may take us to the limit of the known and even of the knowable. We may recognize in them the structures of the x that lives in and through our lives. This is the purport of the statements about myth by Jung and Otto—and about primordial phenomena (Urphänomene) by Goethe—cited in the previous section. And yet mythic forms and images are and must be logical if they are to function within a symbol system, even if they do so in a way that provides glimpses of a reality that transcends it. That a god is capable of assuming human form is in part a sign of his extraordinary power. That mythic forms and images accord with logic contributes to our sense of their deep necessity, a point to which I will return in a moment.

In archaic societies myths perform two interrelated functions bearing on the issues I am now raising—the functions of effecting a detachment from the flux of particular experience, and of relating the individual to a total world. (These functions may also be performed by cultural artifacts other than myths—such as works of art and contemplative practices. Myths may also perform a host of other functions. And some myths may not perform these functions at all. But even if these functions do not offer the basis of an exclusive definition of myth, this admission need not hinder us from singling them out as especially important to an understanding of what myths are and do.)

One can see the function of detachment most clearly in myths of creation, which reveal a deeper and more embracing reality that our personal interests and projects in the world cause us to neglect. Such myths free us, in the words of Mircea Eliade, from a "false identification of Reality with what each of us *appears to be or to possess*" and thus enables us "to approach a Reality that is inaccessible at the level of profane, individual existence."[52] As Polanyi comments on this view of creation myths, "Our personal involvement in the world is *with some parts of the world,* while the conception of creation encompasses the *whole* world—the world that lies beyond or under or through all its parts. The one is concerned with things as parts, while the other ignores these matters and has the totality of all conceivable experiences as its object. . . . In this sense, therefore, myths of creation are untranslatable into terms that apply to things within the world."[53] In reciting or listening to such a myth, according to Eliade, one transcends "the 'historical situation'. In other words, one goes beyond the temporal condition and the dull self-sufficiency which is the lot of every human being simply because every human being is 'ignorant'—in the sense that he is identifying himself, and Reality, with his own particular situation."[54] And so the detachment effected by myths in archaic societies is also an opening to a total world having, for the person entering it by means of the myth, a more objective character. It is this line of reasoning, and this positive valuation of mythic forms and images, that led Jung to consider them expressions of the "objective psyche."

The reader will, however, recall my insistence (in part 5.13) that an objective view of the world is impossible. This coupled with my insistence (just now) on the subjectivity of our living among fictions, and on their fictionality, should raise doubts as to how neatly the term "the objective psyche" resolves issues raised in the preceding section. Further, even if myths in archaic societies may be said to create a total world, we may still wonder how unified or multifarious such a total world is—questions to be explored in the following section. I would emphasize, too, the way in which consciousness not only makes the unconscious conscious (as we also saw in part 5.13), but beyond this helps to form it by being manifest in conscious attitudes to which the unconscious creatively responds. Moreover, the segregation of sacred life that I have just been describing is always incomplete, a failed attempt to realize a desideratum. There is laughter in church, Judas among the Disciples, the altar built for venal ends. We live in divided and distinguished worlds that we nonetheless cannot in our minds and hearts securely divide and distinguish when it seems most important for us to do so.

Still, the butterfly-like life of the psyche is real, indeed in important respects primary and irreducible. And there are important respects in which unconscious processes are primary within that life. Though we experience mythic forms and images as phenomena of consciousness, and though they may in part be consciously created in accord with conscious aims and values, there are also important respects in which they bring unconscious processes to conscious expression. In so doing, mythic forms and images mediate between consciousness and its unconscious background and matrix. Conscious products, they have a resonance of unconscious implications that enables them to point beyond the known. This resonance, apprehended in glimpses, is essential to their efficacy as transformative symbols.

I want now to discuss two characteristics of Shakespearean comedy that are "mythic" in the sense in which I am using the word. They belong to the class of what I have been calling mythic forms and images—appearing here in a nonmythic context, though they also figure in what we would call myths in a more limited sense. Further, they function as formal and final cause—they are structuring elements—in the interactions between consciousness and the unconscious, as such interactions are implied in the drama. The first of these characteristics is the contrivance of events to serve the exigencies of the plot; the second is the weddings concluding the main action. (I have touched on both briefly in part 3.1.)

By "contrivance" and "exigencies" I mean to suggest the radically nonnaturalistic, dancelike movement of the comic form, which unfolds in accordance with what could be called a mythic logic, a logic

307

of higher powers, superior to individual volition. (One may grant at least some manifestations of *mythos* as having a special authority with respect to *logos*—as being in some sense truer. Writers I have cited do this, persuasively. Still, myth has its own form of logic, partly according with the logic followed in mundane affairs.)

For example, in the story of the three caskets in *The Merchant of Venice*, the choice of the correct one can only come last, since with that choice the story of the rival suitors will be wound up. Moreover, since the first casket is of gold, the second must be of silver and the third of lead, since this series is a single, clear, and logical progression. Moreover, when Bassanio declares his love of Portia it is logical, since the Venetian friends share a common fate, that Gratiano should declare his love for Nerissa, offering no more explanation than this:

> My eyes, my lord, can look as swift as yours:
> You saw the mistress, I beheld the maid.
> You loved, I loved. . . .

> [III.ii.197–99]

Further, once Antonio's bond with Shylock is signed, it is inevitable that Antonio's ships should miscarry and the bond be forfeit, since this development accords with the logical principle of fairy tales (described by Vladimir Propp), whereby every explicit injunction in the story is to be violated.

To see the relations between such contrivance and the weddings at the close, we must ask ourselves *what* weddings are an image *of*—to return to Kerényi's question about myths considered in the preceding section. And to begin to answer this question we might consider the feelings and emotions aroused by weddings in real life.

One striking fact about weddings is that they make some people cry. Why? Partly, one may guess, because the bride and groom are making an immense commitment for obscure reasons that one would have to sum up in the unenlightening word *love,* and are doing so while completely unaware of what will result from that commitment. One gains a measure of their ignorance if one imagines a married couple with grown or half-grown children and then thinks back to the wedding of the couple, when those children, in all their particularity and complexity, were, in effect, a cipher, a nothing. Further, though matrimony is a haven, it is better to be well hanged than ill wed, and the tears at a wedding may also be in response to the immense risk with which the scarcely definable promise of marriage is suffused. Moreover, though this was earlier clearer than it is now, there is still an important sense in which marrying is not something two people do, as actions performed by their conscious egos, but is rather something done to them by personal and historical circumstances, by society, and—to use a word I have already applied to the Venetian friends—by fate. But what does *fate* mean in such a connection? It means a formal and final pattern of that which lives in and through our lives, as that pattern is manifest at the limits of the known. Such a pattern is of emotional import.

In what someone takes to be a fateful event, a special value is revealed in a way that seems both fortuitous and the expression of a transpersonal order. There is, it is supposed, a level of reality on which one's future is already known—written, for example, in the Book of Fate. What knows one's future, it is assumed, makes it happen. And what knows it and makes it happen is thought to foretell it by making order out of chance, or by revealing apparent chance as secretly ordered. Refined and elaborated, such "magical" views become metaphysical concepts of the preestablished harmony of the universe. Whatever we may think of such concepts, experiences of fortuitous—magical—order are available to all but the most hardened rationalists among us.

Shakespeare records such experiences, on the one hand, because as a dramatist he is concerned with action, which is formed, which moves to some goal, but which may be dissipated in random events. He records such experiences, on the other, because he is concerned with the soul, which in some of its most important expressions views the world magically. Thus, he sometimes presents twilight subjective states in which the distinction between subject and object does not obtain.

But in Shakespeare's plays events in the outer world, and coming to the subject from others, also sometimes assume the character of magically induced *actions,* or of actions suggestive of magic. In *King Lear,* for example, the storm on the heath *is* Lear's passionate madness. Or rather, between storm and madness there is a causal relation, not so much material and efficient—though also that—as formal and final.

Let us return to our question concerning the relation between the "contrived" logic of Shakespeare's comic design and the weddings rounding out the main action. In a sense the plot of such a play as *The Merchant of Venice* is partly, in effect, the product of a process of reasoning backward from its weddings. The characters are "fated" to be married; the exigencies of the plot force them to that intended end. Marriage is the mythic form of their relation to the unknown, is for them the experienced structure of spirit, from which the formal and final meaning of their lives has been emerging since the outset of the action. To be fated to marriage in this way is to be subject to such higher powers as those that find expression in the nuptials of Zeus and Hera bringing fertility to the fields,[55] or of the Bridegroom Christ and the Church or the soul.

To elaborate upon these remarks about the *x* that lives in and through our lives, I want to comment briefly on two utterances by Jung bearing upon myth as formal and final cause.

The first is the motto he had carved over the entrance to his house in Küsnacht: "Called or not called, God is present." If *God* is understood as, on the one hand, the result of the metaphorical extension we have been considering, and, on the other, as the lived experience of spirit, and if the irreducible discrepancy between these two senses of *God* is kept in mind, the thought expressed in this saying is, I believe, not only true but psychologically invaluable.

The practical wisdom implied by this saying (thus understood) is elaborated in the second of these utterances, in Jung's essay "On the Nature of the Psyche," in which he compares instinct with the infrared part of the color spectrum and "archetype" with the ultraviolet part. One would expect blue to be a more apt equivalent of the spirit than violet, he observes, implying that the ultraviolet of his metaphor stands for the spiritual form of instinct. Spirit would thus be continuous with instinct, and partly of the same nature as it, but without being reducible to it. Since we do not know what thing or multitude of diverse things instinct may be—some 14,000 "instincts" have been proposed—this attempt to ground "archetype" in instinct does not say anything very specific. It nonetheless says something important, which

310

Receptivity, Commitment, and Detachment

Jung summarizes thus: "The realization and assimilation of instinct never take place at the red end, i.e., by absorption into the instinctual sphere, but only through integration of the image which signifies and at the same time evokes the instinct, although in a form quite different from the one we meet on the biological level."[56]

We could imagine the body-ego or body-subject as the infrared part of the color spectrum and spirit as the ultraviolet part. Thus qualified, Jung's remarks about the integration of the image are profoundly true: psychological problems serve the purpose of impelling the person suffering them to make contact with the relevant spiritual factors. These are the mythic forms and images, the souls, spirits—and demons—of lived experience. Such contact must precede integration of spiritual contents, which is in any case possible only to a limited extent, since spirit remains finally "other."

And yet, as the metaphor of the spectrum suggests, "other" need not be assimilated to the "Wholly Other" that the theologian Rudolf Otto regarded as the primary object of religious experience.[57] (Such assimilation would make "other" not violet but blue.) Rather, the otherness that makes persons and things into "It" is first known in the shared life of mother and infant in which "Thou" appears even earlier, and the spirit that can be known as "Wholly Other" can also be known in the intimacy of "nearer to me than I am to myself." (This intimacy is implicit in a central tenet of Meister Eckhart, that "God is in us and we are in God"[58]—an idea to which we will return in the next section, especially in connection with Coleridge.) In relation to the body-ego or body-subject, the image—at the ultraviolet end of the spectrum—is always significantly "other"; yet it remains mine, however much it may sometimes seem not-mine in lived experience.

I wish to conclude these remarks about self, other, and images of meaning by recounting a dream of Henry Newman (whom we met in part 3.3), and by allowing some actions and utterances of Baby Amanda to serve as commentary on it.

The main figure in Mr. Newman's dream, apart from himself, is a woman, "petulant, bright, cheerful, bitchy, snide, and childish," who is perhaps, or perhaps not, identical with a certain well-known actress. She is in charge of a group of children, to whom she is telling a story. The authorities think she is an impostor and are intent on

311

testing their suspicions. Mr. Newman knows that if he and two other men present listen attentively and completely agree with everything the woman says, they will be able to recall the story verbatim, no matter how long it is. He closes his eyes in concentration on the story.

The woman now speaks directly and personally to him, asking, "Do you care for me? Do you love me?" With his eyes closed, he watches her continuing to speak in the same vein, as she moves closer and closer to him. The dream becomes "sexually intimate," and she implores him to love her as they loved one another as children. With his eyes still closed, he tries to embrace her; she is, however, "visually but not physically present."

What Mr. Newman embraces is an animating image, belonging less to the physical world than to the reality of the psyche—an image expressive of the contrasexual component of his own person. That the woman in the dream is an actress—a role-player—or an impostor of an actress, or an impostor of a teacher, emphasizes her quality as image. Further, though the woman is in some sense a copy of a well-known actress in the social world, her image is only secondarily derivative; primarily it is originative—is about Mr. Newman's own capacity to resonate with feminine forms and images inside and outside himself.

Twenty-four-month-old Amanda conducts tea parties at which she serves invisible tea. Sometimes her guests are inanimate (toy Easter Bunny and toy Bear), and sometimes they are real people, who must drink the invisible tea as though it were wet and hot and good-tasting. She and her guests are not making do with what happens not to be real tea—they are translating real tea to the level of image. To make the pretend tea party into a real tea party with real tea would be to destroy the translation.

Recently Amanda's father made her walk with him from the car around the front of the house to the door, while her mother came around the back of the house, where she wanted to fetch something. In an anxious voice, Amanda kept repeating to Daddy, "Mamma will come, Mamma will come," thus saying to herself what he or her mother would say to her. Also, when given the choice between howling about something in displeasure or going to her room, she will sometimes fight back tears, saying, "No, I don't want to cry," or will choose to go to her room in the hopes of composing herself. These are the beginnings of the kind of reflectiveness that means becoming responsive to the images that Jung would place at the ultraviolet end of his metaphorical spectrum. This development has been prepared for by Amanda's rich experience of a mother-infant community in which both partners have collaborated to give her a sense of the self in which the developing ego is grounded. To say "Mamma will come back" is to acknowledge a psychic image of Mamma as a possession of the self.

6.6 How Unitary is One? How Dual is Two? Unus Mundus, Polarity, and the Mother-Infant Relationship

"Out of the One comes Two, out of the Two comes Three, and from the Third comes One as the Fourth": this "Axiom of Maria" recurs over the centuries in the alchemical writings Jung studied so assiduously. This saying describes a coherent, if enigmatic, progression in the numbers from one to four that are so important in our symbolism, in the workings of our minds, and in the physical world. Their importance in the domain of culture and spirit is evident in the various religious and philosophical monisms and dualisms, in the Christian trinity and the three terms (thesis, antithesis, synthesis) of the Hegelian dialectic, and in the quaternity symbolism of much religious art and architecture. The importance of these numbers in the psychological development of the individual is suggested by such terms as the "unit status" of the infant and the mother-infant "dyad," by the triadic Oedipus complex, by the quaternity of father, mother, son, and daughter, and by the symbolism of Four prominent in dreams and in such religious visions as those of Ezekiel, Blake, and the Sioux medicine man Black Elk.

Fundamentally important as the numbers one through four are, certain uses of them give rise to significant ambiguities that easily go undetected.

I wish to discuss some of these ambiguities, which might be suggested by such questions as these: How unitary is One? How dual is Two? Is One prior to Two, or is Two prior to One? What is happening when something is presented as One but is not, or when something

313

is presented as Two but is not? What is happening when Three comes out of Two in such a way as to suppress the Two purportedly necessary for the Third to become One as the Fourth? What, in short, about the thwarted, subversive, illusory forms of the progression from One to Four that in the Axiom of Maria sounds like a natural unfolding? I will hardly make these questions sound less arcane when I remark that the issues they are meant to suggest entail a concern with the *unus mundus* (the alchemical "One World") and the difference between polarity and dialectic. But the issues are psychologically not only real but often as urgent as, say, the pained bewilderment of a crying baby. I will have the mother-infant relationship in mind in my discussion of all the issues I raise.

The 1984 issue of *Harvest,* a journal for Jungian studies, published by the Analytical Psychology Club of London, at various points suggests these ambiguities and a possible perspective on them. Indeed, the issue begins with an exchange of letters between a correspondent and Jung about an extraordinary dream described by Dostoyevsky, in the structure of which the numbers one through four are very important.[59] I wish to comment on articles in the issue that touch on my theme—those by the scholar-critic Kathleen Raine, and the analysts Aniela Jaffé, Bani Shorter, Robert M. Stein, and David Holt.

Raine makes clear that the issues with which I am now concerned have a bearing on the inadequacies of the prevailing scientific world view. She also makes clear that these inadequacies require that we regain the insights of such earlier thinkers as Blake. Speaking of the infinite, coherent cosmos revealed by natural science, she remarks that nothing of its order would be altered or lost "by the transposition of the phenomena from an external and lifeless physical space [which it occupies in much contemporary 'normal science'] to an inner and mental living space." She refers to "what Blake describes as the 'wrenching apart' of an external physical space . . . from an interior and mental space," this process being "the disruption of the original *unus mundus,* the indivisible unity of mind and matter, of man and nature," "a living universe, whose 'Every particle of dust breathes forth its joy.' "[60]

Jaffé focuses on the *unus mundus*—Neumann's "unitary reality" (*Einheitswirklichkeit*)—as it figures in the later theorizing of Jung and

Neumann. Before arriving at the concept of unitary reality, Neumann had regarded the symbolic serpent biting its tail (*Uroboros*) as an image of the unitary condition preceding "the polarised reality of the ego-consciousness that we know, moving constantly within the tension between subject and object, man and nature, or man and his world." He also regarded the widespread myth of the Original Parents locked in embrace as such an image, their unity being "that of the transcendent, God-like existence which is free of all oppositions, the amorphous Ejn Sof, representing both eternal fullness and nothingness." Jaffé remarks about this image, importantly, that it does not simply represent equilibrium but also has in it the creative element of beginning anew. "Out of it flows the cosmos," she writes, "just as, psychologically speaking, consciousness evolves from the unconscious or the ego from the self."[61] This One, then, has polarity and further differentiation actively implicit within it.

In her reflections upon "Giving Birth within a Tradition," concerned with the further development of Jungian psychology, Shorter characterizes psychotherapy in this tradition in a way that implies the *unus mundus.* "The 'whole psychic human being,' " she quotes Jung as saying, "proves to be nothing less than a world, that is, a microcosm, as the ancients quite rightly thought. . . . The psyche reflects and knows the whole of existence and everything works in and through the psyche."[62] Any tradition shares features with such a microcosm, and like the individual must grow and develop. The growth and development of either entails the receptivity and detachment seen in the mother's relation to the embryo and to the growing infant: "The ability to be impregnated, to receive and allow the new and the growing other a place, to ponder the wonder of its arrival and to nurture it in partial unknowing belongs to woman, but so also does allowing detachment from each stage or insight met, held, explored, suffered or cherished."[63]

Stein, like Jung, both differing from Freud, regards the incest taboo primarily not as the result of prohibition by an external authority but rather as the expression of an inner demand for psychological development, though the disposition to such development makes use of external authority and its prohibitions. Taboo is "to set apart"; prohibition separates, and so does the detachment that allows the living creature to be born and to be allowed to pass from one stage to another. In this way the Father World with its prohibitions may be seen to elaborate upon a disposition partly inherited from the Mother World, a disposition originating on a psychic level on which mind and body could be said to be largely one.[64]

Holt, in his approach to dreams, takes Jung's dramatic model of their structure as a point of departure for considering them under the aspect of dramatic performance, with its multiple points of focus and reference.

In connection with Holt's concerns, it is notable that Jung, along lines pursued by Jaffé in her comments on unitary reality, did not presume to know whether there are ultimately many archetypes or only one, since in the unconscious, distinctions between one and many become impossible to trace. Dramatic expression—in the dream itself, as a minidrama, or in the real or metaphorical performance of it—is the result of a differentiation requiring restraint, as this possibility, here, is suppressed and excluded and that one, there, realized and underscored. The actions and the prevailing attitudes of the dream ego (the ego as represented in the dream) are relativized by being regarded not only from its own viewpoint but also from others'—those of other characters, the director, the audience—all trying to apprehend the intention, the affective currents, the meaning of the story being enacted. This "exercise," as Holt calls it, is very much like that of the waking ego trying to maintain a responsible openness to intimations of the self.[65]

Shakespeare frequently took up the common Renaissance themes of the world as a stage and of life as a dream, and sometimes interwove them. Stage play and real life are already interwoven—a play draws its materials from life, at however great a remove, and we partly forget, while also remembering, that it is a play we are watching—as dream and real life, too, are interwoven: while we dream we do not know we are dreaming. And in Shakespeare's interweaving of these themes, we are brought to a liminal or threshold state, in which customary boundaries are relaxed or blurred. What is imaginatively presented in this state is in important ways not a semblance of something else, behind it or reflected in it, but has its own irreducible reality and truth. The degree of liminality sometimes achieved in this presentation is suggested by a remark of the mad King Leontes, in Shakespeare's *The Winter's Tale*, to his queen, whom he has wrongly accused of adultery, "Your actions are my dreams" (III.ii.80). Still, the very portrayal of Leontes' madness affirms the necessity of the kind of imaginative exercise in which the ego acknowledges the relativity of its position. It affirms this by making us aware that such an exercise would be required for him to be cured of this madness and to develop beyond the prepsychotic condition that led to it.

The detachment achieved by imagination used in this way is more closely related to the maternal letting go described by Shorter than it is to paternal prohibition. And this maternal letting go is more closely related to the nonconsummatory mutuality of mother and infant than it is to appetitive strivings expressed in such utilitarian projects as a chimpanzee's ruse to get a banana away from a rival; a two-year-old's project of jamming a high chair and a tricycle together in the hope of making a single, climbable object of them; or President Reagan's fantasy of an impenetrable Star Wars system of defense against missiles.

I now want to consider the bearing of the dramatic perspective on the relations I have been discussing, as I reflect for a moment further about "archetypes."

To talk about archetypes is to essentialize—to construe our experience in terms of essence. We are led to do this by our urge to symbolize—by symbolization as psychic process—and by the genius of our symbol systems—by the symbolic artifacts that embody and in turn shape our motives. This does not mean that the essences thus arrived at are necessarily "mere" fictions—that "archetypes" belong only to the realm of "talking about." But it does mean that they are not located in a supercelestial place—or in the collective unconscious conceived as such a place. Rather, they are in the world, in complex relations among subjects.

What I mean may become clear, first, if we recall that Jung also called the "collective unconscious" the "objective psyche," and, second, if we allow the term "objective psyche" to be qualified by certain utterances by the biologist Jakob von Uexküll. These utterances also usefully elaborate on Goethe's remark (cited in part 6.4) that we see the light of the sun because our eye is sunlike, and there are reasons

317

why it will be well to have them in mind as we turn to matters to concern us in a moment.

According to von Uexküll, we have come to realize that "an objective picture of the world, which does justice to all subjects, must necessarily remain a phantom."[66] Moreover, "there are just as many spaces and times as there are subjects, because every subject is enclosed in its own environment," a point which he strikingly illustrates by insisting that "we can no longer speak of a single sun, shining in the sky, but must speak of thousands upon thousands upon thousands of suns, shining down from the remotest planes of unknown subjects. The suns do not act directly upon one another but act upon our environment through an unknown subject. The sun that makes a swarm of gnats dance is not our sun but a gnat sun, which owes its existence to the eye of the gnat."[67]

Von Uexküll applies this thought to human interactions in another striking figure, from the theater: "When we see our fellow men walking around, they are striding upon our stages. These stages are never identical, and in most cases they are fundamentally different. And we cannot demand to play the same role on other stages that we play on our own."[68]

As a scientist, von Uexküll is concerned with the lawfulness in the relations he has thus described, but his emphasis is on singularity and kinds of singularity, rather than on merger and the obliteration of individual differences in the interests of abstract oneness. And his figure of actors on a stage—or on various stages—is compatible with Holt's contention that looking at experience dramatically keeps perspectives open and preserves their multiplicity.

Playwright, actors, director, and audience collaborate in exploring the mode of action. But this exploration is also a revelation of essence—Oedipus and Hamlet are essences—and so drama is also a form of contemplation.

One contemplates—whatever form one's contemplation takes—within a field of action, a field in which action is demanded. At the same time, one acts within a field of essences, each asking to be contemplated. Since action and essence are interwoven in such ways, philosophers of action, such as Aristotle, and philosophers of essence, such as Plato, tend to talk past one another. Hence the elusiveness of some of the issues I am discussing in this section. My point now is that, despite the necessity for contemplation (discussed in part 5.6), the "dramatistic" view of human motives has the inestimable value of keeping essences alive and in the world and of holding oneness open to singularity and multiplicity.[69]

I wish now to return to some of the ambiguities implied by my initial questions.

There is a long tradition of polaristic thought, going back to Heraclitus and other early Greek philosophers and including in the eighteenth and nineteenth centuries Goethe, Schiller, and Nietzsche in Germany and Blake and Coleridge in England. In important respects Jung belongs in this tradition.[70] In it man and nature are conceived as embodying polarities in some sort of relation to an antecedent or implicit unity. (The answer to the question whether One or Two is prior depends on what aspect of the overall scheme one wishes to emphasize.) There are strong reasons in favor of conceiving the world in this way. And they lead to a concern with the unitary reality discussed by most of the writers I have mentioned earlier.

In his exposition of Coleridge's thought, Barfield argues persuasively in favor of conceiving reality polaristically.[71] Barfield points out that when we use the term *life,* we are speaking of something not reducible to what we have in mind when we say, "Organisms exist." Rather, we mean by *life* a unity antecedent to the phenomena of our experience, a unity that we would describe qualitatively in such ways as a "sense of richness and oneness with all life" (D. H. Lawrence), or an "orgiastic, mystical sense of oneness, of life as indestructibly powerful and pleasurable" (Nietzsche).[72] This antecedent unity—of our fundamental subjective involvement in our experience—is distinct from the kinds of oneness created by the process of abstraction. Coleridge is assuming this prephenomenal oneness when he writes that "every power in nature and in spirit must evolve an opposite as the sole means and conditions of its manifestation: and all opposition is a tendency to re-union."[73]

The polaristic nature of Jung's psychology is evident in many of its central concepts. The attitudes and functions of his typology tend to exclude one another; feeling-toned complexes and archetypes are bipolar—good mother and bad mother imply one another—and much of his thought is concerned with the principle (*enantiodromia*) whereby psychological opposites tend to turn into one another. This emphasis on polarity gives his thought much of its force. Still, thinking psychologically in the most conscious way possible entails being aware of the self-deceptions into which we may fall in our thinking about One and Two.

Our awareness of the antecedent unity of which I have spoken may mislead us as we identify that unity with the kinds of unity created by our symbol systems. In this identification we are inclined to attribute universality to the symbolic One, while neglecting the arbitrariness and contingency implicit in it by virtue of the arbitrary and contingent features of the symbol system producing it. We are inclined to forget, that is to say, that it is a oneness made from specific and idiosyncratic particulars, and has whatever meaning it has in relation to them. Sir Thomas Browne maintained that man lives amphibiously in divided and distinguished worlds. And from a very different point of view Rilke, three hundred years later, acknowledges a related state of affairs:

> *Mit allen Augen sieht e Kreatur*
> *das Offene. Nur unsre Augen sind*
> *wie umgekehrt und ganz um sie gestellt*
> *als Fallen, rings um ihren freien Ausgang.*

> With all its eyes the creature-world beholds
> the open. But our eyes, as though reversed,
> encircle it on every side, like traps,
> set round its unobstructed path to freedom.[74]

We would do well to have these divided worlds and obstacles to "the open" in mind as we carry out our devotions to Christ, Allah, Zoroaster, or whatever other symbol we accept as offering the promise of oneness.

My concern here is with beclouding ambiguities with respect to One and Two but also to Three, which, like One, can—properly but also improperly—serve as a conflict-resolving term.

I would call attention to two dangers of the kind of thinking I have been describing. One is that it may lead to false dichotomies, in which something is presented as Two that is not. Many later Jungians have sensed such dichotomizing in some of Jung's formulations

320

of gender differences, especially as aligned with the polarity of Eros/ Logos. The other danger is that one may be misleadingly impelled to find oneness in order to mitigate the rigors of a dichotomy consciously or unconsciously sensed as an illegitimate split—that something may be presented as One that is not.

I will call this a manufactured as opposed to a natural oneness, a consoling oneness as opposed to a oneness content to go about its business without special regard for feelings injured by all the divisive two-ness in the world. (When some people, including those drawn to Jung, are fascinated by such phenomena as fire-walking, they are finding consolation in the apparent proof that mind and body are one. After all, to be thrilled at the prospect of their being one is to assume that they are two. Among the questions one would like to ask them is, "What kind of relation do you have to your body? What split are you so eager to heal?")

Exaggerations of either oneness or two-ness or both are often at the expense of differentiated feeling, concerned with gradations, transitions, continuity, and coherence.

Very aware of living in divided and distinguished worlds, I remain alert to manufactured and consoling oneness and to the kinds of two-ness that lead to the need for it. This alertness causes me to pause when Jaffé describes unitary reality as the "antithesis" of polarized ego-consciousness, as I wonder what opposition is thus implied and how it got established. More generally, it causes me to reflect on some of the ways in which oneness is manufactured.

The artifact One may sometimes be seen as a product of the genius of language, or the "rounding out" characteristic of any universe— note the oneness in the word—of discourse. One commentator on Pico della Mirandola (1463–94), the energetic "harmonizer of oppositions," while summarizing the Italian philosopher's claim "that the great religious and philosophical doctrines of the world, with all their contradictory ideas of God and the good life, amount to more or less the same thing," compares the doctrines to "Shakespeare's lady who did 'protest too much,' " for they "bear witness to the urgency of the notions they deny."[75] The contradictions are lost in the sense of oneness, and hence ultimacy, awakened by this or that doctrine owing to its internal coherence and its claim to completeness.

As we saw in part 6.2, Bentham in the nineteenth century used the term *archetypation* to describe this sort of rounding out. (Thus, the unifying term *Church* obscures the differences between its component classes, clergy and laity, which in some respects are motivated by radically different personal interests.)

When Jaffé describes Jung as thinking that the *unus mundus* "transcends consciousness and is therefore inconceivable," that "it can neither be grasped nor imagined," that "its reality is manifested only in its effects upon consciousness as a hypothesis," I find myself wondering what the difference is between a hypothesis and a concept.[76] Jaffé's words presume to talk about something—if it is beyond experience, what is it, and what is there to say about it?

Neumann differs from Jung in believing that certain kinds of symbolism give glimpses of unitary reality, and illustrates his contention with a poem by Goethe.[77] In its description of a twilit world in which much is indefinite, the poem does indeed convey the impression of an invisible power permeating everything. Jaffé observes that in the poem "we are shown both the here and now and that which lies beyond, a feature of the symbol of unity."[78] But the poem is what it is in part by virtue of specific and definite images, as when it compares a meadow to a head of hair. Moreover, language and art induce us to look beyond the here and now in many ways, but without completely sacrificing specificity to generality. Though one could class Goethe's poem with other works of art sharing certain features with it, it produces an effect diferent from that of any other verbal utterance, and speaking of "the symbol of unity" does not take one very far in describing, much less in accounting for, that effect. If imagination creates "multeity in unity," in Coleridge's phrase, the specifics of multeity, far from being annulled, are crucial to the imaginative whole compounded from them. Goethe's poem explores a liminal state, but liminality is not oneness. (See again fig. 5.)

When Leontes retorts to Hermione, "Your actions are my dreams," he is creating a spurious unity, since her chaste actions in reality have nothing to do with his jealous dreams. At the same time, he is giving an accurate account of what has happened: her reality has in his mind become assimilated to his fantasies about her. In his stating the matter in this way, he is demonstrating an awareness of what is happening, entailing something like a collusion of his ego, an attempt to abdicate responsibility for what part of him recognizes as not reality but dream. Further, the audience is invited to hear his retort from the position of Hermione, who has just said, "You speak a language that I understand not" (III.ii.78). Thus we see how the dramatic mode of essentializing—in the mode of action—preserves our awareness of complexities and thus creates an ironic context in which a spurious unity is revealed as spurious. The unity described in the poem by Goethe strikes one as authentic precisely because it is expressed in terms of an interplay of perspectives related to that present in the interchange between Leontes and Hermione.

Neumann's reading of Goethe's poem is related to his view that "the child, before the development of the ego, lives in the original unity of inner and outer worlds," a view which is contradicted by a considerable body of clinical and experimental evidence.[79] Infants have the capacity for fusion, but this does not mean that fusion—as in the infant's failure to discriminate between itself and its mother—is the original psychic condition. Just as liminality implies separateness as well as merger, so do the workings of the infantile psyche. Also in this sense One is not prior to Two.

In Coleridge's view, Two as polarity is by its nature productive. And this productivity may take the form of a dialectic, in which two opposing forces or terms give rise to a synthesizing third in a progressive development. Socrates is the model of trust that the play of conflicting ideas will lead to a higher level of truth. And someone recording his dreams over a period of time is hoping to take part in a dialectical interaction between waking ego and dream content that will bring about a change in both. But a dialectic—making a Third out of Two—may also prove illusory, a point made forcefully by the Shakespearean scholar Sigurd Burckhardt, who caricatures dialectics by comparing it with a moment in a seventeenth-century German play based on the story of Hamlet.

In the play Hamlet marches between the characters corresponding to Rosencrantz and Guildenstern, who have pistols aimed at him from either side. Hamlet frees himself of them by suddenly ducking, an action which leads the two courtiers by sheer reflex to shoot one another dead. "The dialectician," Burckhardt remarks, "is not such a fool as himself to take arms against a sea of troubles; he divides his troubles into antitheses and makes them take arms against each other." In other words, "dialectics is an ordering device," which works "by arranging disorder symmetrically." An image of this process is the triad, in which the base points may represent conflict, which is, however, resolved in the apex, representing something like a higher court of appeal. But faith in this process may assume more order than there really is, and may distract attention from the reality and persistence of disorder. Shakespeare, taking a searching look at the problem of disorder in the Prince Hal plays, "had long since discovered that the apex had disappeared or become inaccessible. . . ."[80]

Related observations are made by another Shakespearean scholar, John F. Danby, who writes about *Antony and Cleopatra* that in "the bewildering oscillations of scene, the overlapping and pleating of different times and places, the co-presence of opposed judgments," there is "the logic of a peculiarly Shakespearean dialectic. Opposites are juxtaposed, mingled, married; then from the very union which seems to promise strength dissolution flows." As the lovers come together, "they lapse, slide, and fall apart unceasingly," and "the opposites play through Antony and play with him, and finally destroy him."[81] In this play, too, there is no resolving third term.

Indeed, such thoughts about these plays might lead us to reflect, further, on ways in which the dialectical third term, when it is present, often offers a presupposed pseudoresolution of the tensions between thesis and antithesis. Thus, Marxists describe the conflicts inherent in capitalism in such a way that the outcome of communism is surreptitiously present from the outset.

Moreover, that Two may give rise to a Third engendering conflict that it does not bring to harmony is clear from innumerable instances of triadic envy and the unresolved Oedipus complex.

Many life problems have either double or triple aspects, depending upon how they are viewed. World politics, for example, is largely made up of bipolar oppositions with some sort of third term implicit within them, as is suggested by the Near Eastern proverb, "The enemy of my enemy is my friend." In speaking of a "parental complex," I meant to suggest something of the way in which an apparent opposition—between mother and son, for example—is really a triangle—

of mother, father, and son—and the way in which the same triangle may be manifest as a simple opposition—the son against mother-and-father-as-team.

"Malcolm Roberts" offers a striking example of such ambiguities. A competitive, successful man, he senses that there is something false about his drivenness, which had its genesis in about his third or fourth year, at the time of the birth of his sister. He describes his father as aloof, and his mother as such a masterful manipulator that she gets her way without calling attention to the ruses involved in her doing so. For her, personal worth means being successful, as measured in such conventional terms as having a lot of money and driving a fancy automobile. Mr. Roberts understands that, smothered and seduced by her, he very early made her ambition for him his own.

After the birth of Mr. Roberts's sister, his mother had him sleep with her, ostensibly so that he would not feel that the birth of his sister had made him unwanted. He is totally unable to recall his father's presence in the bed, though he must have slept in it. Nor has Mr. Roberts any ideas of the arrangement of the sleepers in the bed—whether he slept next to his mother with his father on the other side of her, or between his parents, or next to his father with his mother on the other side of him. Tensions one can imagine as pictured in this arrangement include the rivalry of the brother and sister for the attention of their mother, the mother's seduction of her son as a substitute for her husband—as though, with the husband's biological purpose fulfilled, he could now be dismissed from the bower of the Mother Goddess and her son lover— and the father's acceptance of the whole arrangement as justifying his withdrawal from his wife.

The way in which Mr. Roberts's father has been simply erased from his memory of this scene is striking. And surely Mr. Roberts is in need of some new form of connection with masculine values—and with feminine values as well. But it is important to realize that the feeling-toned complexes underlying such problems are bipolar in character.

The interactions of "Linda Randall" and "Margaret Anderson" illustrate this bipolarity. Both have risen socially from their working-class backgrounds. Since Mrs. Randall was brutally mistreated by her mother, her affective ties to her childhood milieu are strong, and she retains a vivid sense of the squalor and deprivation she has known, whereas Mrs. Anderson has seemingly glided very smoothly into a life of elegant good taste and culture. Still, parts of Mrs. Anderson's childhood are erased from her memory in a way closely related to the way Mr. Roberts's father has been erased from his. The two poles of the feeling-toned complex shared by Mrs. Anderson and Mrs. Randall could be called "The Princess" and "The Girl from across the Tracks." When Mrs. Anderson and Mrs. Randall are together, Mrs. Anderson's allusions to Mozart, Wittgenstein, Proust, and Bryn Mawr make Mrs. Randall nervous in a way that leads her to denigrate herself for what she at that moment feels to be her commonness. Thus, Mrs. Anderson is allowed to be The Princess, while Mrs. Randall takes up the role of The Girl from across the Tracks, and the whole complex is dramatized between them. It is important to realize, however, that in taking up that role, and in letting the other side of the tracks into the picture, Mrs. Randall is performing an act of balancing, reflecting the homeostatic aspect of the self. If both Mrs. Anderson and Mrs. Randall could be both The Princess and The Girl from across the Tracks, the activity of the complex would be, in the psyche of each, the expression of a more favorable relation between ego and self than it is when one pole of the complex is being projected onto the other person.

My discussion of the mother-infant dyad and triadic tensions in the blues (in part 3.1) made clear how unstable the relations between Two and Three can be in interactions among people. In individual development, relations between Two and Three are unstable in part owing to the power—and inertia—of the mother-infant bond, as the infant deals falteringly with the arduous task of trying to accommodate the Third in the forms of father, siblings, and other figures of the wider world. (See fig. 9.) But relations between Two and Three are also unstable owing to the infant's resistance to the sacrifice, seemingly demanded by the Third, of qualities that the infant seeks to retain at the urging of the self that knows what is good for itself. (These may include, say, dreaminess conducive of some kinds of play but not of doing school work.) Hence some conflicts that psychoanalysts construe as being between the father (or mother) as moral authority and the supposed paradisal bliss of the mother-infant relationship are more

Fig. 9. Mother cat and kittens. Instability in the relations between symbolic Two and symbolic Three. Twenty-month-old Amanda calls the mother cat in this picture "Mamma" and the three kittens sprawling on her body and forefoot "babies." The kitten touching the mother cat's tail Amanda identifies as "Daddy." (A few months before, when someone in a group including Father, Mother, and friends would ask, "Where's the baby?" Amanda would point to Father.) She recently exclaimed, "Daddy and Mamma and Mamma!" Daddy often seems, in Amanda's interpretation, an only slightly differentiated feature of the Mother World consisting of Mamma and Baby.

Though Amanda's world-view is in need of expansion and revision, it contains what could be called a primitive realism on the level of the self that knows what is good for itself. (Amanda has a clear understanding of what is most necessary for her present well-being and further development: Mother.) Residuals of this primitive realism and this connection with the Mother World are implicit—are tacitly known— in developed feeling and imagination.

327

truly between the Third in various forms and the self that knows what is good for itself. (Dreaminess at school may be preserving a child's authentic individuality—even if inefficiently.)

Accommodation of the infant to the Third of recalcitrant reality is essential. But so is the retaining of residual connections with the maternal ground—so is the retaining of the ability to recover and reexperience those connections in forms appropriate to later stages.

In individual development, Two and Three are also unstable owing to the relative nondifferentiation of the two-year-old's urge to autonomy. Wanting and needing to stand on his own two feet, he often fails to realize that self-sufficiency cannot properly be at the expense of mutuality. Though on a deeper level tenacious of the mutuality demanded by the self that knows what is good for itself, the developing infant is also impelled to grapple with the Third, even to lose himself in it. Thus the two-year-old's attempts at independence contribute to the self-alienation to which his attempts at conformity are also contributing. And thus (as we saw in the example of Jack Wolfstone in part 6.2) the rebel may even work hand-in-glove with social authority in tyrannical form. Still, when things have gone reasonably well for the infant, he has also been given resources for the development of a sense of autonomy that knows itself subject to mutuality. For such a sense to be found and become part of adapted consciousness, it must be lost—deintegration is precisely the assuming of partial perspectives, at the expense of more nearly total but more rudimentary ones, to the end of differentiation. The products of this differentiation are then ideally integrated at a further stage.

I would add to these comments on Two and Three a related one about Two and One.

In regarding the human creature as *homo duplex*, of a dual nature, I have not wished to give assent to one or another of the mind-body dualisms so prominent in Western thought. I have rather meant that if one employs devices of symbolism to achieve a semblance of oneness somewhere—for example, by conceiving of a mind-body unity maximally adapted to its environment—duality will force its way into the picture elsewhere, or will lurk just beyond the edge—for example, in the reality of death. There is a story about the Garden only because the Garden had a snake in it; without the snake, with its capacity for breaking down existing structures, the Garden lacks a story that can be told. The instability of One—the Garden, say—is destined to be realized, just as Two is destined to be transformed under the influence of the Third. But in attending to the instability of the Two, it is important to remain aware of the resources of Two for providing strength, stability, and flexibility for further stages of development. This is notably true of Two in the form of the mother-infant relationship.

I wish to close by commenting on two dreams that may be taken to bear on the development from Two to Three to One as the Fourth.

"James Watkins" is a forty-five-year-old novelist, whose invalid mother died when he was a small boy. Mr. Watkins is at the moment stuck in his writing. He dreams: "In a church with J. T. [a roistering friend of the dreamer during his stormy adolescence]. An attractive woman rubs her breast in an inviting way; the nipple is very pronounced. We go to her house. She is an artist, and on the walls are many marvelous paintings by her. She also has a small child, perhaps two years old. She and I want to make love but are hindered by the presence of the child."

"Mary Thomas" is a thirty-two-year-old social worker, whose mother owned first editions of the Oz books, which she read to her daughter in her very early childhood. Mrs. Thomas dreams that she and her male analyst are sitting on two sofas. He has been reading first editions of the Oz books.

The woman artist in Mr. Watkins's dream offers him an enhanced contact with sources of his own creativity. She also holds out promise of sexual fulfillment and the nourishment of which he was significantly deprived as a small child. But the incest taboo creates a conflict: adult sexuality and the nourishing of infants are to be kept separate. Yet there is a tacit but essential connection between mother and *anima*, or contrasexual soul-image—despite the differences between them; and to be cut off from the inner mother is to be cut off from the richness of the woman artist's paintings. The paintings as imaginative products are related to the Oz books of Mrs. Thomas's dream, these being related in turn to her early bond with her mother. That her analyst is drawn into that bond is propitious.

The Oedipus complex has had its influence on both dreamers. But in the larger view, it is possible to question, as the psychoanalyst Heinz Kohut has done—in the spirit of Loewald (cited in part 1)—not only

329

Feeling, Imagination, and the Self

the importance of, but even the need for, pronounced forms of the
Oedipus complex in individual development and the life of culture.[82]

As we have noted (in part 6.1), Jung and Freud differed about the
nature of psychic energy, Freud regarding it as sexual, and Jung conceiving it in a way that brings it close to interest. And this difference
is important in understanding the development from Two to Three.
When sixteen-month-old Amanda falls into a paroxysm of tearful
anguish at the sight of Father and Mother embracing at the door as
Father leaves for work, Amanda is very probably feeling something
that can only by a very loose analogy be described as sexual rivalry
but is rather upset at losing Mother's undivided interest. Incidentally,
with Amanda's outburst in mind, Neumann's view of the embrace of
the World Parents as "free of all oppositions" seems another instance
of manufactured and consoling oneness, totally disregarding the role
assigned to Amanda in a painful drama.

Interest precedes sexual interest; imagination precedes sexual imagination. Imagination transforms psychic reality, enhancing interest,
giving it new objects, and inducing it to make new links between the
personal and particular and the general. The Oz of Mrs. Thomas's
dream is the place where tensions of life within the family can be
explored not simply in themselves, in their everyday form, but in
relation to wonder and the forces of magical transformation. Her dream
alludes to the affective and imaginative bond between mother and
infant that, alive in the present, gives Mrs. Thomas resources for
working at triadic issues of various kinds within the process of differentiation and integration that Jung called individuation. If One and
Four are symbolic of this process, the mother-infant relationship is
the Two that enables the Third to give birth to One as the Fourth.

6.7 The Felt Oneness of Mother and Infant and the Integrity of the Subjective Sphere

A number of writers, among them the phenomenologists Scheler,
Helmuth Plessner, and Strasser and the psychoanalyst René Spitz,
have regarded feeling and emotion as originating in the experience of
nonintentional oneness, the capacity for which one retains throughout
life. Intellectual activity can be experienced as a form of reaching—
if the emotional equivalent of intellectual reaching succeeds, it be-

330

comes the completed act of what in English is most conveniently called feeling. German-speaking writers such as Scheler can call it *Einfühlung*, which conveys a sense of penetration and being contained, of arriving at a goal. The English translation of Scheler's book on phenomena described by this word renders it as "sympathy," and one could also render it as "empathy."[83] To express the ultimate precondition of the activity named by this word, Scheler employs what is, in effect, a pun, joining *ein*, "in," and *eins*, "one": the precondition of conscious feeling, *Einfühlung*, is one-feeling, *Einsfühlung*.[84] (That oneness may be anything but simple, as we saw in the previous section. That there is also a deep interconnectedness much more primitive than conscious feeling we saw in relation to the emotional "conviviality of the native mind" considered in part 5.4.) In Scheler's view "one-feeling" characterizes the early mother-child relationship and the play of young children.[85]

Since an infant responds to the relatively complex form of its mother's face before it does to a colored dot or a ball, Spitz is led to distinguish between the object and what he calls "the precursor of the object," by which he means a relatively generalized protoform of the mother's face as the infant will later perceive it. "The establishment of the precursor of the object," he writes, "certainly is preceded by increasingly organized responses of the infant to the ministrations of the environment, represented by the mother. . . . This process culminates in . . . the emergence of the smiling response, which represents a conscious, reciprocal communication."[86]

In other words, objective perception grows out of the infant's awareness that the mother-infant dyad is a duality, an awareness that grows, in turn, out of the infant's emotional-toned experience of itself, its mother, and the environment as in some respects a relatively undifferentiated whole.

That this sense of relatively undifferentiated wholeness persists in later life is apparent from the psychology of "Leah Gardner," which also gives a glimpse of what the experience of it may be like for the infant. As a result of early maternal deprivation, Mrs. Gardner has developed an abiding, passionate attachment to animals. She has come to realize that, although she feels herself to be their mother, they also have the significance of "mother" to her: she is to herself, and her animals are to her, both infant-as-mother and mother-as-infant (in ways summarized in fig. 10 and the caption to it).

Plessner regards the original form of feeling as "distanceless imbed-dedness in the object" (*distanzlose Sachverhaftung*), an awareness of contact that excludes the "distance" always presupposed between the subject and the object at which it aims.[90] Strasser, who also uses the word *feeling* to describe the earliest relation between mother and infant, says that in it "the specific subject-object tension does not, as yet, exist." The infant feels his own condition, but he does so only in contact with his mother. Thus, "suckling and mother feel *one.*" In short, "*the feeling subject* [the infant] *feels himself by the fact that he feels his fellow-subject* [the mother]; and reversely, the fellow-subject who is felt is present to the feeling subject by the fact that the latter feels himself."[91]

The objectifying and reflecting mode of awareness is only an " 'up-per layer' "; the original nonobjectifying awareness rises to the surface "whenever the situation appears to the ego in such a manner that he *cannot maintain a distance* (emotion) or whenever . . . *no distance exists* (feeling)."[92] The ego's failure to maintain distance under the sway of emotion accords with such expressions as "falling in love," "sinking into despair," "overcome with grief," "filled with hate." This emotional loss of distance may bring to manifestation an "affect-ego," related to a corresponding "affect-object," as when a jealous person discerns evidence of infidelity where an unjealous person would not.[93] The lack of distance in feeling, however, is of another kind, and requires us to consider the relation between it and the intentional feeling that may include the experience of distance overcome.

The contact and lack of distance characteristic of primary feeling—the precondition of intentional feeling—are not identity, are not fusion into some sort of simple oneness. Rather, they belong to the experience of fellow-subjects who know themselves to be interrelated. Their in-terrelationship is the protoform of all community.

Community entails a rich structure of restraints and boundaries. Rather than thinking of these restraints as primarily imposed upon the individual from "without" in the form of social authority, it is useful to reflect that the brain would explode from neural firing if it were not for the inhibitory functions that "sculpt" the too-richness of

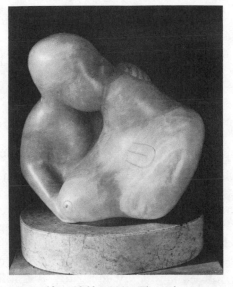

Fig. 10. Henry Moore, *Suckling Child* (1930). The infant nurses as though its mother's breast were part of itself, with the mother's head and the rest of her body entirely assimilated to the act of nursing. The distinction between subject and object and inside and outside is broken down in the process thus depicted. Moreover, the sculpture as a whole appears to the viewer to enter imaginatively and empathically into the experience of the nursing mother and infant, an experience that engages deep-body awareness and that is tactile rather than visual. Yet the stylized female genitalia have a meaning for the viewer that is not part of the infant's experience of nursing.

The female genitalia are one of the most ancient symbols of ongoing, inexhaustible life, as may be seen in numerous Old Stone Age paintings and sculptures.[87] And in these ancient works of art the female genitalia are abstractly rendered as symbolic icons, often as parts of more naturalistic delineations of the female form—exactly as in Moore's sculpture. One "sees" this part of the sculpture in a different way than one does the rest of it. As *Suckling Child* demonstrates, naturalistic delineation encourages an empathic response, whereas the abstraction of the female genitalia as symbolic icon encourages a response in many respects opposed to empathy and forming a polarity with it.[88]

The interplay between empathy and abstraction, with empathic response predominating—along with the breaking down of the distinction between inside and outside and subject and object—evokes a sense of liminality—of thresholds and dissolving margins. Liminal states—which cannot be reduced to fusion, archaic identity, or "oneness"—are fundamental to adult experiences of imaginative transcendence—experiences of the greatest personal and cultural value.[89] In this sense residuals of the early mother-infant relationship are implicitly active in the creation and apprehension of the profoundest products of art and religion.

possible experience—that we come into the world attuned to coherence. We have aleady seen we also come into the world with a sense of self and consequently a sense of boundaries distinguishing self from non-self.

Primary feeling is liminal: in it restraints and boundaries are blurred and weakened. For these to be blurred and weakened, they must be present. In a related fashion, the distancelessness of primary feeling implies distance.

The early maternal deprivation of Mrs. Gardner has resulted in a sustained cultivation of certain qualities of experience that other adults value with less determination—and in a curious sense less consciously. These are qualities mined from the background of intentional feeling. The distancelessness of her relation to her animals implies distance. She knows perfectly well who is to be fed and who is to do the feeding. But she also values the contact and distancelessness accomplished by the feeding, the nonconsummatory mutuality that the satiation of appetite can be made to serve.

Mrs. Gardner knows this state in large part because she sensed it around and beyond her actual experience of her mother. Thus, guided by the self that knows what is good for itself, she has developed a fundamental principle of imagination (to be explored further in the next section, where we will see—and as we will see further in part 6.9—that the same principle, deranged, may also result in untoward developments).

I wish to illustrate the relations of distancelessness to distance in feeling, and of feeling to emotion, by two examples of dramatic acting, performed by the silent-film comedian Buster Keaton and the German actress Helene Weigel.

The audience sometimes responds to Keaton's doings with howls of laughter. Keaton, in contrast, does not respond to his funniness in this way but rather remains firmly in control of every gesture and movement. The response of the audience is emotion; his actions are based on his feeling for certain comic qualities, while his emotional response to them remains firmly in check. He "reads" and expresses those qualities with a measure of detachment. And yet there is a sense in which one is in, or puts oneself into—and is as a result in—what one reads, whether literally or figuratively. (To be moved by a poem is partly an experience of self-recognition, of finding that one was already there in the poem, waiting to bridge the distance between oneself there and oneself reading it, and thus for those two to be one. But one is conscious of the work of composing the poem and of reading it, and is thus conscious of its otherness, which makes the experience of it intentional, and not simply one of one-feeling.)

My example of Weigel is from her performance of the title role in Brecht's *Mother Courage and Her Children*. In the play, Mother Courage has been roaming the countryside with her provisions wagon during the Thirty Years War, trying to stay alive and keep together her family— her mute daughter Kattrin and her two sons—by selling whatever she can to both sides of the combat. Her simple-minded, honest son Swiss Cheese is made paymaster of the Second Protestant Regiment, which is suddenly routed by the Catholics. Swiss Cheese shows up at his mother's wagon with the regimental cashbox, ponders what to do with it, and decides to hide it by the river. Two men appear, looking for the man with the cashbox. Mother Courage, who has had the Catholic flag run up on her wagon, claims that Swiss Cheese had stopped at the wagon only to buy a meal, and that she does not know him. Swiss Cheese claims that he knows nothing about the cashbox. The men do not believe him and take him before the court-martial. Mother Couragage arranges to pawn her wagon to raise money to bribe the judge. Yvette, a whore who frequents the wagon, will offer the bribe, pretending that Swiss Cheese is her lover. But Mother Courage haggles too long, and does not give Yvette a large enough bribe; and as a result Swiss Cheese is shot.

At the close of the scene Yvette informs Mother Courage that she is suspected of being an accomplice of Swiss Cheese and of having the cashbox. Yvette tells her that the men from the court-martial will bring the body of Swiss Cheese to show Mother Courage, so that they can see if she gives herself away when she sees it. Two men bear in Swiss Cheese's body on a stretcher, and the sergeant with them addresses her:

> Here's a man we can't identify. But he has to be registered to keep the records straight. He bought a meal from you. Look at him, see if you know him. (*He pulls back the sheet.*) Do you know him? (MOTHER COURAGE *shakes her head.*) Lift him up. Throw him in the carrion pit. He has no one that knows him.[94]

335

In the production of the play in East Berlin, under the direction of Brecht, this remarkable moment was followed by one at least as remarkable. As the body of Swiss Cheese was carried off, Weigel as Mother Courage looked the other way and opened her mouth. As one member of the audience described the gesture, it "was that of the screaming horse in Picasso's *Guernica*. The sound that came out was raw and terrible beyond any description I could give of it. But, in fact, there was no sound. Nothing. The sound was total silence. It was silence which screamed and screamed through the whole theater so that the audience lowered its head as before a gust of wind."[95] (See fig. 11.)

In Weigel's performance, Mother Courage was almost overcome with horror and anguish in such a way that she lost the distance between the position of her conscious ego and that of the affect-ego that would find release in a scream. But she was not overcome, and she did not lose that distance. Rather, she "went with" the emotional current arising within her, to the extent, and only to the extent, of reading its physiognomy, of exploring the emotional import of the events befalling her, and of bringing to expression her grasp of that import. Her pain inclined her to the lowering of consciousness that would produce a scream, but she countered this inclination by a successful effort at increased consciousness, through which she reached to the wider issues of value needing to be faced. She thus arrived at a complex feeling-judgment of the kind that we will be examining in the next section, one that we might express for her in some such terms as these: "I love Swiss Cheese, but he is dead. I must go on living, because despite this almost overwhelming pain, I want to do so, and because Kattrin needs me. I must succeed in sacrificing the value of the relief that would be afforded me by the direct expression of what I feel in a scream. I must do this for the sake of a higher value, that of my life and Kattrin's."

In this case it was precisely the slight but sufficient distance between feeling and emotion that enabled feeling to maintain the integrity of the subjective sphere by generating an ego attitude that was appropriately detached, committed, impassioned, and ethical. And yet Weigel's Mother Courage was thoroughly *in* the horror from which she was detached, just as Keaton was *in* the vision of the comic that

Fig. 11. The silent scream of Mother Courage (played by Helene Weigel in Berlin in 1949) after she has refused to recognize the body of her dead son. In maintaining silence under the stress of powerful emotion, she demonstrates the importance of inhibition in conscious feeling.

337

he is reading, mapping, expressing. And this "being in" yet being detached presupposes knowledge of the one-feeling of distanceless contact between mother and infant that is the basis—variously—of union, of fusion, of independence within community, and of isolation maintained by the illusion of self-sufficiency.

6.8 The Object in Acts of Feeling

More than just making one realize that one has lost someone precious, grief shocks one with the sudden conviction that part of one's very self has been torn away. Thus (at first) grief heightens one's sense of identity with the person lost. Mother Courage counters this feeling of identity through a powerful act of disidentification: by not surrendering to her impulse to scream, she preserves her concern with the emotional situation in its totality, as comprehended in the complex feeling-judgment ascribed to her in the preceding section. For feeling to maintain the integrity of the subjective sphere in such a way, it must also maintain that of the object. But as Mother Courage's reaction to the death of Swiss Cheese shows, feeling must thus confront issues concerning the ambiguous relations among "Thou," "I," and "it."

To say "Thou" the subject must largely surrender the kinds of wish and will that constitute egocentricity. For such reasons the relation of "I" to "Thou" has been regarded as the most valuable form of relationship between the subject and the "other."[96] But "Thou" is misconstrued when the subject assumes it to be the mirror image of itself in which otherness is annulled, and when the subject forgets that there are other subjects—for example, not only Swiss Cheese but also Kattrin—who must in the same complex configuration also be regarded as "Thou." "Thou" is also misconstrued when the subject forgets that both the subject and its fellow subject as "Thou" are both also "it," that the experience of life is continuing passionate crisis because no one knows for sure that he himself or "Thou" will not a moment hence be shot and thrown into the carrion pit—that impersonal Force will not triumph over personal value.

In this section and the next, I will be especially concerned with the role of feeling in engaging, transforming, and mitigating passionate crisis as it tends toward a derangement of the subject from adequate and authentic forms of relationship between self and world. I will consider how feeling, when it is intentional, takes place in acts, with these entailing emotional expression and emotional understanding as interrelated aspects of the same process. (I can know and, with luck, understand what I feel only if it comes to expression in me.) I will regard reflection and action as interrelated aspects of this process. (An audience reflects on a dramatic action; Hamlet reflects as part of a dramatic action presented to an audience.) In this section I will concentrate on the part played by the object in such an act of feeling, beset as both object and act are by vicissitudes of the subject. In the next section I will concentrate on the feeling-judgments shaping such acts, or taking shape within them.

To speak of acts of feeling is not only to imply distance to be overcome, and possible aberrations bearing upon distance and the lack of it. It is also to imply time as a dimension of emotion and feeling.

Emotional life is in many of its manifestations pulsational, wave-like, rhythmic, welling from the nonego into dimmer and then more lucid ranges of consciousness.[97] It is thus made manifest; but as I meant to suggest by speaking of the nonego and dimmer regions of consciousness, being made manifest is not necessarily the same thing as becoming consciously known. (The person who angrily smashes a priceless cup on the floor may afterward say, "I didn't know what I was doing.") Indeed, important current refinements of emotion theory are based precisely on evidence for the reality of noncognized emotions.[98]

There are thus relatively (or even completely) unconscious emotional acts, and there are acts engaging more conscious reflection, with these implying an awareness of the time in which such acts take place. Time is essential to emotion and feeling generally because of the rhythmic character of primitive emotional expression. Time is also essential to feeling as it becomes intentional, and reflective, because to live consciously in time is to strive for emotionally important things one does not have, or to face the prospect of losing emotionally important things one wants to go on having—including life.[99]

I will now discuss the object in acts of feeling recorded in two literary works germane to our reflections on *Mother Courage and Her*

Children. Both acts of feeling are in important respects failures. But then, the cultivation of proper modes of feeling is a never-to-be completed task, and to record such a partial failure sensitively and in a way that opens it to wider ranges of implication and context is to go far to redeem it. (As for "proper modes of feeling," feeling is proper, and an act of feeling successful, in redeeming as best it can the recurrent failure of feeling that is our lot. As there is no reaching from the pathic to the ontic, we must manage as we can with what we can know of the finally unknowable pathic in relation to our fictions of the ontic, fictions recurrently in need of renewal, as are many of the acts of feeling portrayed in them.) Moreover, that in such matters negative examples may be as forceful as positive ones will concern me in part 6.9. I will comment on parts of Robert Frost's poem, "The Most of It,"[100] and the moment in *King Lear* when Lear comes upon his loyal servant Kent in the stocks.

Frost's poem, very much about the need for the "other" to be objectively "there," begins,

> He thought he kept the universe alone;
> For all the voice in answer he could wake
> Was but the mocking echo of his own
> From some tree-hidden cliff across the lake.
> Some morning from the boulder-broken beach
> He would cry out on life, that what it wants
> Is not its own love back in copy speech,
> But counter-love, original response.
>
> [1–8]

The universe thus "kept . . . alone," assimilated to the subject at the expense of objective features, is undifferentiated and vague, as we may see in various details. (The surface from which the "mocking echo" of the speaker's voice resounds is not a particular cliff but "some" cliff, and is "tree-hidden" at that. "Some morning" is similarly imprecise, and that he *would* "cry out on life" suggests that he did it repeatedly, though at no particular time. Moreover, what we might expect to be a beach covered with boulders is "the boulder-broken beach," a beach broken by boulders, though a beach is unbreakable.)

Having spoken of a "mocking echo" and of life's "own love back in copy speech," the speaker thinks of "counter-love." That he is

340

concerned with love at all is striking, since nothing in the vague jumble described in the opening lines would seem likely to inspire thoughts of love of any kind. "Counter-love" represents a first attempt to imagine something beyond a "mocking echo," and though "counter-love" does not necessarily imply an echo, the phrase also does not rule out such an implication. Hence, the speaker redefines "counter-love" as "original response," which does rule it out. Neither echo nor command, "original response" allows for the integrity, even the unfathomable mystery, of the "other." Indeed, the phrase may even be taken to suggest that the original, basic human act is, precisely, response, that we are creatures in a world that is first given, and that whatever we say or do is on some level in response to that givenness.

The cry of the speaker is, we learn, answered only by the "embodiment" that

> Instead of proving human when it neared
> And someone else additional to him,
> As a great buck it powerfully appeared,
> Pushing the crumpled water up ahead,
> And landed pouring like a waterfall,
> And stumbled through the rocks with horny tread.
> And forced the underbrush—and that was all.
>
> [14–20]

In the phrase "someone else additional to him," the speaker expresses a bland and unsearching view of love, a view that would let simple addition take the place of complex encounter, and that would ignore the unique particularity of the actual "other." The foreignness, autonomy, and crude power of the great, pushing, crumpling, pouring, stumbling, horny, forcing buck is in direct—and compensatory—relation to the superficiality of the speaker's conscious attitude, as a denied but fundamental aspect of reality, the world not amenable to human wish or will, demands to make itself known. Further, while symbolizing qualities of the objective world, the buck, appearing for a moment, then retreating, suggests the power of many poetic and religious symbols to allow only a glimpse of a meaning that, beyond that glimpse and its implications, must remain unknown. In this perspective, the universe kept alone of the first line is what has been appropriated from such symbols in the making of some semblance of

341

a conscious steady state—corresponding, say, to a doctrine formulated on the basis of an original religious experience. The buck could be taken to symbolize the life and meaning that have escaped and that are necessary to counteract the pseudo-self-sufficiency and inanition inevitably present somewhere among the results of that appropriation.

In the second act of *King Lear*, with the stage peopled by Lear, Kent, Lear's Fool, and Lear's alter ego, Gloucester, Lear learns that his evil daughter Regan and her husband Cornwall have put Kent in the stocks. Throughout Lear's speech in response to the discovery (II.iv.98–116), Kent is there for Lear to look at or not as he reflects upon the slight represented by this treatment of his man, and that represented by the refusal of Regan and Cornwall to see him. The latter slight is more direct—it is aimed at Lear, not at his man—but it is also more intangible, since Regan and Cornwall are not present, and since there might be some sort of reasonable excuse for their absence. What is demanded of Lear is an act of feeling that will bring his acute emotional stress to some form of felt coherence by finding realistic and self-syntonic meaning in his situation, along with an appropriate course of action. This act of feeling must do justice to the reality of the object on which it is focused, at this moment Kent. (Later, this focus will expand to include other objects, when Lear encounters Goneril and Regan.) Who or what is Kent? On some level an intimate fellow-subject, a "Thou." (Lear has incurred obligation to Kent by hiring him on.) But "fellow-subject" is a category that Lear grasps at best slightly. And Kent in the stocks is an enigma.

The sight of this enigma is inflammatory, and Lear endeavors to remain patient by not looking at it, but not to look at it is to persist in denial as a mechanism of ego defense. (When Kent told Lear that Regan and Cornwall had put him in the stocks, Lear responded, "No," Kent answered, "Yes," Lear repeated, "No, I say," Kent insisted, "I say yea," and Lear in the continuing—largely contentless—debate said, "No, no they would not!" and, "By Jupiter, I swear no!" and, "They durst not do't; / They could not, would not do't" [II.iv.14–22].) Finally, Lear must admit that the reality of Kent in the stocks cannot be denied, even though admitting it may further require that he accept it as proof of Regan's and Cornwall's slight of him by their refusal to appear. Kent had earlier commanded Lear to "see better": seeing Kent in the stocks is an important early step in Lear's acting on Kent's admonition. Precisely because Lear has so thoroughly reduced the world to an egocentric fiction, it is important that this early step should be the sight of a real person really there. (Later, his education will include hallucinations and delusions.) But what will he now do about the slight to which he has dropped his guard?

Beginning to focus on the slight, Lear says to Gloucester:

> The king would speak with Cornwall. The dear father
> Would with his daughter speak, commands—tends—service.
>
> [II.iv.98–99]

(The Signet editor takes *tends* to mean "awaits," "with, possibly, an ironic second meaning, 'tenders,' or 'offers.' ") Lear is here undecided whether he should speak as the king to a duke or as a father to his daughter—and perhaps whether he should command her or simply announce that he is awaiting her (with the possible intention of "tendering" her service). And to call himself "the dear father" is hopefully, despite evidence, to assume his daughter's kindly disposition toward him.

Ashamed of his indecisiveness, Lear demands, "Are they informed of this?"—thus trying to allow that there may be mitigating circumstances, but this attempt collapses in the middle of the line, as his attention is diverted to his rising passion: "My breath and blood!" But this makes him think of the passion of Cornwall, whom Gloucester has described as of "fiery quality." Lear goes on:

> Fiery? The fiery duke, tell the hot duke that—
> No, but not yet.

By translating the euphemistic "fiery" into the blunt and pejorative "hot," Lear begins to strip away the polite and politic obstacles to the free expression of his passion. This is a step toward knowing that it is there and understanding what it is, but the step does not promise to be part of an act of feeling that would deal with the total situation and its meaning, and would offer him an appropriate course of response. Sensing the danger of the disorienting outbreak of passion he is thus inviting, Lear reverts to granting that there may be mitigating circumstances. Indeed, he now even formulates an excuse in Corn-wall's defense:

> May be he is not well.
> Infirmity doth still neglect all office
> Whereto our health is bound. We are not ourselves
> When nature, being oppressed, commands the mind
> To suffer with the body. I'll forbear;
> And am fallen out with my more headier will
> To take the indisposed and sickly fit
> For the sound man.

Lear thus seizes upon one of the most ancient and dubious reasons for not doing something one does not want to do—that one is "in-disposed," which may indeed mean either that one is ill or, indeed, that one does not want to do it—and pursues it as a generalization about mankind. Like his earlier denial of the obvious—the sight of Kent in the stocks—this shift to generalization serves to cool his rising passion by diverting attention from the personal and tangible. (We might recall that Othello is goaded to murder by the—personal and tangible—"ocular proof" of Desdemona's handkerchief.) This diver-sion ironically strengthens the folly that has led Lear to his present quandary, since what he most needs is precisely a clear perception of the personal and tangible, as distinct from the egocentric fiction that has replaced it. Yet Lear's defensiveness serves a purpose: in speaking of the suffering of the mind—if Cornwall is indisposed it is presumably by a physical ailment—Lear shows himself aware that his own sanity may be at stake. In the whole speech he is allowing himself to see and understand in measured bits that Kent is in the stocks and that Lear is being insulted by Regan and Cornwall, while he simultaneously tests his own capacity for bearing and dealing with what he is thus coming to know. This measuring of the genuine condition of the subject is compatible with an act of feeling, which, however, would need to embrace, more honestly, more elements of the total situation.

The specious excuse for Cornwall vanishes as Lear looks again at Kent in the stocks and exclaims:

> Death on my state! Wherefore
> Should he sit here? This act persuades me

That this remotion of the duke and her
Is practice [= deceit] only.

Rather than trying to ward off his passion, he now imagines un-
leashing it and witnessing its ultimate effect: his exclamation "Death
on my state!" is an incitement and an unconscious prediction of the
destruction of the kingdom. Lear has reduced his "daughter" to "her,"
as he will in a moment translate "her" into the duke's "wife," thus
setting aside the relation of father to daughter, precisely as Regan, to
Lear's disbelief, has set aside the relation of daughter to father. His
setting aside of this relation creates the precondition for revenge.

"Give me my servant forth," Lear commands imperiously but also
impotently, since there is no one here who can do this.

Go tell the duke and's wife I'd speak with them!
Now, presently! Bid them come forth and hear me,

he continues, finally giving way to the climactic expression of his
passion:

Or at their chamber door I'll beat the drum
Till it cry sleep to death.

Lear's passion is thus finally articulated, is objectified in an image
adequate to its intensity; the content of his passion is imagined, and
thus potentially made accessible to feeling. But Lear is close to falling
apart in a way analogous to the way a baby falls apart; hence Lear's
passion is articulated in relation to an affect-ego incapable of assim-
ilating and providing a form of consciousness that can be expanded
by the image thus produced. The ego is as impaired and diminished
as the original object of the whole set of reflections—Kent in the
stocks—has been lost from view.

Lear's image of himself as the agent of his passion—"I'll beat the
drum"—is joined with an image of the causes of his passion, being
locked out— "at their chamber door." His imaginary drumming can
depict the rhythmic nature of primitive emotional expression; yet he
will do the drumming—he will drum with a measure of ego control.
He will beat the drum rather than lay hands on his offending daughter
and son-in-law—his anger will be sublimated—and yet he will be
revenged—his egocentric rage and aggression will be granted full vent.
The image combines a realistic assessment—the sound of a drum

would, in fact, penetrate a locked door—with a fantasy of magically transcending his actual debarment. Rather than awakening Regan and Cornwall—who are depersonalized by not being named—the drum-beats will transform their sleep into death. As the Signet editor remarks, the image also suggests the idea of death following sleep "like a pack . . . of hounds, until it kills it." (There is thus the unconscious irony that Lear is intent on murdering sleep in much the way that Macbeth murdered it.) The emphasis, however, is not on the act of destruction—the mauling and tearing to pieces as by hounds—but rather on Lear's power to cause such an act. Still, there is denial in this construction of the sitution, since the act of which he imagines himself capable must have such results as mauling and tearing to pieces.

This climax of Lear's reflections partly represents a clarification. Abandoning the string of evasive sophistries that have preceded it, Lear has come to know what he really feels, and has expressed it—has come to know it by expressing it. But this clarification entails confusion of another sort, as he loses sight of the reality of the object—first Kent in the stocks, then Regan and Cornwall—and reverts to the egocentric fiction of his omnipotence. With the reality of the object thus devalued, Lear is moving toward the madness that will befall him by the close of this scene.

When Lear does go mad, we see in him a loss of minimal ego boundaries, an invasion of the ego by nonego contents, no longer imaginative but taken literally, a confusion of subject and object in the form of hallucinations, delusions, and magical thinking. His madness overcomes him, but very importantly it also—imaginatively—overcomes us. Since the storm of his madness is presented as an objective storm—not a mental image like that of Lear's drumming—and since the storm is symbolically his madness, we feel ourselves partly taken into his mind, and our viewpoint partly assimilated to his. Yet we do not get wet with the rain, as he does—we do not identify with him in the sense of forgetting that we are in the audience watching an actor performing a role in what is for us a fiction.

In the disintegrating storm of Lear's passion, he loses one important part of his capacity to feel—that of dealing with emotion—another important part of which he had lost by the beginning of the play—that of evaluating properly. Not madly raving ourselves, we must feel for him, with him, on his behalf. We must, for him, imaginatively work to complete successfully an act of feeling that he initiated, then bungled, and in some—flawed—measure completed despite his bungling of it. He must struggle to regain something of the imaginative, detached participation that we in the audience never entirely lose.

Lear declaims that "When we are born, we cry that we are come / To this great stage of fools" (IV. vi. 182–83), leaving us in the audience to try to arrive at proper modes of feeling about him as the "other"—modes that he has largely forsaken. What we are given to feel about includes the image of the raging infant. Thus we are urged to be aware of the larger context including what is now notably lacking, the mutuality fostered by the early mother-infant relationship, and residuals of the maternal presence that can nurture resources of feeling and imagination and thus create a world of fellow-subjects. As mother and infant are together, we human creatures are in one sense all together, even if in another we are each naked and alone on this stage of fools.

In the latter part of the play, the mad king becomes for the first time concerned with the wretched of the earth, with those not agents but victims, those largely reduced to things. One of the wretches is Gloucester's son Edgar, disguised as Poor Tom, the Bedlam beggar. In Poor Tom, Lear believes that he has found "the thing itelf" (III. iv. 105). Part of the irony of this is that Lear has not reached "the thing itself" as some graspable essence—indeed in one sense has not reached the "other" at all—but rather has glimpsed what might be called a provisional form of such an essence, a form belonging to levels upon levels of play-acting and illusion (as an actor plays the part of a character, Edgar, inventing a fiction and playing the part of another character, Poor Tom, within it). In one sense Lear's progress has been like that of the speaker in the poem by Frost, in that both characters at first demonstrate a superficiality of conscious viewpoint requiring a powerful compensatory vision of the "other" insisting on its own reality. And just as we may regard Frost's buck as commenting on the nature of many powerful religious and poetic symbols, so we may regard Poor Tom in his role as "the thing itself" as also commenting on it.

Such symbols compel in part because we sense that their making known (of whatever they make known) is incomplete, that they have further meanings as yet undisclosed. Thus we do not relate to them in transactions that are closed and discrete, like those with a bank teller. We must rather remain open to the abundance to which we have access only when they give it through their self-disclosure. Yet Poor Tom is the image not of abundance but of miserable poverty.

Addressing "Poor naked wretches, wherso'er you are," Lear exclaims, "O, I have ta'en / Too little care of this!" (III.iv.28–33): the image of misery has the power to draw him in the direction in which he needs to go—it has more energetic value than the conscious attitude he is in the process of abandoning. Lear is nearing the paradox that another Skakespearean character, Timon of Athens, expressed in the declaration that "nothing brings me all things" (*Timon of Athens*, V.i.188). These sentiments can be brought into relation with the kinds of religious and poetic symbols suggested by Frost's buck and Edgar as Poor Tom as "the thing itself."

Many religious and poetic symbols are abundant in their implications and in the range of their affective workings. And yet, in the incompleteness of the statement they are at any moment making, they may also be regarded as impoverished. (What a poor, inarticulate thing a cross may be as it marks a place where someone was killed in an automobile accident.) Thus, still another Shakespearean character, Duke Theseus, can watch a play performed by bumpkins and can speak of them as "shadows" mirroring the inadequacy of even the most accomplished art to depict the Real (*A Midsummer Night's Dream*, V.i.211–12). Edgar as Poor Tom as "the thing itself" richly presents these ambiguities and this paradox.

In *King Lear*, as in life, what we seek as "the thing itself" refuses to be grasped, refuses even to retain its contours as a single thing. Ambiguously "I," "Thou," and "it," "the thing itself" can never be securely translated from out of the space of the early mother-infant relationship in which feeling and imagination develop and from out of the inner space such residuals inhabit.

When asked, "Do you want to go to your room until you stop crying?" twenty-six-month-old Amanda, struggling against falling apart, nods assent, goes to her room, and closes the door—reappearing once with dolls in her hand to say, "I'm still crying," then returning to her room. Removing herself and closing her door are attempts at objectification, at finding limits that will separate her from her upsetness. This is importantly a process of dealing with "oughts." Though she is partly inclined to construe these as belonging to the objective order of things, and though part of her is struggling against them, she does not experience them as simply being imposed from without. She seems to feel, rather, that she partly wants "oughts," and that they partly belong to her—or "ought" to belong to her. In their harsh and constraining aspect, they are related to the impoverishment of the symbols we have been considering. And yet (as we saw in part 2.7) limits imply an abundance that is beyond limits. The dolls she plays with while trying to pull herself together are not simply consolation for the discomforts entailed by "oughts." Dolls obey rules, too. (Amanda gives Bear "time out" for pinching her.) And rules belong to play, which gives "I" possibilities for finding a felt and imaginative relation to "Thou" and "it."

The liminality explored in play appropriates "the thing itself," which is known—apart from our self-deceptions about it—only insofar as it is glimpsed in imagination as process. In the same way, it is also known only insofar as it is the provisional object of an act of feeling properly informed with right loving and right hating. In this sense when Lear looked compassionately upon Edgar as Poor Tom, he did indeed know "the thing itself."

6.9 Feeling-Judgments and Feeling-Toned Complexes

At the close of the film *Chinatown*, the detective protagonist played by Jack Nicholson wakes up realizing that he has relived the nightmare of his life by once again trying to protect a woman and by his very actions making her more vulnerable than she would have been if he had done nothing. This moment in the film may be taken as a paradigm of the neurotic condition: injured through early experience, we build up defenses against a repetition of that injury, and these inevitably lead us right to the thing from which we are trying to escape.[101] In this connection one could speak of a repetition compulsion, and indeed, most of the problems that lead people to seek out an analyst have a strongly repetitive character. In trying to understand this tendency to repetition, one may focus on the established and relatively fixed pattern that is being repeated. Or, more prospectively, one may regard the repetition as according with a sentiment to be expressed in some such words as, "If I repeat the pattern one more time, perhaps I may at last bring it to a positive outcome rather than to another of the familiar disastrous ones." In this sentiment there is something more realistic and hopeful than wish—though one may be inclined to call it wish when the outcome again turns out to be a disaster.

I am now especially concerned with the role of emotion and feeling in holding us in patterns opposing the best interests of both ego and self, but also in maintaining the integrity of the subjective sphere despite the sometimes divisive influence of such patterns. And I am concerned, further, with the role of emotion and feeling in the development of a more comprehensive awareness allowing the ego to see beyond such patterns. I will regard these as expressions of the feeling-toned complexes described by Jung in his early work on the association experiment and well known to analysts from their clinical work.[102] And I will give special attention to simple and complex feeling-judgments in mediating in various ways between ego-consciousness and such patterns. Of most interest to me will be complex feeling-judgments as evaluations that play a special role in feeling as—what it ideally is—differentiated relatedness of ego to self and person to world.

By way of background to a further exploration of these matters, I would stress the primacy of emotional elements in our experience in general, and of feeling in our experience as it becomes conscious. And I would also stress the globalization and attraction and repulsion in emotion and feeling. Writing in the 1920s, the German psychologist Felix Krueger, elaborating on the work of the early Gestalt psychologists, insisted that "isolated sensations, perceptions, relations, also memories, clear ideas, decided volitions—in brief all experience-organization (*Erlebnisgliederung*)—split off only after some time from the diffuse tendencies of emotion, and . . . they always remain functionally dominated by them. In any case they always remain more or less imbedded within the emotion, which, as it were, fills in the 'gaps' in the total experience. . . ."[103]

Both emotion, as Krueger is using the word—and feeling, when he describes it as "the maternal source" and "fertile soil" of psychic life—include nonintentional, or objectless, moods. Indeed, insofar as

350

intentional feeling, or feeling in relation to an object, develops out of a matrix or in relation to a background, moods—belonging to that matrix or background—precede and are fundamental to its development.

To be happy or sad about something, I must be happy or sad, but being happy or sad belongs to a different level of experience from being happy or sad about something. (I may have no idea what I am happy or sad about—if I am happy or sad about anything.) I may call my sadness "depression" and consult a psychiatrist about it. Together we may bring to conscious awareness a persuasively plausible reason, based on my life-experience, for my sadness—a reason that had not occurred to me. This new view of myself might alter my mood dramatically, or might not alter it at all. If he prescribes medication that alters my mood in ways not at all understood by me and little understood by him, this procedure takes place at a vast remove from what I mean when I say about my experience, as I recognize it to be authentically and subjectively mine, "I was sad about x."

Mood also persists as nonintentional residue of intentional feeling. For example, one may feel grief owing to the death of a loved one, and in time one's grief may be gradually transformed to a mood of vague sadness no longer related to the missing loved one. For such reasons various writers have imagined a fountain in which the rising jets of water are intentional feeling-acts and the water in the basin is nonintentional mood.[104] Also for such reasons, Strasser speaks of the "transobjectivity and transsubjectivity of disposition" or mood—an important element of much art, indeed of much experience in general.

What Strasser means by this phrase he illustrates by a simple folk song, which speaks in the first stanza of a dark cloud and coming rain, in the second of weary and dying flowers and of things wasting away in the sunless forest, and only in the last of the singer's separation from his beloved and the resulting heaviness of his heart.[105] One might say that the song describes a process in which someone projects his feelings and their implications onto the objective world, then becomes conscious of their reason, and in that sense their cause; and indeed, consciousness is often thus created by way of projection.[106] But this description implies a distinction between subject and object, and between intentionality and nonintentionality, that does not reflect our experience of the song.

351

Feeling, Imagination, and the Self

One may psychologize and philosophize (and theologize) along various lines about the transsubjectivity and transobjectivity of mood. But surely we understand the phrase, in part owing to what we know of the felt oneness of mother and infant (discussed in part 6.7). One could also say, however, that the transsubjectivity and transobjectivity of mood precede the mother-infant relationship in being among the fundamental potentialities of the self that knows what is good for itself. In this view the mother-infant relationship takes them up from the self that knows what is good for itself, and in that relationship they are realized in an indirect, and sometimes a direct, relation to the evaluative self as *spiritus rector*, or guide of proper development.

If this seems to raise the question of "where" the self that knows what is good for itself is (or was), the answer must be, Not in any simple way inside the person. This answer is suggested by the terms *transsubjective* and *transobjective* when applied to moods emanating from deep regions of the self. (To speak this way is no more mystical than to say that the "fit" between organism and environment, as studied by ethologists, is transsubjective and transobjective, in that the organism finds significance in only a highly selected part of its environment, this selection reflecting complex patterns of relationship far more comprehensive than that between this particular organism and its particular environment.)

This view of mood in the mother-infant relationship seems to me congruent with Spitz's description (cited in part 1, n. 23) of the "coenesthetic reception" dominant in the first months of life—a form of communicative interaction not based on focused awareness.

By emotional globalizing and emotional attraction and repulsion I mean, most simply, that psychic life consists of parts and wholes of various kinds, that parts are taken up in wholes, that wholes break down into parts, that there is attraction and repulsion among various parts and wholes, and that emotion plays a role in all of these processes and relations—which can be, and have been, psychologized and philosophized (and theologized) in various ways. We may discern in such globalizing the totality-character of some moods. As for such attraction and repulsion, we might think of conscious sympathy and aversion, and of certain phenomena of perception that have been shown to be matters of interest, lack of interest, or antipathy, all of which are emotional. (Lack of interest may be regarded under the aspect of emotion.)

Of special importance to the concerns of this book are the emotional globalizing of the infant, its falling victim to massive impulses of attraction or repulsion, and the efforts of the mother to moderate these impulses and hold them within a frame of coherence. (The infant does not know, "I feel hunger pains, but it is now 4:40, and I will be fed at 4:45, only five minutes away, because Mother cannot be here sooner." Nor can Mother explain this to him.) Mother must shape these emotions, give them objects, assign reasons for them, and set limits to them, in such a way as to bridge extremes, and to encourage the development of an intermediary range of emotional qualities, containing shades and complex mixtures of the extremes. Much of this shaping is done in the mode of coenesthetic reception. Though, as I have said, in many respects the mother guides this process, it is in other respects a true collaboration, with the infant trying to help its mother, as it has been doing since shortly after birth. (Thus self and ego, or incipient ego, come to expression in and through their relationship with no fixed assignment of roles to either mother or infant.)

This shaping of emotion through the collaboration of mother and infant is the beginning of the complex feeling-judgments to be discussed in a moment. The same development establishes the basis for the creation and comprehension of imaginative symbols.

What I have just said about mood should suggest that emotional nonintentionality and emotional intentionality are sometimes mutually exclusive and sometimes not. Indeed, they are sometimes indistinguishable. This is exactly as conscious and unconscious are sometimes mutually exclusive—justifying Coleridge, Jung, and others in thinking polaristically (as we saw in part 6.6)—and sometimes not. (A dream is conscious experience but may depict matters otherwise unknown—unconscious—and highly at odds with conscious values. If I ski well, do I do so consciously or unconsciously?)

Jung's association experiment consists of a list of 100 common stimulus words, which are read by the experimenter to a subject, who is to respond with the first word that comes to mind. The response (or lack of response) is recorded along with the reaction time, measured

353

with a stopwatch in fifths of a second. After the list has been completed, the experimenter asks the subject to try to remember his original response to each word, and reads the list again, noting correct and faulty recollections and instances of no response. The results are then scored according to various criteria, and often the subject is asked for reasons for various responses.

Though Jung at first thought the experiment might be useful in psychiatric diagnosis, he early came to focus on disturbances in the normal process of association, as these are caused by what he called feeling-toned complexes. Such complexes are bundles of psychic elements of various kinds—sensations, ideas, memories—bound together by a shared feeling-tone (let us say, of admiration, sexual desire, anger, resentment). This feeling-tone is roughly equivalent to its energetic value, which can in some measure be objectified and even (within limits) quantified. Thus the activation of a complex can be detected by various aberrations in the normal process of association that Jung called "complex indicators," such as delayed reaction to the stimulus word, responses in a foreign language, "clang" responses—based on sound rather than on meaning—exclamations ("Oh!"), and faulty recollection of the initial response.

Delayed reaction is one indication that complex-influenced disturbances have an important temporal dimension, another such indication being signs of the perseveration of a "constellated" (or activated) complex. This means that when a nonego complex has begun to interfere with the operations of the ego, the interference tends to continue. Thus when one stimulus word provokes a delayed reaction, the stimulus words immediately following tend also to provide delayed reactions; and often the meanings of the following responses are more related to the meaning of the stimulus word that provoked the first delayed reaction, or to the meaning of the word in response to it, than to the meanings of the succeeding stimulus words. Since the feeling-tone is in certain respects the essential constituent of a complex, the perseveration of its influence should surprise no one who has felt himself mistreated and then tried to deal with his annoyance by putting it out of his mind. Complexes, in any case, originated in the past, so that the perseveration recorded in the association experiment is simply a recent expression of their persistence in time.

Receptivity, Commitment, and Detachment

Delayed reaction times and perseveration in the association experiment are instances of the emotional globalizing of which I have been speaking. It may also be seen in the tendency of the complex to spread in the sense of becoming enriched with more and more associative material, progressively remote from the ostensible core meaning of the complex. (When performing the association experiment with a young woman subject, I was baffled when the stimulus word *carrot* upset her so much that she could not respond at all, and the succeeding stimulus words provoked strikingly disturbed associations. She, it turned out, had been engaged to marry a young man; the engagement had been broken off, and she had returned to him the diamond ring he had given her, diamonds being measured in "carats.")

Emotional attraction may be seen in the interference of the nonego complex in the field of the ego—as though the nonego complex "wanted" to merge with the ego or appropriate it. Such attraction is also part of emotional globalizing, as bits of psychic material come to form more and more associative links. Emotional repulsion may be seen in the very existence of nonego complexes incompatible with the ego, and in the defensive operations of the ego to keep them at bay. The detective protagonist of *Chinatown* has a savior-of-women complex that he tries to disown, but he wakes up to find that he has identified with it. Something of the same thing is true of Art Pepper and Dr. Smile, indeed of most people of whom I offer psychological vignettes in this book.

In view of the relativity of emotional nonintentionality and intentionality, and of conscious and unconscious, what I have so far said about emotional attraction and repulsion presents an oversimplified picture of a subject—the ego—standing over against an object (albeit an "inner" object)—nonego complexes. Actually, nonego complexes may be conscious or unconscious. (Someone may have stagefright—the expression of a complex—know his stagefright inside out, and still have stagefright.) The ego itself is in Jung's illuminating if paradoxical view a complex among other complexes—one to which the sense of "I" adheres, though this distinction, too, is relative, since nonego complexes may convey a sense of "I"-ness, when they are personified in dreams, for example, or when they develop into the splinter psyches manifest in extreme forms of psychopathology. And education is in important respects a process of forming complexes constituting "character" and good habits.

In Jung's investigation of complexes, he was concerned with emotional intentionality. More specifically, he was concerned with intentions in relation to counterintentions. About this it is important to note that there are no intentions without at least implicit counterintentions. Psychologically as well as physically, the shadow is born with the light—nonego complexes incompatible with the ego are born with the ego.

Counterintentions are directly and indirectly created by the Father World and its representatives, chiefly Father. (The paternal "Thou shalt not" and the recalcitrance of objective reality may counter the intentions of the incipient ego, and internalizing the "Thou shalt not" and learning about the world create a shadow of intentions counter to those of the ego in its compliance.) But even before this, counterintentions are "given" as part of the Mother World. This is because (as we saw in part 6.6 in connection with the views of Coleridge) nothing comes to phenomenal manifestation except in relation to polarity. (See again fig. 3.) And it is in the Mother World that phenomena are born.

Phenomenal manifestations of polarity are, it is true, hierarchically organized. But this state of affairs, too, is "given"—if by anything, then by the Mother World. (There is order in nature—and its order is in many respects hierarchical—whether or not an enthroned god is imagined as creating or imposing it, and declaring "Thou shalt not" in the process.)

The principle of the Father World may emerge from the Mother World and reach beyond it. But the more it reaches beyond it—say, in the exploration of outer space—the more it needs transcendence in the form, precisely, of the Mother World—say, in the exploration of ecosystems and the depths of the sea.

My reason for expressing myself in these mythic terms (and for thus prefiguring part 6.12) is to propose a general view of the instances of inner and outer conflict shortly to be discussed. In this view the feeling-tone of feeling-toned complexes belongs to the array of emotional potentialities having their primary and natural context in the mother-infant relationship. (In Krueger's formulation, feeling is the "maternal source.") That relationship is the most fundamental shaping influence on the capacity for making feeling-judgments. As this capacity develops, it must deal with the aspects of reality I am symbolizing as the Father World—and specifically with the tensions conducive to complexes that the Father World brings into personal development. But the differentiation of feeling, and especially of the capacity to form complex feeling-judgments, is of primary importance if one's ego is to find the kind of relationship to one's complexes that will further individuation. The concern for transitions, gradations, and coherence characteristic of complex feeling-judgments is first developed in the feeling relationship of mother and infant.

Complexes easily result in a lowering of consciousness. Any developed conscious function such as intellectual thought may serve to mitigate the influence of complexes (when they are adverse). Still, the desideratum of proper feeling is unavoidable: when complexes impair evaluation and relatedness, a restoration of more adequate feeling is called for. (Such impairment may result in deintegration, which may, in fact, be a good thing—as when someone angrily quits a job he will be well rid of. But this complication does not in the larger view obviate the need for proper feeling.)

A simple feeling-judgment is an emotional evaluation that stresses one value in relative isolation from others, or that employs a single, and therefore simple, scale. "Thou shalt not" is an example of such a judgment, because it singles out x as important to avoid, without consideration of the degree to which it should be avoided, the importance of avoiding it in comparison with that of avoiding other things, or mitigating circumstances. (I choose the example because of its clarity, not because I regard it as paradigmatic in the sense of being the primary factor in the organization of our conscious emotional experience. Both the natural and the human worlds have intentions and counterintentions, impulses, and checks and balances of all kinds, only some of which are clearly related to a humanly—and authoritatively—imposed "Thou shalt not.") "I love my country" is a simple feeling-judgment like "Thou shalt not" but in positive form. "My country, right or wrong" implies that such simple feeling-judgments are often both too global and too partial, and thus, since on some level one knows this, are defensive.

Often, though—and often properly—simple feeling-judgments do admit of complexity. When I say, "I love my child," I am expressing a global judgment that nonetheless leaves me free to be momentarily cross when, at the age of two years, she smears my eyeglasses with strawberry jam. Indeed, simple feeling-judgments are implicit in all commitment and are thus of fundamental importance in the individuation process.

A complex feeling-judgment, in contrast, weighs one value against others, or weighs values on more than one scale. The rudiments of such a judgment may be seen when eighteen-month-old Amanda wades into cold water, obviously weighing her displeasure in its coldness against her pleasure in its wetness.

A more developed—and to my mind paradigmatic—example is offered by eight-year-old "Margaret," whose grandfather has died, and whose grandmother has remarried in what some people regard as unseemly haste. When asked whether she finds this good or bad, Margaret replies that she finds it in some ways very good and in some others bad. Her reply has laid the basis for a complex feeling-judgment that will help her to accommodate feelings of various kinds while adequately taking into account that her own subjective standpoint and that of her grandmother must necessarily be different. Margaret does not simply like or simply dislike her grandmother as a result of her remarriage, nor does she experience depression, rage, or fear. Rather, she can entertain a play of various feelings as distinct from the rush of a single emotion. The complex judgment in which these feelings are resolved serves Margaret's adaptation to a new and complex situation.

Margaret's reply that she finds her grandmother's remarriage in some ways good and in some ways bad is, very importantly, not an expression of the ambivalence described by psychoanalysts. On the contrary, complex feeling-judgments lessen the likelihood of ambivalence. The example of "Alice Kendall," who is white, and her boss and close friend, "Ed," who is black, shows how the making of a complex feeling-judgment can bring coherence to an emotional situation that might otherwise become chaotic.

358

Receptivity, Commitment, and Detachment

Alice's father, a wealthy businessman, was offended when she wrote her parents a letter addressed to Mary and James Kendall instead of to Mr. and Mrs. James Kendall. Recently her mother had expressed the desire to be addressed as Mary Kendall, so that Alice was, in fact, complying with her mother's wishes. In reply, her father wrote two curt notes to her on small pieces of memo paper from his office. In these he insisted that any man has the right to at least the minimal respect that goes with being called "Mr." He pointed out that she has black friends, and proposed that she ask them how a black man feels when he is not given that respect. If his daughter is not willing to address him as "Mr.," she should, he insisted, address her letter simply to her mother, who would then relay their contents to him.

Alice showed these notes to Ed, who was even more appalled than she by her father's pitiable clinging to his persona as he begged crumbs of respect from his daughter. Her parents, I should note, have met Ed and find him a fine man, but they disapprove of her relationship with him because he is black. Nothing that Alice has been able to say in praise of him has lessened their disapproval.

Ed insisted that Alice immediately write her father describing some of her father's good qualities and expressing gratitude for things he has done for her. Alice tried and tried but could not think of anything good to say about him. Ed then searched his own memory and reminded Alice of good things she had told him about her father in the past. He urged her to write the letter whether she wanted to or not. While Ed supplied materials for it, tears streamed from his eyes, as he was deeply aware of pleading for someone who had profoundly hurt him. Again, Ed's attitude toward Alice's father was not ambivalent. It was the expression of a complex feeling-judgment in which various emotional currents were taken into account and in which facts were assessed as to their relative importance according to various criteria.

The value of Ed's capacity to make complex feeling-judgments is especially clear in contrast with the simple feeling-judgments of Alice's father, and the contrast shows something of the bearing of both kinds of judgments on feeling-toned complexes.

Mr. Kendall's attitude toward black people is very possibly a conscious conviction for which he could offer some sort of rationale. But it is also very likely based on a complex with unconscious roots, one that might be revealed in response to a stimulus word such as *black* in an association experiment. Simple feeling-judgments—such as "Blacks are inferior"—may be entirely compatible with a complex—such as a complex of antipathy to blacks. Indeed, such a judgment may be part of the complex. Thus the judgment offers no resistance to the invasion of the ego by the complex, to the disorientation of the ego by the emotional charge (the feeling-tone) of the complex, and hence to the usurpation of the ego by the complex. A complex feeling-judgment, in contrast, typically contains one element that is in some measure compatible with the complex and one or more that are not, so that the judgment partly inhibits the direct expression of the complex. Subject to this inhibition, tendencies to such extreme responses as revulsion and total identification (with the contents of the complex) may give way to imaginative sympathy. (Complexes are often curiously "intelligent" when one has the right relation to them—when they are not blind and blinding.)

If the stimulus word *black* would not get an indifferent response from Mr. Kendall, surely neither would it from Ed: if Mr. Kendall has a "black" complex, so, in some form, has Ed. But surely this complex in Ed is the basis of a complex rather than a simple attitude, and he surely also holds complex attitudes toward other elements of the complex. (Despite the broken family of his own childhood, "the integrity of families is important." Despite his own missing father, "one's father should be honored." Despite the personal affront to him, "individual interests should be subordinate to a community of decent people." Despite his tears, "more moderate and socially oriented feelings and emotions should prevail." Despite his role as victim of Mr. Kendall's bigotry, "bigots, too, may be victims, and any victim who is in a position to help another victim should do so.")

In Ed's dealing with Alice's problem, he was vigorously exercising the "as if" mode of imagination; indeed, using real-life materials to real-life ends, he was an artist of a high order. As this reflection should suggest—as should my example (in part 6.7) of Mother Courage's complex feeling-judgment with regard to her dead son—the making of adequate feeling-judgments is a major concern, and even theme, in many kinds of art. Before returning to a few more events of real people, I want to explore the making of complex feeling-judgments in a Shakespeare sonnet and in *The Winter's Tale*. The moments in this play that I will discuss are especially revealing about the relations between feeling-toned complexes and complex feeling-judgments.

Shakespeare's thirty-fifth sonnet presents to his male friend Shakespeare's own response to something troubling, not clearly identified, that the friend has done:

1 No more be grieved at that which thou hast done:
2 Roses have thorns, and silver fountains mud,
3 Clouds and eclipses stain both moon and sun,
4 And loathsome canker lives in sweetest bud.
5 All men make faults, and even I in this,
6 Authorizing thy trespass with compare,
7 Myself corrupting, salving thy amiss,
8 Excusing thy sins more than thy sins are;
9 For to thy sensual fault I bring in sense—
10 Thy adverse party is thy advocate—
11 And 'gainst myself a lawful plea commence.
12 Such civil war is in my love and hate
13   That I an accessory needs must be
14   To that sweet thief which sourly robs from me.

The word *grieved* in the first line has a double meaning, as we find out in the course of the poem: the friend has done something he feels, or ought to feel, "grieved" about, but the poem as a whole is about Shakespeare's grievance concerning the "amiss" (error) or "fault" of his friend. Ostensibly Shakespeare is saying that the grievance is past, forgiven, and ready to be forgotten. If this is what he meant, the sense of the poem would be, "Hurt as I was at the moment, I realize upon reflection that there are reasons for what you did and that, in any case, I had exaggerated its importance." Instead of expressing such a sentiment, the poem, rather, records, indeed enacts, the process by which the poet puts his grievance in some measure behind him, a process of stating a complex feeling-judgment in which the basis for the poet's initial disapproval of his friend's act is neither denied nor softened but emphatically affirmed.

Indeed, in the larger view, the sonnet is an expression of condemnation. Importantly, the condemnation is not a simple feeling-judgment in which Shakespeare closes himself off from his friend. Rather, it is a complex feeling-judgment expressive of what one Shakespearean commentator has called "the open heart": Shakespeare's heart declares itself both angry and still accessible.

I like to imagine that the first line, "No more be grieved at that which thou hast done," is being addressed to someone who has no idea that he has done anything he should grieve about, or in any case, that anyone else knows that he has done it. (Imagine someone quite at peace with himself shocked at being told, "I know you have been having sleepless nights about that dreadful thing you did, but it is really time for you to put aside your guilty worries about it and get on with your life.")

In the next lines (2–4) Shakespeare takes beautiful things ("roses," "silver fountains," "moon and sun," "sweetest bud") and reminds us of their links with ugly or at least more problematic things ("thorns," "mud," "clouds and eclipses," "loathsome canker"). Notably, the latter are poetically more powerful. "Silver fountains" are an Elizabethan commonplace; "silver fountains mud" is jarring. He might have written, "Clouds and eclipses hide both moon and sun," which would suggest that clouds go away, leaving the moon and sun. "Clouds and eclipses stain both moon and sun," in contrast, implies that these obscuring things have a real and permanent effect. In the same vein, "sweetest bud" is quite pallid in comparison with "loathsome canker."

"All men make faults," Shakespeare declares (in line 5), as though intending to argue, assuagingly, "Though what I have said so far is true, everyone has faults." Instead, he points the accusing finger at himself for excusing his friend too readily, saying, in effect, "You are guilty for what you did; I am guilty for forgiving you." "Authorizing thy trespass with compare" (line 6) means roughly, "In citing similar cases in your defense, I simply authorize what you did." He goes on to say (roughly), "I corrupt myself in excusing you" (line 7), adding (roughly) that "in going so far in forgiving you, I engage in an exaggeration greater than that expressed in what you did" (line 8).

In line 9, "For to thy sensual fault I bring in sense," *sense* has the connotation of reason, so that Shakespeare is saying (roughly), "Reason, which is the higher faculty, I am corrupting in arguing on your behalf for what might have been a sin of appetite." For the first time announcing that he is really against what his friend did, Shakespeare

362

reminds his friend that he, Shakespeare, has been arguing in his defense. "And 'gainst myself a lawful plea commence" (line 11): as the friend's advocate against a hypothetical adverse party, Shakespeare, who disapproves of what his friend has done, is arguing against himself, as he has been doing all along. It is now clear, however, that he has been arguing against himself.

As I have said, ambivalence is not differentiated feeling. "Such civil war is in my love and hate" (line 12) expresses ambivalence, not to recommend it, not to propose it as a solution, but to admit that it is Shakespeare's momentary condition. But to acknowledge that condition within the context of such a complex larger statement is, one could say, an expression of differentiated feeling.

"That I an accessory needs must be / To that sweet thief which sourly robs from me" (lines 13–14): Shakespeare confesses to being an accessory, which he "needs" must be, whether he were to remain silent or, as he has done in this sonnet, say too much in his friend's defense.

The concluding mention of "that sweet thief which sourly robs from me" admits that, despite all the implications of legal procedures, the matter is finally very personal. Shakespeare is saying (roughly), "I am personally hurt in a way that gets into imponderables"—essentially triadic. It may not be very grown-up to feel, "X should like or respect me; instead X gives the liking and respect to Y, and so I am being robbed of it," but his feeling belongs to the range of what we feel, if we feel fully. (A main theme of this book is that being grown-up is not everything; in any case, recognizing one's infantility can initiate release from the neurotic condition described at the beginning of this section.) Shakespeare is saying (roughly), "I am ambivalent, my ambivalence is personally motivated, and it arises out of the kind of predicament I have so fully described." To express a feeling situation in such a differentiated way is an act of differentiated feeling, even if the sonnet describes an attempted feeling-act—to find a resolution to the poet's dilemma—that ends in stalemate. This is one of many literary works exploring the feeling dimension of experience when practically no other form of action is possible.

The main action of The Winter's Tale begins with an outburst of madness in which the ego of one of the principal characters, King

Feeling, Imagination, and the Self

Leontes of Sicilia, is possessed by a feeling-toned complex. In keeping with Jung's important realization that psychic problems are to be dealt with not so much directly as through a broad increase in consciousness, much of the rest of the play dramatizes the creation of a larger world than that visible at the beginning, a world providing a more complex and flexible framework of evaluation than that which led to Leontes' madness.

As the play opens, Leontes is being visited by a childhood friend, King Polixenes of Bohemia. Having stayed for nine months, Polixenes makes preparations to leave, but Leontes begs him to stay longer. When Polixenes refuses, Leontes urges his wife, Hermione, to plead the case for staying. She does so, successfully. When Leontes reflects on her success, after his failure, and sees her and Polixenes holding hands, he from one moment to the next goes mad. (Nothing in the play suggests that anything improper has gone on between Hermione and Polixenes.) I will quote the speech expressing the outburst of Leontes' madness—and some following—to show how a complex may overwhelm consciousness, may refuse one's efforts to push it away, and may instead drag one again and again into it. Leontes exclaims, in an aside:

> Too hot, too hot!
> To mingle friendship far is mingling bloods.
> I have tremor cordis on me; my heart dances,
> But not for joy, not joy. This entertainment
> May a free face put on, derive a liberty
> From heartiness, from bounty, fertile bosom,
> And well become the agent—may, I grant;
> But to be paddling palms and pinching fingers,
> As now they are, and making practiced smiles
> As in a looking glass; and then to sigh, as 'twere
> The mort o' th' deer—oh, that is entertainment
> My bosom likes not, nor my brows.
>
> [I.ii.108–19]

The words that signify the firm intrusion of the complex into the field of the ego are *mort o' th' deer* (a horn call announcing the death of a deer) and *brows*, both of which have a bearing on Leontes' sudden obsession with the thought of being a cuckold, and hence, in the

Elizabethan metaphor, growing horns. The perseveration of the complex may be seen in the recurrence of animal imagery in several of the next lines. Thus, a moment later he remarks to his young son,

> We must be neat—not neat, but cleanly, captain:
> And yet the steer, the heifer, and the calf,
> Are all called neat. Still virginaling
> Upon his palm? How now, you wanton calf,
> Art thou my calf?
>
> [I.ii.123–27]

As soon as he uses the word *neat* to mean tidy, he senses its application to an animal—we have retained this use of the word in *neat's-foot oil*—and tries to ward off the association by translating *neat* into *cleanly*. But the association is too powerful for him to deal with in this way, and so he spells out the implicit thought, putting it in a general form that, by intellectualizing it, gives him a bit of distance from it. But the association is strong enough that it draws his son to it as his "wanton calf." (Indeed, "boy" belongs to the complex both in signifying his son and his own immaturity as "boy eternal" [I.ii.65].)

When Leontes' son consents to be called his "calf," Leontes demurs, saying:

> Thou want'st a rough pash, and the shoots [= horns] that I have
> To be full like me . . . ,
>
> [I.ii.128–29]

then goes on thinking about his son and jealousy, referring to his wife as "dam," a female breeding animal, and ending his speech thusly:

> And that to the infection of my brains,
> And hardening of my brows.
>
> [I.ii.145–46]

In the last line Leontes again imagines his own brows sprouting horns.

Significantly, when Leontes' wife Hermione notices that "He something seems unsettled," she remarks, "As if you held a brow of much distraction" (I.ii.147 and 149). As I implied in my remarks (in part 6.6) about affect-ego and affect-object, complexes are bipolar. (*Whitey* and *nigger* form an intrinsic pair. A whiny, sullen young man lolling in his mother complex exerts a great pressure on any older man

365

to become the tyrant father—the young man expects, wants, demands, needs that the older man play that role and seduces him into playing it.) The transsubjectivity and transobjectivity of mood may be thought to include the kind of unconscious contagion of the complex that is expressed in Hermione's gaffe.

One important theme in the rest of the play is the reeducation of Leontes, first in the form of the restoration of his sanity, and then in contrition and a general enhancement of feeling as evaluation and relationship.

After Hermione has been thrown into prison as an adulteress, she there gives birth to a daughter. Her waiting woman Paulina then takes the baby to Leontes, thinking that the sight of it will soften his heart and restore his sanity. That it instead enrages him to the point of first wanting it thrown into a fire and then ordering it to be left in a desolate place is a measure of his insanity and of how truly evil it is in its effects. The death of his son and the apparent death of Hermione shock him to his senses, but the issues resulting from his loss of judgment are resolved in part indirectly through the workings of time, "great creating nature," and the influence of Paulina and Hermione. Hermione's daughter, Perdita, who grows to adulthood in the course of the play, has a symbolic value important in conveying to the audience (if not to Leontes) a sense of the needed resolution. While Leontes is still raging in his delusion, Paulina and Hermione have the unpromising task of trying to reason with him, and they do so in ways that dramatize the process of forming complex feeling-judgments, which will be necessary to save whatever can be saved from Leontes' folly and tyranny. This process is evident in speeches of Paulina and Hermione in which they employ such constructions as these: as _____ as _____, more _____ than _____, less _____ than _____, with the blanks filled in by the words *honest, mad, rotten, sound, tyranny, innocent, patience, true, unhappy, love, disobedience,* and *gratitude.*

Thus, when Leontes calls Paulina "A most intelligencing bawd," she replies,

> Not so;
> I am as ignorant in that as you
> In so entitling me; and no less honest

Than you are mad; which is enough, I'll warrant,
As this world goes, to pass for honest.

[II.iii.68–72]

And a moment later she refers to the root of Leontes's opinion,

which is rotten
As ever oak or stone was sound.

[II.iii.89–90]

When Hermione speaks in her own defense in court, she declares,

if powers divine
Behold our human actions—as they do—

[III.ii.27–28]

emphasizing the conditionality and the more embracing viewpoint that are lost from Leontes' consciousness, and then goes on:

my past life
Hath been as continent, as chaste, as true,
As I am now unhappy; which is more
Than history can
pattern. . . .

[III.ii.32–35]

These comparisons imply a process of weighing. (As Hermione remarks a moment later, "For life, I prize it / As I weigh grief, which I would spare" [41–42].) But the things weighed (chastity, unhappiness, life, grief) lead us into realms of emotion and value that in important respects challenge the logical form of comparison. Such comparisons as that between chastity and unhappiness reveal the poverty of language and the oversimplification of logic in dealing with issues in these realms. Chastity and unhappiness can be only indirectly compared, as elements of a complex situation consisting of values to varying degrees compatible or opposed and of emotional currents similarly compatible or opposed, as these values and emotional currents bear on complex relationships. What is needed are feeling-judgments complex enough to deal with such complexity. The speeches I have been discussing, straining the limits of the sayable as they do, convey a sense that one must deal with such complexities both more complexly and more simply, that much of the complexity required of feeling is

367

Feeling, Imagination, and the Self

accomplished by a direct emotional apprehension of value, by simply seeing what is there. In an entirely different mental realm from the "ocular proof" of the handkerchief that deceived Othello into believing that Desdemona was unfaithful, Hermione's goodness, like Desdemona's, is simply "there," to be perceived by anyone with an open heart—and with the quality of feeling *The Winter's Tale* is demanding of its characters and its audience.

Indeed, breaking down habitual feeling-judgments—involving emotion and value—is essential to the overall effect of the play. Thus, one of the characters, Paulina's husband Antigonus, is eaten by a bear, and the clown son of a shepherd reports this event while it is happening. At the same time a wrecked ship is sinking with its crew, and the clown in his narrative must comically go back and forth between the calamity of Antigonus and that of the ship. The audience laughs at both. At the same time, the shepherd finds the baby Perdita with a casket of jewels, so that the audience, like the shepherd and his son, is given the task of responding emotionally both to things dying and at the same time to things newborn. Indeed, at the close of the play, as a series of apparent marvels is revealed, Paulina hears her husband's death confirmed, with the detail that "he was torn to pieces with [by] a bear," at the same time that she must respond to various occasions of joy. Shakespeare has a witness recount the scene thus:

> But, oh, the noble combat, that 'twixt joy and sorrow was fought in Paulina! She had one eye declined for the loss of her husband, another elevated that the oracle was fulfilled. She lifted the princess from the earth, and so locks her in embracing as if she would pin her to her heart, that she might no more be in danger of losing.
>
> [V.ii.74–80]

The close of the play effects a modification of habitual feeling-judgments through an imaginative awareness (discussed in part 5.8) that life continues despite death, that we may participate in this continuing life (though not appropriating it to ego-determined ends), and that its continuance and our participation in it are causes for wonder.

I will conclude with two real-life vignettes illustrating how the constellation of a complex may impair the making of an appropriate

368

feeling-judgment despite the best efforts of the ego to make it; and how dreams, linking the ego to the psychic depths, may offer materials for the making of a feeling-judgment that will mitigate the disruptive effects of a complex. The mother-infant relationship will be seen to be important in the background of both the complexes and the feeling problems I will be describing.

When Mrs. Gardner (discussed in part 6.7) on some level regards herself as infant and mother in relation to her animals, whom she regards as infant and mother in relation to her, her abandonment complex is tacitly active in a way that is entirely consistent with a realistic appreciation of her animals and of the life she shares with them. But she has also found herself in relationships with men who have turned out to be weak and irresponsible, and years ago she took upon herself the task of trying to better these relationships through her own psychotherapy, in the course of which she once dreamed that she was embracing one of these men and could see in the mirror that his and her heads were transposed. Such a dream would seem to suggest that her relationships with men tend to become symbiotic, with a resulting confusion about what belongs on each side of her ego boundaries and theirs. And such confusion would seem symptomatic, in turn, of an archaic identity with her much-needed but frighteningly absent mother. It is one thing, and a valuable one, when mother and infant share roles as they do in Winnicott's description of the nursing couple (quoted in the caption to fig. 4). It is another, and more problematic one, when a yearning for such a sharing of roles takes the form of a complex obtruding into the field of Mrs. Gardner's ego in her relations with men.

What I have been saying fits certain moments in Mrs. Gardner's sometimes problematic but also rewarding relationship with her present husband. In moments of stress she is inclined to feel that he is the infant in great need of maternal care, without which he, the infant, who is also the mother, will abandon her. Thus in such moments she oscillates uncontrollably between feeling herself the mother and feeling herself the abandoned baby.

Recently Mrs. Gardner found herself anxious and depressed after her husband had failed to come home one night at the expected time. In response to his tardiness, her mind was flooded with elaborate

369

fantasies of the mishaps that could have befallen him. He finally appeared, giving a reasonable explanation of his lateness, and commented, "You weren't worried, were you?" to which she replied, "Well, I was worried for a minute," thus restraining herself from telling him how agitated she had been. The next evening they failed to coordinate their plans as to which of them was to do what in the way of grocery-shopping for dinner. Already somewhat anxious and depressed—the lingering effects of her upset the evening before—she was made even more so by this misunderstanding, though the inconvenience it caused them was slight. She remained anxious and depressed the next day, when she discussed these events and her reaction to them with her analyst, who was thus confronted with a delicate task in responding to her account.

Part of what made the talk delicate was that the maternal quality embodied in such a complex, or at least in such a complex when it is obtruding in such a way, is not of a very high order. I think of this sort of maternal quality as "reconstituted mother," on the analogy of reconstituted orange juice, made by squeezing orange juice, subjecting it to various mechanical and chemical processes that reduce the juice to concentrate, then mixing the concentrate with water to create an imitation of the original orange juice. Since reconstituted mother is inferior, the person manifesting such a maternal quality feels inferior about manifesting it. Yet neither Mrs. Gardner nor the analyst could see anything to do but perform their parts in a variant of a script that might be called, "Here I Am, Doing It Again." Not at all surprisingly, calling attention to the familiar pattern led Mrs. Gardner to exclaim, "It is hopeless. My whole life is a botched job. I can never get out of this. I'll be doing it again and again." Here we see the emotional globalizing of which I have spoken, leading to the creation of an overly global, and overly partial, simple feeling-judgment.

This inadequate feeling-judgment offered a point of departure. With the help of her analyst, she gave her attention to how inadequate this feeling-judgment was, and to how very far from being a botched job her life actually is. This might sound like cheering her up, which is generally a poor way to respond to someone who is depressed, but it can be regarded more accurately as an attempt to replace an inadequate feeling-judgment with an adequate one. The further aim was to make it possible to discuss feeling issues closer to the core of the complex, a discussion which would make her aware of the margin of choice left to the ego despite the complex. Thus, for example, she considered what she might have said when her husband commented, "You weren't worried, were you?"—what she might have said, more specifically, that would have expressed more respect for the reality and the deep implications of what was going on in her and between her and him.

It is important to add that Mrs. Gardner has had success in being a good enough mother to her children. She has been able to have it because good enough mother and reconstituted mother can coexist in the same person. But good enough mother is quietly good enough, whereas reconstituted mother is touchy about her deficiency, and thus sometimes allows adapted feeling to be subverted by a complex.

Thirty-year-old "George Jackson" works as an administrative assistant in a reformatory. Mr. Jackson is seeing an analyst partly in the hope of bringing some tranquility to his family life, in which there are violent eruptions between him and his abusive ten-year-old son, who has been referred to a child psychiatrist. In these altercations Mrs. Jackson usually supports her son against her husband. As an example of the kinds of tensions that beset the family: Mr. Jackson looks out the window to see the ten-year-old boy using the neighbor's power lawn mower. Mr. Jackson tells his son that the instrument is too dangerous, and forbids him to use it. In response, the boy explains that he is saving up money to buy a power mower of his own. Mrs. Jackson sides with her son.

Mr. Jackson's mother died when he was very young, and he was brought up by his sadistic stepmother, who labored mightily to convince him of his worthlessness. She would banish him to his room, and when he had to come out to go to the bathroom, she would say such things as "What an ugly kid! Go back to your room so I don't have to look at you." When he was about sixteen, he responded to her years of mistreatment by physically beating her up. At about the same time, he took all his clothes and other possessions to the edge of town and burned them.

371

Mr. Jackson idealized his father and followed him everywhere. But his father dealt with his stepmother for the most part by staying away, thus giving his son no help in his son's troubled relationship with her. After high school, Mr. Jackson worked for years as a checker in a supermarket, then suddenly quit in anger at his treatment by an authoritarian boss. In the weeks of unemployment following, he went through a mild psychotic episode that left no observable aftereffects.

The judgment "ugly" figures both in Mr. Jackson's conscious attitude and in the life of an autonomous complex. Though he is highly intelligent and has read many books, he speaks with atrocious—ugly—grammar, thus openly revealing the undisciplined other side of his nature as a scrupulously fair disciplinarian. He has decided that people find him attractive and look at him admiringly; so, he is not consciously afraid of being ugly. Still, he remains strikingly sensitive to ugliness. Thus, when he finally noticed a small Hopi Indian figurine of a Mudhead clown in the study of his analyst, he exclaimed, visibly shocked, "My God, that's ugly! It's grotesque!"

Once he was for days in an irritable mood, in which he burst out in anger at people with whom he worked. This irritability was preceded by several days of extreme sensitivity to sensory impressions, during which if someone hit a spoon against a cup, he almost jumped out of his skin. While still irritable, he was in a store with a male friend and the friend's baby, which Mr. Jackson was holding while showing the baby a pet parrot. Usually he finds parrots very ugly, but as he showed it to the baby, it seemed to him extraordinarily beautiful. He felt a great flood of pity for it, thinking that it should be in the jungle, where it would be free. Surely he saw himself in the ugly-beautiful parrot, and the pity he felt for it is related to concern and self-forgiveness he would need to feel if he were to arrive at an adequate complex feeling-judgment of himself and the value of his life. But Mr. Jackson is also capable of sentimentality, and it would surely also be right to detect in that pity, "loud" as it was, traces of sentimental "reconstituted mother."

Indeed, his life is to a notable extent governed by various inner figures personifying forces in a network of complexes. Among these figures are the arbitrary male authority; the good father, who is idealized and unreliable; the abused child; the disobedient child; the punishing stepmother; and a version of "reconstituted mother," full of archaic, overblown, and sentimental feeling. His problematic relations with male authorities he understands relatively well. He understands less well the way in which the occasional collapse of the internalized male authority calls forth the angry mother. And he understands even less well the way in which the disobedient child becomes the abused child calling forth the pitying, "reconstituted" mother. One of the ways in which he seems to be seeking to modify the influence of these figures as disruptively autonomous agents is by developing a capacity for making complex feeling-judgments. The following dream of his can be regarded as concerned with this task.

Mr. Jackson dreamed that he was swimming across Green Lake in Seattle, a lake a mile or so in diameter. He swam carrying his ten-year-old son, and discovered that he could do this very well, though his son was at first uncertain whether this was fun or whether he should be afraid. The dreamer said that in the dream, "I was surprised that I was not afraid." Apparently that feeling communicated itself to his son who as a result remained calm. The dreamer swam the rest of the way across the lake, got up on the other side, and then put the boy down.

When his son began crying, Mr. Jackson said, "Look, that's nothing, that's nothing"—about his feat of carrying his son across the lake. But then he immediately corrected himself, saying, "Actually, Son, that was very hard." But in reporting the dream to his analyst, he remarked, "I immediately took it [the difficulty] for granted."

Talking further about the dream, he commented, "If I could redo that dream, I would have myself feeling happy that I'm swimming across the lake with my son and able to do it, because, when I do good things, I just take them for granted. I should give myself more credit, and I wish that in the dream I had." A bit later he remarked, "Well, I think you know that part of me is a screwed-up kid, and I think that is symbolized by my son. If I take good care of it, it will be all right. It doesn't have to hold me back from even remarkable accomplishments, but I have to take care of it." In the dream, taking care of it meant being surprised that he was not afraid, and transmitting the feeling of not being afraid to his son.

Adequate feeling-judgments are created by differentiated feeling. Its workings include registering emotional currents (feelings and emotions) in their relation to psychic contents (sensations, images, thoughts) that can, and often must, also be grasped nonemotionally. Its workings also include evaluating emotional currents and using them to evaluate, especially under the aspect of relationship. To be surprised that one is not afraid is to give a new accent of value to one's lack of fear. To have the fear gone from his relationship with his son, and to know that it is gone, means for Mr. Jackson to be able to support his son in the right way. Not being afraid is linked with giving himself credit for not being afraid, and for swimming well. To give himself credit belongs to the margin of freedom left to his ego despite his complexes. The complex feeling-judgment giving Mr. Jackson this credit is at first emotional (being surprised). It is this, moreover, as an expression of the relationship of ego to self. But his feeling-judgment is then articulated as an attitude of the ego about self and world, and about relationship: giving credit to himself, Mr. Jackson must take care of the screwed-up kid, who is his son and also himself. Though ostensibly about father and son, this attitude echoes a mother's caring for her baby. In this attitude Mother cares for Baby in more nearly the right way than in Mrs. Gardner's anxious depression about her husband or in Mr. Jackson's pity for the parrot.

6.10 A Good Reason for Representing Disordered Feeling

The turbulent personal life of Scheler would hardly seem to bear out his status as an important writer about ethics. Indeed, the scandals arising from his relations with women caused him to be removed from his posts at one university and then at another, and to be reprimanded by the Archbishop of Cologne, where he taught Catholic moral philosophy. To the archbishop he is said to have replied, "I only point the way; a sign doesn't have to go where it points." As one writer has observed about Scheler, "In a relativistic age, he taught a theory of absolute values; yet he not only failed to live by the values he taught, but freely adapted his philosophical theories to the endless changes in his personal life." Moreover, his "*intellectual* career was equally disordered."[107]

A characteristic concept of Scheler's is that of *Wertgefühl*, value-feeling, as a distinct mode of cognition. He planned to write a study of what Pascal called the *désordres du coeur*, the "disorders of the heart" that Scheler knew so well.

In television interviews a contemporary playwright, who also knows about such disorders, displays an arch and sardonic manner, unsurprising in view of his plays, in which the characters interact in pettily fiendish ways.

Whereas Scheler did not in any overt way move in the direction of the positive values to which he pointed, this playwright does not point to them. Should he? What is the relation between Scheler's disordered personal life and his quest for absolute values? Do his life and his work add up to such an incoherent, self-contradictory whole that it should be disregarded with the comment, "Physician, heal thyself?" Is there no significant difference between his case and that of Dr. Smile (considered in part 1)?

In drama more generally, an array of troubled characters—representing a sampling of the contents of a psychiatric textbook—often do reprehensible, even monstrous things to one another. In this, drama accords with art in other genres in its concern with human brutality and debasement. What are the reasons for such representations of disordered feeling?

One reason—happily not yet the one to which the title of this section alludes—is to wallow in it for the sake of feeling *something*—of feeling anything other than boredom. Thus, one critic has observed that in the plays of such Elizabethan and Jacobean playwrights as John Fletcher and Philip Massinger "there is a coarsening of the feeling (which is accompanied, inevitably, by a coarsening of the poetic fibre) together with an increased dexterity in the manipulation of the emotional effects of narrative and character."[108]

In such plays emotion is presented sensationally, with the playwright little concerned that his various emotional effects be consistent with one another, or with an overall moral vision. Thus, a death may be presented tragically, but a character may then comically fall in love with the corpse. "Provided the characters are feeling intensely all the time, it does not much matter how or why."[109] Indeed, another writer has accused Fletcher and his collaborator Francis Beaumont of creating "a world of refined sensationalism where only the given moment counts because no overall pattern of meaning exists."[110]

375

One may judge their plays in such a way, and may decide to pass them by in favor of better ones. Yet some of the better ones have the same kinds of content in the form of disordered feeling, so that it is hard to see where lines of discrimination should be drawn. (This may be seen, for example, when some reviewers judge a certain current film as pretentious sensationalism, whereas other reviewers praise the same film as art.) I am concerned with why there should be such mixed and ambiguous cases, and why some notable works of art should, in their representation of disordered feelings, share elements with works of emotionally exploitative kitsch.

One way to approach such questions is by way of a distinction to be found in Aristotle between pathic and ethical motivation, between acts that are relatively inarticulate in being largely the expression of what I have been calling the pathic ground, and acts that more strongly engage reason and conscious will.[111]

When a dramatic character comically falls in love with a corpse, or when a tough television detective punches a criminal senseless, the pathic motivation is very prominent, the ethical motivation not— such characters are driven, without much concern for why and for what their drivenness means.

That the ethical motivation of such actions is slight is, nonetheless, ethically significant, whether or not the works in which they occur attend to this significance or lack of it. Indeed, precisely this ambiguity—that something not presented as ethically significant in an overt way may be felt as ethically significant—can be very important in a work of art. (Samuel Beckett's *Waiting for Godot* is overtly concerned with the boredom, anxiety, discomfort, fear, and pain of Vladimir and Estragon. The play, however, has ethical implications fundamental to its effect on its audience.)

When Mother Courage mutely denies that she knows her dead son, or when Oedipus realizes that he has killed his father and married his mother, the motivation of the action, and of our response to it, is in the highest degree both pathic and ethical. In our response to such dramatic moments, what we already know ethically—for example, that human wish and will are often of little avail—is not only enlivened by energies released through passionate crisis, but is transformed by being drawn into complex feeling-judgments resulting in a new perception of value. In the process what had seemed, or for all practical purposes had been, emotional urgency has become cognitive, serving ethical awareness. That such judgments can emerge in such a way we have already seen in Mr. Jackson's reflection (in part 6.9) that he was surprised, in his dream, that he was not afraid. My purpose now is to focus on the way in which such a process may be initiated through an experience—often mediated by some sort of representation—of disordered feeling. I will illustrate this process by an account of "Nicoletta Wolff."

Mrs. Wolff belongs to a large Austrian family owning a family plot in a certain cemetery. After some years abroad, Mrs. Wolff visited the cemetery and was incensed to find that the mother of her father's second wife had been buried in the plot near Mrs. Wolff's mother— her father's first wife—and Mrs. Wolff's maternal grandmother. Mrs. Wolff remarks about the incident, "I had not had the remotest idea that I had such a strong sense of propriety in these matters, or indeed what that sense of propriety was, until I felt it violated." Her extreme annoyance, in effect, worked to reveal the till then undisclosed values that would explain it.

In his analysis of physical properties, Aristotle speaks of "form by privation,"[112] a concept that can be applied to affective life in a way that has a bearing on the representation of disordered feeling. If we touch something cold we know that it is cold—its coldness is a "positive form"; but we also know that it is not hot—this is its "form by privation." The relation between these two kinds of form makes change—becoming—possible. That is, an actual thing possesses not only its positive form but also, potentially, its opposite form by privation, which is part of the dynamism that brings the positive form to manifestation. (This concept clearly belongs in the tradition of polaristic thinking, represented by Coleridge, Jung, and others, that we considered in part 6.6.) Just as we know cold to be not hot, to enter empathetically into the suffering of Vladimir and Estragon is to know how reduced and isolated the human person has become in them. To know this is to know the reduction and isolation of these characters as a betrayal of our own potential larger selves and of community. The play thus makes us give value to the qualities we experience as betrayed.

In *The Birth of Tragedy* Nietzsche expressed a related thought, more directly bearing on phenomena of pathos and ethos than is Aristotle's physical form by privation. Speaking of the "Apollinian precision and lucidity"of the language of Sophocles' heroes—as a primary expression of "Greek cheerfulness"—Nietzsche remarks that "we immediately have the feeling that we are looking into the innermost ground of their being, with some astonishment that the way to this ground should be so short. But," he continues, "suppose we penetrate into the myth that projects itself in these lucid reflections: then we suddenly experience a phenomenon that is just the opposite of a familiar optical phenomenon. When after a forceful attempt to gaze on the sun we turn away blinded, we see dark-colored spots before our eyes, as a cure, as it were. Conversely, the bright image projections of the Sophoclean hero . . . are necessary effects of a glance into the inside and terrors of nature; as it were, luminous spots to cure eyes damaged by gruesome night."[113]

This description has implications with regard to ego, self, passionate crisis, and feeling.

It is an inescapable part of our condition as flawed, mortal creatures that we stand in some sort of relation to a dimension of reality that can be symbolized by "the inside and terrors of nature."

The ego can never have anything as its secure possession: whatever the ego has it may be asked to surrender, or may have forcibly torn from its grasp. Thus delivered up to passionate crisis, the ego defends itself by creating and believing in false unities of various kinds (instances of the manufactured and consoling oneness discussed in part 6.5). These fictions of permanence and sufficiency have the ego as their primary object but also embrace its ties to the objects of this world. In such forms as the pseudoparadisal bliss of reconstituted mother, these fictions impoverish feeling.

False unities must be violated for truer ones to emerge—just as less adequate forms of the personality must be abandoned for more adequate ones to develop. (It is my conviction, confirmed by years of experience as an analyst, that people rarely make the major developmental changes demanded by the principle of individuation unless they are forced to do so, unless something akin to "the inside and terrors of nature" gapes in the path before them.) Sacrificing false unities entails the risk of pain, unavoidably a part of the intensification of feeling that allows new and more adequate values to be perceived or old ones to be perceived in a new and more adequate way. Depth of feeling means openness to the world. Openness to the world is openness to pain.

The Dionysian blinding and dismemberment described by Nietzsche corresponds on the level of mythic forms and images to the painful shock of discovery of the burial site of Mrs. Wolff's stepmother's mother. Her articulation of her values with regard to such matters corresponds on the personal level to a realization of the harmony and clarity associated with Apollo. This realization began in Mrs. Wolff with an experience of disordered feeling that might be voiced as, "This feels wrong to me." But is this the way to put it? Is it not rather that her feeling was appropriate but the facts offensive to it were not? Once again we must remind ourselves of the level of our experience on which the distinction between subject and object is fluid, on which the difference between "This feels wrong to me" and " I feel wrong to myself" cannot, at least for moments, be clearly drawn. (Thus if we hear an unfunny dirty joke, we feel dirty.) Passionate crisis is not simply the result of a failure of adaptation, though we know it most overtly in such failures. Rather, passionate crisis is an irreducible and unpredictable element in our relation to the pathic ground. We are implicated in the pathic ground—we belong to it, and it belongs to us—and so we are implicated in passionate crisis.

Ego-consciousness is always one-sided, always in need of being redressed. Thus adequate feeling judgments are in general brought forth against a background of disordered feeling. And such judgments stand in a real if tacit relation to inadequate feeling-judgments needing to be countered and replaced by them. In the view of Shakespeare and Milton, virtue is active—it is not "fugitive and cloister'd," in Milton's phrase.[114] In a related fashion, feeling is active, engaged in redeeming the disordered feeling into which it is the lot of all our feeling-judgments to fall.

I have been describing feeling as a process in which the ego participates, something the ego partly "does," but a process fundamentally rooted in the self. And in speaking of Aristotle's form by privation and Nietzsche's Dionysian blinding, I have implied the compensatory relation obtaining between consciousness and unconscious processes and contents, this compensation being an expression of the self, and thus of the self that knows what is good for itself. Because of this compensatory relation, representations of disordered feeling can enhance adequate feeling.

What then about watching a dramatic character comically fall in love with the corpse of someone who has died tragically? What about watching a tough television detective punch a criminal senseless? What about watching a pornographic film in which the murder of a woman is presented as erotically exciting? Such representations of disordered feeling can hardly be imagined to enhance adequate feeling.

Watching Vladimir and Estragon is different, because positive feeling-values are implicit in Beckett's play, even if we apprehend them by means of an affective counterpart to form by privation.

Practically speaking, however, despite the evidence of such a play, not every negative has its positive: there are some situations pervaded by bad feeling that one cannot better but can only leave. Adequate feeling then demands the simple feeling-judgment of a decision to leave them.

Just as not all dross is to be alchemically transmuted into gold, not all disordered feeling is redeemable. Rather, some of it is destined simply and also richly for a cancer-like proliferation of itself. Our capacities for degradation are enormous, and we all carry them within us. Our suspicion that this might be so is one reason for clinging to our deluding fictions. It is also a reason for cultivating the forms of art, religion, and human interaction that subvert those fictions by enhancing feeling as an accomplishment on behalf of our better selves and our hopes for a better world.

6.11 Imaginative Response to the Banalization of Feeling

On his deathbed Goethe is reported to have implored, "*Mehr Licht*," "More light": more life, more consciousness, more participation in the cosmic principle of light. Goethe's dying words inspired a joke about a nouveau-riche aspirer after culture who on his deathbed tried unsuccessfully to imitate Goethe by imploring, "*Mehr Beleuchtung*," "More artificial lighting." Much of religion is devoted to the partly paradoxical twofold enterprise (considered in part 5.2) of making the

Receptivity, Commitment, and Detachment

profane sacred—as when bread and wine are transformed in the Mass—
and of establishing reliable forms of relationship to the sacred—as
when the Mass is regularly repeated for the benefit of those participating in it. That is, religion often magically tries to transform ordinary
light into the divine Light, in order to use the divine Light to operate
electric lamps. Thus religion may foster the "sclerotic consciousness"
it is ostensibly seeking to break down. [115]

A similar dilemma arises more generally in the life of feeling and
emotion: motivated by fear of passionate crisis, one may develop feeling into an agreeably stable psychic function that is also disagreeably
conventional and lifeless, as, for example, one relies automatically on
feeling-judgments no longer suitable. Disorders of feeling are averted
by its banalization. As a result, emotion is buried or split off—though
it may be sensed to loom autonomously and chaotically. Threatened
with stultification in the resulting emotional impoverishment, imagination may react by engaging in an act of introversion revealing
images emotionally powerful enough to effect an alteration in the
prevailing conscious attitude. I will now examine a poem by Wallace
Stevens and one by Georg Trakl illustrating this process of renewal.

The poem by Stevens I wish to discuss is "Gubbinal":

> That strange flower, the sun,
> Is just what you say.
> Have it your way.
> The world is ugly,
> And the people are sad.
>
> That tuft of jungle feathers,
> That animal eye,
> Is just what you say.
>
> That savage of fire,
> That seed,
> Have it your way.
>
> The world is ugly,
> And the people are sad. [116]

To call the sun a flower is a radical condensation of cause as
necessary condition (the sun) and effect (flower). This metaphor is

made all the more striking by the qualification "strange," which implies that the speaker is already engaged in a train of thought in which the world consists entirely of flowers: the sun is the strange flower among other flowers—as a flower, the sun is strange when compared with other flowers. The sense of process thus suggested is heightened by the demonstrative pronoun *that*—"That strange flower"—which suggests an act of pointing, of singling out. The alliteration of *that* and *the*—"That strange flower, the sun"—also intensifies the link between sun and flower.

The phrase *jungle feathers* also suggests a condensation—perhaps of "feathers of some jungle bird"—with the implication that the jungle is now being seen as a bird. (Leaves and flowers are like feathers.) Moreover, *tuft* suggests fur rather than feathers, as though the speaker is in the process of pondering whether what he is trying to imagine is bird or animal. In the next line, "That animal eye," the speaker retracts his tentative suggestion (made in "feathers") that what he had in mind was a bird. He also seems to be now trying to gain a more differentiated view of what he had first imagined in the condensed form of flower-sun, as though sorting it into its component parts (tuft, feathers, eye). The alliterative repetition of *that* and *that*—"That tuft of jungle feathers, / That animal eye"—intensifies the link between tuft and eye, so that we may glimpse a tuft of fur/feathers with an eye at the center of it.

These complementary processes of differentiation and concentration are continued in the next stanza, in which the danger implied by the jungle animal is further emphasized in "That savage of fire." Anthropomorphizing the sun, and thus establishing a human kinship between the speaker and it, might be seen as an attempt to depotentiate its danger, but the resulting "savage of fire" is also awesome—who would want to encounter him? And uneasiness about this disturbing image may be one reason why the speaker proceeds to "That seed." That this sun-fire-man is "savage" also calls attention to the affect generated by the whole process of imagining these things ("savages" being people who are thought to give way to their emotions).

In a final imaginative thrust in the form of "That seed," the speaker, in effect, returns to the metaphor of the sun as flower. But this time he has stripped the flower to its essence, and has heightened the

382

metaphor by bringing in an element of potential opposition, since flowers bloom in the sun, whereas the seed is destined for the dark earth. The alliterative repetition of *that*—"That savage of fire, / That seed"—equates "savage of fire" and "seed." With this the speaker has gone as far as he can go in expressing the essence of his imaginative experience of the sun.

In keeping with my emphasis on mother and infant throughout this book, it is worth noting about this final metaphor that in most mythical representations of the sun it is masculine, often associated with such qualities as conscious discrimination and justice. In this poem, in contrast, the sun is buried like an embryo in the maternal earth. This makes sense because for imagination to renew itself, it must make contact with the maternal depths of the unconscious—the unconscious as the "matrix of consciousness."[117]

Consider the lines

> Is just what you say.
> Have it your way.
>
> The world is ugly,
> And the people are sad.

These lines are as important to the overall effect of the poem as those about imagining the sun. Indeed, we partly have the impression that the lines just quoted are spoken by another voice than the one speaking about the sun, so that the poem is, in effect, a dialogue between representatives of two dissimilar attitudes. We will see, however, that the relations between the voices are more complex than this description implies.

"The world is ugly, / And the people are sad" seems a simple, global feeling-judgment of a dim and unsearching sort. The words seem spoken by the prosaic voice of a nonpoet, or of the poet's nonpoetic self—in any case, the voice of someone dejected as he contemplates what Stevens in another poem ("The Man Whose Pharynx Was Bad") calls "the malady of the quotidian."[118] The dimness of this speaker is suggested by "the people": if the speaker is to say "the people," instead of "people" or "some people," the definite article *the* asks for specification (such as "the people next door") that it does not get. In any case, being so general, with the subject so poorly defined, the statement that "the people are sad" is vapid and sentimental.

That the relations between the two voices is nonetheless complex and partly very ambiguous is suggested by the word *just* in "Is just what you say." *Just* may mean "merely," with the prosaic voice dismissing the poetic voice for the arbitrariness of its description of the sun. Or *just* may mean "exactly," with the prosaic voice granting the excellence of the description but still insisting on the ugliness and sadness ignored in it. "Have it your way" could also express shoulder-shrugging dismissal, but then, too, it could express concurrence with the poetic *way*—"Have it *your* way"—while insisting that it is not all-sufficient. Still, even if the prosaic voice is—perhaps "unconsciously" and despite itself—in some measure giving the poetic voice its due, the prosaic voice is doing so as part of its own vague complaint.

The distinction between the two voices breaks down in other ways as well, as may be seen with regard to the stanzaic pattern. No stanza is given completely to the poetic voice: each of the three stanzas in which that voice speaks includes one line belonging to the other. Further, the fourth stanza,

> That savage of fire,
> That seed,
> Have it your way,

is a tercet, followed by the couplet

> The world is ugly,
> And the people are sad,

whereas the pattern of the first three stanzas—tercet, couplet, tercet—would lead us to expect the fourth stanza to be a couplet and the fifth a tercet. The reversal of the expected pattern has two main effects. First, it suggests that the imagination manifest in "That tuft of jungle feathers, / That animal eye" is so intense that it impetuously leaps ahead to "That savage of fire" without pausing to repeat the couplet, "The world is ugly, / And the people are sad." And second, this reversal keeps the poem from concluding with a tercet concerned with imagining the sun and instead gives the last word to the prosaic voice uttering precisely that complaining couplet. And so the poem records an act of passionate imagining that vivifyingly draws contents from the psychic background into the sphere of the ego. But at least half of the problem posed by the poem is that of transforming a banal feeling attitude, and this transformation does not in any clear way take place.

A certain leader of "self-actualization"groups who recorded dreams and other products of her inner life in many notebooks found herself in a personal crisis in which she had to declare herself a cynical fraud, a mask with nothing behind it. As her notebooks attested, her imagination had been busy, but in curious isolation from the concerns that let to her crisis. In Stevens's poem the isolation between the two voices is less complete—as we have seen, ambiguities of the prosaic voice may suggest agreement with the poetic voice, and every stanza devoted to imagining the sun contains one prosaic line. Still, the attitudes expressed by the two voices remain dissociated. Rather than suppressing the prosaic voice, however, which would have been one way to deal with the problem, Stevens makes the contrast between the two voices central to the overall effect of the poem. The poem is thus an account of success-within-failure, the success being the vigorous workings of imagination, the failure being the continuing banalization of feeling. (Such failure might encourage one to give up on feeling and to glorify imagination, with the result of aestheticism, the dangers of which we noted in part 2.6. Though ambiguous, "Gubbinal" does not encourage this kind of giving up on feeling.) The poem, then, contains something of the same duality we saw in Frost's "The Most of It" (discussed in part 6.8), the difference being that Frost is dealing with the problem of the "other"—of whether the "other" is really there, and of what its nature is—whereas Stevens is dealing with the problem of finding an adequate relation to inner resources of vitality and meaning. The issues treated in the two poems are different but closely linked.

The poem by Trakl I wish to discuss is "Die Sonne," "The Sun."

Täglich kommt die gelbe Sonne über den Hügel.
Schön ist der Wald, das dunkle Tier,
Der Mensch; Jäger oder Hirt.

Rötlich steigt im grünen Weiher der Fisch.
Unter dem runden Himmel
Fährt der Fischer leise im blauen Kahn.

Langsam reift die Traube, das Korn.
Wenn sich stille der Tag neigt,
Ist ein Gutes und Böses bereitet.

Wenn es Nacht wird,
Hebt der Wanderer leise die schweren Lider;
Sonne aus finsterer Schlucht bricht.

Daily the yellow sun comes over the hill.
Beautiful is the forest, the dark animal,
Man; hunter or shepherd.

Reddishly the fish climbs in the green pond.
Under the round sky
The fisherman moves quietly in the blue skiff.

Slowly the vines, the grain, ripen.
When the day draws silently to a close,
Something good and evil is prepared.

When it is night
The wanderer gently raises his heavy eyelids;
Sun breaks out of a dark chasm.[119]

Trakl's poem, like Stevens's, is concerned with an "inner sun," and also calls to mind mythic associations of the sun: those of the sun with a boat, of the sun as a fish, of the sun held captive in various ways. (In the Egyptian "Book of the Dead" there is reference to, in Jung's words, "the sun-ship, which accompanies the sun and the soul over the sea of death towards the sunrise." In a vase from the Cyclades, between 2500 and 1100 B.C., the sun is surrounded by the sea and four fish; in a porcelain plate by the twentieth-century artist Piero Fornasetti the sun is itself a fish. Mythical seagoing solar figures are "enclosed in a chest or ark for the 'night sea journey.' ")[120] Though Trakl's poem is not implicitly a semidialogue, as is Stevens's, it does record a series of imaginative transformations concerned with resolving opposition by means of a unifying symbol. And Trakl's poem goes much further than Stevens's in making these transformations actually affect the opposition creating the need for them.

Receptivity, Commitment, and Detachment

The first line defines the sun by a color (yellow) and by the sun's repeated act of rising over the hill. This line, following the title, "Die Sonne," "The Sun," establishes the sun as the subject of the poem. The verb for the rising of the sun, *kommt*, "comes," is, however, bland: the point of the line is apparently to record a prosaic action endlessly repeated, an act inspiring no special feeling. Moreover, our expectation that the whole poem will be about the sun is disappointed by the next two lines, which shift attention to another subject:

> *Schön ist der Wald, das dunkle Tier,*
> *Der Mensch; Jäger oder Hirt.*

> Beautiful is the forest, the dark animal,
> Man; hunter or shepherd.

This subject is immediately shrouded in mystery, owing to the ambiguity of the syntax. The poem could be saying in an elliptical way, "*Schön is der Wald; schön ist das dunkle Tier; schön ist der Mensch,*" "Beautiful is the forest; beautiful is the dark animal; beautiful is man." But the series of nouns can also be read as appositives, so that forest, animal, and man are condensed into a single thing: "Beautiful is the forest–dark animal–man." In comparison with the sun of the first line, this composite thing is obscure, possibly because undifferentiated. But in calling it beautiful even before it is identified, the poem attributes to it a value that cannot simply be set aside in praise of the sun, which has not yet had a value attributed to it. The extent to which our attention is deflected from the ostensible subject of the poem, the sun, becomes clear if we reflect how natural we would have found it if the first line had been followed by the judgment that the sun is beautiful. The first lines, in effect, establish a polarity with no intermediary terms: if the sun goes on rising daily, and if the forest–dark animal–man goes on being beautiful in its own right the two will remain closed within distinct processes having no influence upon one another—in a way that may remind us of the poem by Stevens. For this distinction to break down, the sun will have to rise *within* this mass. The movement of the poem is toward the rising of an "inner" sun.

The qualifications of man as "*Jäger oder Hirt*" ("hunter or shepherd") may seem the beginning of a differentiation, but this impression is misleading: the hunter belongs to the forest and dark animal, whereas the shepherd represents a different—pastoral and less "primitive"—level of civilization; the poem judges both beautiful, with no distinction made between them. But the implication of this is that the shepherd is being assimilated to the dark forest, basically inimical to him and his flocks.

The first line of the second stanza, "*Rötlich steigt im grünen Weiher der Fisch,*" "Reddishly the fish climbs in the green pond," is clearly meant to echo the rising of the sun, to correspond to it, to be an equivalent of it. The pond that "should" be blue is instead green, the color of the forest. In view of this, the blue of the skiff is startlingly strange. Perhaps its blue is the color of the sky, to which no color is attributed.

The second stanza seems a transformation of the first also in that the new poetic character, the fisherman, carries on activity comparable to the activities of the hunter and the shepherd. Woods and water can both be symbolic of the unconscious—the general index to Jung's *Collected Works* points to much argumentation and evidence concerning this symbolism—but the second scene implies a progression in that the fisherman has the means to reach down into the depths of the pond there to catch fish, which represents a lower evolutionary level—hence a deeper level of unconsciousness—than the dark animal of the forest. It is from the depths of the unconscious that we might, on the basis of our knowledge of dreams, expect the new symbolic content, the transformed sun, to arise. But the fisherman is under the round sky, which reminds us of various archaic world-views in which the sky is a bowl or disk: he is in the maternal "Great Round"of fate described by Neumann—the fisherman is unconscious.[121] He has not made connection with the sun-fish. Indeed, nothing in the stanza tells us that he sees it, or is aware of its existence, though there is an implicit relation between him and it, as there was between the hunter and the dark animal in the first scene. But we, the readers, are aware that unconsciousness prevails; we are aware of the fish, and aware that the fisherman is unaware of it.

In the third stanza—"*Langsam reift die Traube, das Korn,*" "Slowly the vines, the grain, ripen"—we are brought to agriculture (after our glimpses of hunting and pastoral forms of life). As the vines and grain ripen, the sun that caused them to ripen is setting. Ignoring day, the poem thus moves from dawn to dusk, because the speaker clearly is interested not so much in the sun itself as in its relations to obscurity. Moreover, dawn and dusk are symbolically linked qualitative movements, as may be seen in myths in which the solar hero enters the night sea and rises from it at dawn.

"*Wenn sich stille der Tag neigt, / Ist ein Gutes und Böses bereitet,*" "When the day draws silently to a close, / Something good and evil is prepared": "Something good and evil" suggests such lines from Shakespeare's *Macbeth* as Macbeth's "So foul and fair a day I have not seen," and the Witches' "When the battle's lost and won" (I.iii.38; I.i.4). These lines might seem reprehensibly conducive to moral equivocation. But such ambiguities also belong to a legitimate way of looking at things, a way in which values are indeed relative: for one side to win a battle, the other side must lose, and the winning side may also lose in brutalizing and otherwise corrupting itself in order to win. If there is good, there is also evil, and there are perspectives from which they seem as much complementary aspects of the same reality as are winning and losing the same battle. There is a banalization of feeling that comes of avoiding such ambiguities, while minimizing the extent of the cruelty, suffering, ignorance, and pettiness in the human lot. If Trakl's poem records a descent into the unconscious, it also records an expansion of consciousness, as we come to consider aspects of a reality "behind" or "beneath" that described in the matter-of-fact report that "Daily the yellow sun comes over the hill." And such an expansion characteristically reveals precisely the kinds of ambiguity we have been considering.

Finally, when it is night—rather than at dawn—the wanderer lifts his heavy eyelids, and the sun breaks out of its chasm. The sunrise, first presented as something prosaic (in the first line of the poem), and then as something muted, translated into a strange mode and possibly unseen (the sun-fish rising in the pond), becomes a miraculous blaze, as the sun breaks out of the darkness imprisoning it. Presumably it is the wanderer who is granted this vision because the hunter, the shepherd, and the fisherman are all engaged in activities that, though solitary, imply participation in the human community, whereas the wanderer, in contrast, has withdrawn to the outer limits of such participation. Of these four characters, the wanderer asleep represents the maximum participation in the obscurity that is one of the themes of the poem.

This obscurity annuls the relation of cause and effect between the opening of the wanderer's eyes and the rising of the sun. Indeed, the poem suggests the possibility that the sun rises in part *because* he has opened his eyes. There are parallels to this in the widespread symbolism according to which spiritual awakening is represented by the sunrise. The close of the poem might make us think of the symbolic image of the human eye superimposed on the sun, as it might even of Meister Eckhart's saying, *"Das Auge, in dem ich Gott sehe, das ist dasselbe Auge, darin mich Gott sieht; mein Auge unde Gottes Auge, das ist* ein *Auge und* ein *Sehen und* ein *Erkennen und* ein *Lieben,"* "The eye with which I see God is the same eye in which God sees me. My eye and God's eye are *one* eye and *one* seeing and *one* knowing and *one* loving."[122]

A man opening his eyes to the light of the sun could be an image of waking consciousness, and the last two lines of the poem in part present such an image. But since the wanderer's eyes are implicitly identical with the sun, and since this waking is taking place in the darkness of night, the action could be taken as symbolizing a total identification—the establishment of an archaic identity—between the wanderer and the cosmos. The concentration effected by this ambiguous image is thus related to that of Stevens's calling the sun "That savage of fire, / That seed," with the difference that Stevens does not treat the relation of the subject to that metaphorical fire-seed imagined as an object.

One might define a miracle as an extraordinary event seen in its extraordinary significance. (An ordinary event—the birth of a child, the rising of the sun—is extraordinary, indeed miraculous if we are disposed to see its extraordinary significance.) If miracle dies it can only be revived by a reawakening of the sense, conveyed by the poem, that the "real" sun is both inner and outer, and that the merely outer sun is a simulacrum created in part by an impoverishment of imagination and feeling (as we saw in part 6.5 in connection with the contrast between the lifeless order of "matter" and the living universe).

Receptivity, Commitment, and Detachment

With regard to "archetypes," it is worth noting that mythic overtones (the sky as round, the sun moving through the water, the sun enclosed) play a part in our response to this poem, but that they reach us only through a complex structure, which wakens, disappoints, and fulfills minute expectations based on the specific language of the poem. Trakl somehow *saw* the "archetypal" image of the sun. But as it is embodied in that structure, he—out of the particulars of his own life experience and his situation in the world—also created it.

Having taken the banalization of feeling as our point of departure for a consideration of these two poems, it might be well to glance at the question of when, developmentally, such banalization begins. A sad but compelling answer is that its beginnings are concomitant with the consolidation of the ego. When twenty-six-month-old Amanda on rare occasions intones, "I want my Mommy, I want my Mommy, I want my Mommy, I want my Mommy, I want my Mommy, I want my Mommy, I want my Mommy," she is, in her exercise of egoistic will, reducing Mother to meaninglessness in a way related to that in which words are reduced to it in experiments in which a stimulus word is repeated until the subject signals that it has become meaningless.

Self and ego play through the early mother-infant relationship in such complex ways that one cannot at all simply assign self or ego to either one or the other member of the couple. Still, "I want my Mommy" (repeated endlessly) is at least in part an attempt of the smaller (Amanda, the incipient ego) to appropriate the larger (Mother, the self) and to make their relationship, thus egoistically reconstituted, into a steady state. Amanda, in her way, would already use the divine Light to operate electric lamps. But this tendency is also being countered by the development in her of capacities for increasingly complex imagination and feeling.

Differentiated feeling gives rise to appropriate feeling-judgments like those considered in foregoing sections. Such poems as these by Stevens and Trakl revivify feeling by representing an imaginative experience of trying to arrive at such judgments, or at least of sensing the need for them, while the poems at the same time bring to imaginative expression affect-images establishing contact with the psychic depths.

Feeling, imaginatively embodied, is open to emotion, imaginatively embodied. This nearly circular way of speaking calls attention

391

to the paradoxical role of our bodies in our experience, especially in relation to emotion. We are "body-subjects"—are body—and our experience becomes body. (The old soldier's battle scars and the aches of his once-broken bones are but a striking example of how we all physically become what we live, do, think, and imagine, consciously and unconsciously.) Yet psyche needs to modify—to sublimate—bodily urgency, in large part owing to the unconscious basis, and hence the autonomy, of emotion. (The reader will recall the metaphor of the color spectrum, discussed in part 6.5.)

Attempts to conceive an intermediate realm between body and spirit include the subtle body of Eastern tradition and the Christian Incarnation—and the Holy Ghost mediating the Incarnation. Many mythic forms and images—and works of art such as the poems I have been discussing—convey a sense of this intermediate realm. Insofar as phenomena in some way or other belonging to it become conscious, and do so in a way that adequately grants their reality, they are felt and imagined. In feeling them, one remains aware of their emotional implications. In imagining them, one attends to their formal properties, their nature as images, capable of "higher" transformations, while retaining their links with the psychic depths and the depths of the body.

Imagination, then, supports feeling in an emotional "reading" of the world that is distinct from the overwhelming of the ego by emotion. Further, the exercise of imagination protects feeling from banalization and from disorders resulting from passionate crisis or from attempts to ward it off.

Feeling also entails imagination in the sense that without imagination I can neither feel *with* nor feel *for*, and hence cannot properly evaluate and relate to the "other." Feeling implies being able to see with the other person's eyes, as Mother sees with Baby's.

Feeling and imagination are thus interrelated aspects of a complex process reaching from primitive empathy and sympathy, the "conviviality of the native mind"—see again figure 5—to the symbolization to be found in the finest products of art and religion. And the imagination issuing in the feeling that fosters community is continuous with the imagination creating such poems as these, largely about introversion.

392

The poem by Stevens makes clear that imagination and feeling, despite the complexity of their interrelations, are often distinguishable practically. Still, their interrelations, sometimes indistinguishable, are essential to what imagination and feeling are.

The soil of feeling Stevens describes may be too impoverished to support the imaginative sun-seed planted in it. And the awakening sun-eye of the wanderer Trakl describes may be so far from participation in community that he will not be able to find a path to it. Or, to put the same state of affairs in another perspective, the feeling and imagination prevailing in a person or a society may be too impoverished to apprehend and assimilate the powerfully vivifying symbol. There are mythic descriptions of this failure—the ignoring and despising of Christ—as there are mythic descriptions of the banalization of feeling resulting from willful attempts to make the relationship of ego to self a steady state—"And from the days of John the Baptist until now the kingdom of heaven suffereth violence, and the violent take it by force" (Matt. 11:12). To describe such failure and such banalization, mythically or poetically, is to stand—perhaps a fraction of an inch—outside them. That slight distance may amount to the difference between abandoning the symbol to incomprehension and being true to it in a way that furthers its life.

6.12 Mother World, Detachment, and Receptivity

Psychologically we first inhabit the Mother World of infancy, from which we must detach ourselves, the best form of detachment being one that leaves us receptive. Still, the title of this section describes not a simple progression but a complex set of relations. This is apparent if one pauses to think of the various elements that go to make up such detachment. These include the detachment that characterizes the infant as an individual, separate from its mother, from the outset. They include the striving of the two- to three-year-old for independence or psychological "separation" from its mother.[123] They include the mother's fostering of detachment by letting the infant go (discussed in part 6.6). And they include the relative independence of Father and Mother from one another, with Father especially providing a model of being able to enter, leave, and reenter the relationship of mother and infant.

Further, just as there are mythic forms and images of the mother-infant relationship, so there are those of the separation of the infant from the mother—for example, in the heroic feats of the child hero—and of the Father World from the Mother World—for example, in the Hebraic insistence on the supremacy of God in the sense of his detachment from everything having to do with the worship of the chthonic mother goddesses. And these mythic forms and images also, if indirectly, influence the form of the developing person's detachment from the mother. (When I speak of "Mother World" I am referring to the personal relationship with the mother but mean also to imply mythic forms and images of that relationship.)

Detachment from Mother is necessary for the autonomy of the developing individual, but the matter is more complex than this simple statement suggests for the further reason that autonomy is not something in itself but is part of a polarity the other element of which is relatedness. (Angyal poses the polarity as one of "autonomy" and "heteronomy."[124]) Thus, one must detach oneself to become autonomous but must also, and partly at the same time, detach oneself from one's detachment in order to be related to others and the self. (In part 3.4, about the blues, I spoke of detaching oneself from the kind of detachment that is characterized by emotional noninvolvement and depersonalization. I am now speaking more generally of the interplay of detachment and nondetachment that is essential to feeling and imagination.) Though individuation requires that one stand on one's own two feet and look at the world with one's own eyes, it is nonetheless a fact, grim or delightful but in any case incontrovertible, that we are dependent, and are independent only within dependency—our narcissistic predilections notwithstanding. Since our most powerful and determining experience of dependency is at the beginning of our lives, and since it is drawn on in one way or another in all further steps in individuation, it is one of our greatest deluding fictions to believe that we can or should ever entirely leave the mother-infant relationship.

The whole mother-infant relationship is alive in the incipient ego's attempts to arrive at a form of autonomy that will keep it adequately related to the self. The way in which it is so is illustrated by various actions of twenty-six-month-old Amanda, by which she means to demonstrate her autonomy, and thus convince herself of it—among them, refusing to get dressed and hiding herself among clothes racks in crowded shops. In less willful moods, Amanda solicits her mother's help in controlling her own body. Thus, Amanda says to her mother, "Tell foot not to go down," or "Tell hand to reach," or "Tell mouth not to bite hand."

One might regard such utterances as largely the outcome of Amanda's internalizing of prohibitions. Though these are indeed being internalized, "Tell hand to reach" is not a prohibition, and what is happening does not simply concern relations among a developing ego, developing internalized prohibitions (or superego), and impulses. A sense of self is also being imaginatively elaborated, and Amanda is trying to find a—felt and imaginative—form of autonomy that will allow her, as ego, to retain and enhance that sense of self.

There is, moreover, an implicit connection between such early explorations of the negative and certain important cultural products. The child—to summarize—masters the prohibitory No in two ways, thinking, "I am strong enough and enough myself to know and follow rules," but also, "I am strong enough and enough myself to disobey them." Quite apart from affirming the power of the ego, saying "no" to No is also for the child a part of denying the here and now in favor of the rich and complex reality made available through imagination. (I am regarding imagination as a constructive power and am for the moment ignoring the notable ways in which ignoring the here and now may amount to self-deluding evasion.) In the domain of culture there are mythic representations of this reality, which is one of abundance undiminished by prohibitory restrictions. Thus, the Aranda of Australia celebrate intervals of ritual orgy during which all prohibitions are suspended in a symbolic return to the paradisiacal "freedom and beatitude of the ancestors" who once roamed the land.[125] In saying "no" to No, the child is in part developing the imaginative capacity to gain contact with related forms of abundance. (I am also for the moment ignoring, as largely another story, how vulnerable and problematic that contact may in turn be.)

Accordingly, a better way to understand Amanda's utterances is to comprehend them as articulating a feeling Amanda has had all along, not just about the workings of her body but about her very being, and thus about relations between ego and self. That is, Mamma should perform the functions of Amanda's incipient ego. Yet Amanda, as ego, should tell Mamma to perform them. Further, Mamma and Amanda are thus collaborating to further Amanda's fulfillment of what they both feel to be the *telos* of her life, expressive of the self, as that *telos* is manifest in problems of a certain developmental stage. The reader looking again at figure 4 will see that the reciprocal "mirroring" of mother and infant established much earlier, indeed close to the beginning of the infant's life, is still providing the model for Amanda's attempts to achieve autonomy.

The autonomy demanded of the ego by the self is not independence. The detachment that recognizes the limit of one's autonomy also recognizes relationship and takes place within it. No stage of individuation reaches entirely beyond the pattern of relationship visible in these interactions between Amanda and her mother.

At about the same time that Amanda is saying such things as "Tell mouth not to bite hand," she is also saying such things as "I am Mary Lou's cat; I am not Mary Lou's cat" and "That [tree] is not a tree, it's a diggle-daggle." The "not" in her utterance about not being Mary Lou's cat surely draws much of its force from Amanda's growing sense of imposed rules and prohibitions—"person" meaning to her someone who does or does not do what she is told. A sense of self originates not in the incipient ego, however, but in the self, and a sense of self is inseparable from a sense of relatedness. Knowing that she is not Mary Lou's cat creates the precondition of Amanda's imagining that, on the contrary, she is Mary Lou's cat. In lending her own sense of self to the cat, she is imaginatively engaging in the opening, letting go, surrendering essential to important deep forms of relatedness that are one of my main concerns in this section.

Imagining entails surrendering oneself, as one relates—for example, to Mary Lou's cat—in ways that keep the sense of self from being too narrowly egoistic. In the second to third year of life, the prohibitive "Thou shalt not" is contributing to the establishment of a socialized, and restricted, self. To be Mary Lou's cat, imaginatively, is for Amanda to ignore many rules and prohibitions that she is coming to recognize. (Mary Lou's cat, for example, allows itelf to come and go as it likes, to sleep on the top of the bookshelf, and to tyrannize

396

other cats—these actions being exemplary of the kinds of things Amanda is not allowed to do.) Imagining being Mary Lou's cat is thus transcendence in the sense of keeping Amanda imaginatively in touch with potentialities of the self that are being restricted in the course of socialization. To say this is to say something more and different, it should be noted, than that socialization is thwarting Amanda's impulses to do this or that, and that imagination allows her to satisfy them in wish-fulfilling form.

That is, though rules and prohibitions are indeed of fundamental importance in the shaping of the ego, it is a derivative of the self, and rules and prohibitions are also in an important sense secondary to a sense of self—and to a sense of limits, boundaries, rhythms—preceding awareness of "Thou shalt not." As we have seen (in part 4.4), the self can, as an archaic or emergency ego, act on behalf of a severely impaired ego—this shows the primacy of the self. As we have also seen, such manifestations of the self clearly imply a distinction between self and not-self—it is against not-self that self seeks to defend itself. Rules and prohibitions may help define the ego but may also help define the self's relations to not-self.

Self is infinitely surrounded on all sides by not-self, and not-self is in that regard the more embracing term. But self must find in not-self things that are compatible with self, that can be appropriated by it, that will nurture and enhance it. And in this sense, self is the more embracing term. In this second sense, self may be said to use non-self as a category of judgment in an evaluative process aimed at furthering the self to the end of individuation. Variants of "Thou shalt not" are partly assimilated to the sense of self in this evaluative process, but the process is not for this reason reduced to one of internalizing social rules and prohibitions. (To be Mary Lou's cat and not to be Mary Lou's cat is to be on both sides of the line between self and not-self. Since Mary Lou's cat does the kinds of things Amanda is not supposed to do, issues of "Thou shalt not" are being touched upon, but they are secondary to being imaginatively on both sides of that line.)

The variants of "Thou shalt not" that Mary Lou's cat ignores, and that Amanda would partly like to ignore, are related more broadly to assumptions of all kinds about what constitutes reality—such as that

397

the sky is "supposed" to be blue—many of which are as arbitrary, and as much the expression of vested interests imposing themselves, as are the rules and prohibitions Amanda is tempted to challenge. To challenge them is to test and hence foster ego strength. Calling a tree a "diggle-daggle" does this, too, but in the more general way of questioning the conventions by which we name parts of the world and thereby possibly impoverish it. Quite apart from fostering ego strength as usually understood, however, such playing with rules is a way of actively honoring the openness, letting go, surrendering necessary for the self to be known to the ego. "I am Mary Lou's cat; I am not Mary Lou's cat" expresses an awareness that the ego will have to assume many forms in order to remain appropriately related to the different aspects of the self activated at different moments and in different stages of life—and hence will have to open and partly dissolve in the process of being again and again re-created.

A moment ago I spoke of the reciprocity of mother and infant as a form of "mirroring," a metaphor that is acceptable only if we remain aware that this reciprocity is under the aspect of mutuality as a form of relationship drawing on more than enough. To say that the mother and baby feeding one another in figure 4 are giving oatmeal *back* to one another would be absurd. Rather, they are giving it not back but *on,* an assertion that makes sense if one reflects that the oatmeal in this form of play is not so much oatmeal as it is "life." The circle formed by their actions is expansive—they are giving life on. Babies represent to us concentrated essences of life. It is their nature to grow and expand, and in accommodating to her baby, a mother must surrender to the rhythms of its doing this. Twenty-six-month-old Amanda's developing imagination is engaged in reaching out, and thus creating a larger world, increasingly ordered, but in such a way that the ego as part remains open to the self as whole, even as the ego seeks to develop the autonomy required of it by the self. Surrender plays a part in this imaginative expansion.

Surrender is hardly a simple matter for Amanda, however. Sometimes she fights sleep with fanatical determination, thus demonstrating a thoroughly onesided understanding of the rigors of the ego, striving to be always vigilant, always in control, an attitude resulting in confusion and falling apart. Still, she can also let herself drift off into sleep, and her doing so is a paradigm of a fundamental mode of the ego responsive to the self, to which the ego can open but which it cannot vigilantly and controllingly seize.

I now want to consider various poems—by Rilke, William Wordsworth, Conrad Ferdinand Meyer, and Andrew Marvell—bearing on Mother World, receptivity, and detachment. My discussion of them is intended to show how some of the psychological processes I have been discussing with regard to Amanda figure in later stages of life. I will especially be concerned with letting go as a quality fundamental to a valuable form of consciousness.

The tenth of Rilke's *Duino Elegies* is about the land of death, or rather about a land in which life is not divided from death.[126] There the newly dead are introduced to concentrated essences and subtle refinements of feeling and emotion, chiefly pain, sorrow, and grief. In keeping with what I have said (in part 3.1) about pain as the price of openness, the poem satirizes people in the "City of Pain" who defend themselves against such "negative" emotions by means of artificial devices to maintain happiness. In this land, as one of the personified "Laments" explains, it is still possible occasionally to come across a lump of "polished original pain, / or of drossy petrified rage," signs of the earlier riches of the land. In the course of the poem, a newly dead youth, now no longer one of the "wasters of sorrows," "climbs to the mountains of Primal Pain." The poet remarks that if the endlessly dead, whom the youth is now joining, could awaken an adequate response in us,

> . . . sie zeigten vielleicht auf die Kätzchen der leeren
> Hasel, die hängenden, oder
> meinten den Regen, der fällt auf dunkles Erdreich im Frühjahr.—

> Und wir, die an s t e i g e n d e s Glück
> denken, empfänden die Rührung,
> die uns beinah bestürzt,
> wenn ein Glückliches f ä l l t.

> . . . they'd be pointing, perhaps, to the catkins, hanging
> from empty hazels, or else they'd be meaning the rain
> that falls on the dark earth in the early Spring.

Feeling, Imagination, and the Self

And we, who have always thought
of happiness climbing, would feel
the emotion that almost startles
when happiness falls.

[107–13]

The crucial word here is *fällt*, "falls." Rilke's English translators comment on the passage: "The happiness of the dead is passive rather than what we commonly understand by active; it consists in complete submission to universal law, in their allowing themselves to fall into the depths of Being, into that 'open' from which . . . we are always turning away."[127]

The poem presents falling, first, as a category of the world—there are drooping, falling things, just as there are rising, aspiring ones—and second, as a potentiality of human experience—rather than rising and aspiring oneself, one can concentrate on the drooping, falling things, and can experience one's kinship with them. As a result, the ego opens in various senses, among them that of becoming newly aware of underlying currents of feeling and emotion. This awareness reveals a fine structure—one of the Laments is wearing "Pearls of Pain and the fine-spun / Veils of Patience" (52–53)—but is also open to the vast rawness of emotion continuous with that fine structure—the City of Pain is built upon the reality represented by chanced-upon lumps of pain and rage, and the last we hear of the newly dead youth is of his ascent into the mountains of Primal Pain. Not surprisingly in view of the argument of this book, in the sky appears a shining " 'M, / standing for Mothers' " (94–95) and the feminine gorge gleaming in the feminine moonlight is "the source of Joy" (99), which among men is " 'a carrying stream' " (101). If one lets go, there will be pain, but one will be carried, as the infant is carried by its mother.

That the feminine and maternal element of the moonlit gorge is a "carrying stream" might remind us of the image of the sage in a boat drifting on a stream in many old Chinese paintings. Indeed, the spirit of this elegy is akin to that of the *Tao Teh Ching*, in which we read,

Know the masculine; cleave to the feminine.
Be the valley for the world.
To be the valley for the world,
        do not swerve from your innate nature
        and return to the state of infancy

400

and

> I alone am different from the rest in that I value
> taking sustenance from the Mother. [128]

Asking the reader to have in mind the image of the Chinese sage drifting in his boat, I wish to contrast verses by Wordsworth and Meyer.

In the first book of *The Prelude* (1850), Wordsworth describes stealthily taking a boat and rowing out into a moonlit lake. In his description he—unlike the drifting sage—emphasizes his own activity, dominated by focused consciousness:

> But now, like one who rows,
> Proud of his skill, to reach a chosen point
> With an unswerving line, I fixed my view
> Upon the summit of a craggy ridge,
> The horizon's utmost boundary. . . .

[367–71]

As a result of the poet's "act of stealth / And troubled pleasure," his boat moves,

> Leaving behind her still, on either side,
> Small circles glittering idly in the moon,
> Until they melted all into one track
> Of sparkling light.

[364–67]

A state of moonlike, symbolically feminine receptivity is thus constellated in the background of the ego's activity. As a result, a huge bleak peak,

> As if with voluntary power instinct
> Upreared its head. I struck and struck again,
> And growing still in stature the grim shape
> Towered up between me and the stars, and still,
> For so it seemed, with purpose of its own
> And measured motion like a living thing,
> Strode after me.

[379–85]

And for days thereafter, the poet's "brain / Worked with a dim and undetermined sense / Of unknown modes of being" (391–93). [129]

401

Surely it is because the focused activity of the poet's ego is so strongly emphasized, and because the opening of his mind to "unknown modes of being" is correspondingly so unwilled, that that opening is so threatening, even appalling. But it is also possible for the ego to let go—for one to offer one's will to the opening that one feels taking place. We may see this in Meyer's "Eingelegte Ruder," "Shipped [or In-Drawn] Oars," which has a very different emotional tone from the lines by Wordsworth:

> Meine eingelegten Ruder triefen,
> Tropfen fallen langsam in die Tiefen.
>
> Nichts, das mich verdross! Nichts, das mich freute!
> Neiderrinnt ein schmerzenloses Heute!
>
> Unter mir—ach, aus dem Licht verschwunden—
> Träumen schon die schönern meiner Stunden.
>
> Aus der blauen Tiefe ruft das Gestern:
> Sind im Licht noch manche meiner Schwestern?

My shipped oars are dripping, drops are falling into deep water.
   Nothing that distressed me! Nothing that gave me pleasure! It is today, a painless day, that is trickling down.
   Below me—ah, gone out of the light—my more beautiful hours already dream.
   Yesterday calls up from the blue depths: are there more of my sisters up there in the light?[130]

Here the poet—more like the drifting sage than was the frightened Wordsworth—has drawn in his oars, and acquiesces to the "unknown modes of being" that open to him, or within him, as a result. The past has become identical with the water supporting his boat, and in that water the more beautiful of his hours "dream," nurturing consciousness in the way that dreams may do. That yesterday calls from the blue depths to its "sisters" in the light tells us that the mode of consciousness being described is symbolically feminine, and capable of receptivity, openness, and letting go. One may be detached by walling oneself off; one may also be detached by being receptive and open, and by letting go.

Such receptivity is the subject of another poem by Meyer, "Der römische Brunnen," "The Fountain in Rome":

> *Aufsteigt der Strahl und fallend giesst*
> *Er voll der Marmorschale Rund,*
> *Die, sich verschleiernd, überfliesst*
> *In einer zweiten Schale Grund;*
> *Die zweite gibt, sie wird zu reich,*
> *Der dritten wallend ihre Flut,*
> *Und jede nimmt und gibt zugleich*
> *Und strömt und ruht.*

> Up soars the jet and, falling, fills the circle of the marble bowl, which veils itself and overflows into the bottom of a second bowl;
> The second becomes too rich, welling up it gives its tide to the third, and each one takes and gives together, and streams and rests.[131]

This poem presents as a single process the soaring of the water, its falling, the filling of the bowls, and their being filled, a process in which action becomes reception and reception, action. Fullness thus seeks and finds fulfillment in itself. Though the water "veils" itself, though its flow has a melting and blending quality related to that of the moonlit water in Wordsworth's poem, the psychic state described by Meyer is one of union, with the ego diffusely but powerfully conscious, rather than one of fusion and unconsciousness. Taking place largely within the maternal "round" of the bowls, but also going beyond, and being allowed to go beyond, such containment, the process depicted in the poem implies the nonconsummatory mutuality of mother and infant.

In Marvell's "The Garden"[132] there are (in stanza V) falling objects corresponding to the falling water of Meyer's fountain, but they are more differentiated—various objects are enumerated—and their actions, too, have more specialized aims and accents of value:

> What wond'rous Life is this I lead!
> Ripe Apples drop about my head;
> The Luscious Clusters of the Vine

> Upon my Mouth do crush their Wine;
> The Nectaren, and curious Peach,
> Into my hands themselves do reach;
> Stumbling on Melons, as I pass,
> Insnar'd with Flow'rs, I fall on Grass.
>
> [33–40]

The speaker is overpowered, as was Wordsworth on the moonlit lake, and falls, reminding us of the falling in Rilke's elegy. The overpowering in Marvell's poem, too, results in an opening to "unknown modes of being": since real apples, grapes, nectarines, and peaches do not behave in this way, these must be somehow imaginary, fruits of the mind. Indeed, "the Mind, from pleasure less, / Withdraws into its happiness" (41–42)—the mind detaches itself. And yet this detachment is not abstraction but an opening to sensuous particulars.

The speaker is in an important sense reduced to a state of extreme infantile helplessness. He loses his power of locomotion, usually acquired during the first several months of life. Since the grapes press themselves to his mouth, and the nectarine and peach place themselves in his hands, the poem does not describe him as even grasping them—even a seventh-month premature infant being capable of a strong hand-grasp at birth. The garden induces rest: ". . . all Flow'rs and all Trees do close / To weave the Garlands of repose" (7–8). And yet, though the speaker upbraids others for being "busie" (carving names in trees, being driven by the heat of passion), his mind, still using language—despite his infantile helplessness—is and remains highly active. Moreover, the relations between the activity of his mind and that of the fruits in the garden are strange and ambiguous.

Whereas in stanza V the fruits give themselves to the speaker, in stanza VI

> The Mind, that Ocean where each kind
> Does streight its own resemblance find;
> Yet it creates, transcending these,
> Far other Worlds, and other Seas;
> Annihilating all that's made
> To a green Thought in a green Shade.
>
> [43–48]

Thus, the creative powers of the mind turn out to be strangely destructive. But what is the nature of this destruction? "Annihilating all that's made / To a green Thought in a green Shade" might be taken to describe an act of abstraction from the sensuous reality of the garden, an act destroying the minute particulars of that reality in the sense that the mind does not attend to them. But regarded differently, this annihilation might be taken to imply the movement of the mind into a mode of receptivity in which more overtly active kinds of ego-functioning are inhibited. We might thus regard stanza VI as summarizing the transformation of attitude that has, in fact, been the precondition for the strange behavior of the fruits and for the creation of "Far other Worlds, and other Seas," a transformation in which inside opens to outside, and subject to object, as shade acquires the color of leaf, and as thought acquires the color of the transformed shade.

Though the speaker presents this as an act of radical destruction— of "all that's made"—his view of it may reflect the judgment of an ego so willful, independent, and "busie" that, like the ego of Wordsworth in the boat, it must be overpowered to be made receptive. In this view of the stanza, what is being destroyed are conventional outlines, boundaries, categories discriminated by the ego active in certain of its characteristic ways. But falling and letting go, even while seeming like annihilation, allow the ego to become receptively attentive to processes in the psychic background:

> Casting the Bodies Vest aside,
> My Soul into the boughs does glide:
> There like a Bird it sits, and sings,
> Then whets, and combs its silver Wings;
> And, till prepar'd for longer flight,
> Weaves in its Plumes the various Light.
>
> [51–56]

The activity sacrificed by the ego in becoming open to the garden is thus regained by the soul, now busy at its birdlike grooming. But the transformations recorded by the ego are also transformations *of* the ego. Without the receptive participation of the ego in the movements of the soul, they would not be known, and for all practical purposes would not take place. Just as the self, for its realization, needs the ego, so the ego, for its realization—for its growth, stability, adapted functioning, and pliability—needs the soul. And the soul is knowable only in the receptive mode.

Feeling, Imagination, and the Self

The poem does not describe the "longer flight" of the soul, presumably into some pure transcendence. Rather, the image of the bird poised for flight reminds the speaker of the happy state of Adam in the Garden of Eden before the creation of Eve:

> To wander solitary there:
> Two Paradises 'twere in one
> To live in Paradise alone.
>
> [62–64]

We are thus brought back to a state of relative nondifferentiation: between masculine and feminine (with Eve still one of Adam's ribs), between ego and other (there are as yet no others), and between consciousness and the unconscious (since there are as yet none of the tensions that make consciousness necessary.) This turn of the speaker's thought makes sense owing to the soul's essential links with such states of nondifferentiation. Aware of these links, German writers of the Sturm und Drang (storm and stress) period (ca. 1700–1801) were concerned with *Ungeschiedenheit,* "undividedness," and with—one of their favorite words—*Dumpfheit,* "dimness, obscurity, hollowness, dullness." Indeed, the young Goethe apostrophizes Fate as being most clearly manifest "*in reine Dumpfheit,*" "in pure [as distinct from cloudy] dimness."[133] And surely there is, further, a relation between such undividedness and dimness and the Taoist ideal of being the "uncarved block."[134] Still, the writing and reading of Marvell's poem are conscious acts, and it is as conscious *homo duplex* that we trace the imaginative transformation described in it.

The final stanza (IX) presents a summary view of the larger transformation recorded in the poem:

> How well the skilful Gardner drew
> Of flow'rs and herbes this Dial new;
> Where from above the milder Sun
> Does through a fragrant Zodiack run;
> And, as it works, th' industrious Bee
> Computes its time as well as we.
> How could such sweet and wholsome Hours
> Be reckon'd but with herbs and flow'rs!

The poem as a whole has recorded a movement somewhat like that from waking consciousness to dreaming to waking consciousness,

406

a movement resulting in the kind of transformation one has in mind when one decides to "sleep on" a problem in the hope of waking with a more adequate view of it. The sun running through the zodiac of herbs and flowers represents the product of a related transformation. That is, time can be abstract and mechanical in ways lethal to the life of the soul, and ego-consciousness can be too sharply discriminating, as in bright sunlight. But at the close of this poem, in contrast, time is no longer just measured quantitatively in fractions of hours but is rendered qualitative by being assimilated to the archaic magical symbolism of the zodiac. Moreover, the herb-and-flower fragrance of the zodiac appeals to the "primitive" sense of smell, thus further countering the tendency to conceive time abstractly. The "milder Sun" partly symbolizes consciousness correspondingly transformed.

Rather than towering above the Earth in the assertion of its own power, the symbolically masculine sun is now partly the agent of the round and hence maternal zodiac within the maternal garden. The sun is now "milder" presumably because it has partly been made feminine in this way. Further, owing to the nature of the relations between ego and self, the character of the self as it manifests itself is partly determined by the attitude of the ego. And so one can say that the sun as the self is now "milder" in the sense of being more receptive in the manner of mother and infant to one another, and that the sun now is this as a result of the transformation of the ego of the speaker recorded in the poem as a whole.

Meyer's Roman fountain and Marvell's garden are images of abundance. Abundance is there, but in neither poem is it actively *taken*. (Meyer's fountain simply fills itself to overflowing, and the speaker's activity in the poem is limited to seeing appreciatively and describing the process. In Marvell's garden the grapes press themselves to the speaker's mouth, and the fruits put themselves into his hands, without his doing anything to get them.) In very important ways life must, of course, be taken to be lived. (The hungry and thirsty person must take the fruit and water to eat and drink them.) And more mature levels of psychological development require commitment, which entails taking. (A child takes responsibility for many things. A man and woman take one another in marriage, which means that they will take care of one another and their children.) Commitment is essential to the ethical life, which is measured. (Narcissistic personalities are in-

407

capable of commitment and are deficient in the sense of measure that would make them know that choices must be made and would help shape the grounds for choosing.)

Indeed, the images of the overflowing fountain and abundant garden have their meaning in large part in relation to the speakers', and our, knowledge of limits. Still, these poems are not about the giving back of life, or about the kinds of limits that provide the measure of such giving back. Rather, they are about the giving on of life. And the receptivity I have been discussing is a fundamental component of our knowledge of that giving on.

There is a sense in which life can be, and is, measured. (Marriage regulations in many societies assure that the numbers of living members of families, clans, and other groups are kept relatively constant. Insurance companies make a business of measuring life. Such social upheavals as wars are influenced by the numbers of living people in relation to food supplies.) This measuring of life has the character of barter. But barter is not the only form of exchange—there are also forms of gift exchange. One striking form of gift exchange is that of the Kula practiced among the inhabitants of a ring of islands near New Guinea.[135]

In the Kula each person has gift partners, but the gifts are not exchanged in a way analogous to barter but rather travel in a larger ring of gift exchanges, with each person retaining a gift for a limited time before handing it on further in the ring. Though there is equilibrium in the overall system of the ring, the individual exchanges entail the unexpected, since the potential recipient is dependent on the giver for the gift that he does or does not give. "A man who owns a thing," the anthropologist Bronislaw Malinowski writes, "is naturally expected to share it, to distribute it, to be its trustee and dispenser," for the natives feel that "to possess is to give."[136] There may be individual disappointments in specific workings of the system, but on the whole it clearly presupposes gratitude and trust in the process embodied in it. The whole institution could be taken as symbolic of the giving on of life.

Of course, life is limited by the great enigma of death. And awareness of mortality is part of the sense of measure that makes us ethical creatures. But (as we saw in part 5.8) there are also respects in which death and life are not two sides of an equation but life is, rather, the more embracing term. When a certain man wished to defer following Jesus because the man needed to bury his dead father, Jesus replied, "Follow me; and let the dead bury their dead" (Matt. 8:22). I take Jesus to mean that life should go with Life. I am now speaking of the larger life that cannot really be measured in any way, including the way that might balance a certain sum of life against a certain sum of death.

In the larger life (a topic we considered in relation to mythic forms and images in part 5.8), life may even be said to give itself on. One may participate in this giving on. One does so by being open to it. The receptivity of mother and infant to one another, and the gratitude that is part of their nonconsummatory—and in that sense unlimited—mutuality, is the primary model of such openness.

To participate in the larger life one must take risks. And courageous and responsible risk-taking cannot be reduced to a mechanical technique assuring a particular result. Rather, when facing such risks, one would do well to heed the advice offered in a song sung by the country-western singer Kenny Rogers about "The Gambler," who knows—about cards—"when to hold 'em," "when to fold 'em," "when to walk away," and "when to run," and knows, further, that "You never count your money / While you're sittin' at the table." This is nonspecifiable knowledge. To try to specify it—to codify it, for example—will not give one greater access to it than one has to it in its nonspecified form. Certainly in speaking affirmatively of the larger life I have not meant to imply anything as simple as that if one glimpses the larger life one should necessarily try to seize it and that then all will necessarily be well.

An older man, married and with children, and a younger man, also married and with children, have never recognized homoerotic feelings in themselves, but there is a strong current of shocking but undeniable attraction between them. When they finally give way to it to the extent of embracing one another in a way that they both must recognize as more than a friendly hug, the older man feels like a small boy being taken into the arms of his neglectful and absent father, whereas the younger man feels that he has assumed the role of father that he has not within himself assumed in relation to his wife and children. For both men this is a moment of reaching out to possess something enlarging that is, and needs to be, theirs.

A man and woman—married to others—meet and see in each other the best of which each is capable—undistracted by the kinds of "inferiorities" they share with everyone else. Having the best of oneself seen in such a way is an experience of abundance, as is seeing the best in another. The man and woman know *their* abundance to be of something remarkably and uniquely good, and in an important sense it is for them of another order than sexuality as appetite. Without having been sexually intimate with one another, they become celibate in relation to their spouses. This shows that the two orders—of knowledge made possible by mutuality, and of appetite—finally, if mysteriously, meet.

A younger woman who has been with them together remarks, "The two of you have a secret: so much goes on between you, even when you are just sitting together quietly." She has realized that they not only see the best in one another but seek to call it forth and affirm it. She does not mean that what goes on between them is simply their secret—she means that it is a secret about human life and the possibilities it holds, perhaps even for her. She and they know that what they have discovered is part of something larger than their private world.

Part of their secret is that their mutual interest and respect opens them to moments of communion that accord with an observation of the psychoanalyst Leon Wurmser. Writing about ways in which very early drives to look and to exhibit oneself become integrated in higher forms of mental life, he remarks that "love at its most mature and richest brings . . . [these drives] to their greatest unfolding and gratification. In a sense love at its peak means being as fully accepted as humanly possible in the wish for enriching self-expression and in the desire to be gloriously and abidingly fascinated and impressed—and to have reciprocity in this on uncounted levels of communication and attentiveness."[137] That such experiences may take the form of deluding sentimentality and idealization—as one of the psychoanalytic mechanisms of ego-defense—does not rule out the possibility that they may also take forms that are profoundly truth-revealing. As I have insisted (in part 4.7), one's wariness about idealization may blind one to valuable parts of reality that can only be known through simpler and more complex—and deeper—openness.

In feeling that the man and woman have a secret, their young friend also senses something important related to the incommunicable quality of individuality (alluded to in part 2.7 regarding Aquinas's view of the heart)—and perhaps finally indistinguishable from that quality. I mean that there is a silence—an incommunicability—of intimate communion as there is of aloneness. Thus in their "I love you," lovers know their words to fail them. And thus Shakespearean comedies end in weddings, in part as though to say that what will now develop between the lovers in the intimacy of marriage must, while that intimacy obtains, fall ouside public representation.

To speak this way is, of course, to link communication with speech. But this requires the qualification that another, affective, form of communication, one of the main concerns in these pages, is the primary basis of our access to the larger life insofar as it is known in intimate communion and in relation to our individual, yet open, selves. Unlike the "I love you" of lovers, the words of Mother and Baby do not fail them, because speech has for them no special privilege over nonspeech. What matters to Mother and Baby is giving expression to the affective bond drawing them into and out of the world in countless ways, as the two are together afforded glimpses of shifting, often enlarging patterns of interconnection, which are momentarily known as "mine" and "ours," yet are allowed transformation into further patterns.

The man and woman with their secret, and in their plight, have thus seen and known much to which I have been at pains to give value. But to know what they know in its depth—and in some measure of "Greek cheerfulness" (discussed in Part 6.10)—is also to know the direness of what may ensue from their actions.

Like the two embracing men, the man and woman with their secret are in danger of making messes and causing hurt. Sometimes making messes and causing hurt is the proper way to enact the dictates of the self that knows what is good for itself, as one struggles beyond the mess and the hurt to an embodiment of the larger life as I have been describing it. But the mutuality in which the self finds fulfillment also embraces a larger order of community. And just as the self sometimes dictates that I give up what I want for myself alone, sometimes it dictates that I give up what two—or three or four or five—of us want for ourselves alone at the expense of a larger order of community.

Life asks to be taken, but it also asks to be given on. And sometimes the proper form of giving on entails not taking, entails conserving and sacrifice. As we have seen (in part 2.7), life must sometimes be lived under the sign of Decrease. And in the words of Shakespeare's Timon of Athens, sometimes it is precisely nothing that "brings me all things." That such reduction sometimes needs to be an important part of life as it is wisely given on may be seen in the negative examples of political leaders and other wielders of power who refuse to relinquish it till long after the time has come for them to do so.

As I have noted (in part 6.5 about the weddings closing such plays as The Merchant of Venice), the relation of the individual to the larger life may assume a comic form. But it may also assume a tragic one. King Lear's attempt to find the larger life in the superlatives of his daughters' declarations of love was self-destructive folly. And the commitment of Socrates and Jesus to their visions of the larger life brought about their deaths.

As I have maintained (in part 2.4), the self tells one frequently and precisely how to live. But its messages need to be read with the eyes, intuition, and gut sense of the gambler, and with the ears of Ornette Coleman's musicians (discussed in part 6.3), as they listen for the emerging direction of their music. Like the gambler in relation to his concerns, these musicians are aware that "noise" is the only source of "new information," in their case about the workings of the spirit creating their music. There is a more than fanciful connection between such noise and the squalling of a baby. I mean by this that making music in the way they make it, like making music in many other ways, entails immersion in the affective dimension. And developmentally, consciousness of this dimension comes to be in significant ways differentiated as mother and infant learn to make noncommunication in such forms as acute distress into communication. But not all chaos can be ordered, not all meaninglessness can

412

be made into meaning, and not all limitation can be made to yield to abundance.

An acquaintance once told me that when he was in a Nazi concentration camp, he vowed that if he ever got out, he would be profoundly thankful for a simple bowl of soup. I asked him if he had then forgotten his vow, and he readily admitted that he had. But he insisted that he also again remembered it. Through the blessing of his remembering of his vow, a bowl of soup became abundance, framed and made more manifest by limitation.

A man emotionally half-paralyzed with pain attendant upon a crumbling marriage must move his belongings from his strife-torn house. A friend arrives with a truck and four friends of the friend, unknown to the man, and they move his belongings. He will never see the friends of his friend again. An impecunious young concert pianist has a teacher who does not charge her for the countless hours he spends in helping her. He is repaid by her growing excellence as a musician and the conviction that she will someday help someone as he has helped her. A man in analysis with an older analyst one day realizes that what happens between them does not take the form of arriving at an insight that is then confirmed by the analyst in a completed transaction that allows a new transaction to be initiated. Rather, their relationship is based on the sense of a larger life that both of them have and that they foster in one another through feeling and imagination. In such ways as these, under the aspect of a larger life, life is given on.

Schelling claimed that the great problem of philosophy is why there is something and not nothing.[138] In saying this, he was in a special way taking up the distinction between being and nonbeing that figured in the earliest philosophies of Greece. But he is using that distinction to call attention to the fact that there *is* something and not nothing.

Our affective attunement to the world into which we are born assumes that we do not start out from deficits that need to be made up—from nothings that need to be replaced by something—but rather that there is more than enough, that being is full of itself. Confirmation of these assumptions early in life gives us the strength and courage to

413

deal with limits including those that may threaten us with death or nonbeing, or that we may have to cross to enter Rilke's City of Pain. Rilke's poetic depiction of death as containing life reflects a highly archaic way of feeling and imagining.[139] Though their products are unsusceptible of empirical proof, such ways of feeling and imagining have the psychological justification that self is more embracing than ego, and that life is given by—and in the broadest sense lived through—the self. There will finally be death enough to kill us, and we will have ample occasion to learn much about deprivation, misery, and the reality of evil before it does. But the orientation of the self that knows what is good for itself is toward Life, and so is the affective organization of our experiences, including our capacity for passionate crisis.

One of Amanda's favorite books is *Goodnight Moon,* about a baby rabbit's saying goodnight to all the various objects in his room, including "a comb and a brush and a bowl full of mush / And a quiet old lady who was whispering 'hush,' " as he goes to sleep.[140] Toward the close of the story, the rabbit says, "Goodnight nobody," depicted by a blank page, and finally, "Goodnight stars," "Goodnight air," "Goodnight noises everywhere." Saying goodnight to nobody and to air is like the apostrophe to nonbeing as the ground of being that is embodied in the philosophy of Schelling, or the "God beyond God" of the theologian Paul Tillich (influenced by Schelling), or the Void of the Buddhists. But this representation of nonbeing is treated in the story as no more exceptional than the objects in the house, some customary (a bed, a rug), some very strange (a grandmother rabbit knitting, a rabbit house with a tiger-skin rug on the floor). Indeed, this nothing of air is addressed in the same familiar, intimate speech that Mother is using to tell Baby goodnight. To address the nothing of air and noises everywhere is in one sense to ascend to a high level of abstraction. But in another sense, it is to insist that intimacy, and with it feeling and imagination, extend to the most rarefied contents of Baby's developing consciousness. And it is to insist that, as consciousness develops, feeling and imagination remain open to the self and able to find intimations of its life in even the nothing of silence and the hints of undefined somethings within it.

Wordlike but nonverbal, the noises addressed by Mother belong to a level of experience prior to the distinction between word and thing. Such experience in early life is the developmental basis of a form of transcendence to which sages and technicians of the sacred in many times and places have aspired. It is also the developmental basis of a form of cognition that important contemporary scientists have felt the need to cultivate in their attempts to grasp the nature of physical reality.[141] Such cognition emphasizes the unbroken wholeness of the universe, in which the whole does not simply consist of parts in mechanical interaction. Rather, the whole is enfolded in the parts, which are all interconnected in ways transcending the conceptions of time, space, and causality prevailing in classical physics. And importantly, the recent holographic view of physical reality I am now summarizing also accords with aspects of the mother-infant relationship that I have stressed throughout this book. For both mother and baby recognize that they are "partners" who are never really "apart," and that, though each is a part of the other, each is also a whole, while being, further, a part of the greater whole comprising both.[142]

Mother's blessing in the form of "Good night" reaches beyond the dissolution of commonsense understanding to include the unconscious expressed in the blankness of deep sleep and the imaginative activity of fantasy and dreams. Mother is helping to instill in Baby the trust that it is safe to abandon oneself to such blankness and to dreams that might include tigers as large as the baby rabbit's tiger-skin rug. This is also, by implication, the trust that Baby will find its own relation to the self that knows what is good for itself.

Twenty-eight-month-old Amanda occasionally speaks in an odd way that sounds like a cross between her baby speech and an imitation of baby speech on the part of a child no longer a baby, though she is not herself capable of older-child speech. Unnatural-sounding but not really what one would regard as affected, Amanda seems in such moments unable to find resources, of irony, pathos, or even sentimentality, adequate to express her affective relation to babyhood. It is as though she is no longer always sure how to take her own enactment of the role of baby.

As Baby's third birthday approaches, both Mother and Baby feel moments of nostalgia for the babyhood that is being put behind them. Are they also relinquishing their immediate awareness of the self that knows what is good for itself, and do they feel twinges of regret about doing this?

Feeling, Imagination, and the Self

Twenty-eight-month-old Amanda still says such things as "My feet were sad but now they're happy—I happied them," after she has walked into an icy puddle and then had her feet bathed in warm water. And she still does such things as allowing one stocking to be put on but not the other because it is a cat. But some of such imaginativeness will have to be sacrificed to the consolidation of the ego and the malady of the quotidian. Amanda will have to learn not to walk into parking meters. And sadly, she will probably also have to lose some of the affective acumen that enables her to report about such a mishap, "I cried because I was so angry." (That is, she will probably have to become so adult as to feel impelled to translate such an assessment— a rudimentary complex feeling-judgment of a powerful kind—into the conventional but inaccurate simple feeling-judgment "I cried because I was so sad.") And so the self that knows what is good for itself will at moments have cause to know itself belied. But then what is forgotten in such moments can in principle be remembered.

Moreover, such losses are the deintegrative side of a process resulting in important gains. Parking meters are relentless in dictating the terms on which they are to be negotiated. Moreover, one must have an ego and a secure self-identity to be able to feel and imagine one's way into the common sense-defying but meaningful perspective—known, for example, in dreams—in which each one of us is not one but two or many, and in which this now is interwoven of many times—past, present, and future. Transcendence requires something to be transcended and an ego conscious of the transcendence.

Transcendence is partly return. The poems discussed in this section make clear that it is possible, indeed often essential, for people in later stages of life to recover access to psychic levels so prominent in Mother's and Baby's early experience of one another. And the materials explored in the other sections demonstrate the importance of the evolving mutuality, the sense of abundance, and the self-authentication nurtured and formed in the first two years or so of life. Still, it is very important to regard the ego development of the two- to three-year-old as including important gains not only in the capacity to deal with parking meters but also that for being true to the main values affirmed in the course of these pages.

416

Thus thirty-month-old Amanda, being held in her mother's arms, hits her mother's breastbone, begins crying, pauses to say that she is crying because she hurt herself, resumes crying, and then corrects herself by explaining that she is crying because she hurt her mother. The capacity for active sympathy Amanda thus demonstrates is hardly in any simple way the result of her having been taught by others, and having introjected, a "Thou shalt not"concerned with hitting people. Infantile egocentricity and ruthlessness have in this transaction given way to responsibility and fellow-feeling. But as we have had occasion to see, this relatively mature mutuality is not simply a new development but is the culmination of many developmental steps from the very beginning of life. This mutuality is thus in important respects an artifact, an achievement, but is also the product of an unfolding, the realization of something "given."

The feeling that thirty-month-old Amanda shows in her concern about hurting her mother is linked with a form of imagination that will allow her to say, "I am Dollbaby's Mommy, and I am going to work," and then perform the role with verve and consistency, as she makes important-sounding telephone calls. (She has given Dollbaby to her mother, saying, "You take her, Dad—I don't want her.") Amanda now clearly grasps the "as if" component of the symbolic attitude that sustains a felt and imaginative relation between ego and self.

Some of the complexities we have been considering are well expressed in the figure of the mythical child, whose fate includes abandonment, but who nonetheless proves invincible.[143] Cast off as an infant, Perdita (the "ruined" or "lost" one) was saved by life-affirming forces countering Leontes' intentions that she die. The self that knows what is good for itself put her where she would be nurtured by natural plenitude and community. We feel that the baby Perdita is life itself—certainly for the Old Shepherd picking her up, she represents the quintessence of the life that will survive him. Something in us compels us to feel that it is in the nature of life to strive to give itself on, and we apprehend that giving on under the aspect of the larger life of which the baby is the emblem. That is why our experience of babyhood is one of the sources of the God-image paradoxically taking the form of smaller than small—vulnerable to deintegration, passionate crisis,

417

and dangers of all kinds—but also bigger than big—open to the vast world in which the self lies hidden but everywhere revealed.

6.13 Symbol-Formation at Thirty-Six Months

Thirty-six-month-old Amanda is still capable of reverting to a Mamma-crisis (of a kind described in part 6.1) when her mother, who has been attending to guests, some unknown to Amanda, goes into the bathroom alone. But Amanda now also extends the same exclusiveness to others. And in so doing, she exemplifies with increased complexity the importance (already noted in parts 6.6, 6.7, and 6.12) of infantile residuals supporting a more general sense of two-ness.

Thus when Amanda and Auntie Patty are rolling a beach ball to one another—in a game Amanda has initiated—she is upset when anyone else, including her mother, intervenes to make the ball move not back and forth but in a triangle. In the same vein, when she addresses a question to her mother and her father answers it, she objects vehemently. In both cases her protestations imply clinging to Mamma (whom Auntie in a measure represents). But when her mother answers a question she has addressed to her father, Amanda objects just as vehemently.

Amanda's protestations implicitly declare to Auntie and to whichever of her parents she has asked a question, "I want there to be clear rules." But very importantly, they implicitly declare further, "I want us both to give our undivided attention to one another and to every detail of what we are doing together." Nurtured in the mother-infant relationship, thirty-six-month-old Amanda's demand for mutuality now exists in its own right and cannot be reduced to clinging to Mamma, though Amanda sometimes frantically clings to her. And this further implicit declaration—about undivided attention—expresses a demand for the personal commitment, mutuality, feeling, and imagination necessary to later experiences of one's fullest humanity.

Thirty-six-month-old Amanda also, when there has been no mention of monsters, commands her grandfather, "Stay a Daddy—don't be a monster!" And this command also relates to her insistence that her ball game be limited to Auntie and that her question to her father be answered by her father and not by her mother. With this command to her grandfather, too, she is insisting that rules prevail and that the identities they are supposed to maintain do, in fact, persist. (Grandpa should stay a Daddy.) But she is also aware that these rules and identities may be subject to transformation. (Grandpa might become a monster.) And so she is affirming but also challenging her own sense of propriety—what if Grandpa *were* a monster?—in a way that reaches beyond conventional decorum toward deep questions of how and why, and whether, things are what they should properly be.

And so Amanda's command to her grandfather is, further, concerned with the reality of evil as distinct from good. (Monsters are bad.) But it is also concerned with the possibility that rules based on presumably good (if inscrutable) reasons may, when applied by Daddies, turn out to be monstrous with the evil they are meant to hold in check. (Daddies may become monsters.)

Clearly, as well, Amanda's very notion of "monster" implies a suspicion that evil may be ultimately impersonal. (Rain falls on the just and the unjust. Monsters regard children not as persons but as food.) Yet monsters are also personal. In the child's "animistic" frame of mind drawn on in Amanda's command to her grandfather, one knows that powers, as distinct from things, are living subjects more assimilable to self than to the not-self of death or nonbeing—that monsters are more like "me" than they are impersonally evil.

To the imagining ego of Amanda, then, the notion of "monster" blends personal self and the not-self of impersonal evil into a largely undifferentiated whole. And as though pondering this blend, Amanda implicitly knows that if disaster is to be averted, self rather than not-self must remain the embracing reality—that Grandpa must stay a Daddy, holding within himself whatever potentialities he has for being a monster. And so monsters, thus glimpsed but not allowed to become thoroughly real in the here and now, can be harmless or even benign.

Amanda commands that Grandpa stay a Daddy: she makes his doing so into a rule implying further rules within a more general symbolic context. As we saw with regard to *Goodnight Moon* (in part 6.12), and as Amanda thus continues to know, there is a core of self that is not removed from the world by the symbol systems, with their component rules, that place us in it. We are—but also are not—alienated from the world. Indeed, Amanda can employ the kinds of rules—"Stay a Daddy—don't be a monster!"—that will be greatly elaborated in her further engagement with the Father World. But she can make them serve the special end of preserving the intimacy so richly explored with her mother and so necessary to the unfolding of the self. "Stay a Daddy," she seems to be saying, "so that I can be intimately related not just to Mamma but also to you."

Amanda senses that the self cannot be preserved in stasis—monsters demand alertness and agility—and that the dynamism of the self, with its emotional currents, is in important respects known only through feeling—Daddy and monster are affective realities first and foremost. Thus the symbolic understanding developing in Amanda extends and transforms but does not supersede the more overtly affective awareness prevailing in the mother-infant dyad.

While reaching ahead in symbolic understanding, Amanda, then, also retains contact with earlier levels of affective awareness. Indeed, she is sometimes impelled to reach back to them—even to dive into them (for example, when one of her Mamma-crises, manifestly self-induced, is not just demonstrative for the fun of it but is genuinely felt: she *needs* a Mamma-crisis just now).

Such a Mamma-crisis as that provoked by the recent disappearance of Amanda's mother into the bathroom is partly, in effect, a reminder of Amanda to herself: "Don't forget this dimension of things—don't be tricked into growing up in a way that denatures affective reality to make it safely predictable." Yet there must be predictability. Her command to her grandfather, "Stay a Daddy—don't be a monster!" pleads both for the predictability of a Daddy and for the imaginative glimpse of unpredictable monsters it makes possible. In important ways, it should also be noted, her sense of a father's predictability is not a novel acquisition but has been extended to him owing to the stability of her relationship with her mother—it is something he, as its new object, is partly inheriting from her.

A Grandpa who can stay a Daddy but who might be a monster is an instance, on an early developmental level, of a kind of transformative symbol essential to religion, art, and individuation. Such symbols, emerging in fantasy, serve to bridge oppositions; they make the unknown known—but without presuming to master and diminish its essential unknownness, and they deploy psychic energy, especially in the interest of emotional coherence. (We have considered such symbols in part 6.3 and elsewhere.) Like the Grandpa of Amanda's command, such symbols may be overtly paternal. Yet even then, when they are felt, and are imaginatively real and efficacious, they are, in their invocation of infantile residuals, always close to Mother. These last sentences could be read as glossing Jung's characterization of the unconscious—in his view the ultimate source of such symbols—as the matrix, or mother, of consciousness.

Self and "other" are together from the beginning. Both are to be known, and both are known most fully in intimacy. We reach out intimately to what is given in the here and now. Yet intimacy, not thus confined, is a quality of knowing that can inform everything known. (To say, "Goodnight noises everywhere" is—as we may have surmised in part 6.12—to try, and fail, to imagine how far intimacy may extend.) Seeing with new eyes, a man and woman may, in intimacy, surrender themselves to one another and to their transforming love. And so, a contemplative may, in intimacy, surrender himself to his transforming talisman of the Void. Yet all such later disclosures of value to feeling and imagination are prefigured in the intimacy of mother and child, which they tacitly but actively imply. The intimacy of mother and infant suffuses such moments in the life of the self.

6.14 Giving On: From Mother to Daughter-as-Mother to Infant to Adult

Writing about the ancient Greek maiden goddess, the *Kore*, Kerényi makes the important observation that the pair comprised by Demeter— the Earth-Mother goddess—and her daughter Persephone—abducted by the god Hades to the Underworld—are really different forms of the same figure.[144] On the human plane, the duality-in-unity of mother and daughter is interrelated with the duality-in-unity of mature daughter-as-mother and infant. (Every woman who becomes a mother assumes a new relationship to the motherhood embodied for her by her own mother.) Together these interrelated pairs—of mother and daughter, and of mature daughter-as-mother and infant—provide a model of the giving on of life (discussed in part 6.12). And experiences taking place primarily within this female biological—and psychic—succession are fundamental to the meaning of the giving on of life.

421

Feeling, Imagination, and the Self

When Amanda was eighteen months old, her mother had an experience that she began to record in a letter to her own mother. She began her letter by describing sitting in a café where she saw another woman having coffee with her mother, and expressed the wish that she and her mother could have frequent occasion to meet in such a way. She continued:

> I wonder if you can imagine how having Amanda is for me an almost constant reminder of you—maybe you felt the same way when your babies were little. Amanda makes me sense in a diffuse way how you must have been with me, because I can't actually remember it, but what stirs in me is such a warm, joyous, enveloping love that I know I must have had that, too. It's funny that we can't remember in a precise way what is probably the most important time of our lives, those first two years when we're forming so many ideas about what the world is like. But Amanda has brought back to me so strongly how I *felt* then, which was very much loved and cared for, delighted in and fussed over. That's also a part of why I'm doing the same for her now. I am so aware, many times, of passing something *on* to her.

Amanda's mother then tried to convey, as memory or image, the quality of the experience she wished to describe:

> A curious side effect is that often, now, when I think of you, I see your face so clearly as it was when I was really small—your hair pinned back, and the glasses you wore then, and the red lipstick, and especially your smile. It's hard to realize that that vivid image I have of you, so imprinted on some part of my mind and heart, is of you when you were younger than I am now. Time can play such tricks. But anyway, I think that without Amanda I might very well have missed this sort of rediscovery of you—not that I was unaware of those things I've mentioned, it's just that the intensity and frequency of those images of you are surely connected to Amanda's being here—that's even another reason I have for being grateful for her.

Some such thoughts as these passed, in rudimentary form, through Amanda's mother's mind, and then she forgot them. When they passed through her mind again, it occurred to her to try to express them in a letter. If she had not written the letter, she would, she is sure, have forgotten them again. She began the letter but left it unfinished—she never sent it—and forgot that she had written what she had. She

422

probably would have completely forgotten the letter and the experience it attempted to describe, had she not accidentally come upon the letter in a pile of papers when Amanda was thirty-six months old. Amanda's mother thus demonstrates the wavering of most of us, most of the time, between remembering and forgetting things it would be greatly worth our while to remember. This is not necessarily to imply, however, that Amanda's mother "should" have remembered precisely, and have recorded, the experience that had flitted in and out of her awareness in such a butterfly-like way. The issues raised by her amnesia and anamnesis (Gr. *anamnēsis*, a calling to mind) are too complex and fundamental to accord with such a "should."

To begin with, what she did write was, she realized, at a considerable remove, not only in manner but also in content, from the experience she wished to describe. That experience was of her mother looming over her, as though she were tiny, lying on her back, being looked down upon. What she wrote conveyed nothing of this weird spatial dislocation—as it must seem to be in an adult perspective. Was what she called to mind a conscious memory? If not, what was it? Her problem in describing it is obviously faced by the adult man (described in part 5.4) who related his recollection, from the third to fourth year of life, of a room having "an aura of solemnity"—words that would have been incomprehensible to him at that age. Amanda's mother's experience was elusive for other reasons as well.

Being conscious of something does not necessarily mean holding it in focused awareness, as we may see by considering again the marriages (discussed in part 6.4) that conclude Shakespeare's comedies. The play ends, and the further lives of the couples about to be married are left unrepresented. But the playwright's silence about them tells us nothing about the meaning or importance of those lives or about the depth of the married couples' love. Rather, we may assume that their love, freed from the besetting—and easily representable—problem of whether a relationship can be established in which their love can be lived, may now be lived—largely unrepresented—in their relationship. This may mean—to generalize—that to the eyes of outward observers the mature love of husband and wife is much of the time invisible, and that even to the couple themselves it is much of the time known tacitly.

423

To know something tacitly is, nonetheless, to know it, often in a way that draws on otherwise undisclosed depths of feeling and imagination—and of access to the self. The mature love of husband and wife may be said to have been transformed from overt act to subtle essence, much as the charged experience of love between Amanda's mother, as a baby, and her mother was transformed into something more like a tranquil stream than a cresting wave. But what is like a tranquil stream may—in both the married lovers and in Amanda's mother—be transformed further in ways that produce cresting waves of recognition—of a calling to mind.

The tranquil stream of which I have just spoken is not the unity of nondifference: the experience Amanda's mother wanted to describe to her mother was one of two agents in an intense interaction. Though psychic nondifference, or archaic identity, is real in the mother-infant relationship, the lifelong process of individuation consists largely of disidentification—of rendering archaic identity, and later identifications based on it, conscious.[145] The duality-in-unity in Amanda's mother's mind as she wrote is surely as much duality as unity.

Duality is implicit in reflection, and hence in the development of psyche as an autonomous realm of experience related to vital processes but distinct from them, and—further—in the development of consciousness as relatively independent of the unconscious.[146] The products of this unfolding process of reflection are, in lived experience, substantial. (The ideas that led hundreds of cult members at Jonestown, Guyana, to kill themselves were as real as the poison they took to do it. When Macbeth asks, "Is this a dagger which I see before me . . . ?" [Macbeth, II.i.33], he is free to question what he sees, but he is not free not to see it—his questioning cannot completely dissolve its substantiality. Yet in another sense, products of psyche and of consciousness are startlingly evanescent—"Swift as a shadow, short as any dream, / Brief as the lightning in the collied night . . ." [A Midsummer Night's Dream, I.i.144–45].) What is called to mind, or what calls itself to mind, however sharp-edged and enthralling for the moment, remains poised on the verge of the forgetfulness that washed over Amanda's mother's memories of her mother.

We may experience our lives as entities, beginning and ending, in the same double way: as all-importantly real and enduring, and as a bursting bubble or a blown-out flame. Life goes on in an unbreakable chain, yet our experience of this chain may be as fleeting and as verging on forgetfulness as Amanda's mother's experience of the giving on of life that she knew—years ago and again now—in relation to her mother.

The distancing implicit in the reflection of which I have been speaking—the reflection that sustains the autonomy of psyche in relation to vital processes, and that distinguishes consciousness from the unconscious—undergoes a special, and fundamentally important, elaboration in the Father World. Amanda, like every child, will have to come to terms with a father whom she will never know in the intimacy in which she has known her mother—a father who will never have been an "archaic object" of desire in the way her mother has been, indeed, will not have been such an object at all. And precisely as something totally other than such an object, "the father figure was bound to have a richer and more articulated destiny that the mother figure" (in religious and cultural history); and "through sublimation and identification the symbol of the father was able to join with that of the lord and that of the heavens to form the symbolism of an ordered, wise, and just transcendence."[147]

The full presence of the father in the psychological picture deserves separate treatment—I am working on a version of it—for which I hope this book has helped to prepare the way by calling attention to important neglected phenomena, questioning some received wisdom, and offering alternative viewpoints. For the moment I would comment on the father as the agent of a characteristic form of transcendence only that, along with freedom, it can bring perturbation and perversion; that for it to bring freedom expressive of our fullest humanity, what it brings must be grasped in something of the openness and receptivity inherent in the mother-infant relationship, and that, consequently, for it to bring such freedom, it must be able to present itself in forms that can be grasped in this openness and receptivity.

In playing the game, "I'll be the Mommy, You be the Baby," with her mother, Amanda is, as it were, reaching toward the kind of experience her mother tried to record in her letter to her mother—an experience of the unbreakable chain of life perceived—fleetingly—through imagination and feeling. This chain of life can be conceived

425

as a giving on, but it must be realized that giving on is far more complex and paradoxical than that of mother to daughter-as-mother to infant to the adult retaining something of the infant's openness and receptivity.

Fordham remarks that the main business in life of tiny babies "is to make you fall in love with them."[148] And as Grusha in Brecht's *The Caucasian Chalk Circle* feels herself yielding to the impulse to pick up an abandoned newborn baby—certain that doing so will bring her danger, misery, perhaps death—she exclaims, "Fearful is the seductive power of goodness!"[149] Making us fall in love with them, seducing us into an ethical commitment to them, making us come alive in new ways, babies, too, give life on. (To note that in doing so they consume life—for example, by wearing their parents out physically and burdening them with financial and other worries—is to be reminded that we struggle with limited resources even while being aware of the free grace surrounding and sometimes suffusing the struggle.) Babies as I am now describing them belong to the larger life (discussed in parts 5.8 and 6.12), and the people I have depicted as choosing it share an awareness that the price of admission to the larger life is sometimes appallingly high.

Babies give life on by enticing their parents and other adults into intimacy and a form of personal engagement that is unbounded immediate pleasure, transcendence, and readiness for commitment. And so the baby becomes an image of the self, touching the adult person in a way that inspires an ethical awareness more essential to our fullest humanity than any based on introjected notions of "Thou shalt not." Far prior even to premonitions of such forms of "No," with their implications of the Father World, Baby announces, in effect, "I—as Life—Am." And so the baby enters into the rich drama of its interaction with its mother, shaping its, and our, fundamental and enduring, and always primarily affective, awareness of life as being given on. Religion and culture have no deeper root in our creatureliness than this.

Notes

Part 1

1. The divine child is treated in C. G. Jung, "The Psychology of the Child Archetype," *CW* 9.i (2nd ed.), p. 151–81. See also C. Kerényi, "The Primordial Child in Primordial Times," which appeared with Jung's essay in Jung and C. Kerényi, *Essays on a Science of Mythology: The Myth of the Divine Child and the Mysteries of Eleusis*, rev. ed., trans. R. F. C. Hull (1963; Princeton: Princeton UP, 1969), pp. 25–69.

2. For the relationship between the infant's grasp of "give and take" and its acquisition of language, see Jerome S. Bruner, "Early Social Interaction and Language Acquisition." In *Studies in Mother-Infant Interaction*, ed. H. R. Schaffer (New York: Academic, 1977), pp. 271–89.

3. See John O'Neill, trans., *Themes from the Lectures at the Collège de France, 1952–1960* (Evanston: Northwestern UP, 1970), p. 80.

4. *On the Song of Songs*, vol. 1, trans. Kilian Walsh (Kalamazoo, MI: Cistercian, 1976), p. 136.

5. *Paradise Lost*, IV.44–57, in Merritt Y. Hughes, ed., *John Milton: Complete Poems and Major Prose* (New York: Odyssey, 1957), pp. 278–79.

6. In his *The Religion of the Greeks and Romans*, trans. Christopher Holme (London: Thames, 1962), pp. 141–54, C. Kerényi discusses Gr. *theoria* as meaning "looking" or "viewing," especially in relation to the "show" of godliness enhanced by religious festivity. And Owen Barfield remarks that the Greek word "meant 'contemplation' and is the term used in Aristotle's psychology to designate the moment of fully conscious participation, in which the soul's *potential* knowledge (its ordinary state) becomes *actual*, so that man can at last claim to be 'awake' " (*Saving the Appearances: A Study in Idolatry* [London: Faber, 1957], p. 49).

7. *Chaque fois que l'aube paraît*, trans. Roger Shattuck, who cites the passage in his *Proust's Binoculars: A Study of Memory, Time, and Recognition in A la recherche du temps perdu* (New York: Random, 1963), p. 120.

8. Proust's introduction (1906) to Ruskin's *Le Sésame et les lys*, trans. Roger Shattuck; cited in Shattuck's *Proust's Binoculars*, p. 152.

9. *Devotions upon Emergent Occasions*, ed. John Sparrow (Cambridge: Cambridge UP, 1923), p. 98 (I have modernized the spelling).

10. See Art and Laurie Pepper, *Straight Life: The Story of Art Pepper* (New York: Schirmer-Macmillan, 1979), pp. 309–10 (after release from San Quentin), 84–86 (self-esteem and addiction), 3–23 (childhood).

11. These remarks on personal knowledge are based on the treatment of the subject by the philosopher Michael Polanyi in *Personal Knowledge: Towards a Post-Critical Philosophy* (Chicago: U of Chicago, 1962) and other books.

12. Hans W. Loewald, "Ego and Reality," *International Journal of Psycho-Analysis* 32 (1951): 18.

13. Edward H. Schafer, *The Divine Woman: Dragon Ladies and Rain Maidens in T'ang Literature* (Berkeley: U of California, 1973), p. 22.

14. Schafer, *Divine Woman*, p. 6.

15. Freud, "Project for a Scientific Psychology," *The Origins of Psychoanalysis: Letters to Wilhelm Fliess, Drafts and Notes: 1887–1902*, trans. Eric Mosbacher and James Strachey, ed. Marie Bonaparte, Anna Freud, and Ernst Kris (New York: Basic, 1954), p. 379.

16. René A. Spitz, *A Genetic Field Theory of Ego Formation: Its Implications for Pathology* (New York: International UP, 1959), p. 22, apparently based on Kai Jensen, "Differential Reactions to Taste and Temperature Stimuli in Newborn Infants," *Genetic Psychology Monographs* 12 (1932): 361–479.

17. T. G. R. Bower, *The Perceptual World of the Child* (Cambridge: Harvard UP, 1977), pp. 23–30.

18. Kenneth Kaye, *The Mental and Social Life of Babies: How Parents Create Persons* (Chicago: U of Chicago, 1982), p. 53.

19. Michael Fordham, *The Self and Autism* (London: Heinemann, 1976), p. 34.

20. Fordham, *Self and Autism*, p. 54.

21. Fordham, *Self and Autism*, p. 54.

22. Fordham, *Self and Autism*, p. 13.

23. Speaking of this form of experience—and of relationship—between mother and infant, Spitz calls it "coenesthetic reception," "coenesthetic" being derived from Greek elements meaning "common" and "feeling." Webster's *Deluxe Unabridged Dictionary* (2nd ed.) defines *coenesthesis* as "in psychology, the mass of undifferentiated sensations that make one aware of the body and its condition, as in the feeling of health, illness, discomfort, etc." But Spitz thinks of these early coenesthetic processes in the context of the mother-infant dyad, within which they form a basis of communication. In calling these processes a form of "reception," rather than of "perception," he means to indicate that they occur on a level prior to the distinction between perception and affect. See Spitz's "Diacritic and Coenesthetic Organizations: The Psychiatric Significance of a Functional Division of the Nervous System into a Sensory and Emotive Part," *Psychoanalytic Review* 32 (1945): 146–62; "The Primal Cavity: A Contribution to the Genesis of Perception and Its Role for Psychoanalytic Theory," in *The Psychoanalytic Study of the Child* 10: 215–40; and *The First Year of Life: A Psychoanalytic Study of Normal and Deviant Development of Object Relations* (New York: International UP, 1965), pp. 4 n., 44–46, 53, 134–38.

Part 2

1. In the words of the French poet Arthur Rimbaud, "*Je est un autre*," "The I is another" (my translation); see his May 1871 letters to G. Izambard and P. Demeny

in Oliver Bernard, trans. and ed., *Rimbaud* (Baltimore: Penguin, 1962), pp. 6, 9. ("We are members one of another" [Eph. 4:25].) As Jung has remarked in "The Psychology of the Transference," *CW* 16 (2nd ed.), p. 244, "The unrelated human being lacks wholeness, for he can achieve wholeness only through the soul, and the soul cannot exist without its other side, which is always found in a 'You.' "

2. Jung speaks of "the reality of the psyche" in many places, meaning by the phrase that psyche is not derivative and secondary but, as the precondition of our experience, could rather for all practical purposes be translated as "reality."

3. For an almost identical incident, but within the framework of fools and folly, see the author's *The Fool and His Scepter: A Study in Clowns and Jesters and Their Audience* (Evanston, IL: Northwestern UP, 1969), p. 3.

4. Wilhelm von Humboldt, *Linguistic Variability and Intellectual Development*, trans. George C. Buck and Frithjof A. Raven (1836; Coral Gables, FL: U of Miami, 1971), pp. 39–40.

5. *Discours sur l'origine et les fondements de l'inégalité parmi les hommes* (1755; Paris: Editions Sociales, 1954), p. 115.

6. This translation—the phrase has been translated other ways—is offered by Roger Shattuck, *Marcel Proust* (New York: Viking, 1974), p. 97, n. 3. For Montaigne's essay, see Donald M. Frame, trans., *The Complete Works of Montaigne: Essays, Travel Journal, Letters* (Stanford: Stanford UP, 1980), pp. 478–502; the passage concerned is on p. 480. This soul error is a major form of the disordered feeling discussed in part 6.10 of this book.

7. *Saint Chrysostom: Homilies on the Gospel of St. Matthew*, in Philip Schaff, ed., *A Select Library of the Nicene and Post-Nicene Fathers of the Christian Church* (New York: Christian Literature, 1888) (hereafter cited as *Select Library of Nicene and Post-Nicene Fathers*) 10:344.

8. What Rousseau's singers and dancers became has been accepted as basic human nature by many writers, among them the contemporary literary critic René Girard, who describes several varieties of human desire, all of which are enacted not simply by a subject in relation to a desired object, but also by a rival of the subject. Rivalry is not a matter of two subjects desiring the same object; rather it is the rival's desiring of the object that makes the subject desire it (*Violence and the Sacred*, trans. Patrick Gregory [Baltimore: Johns Hopkins UP, 1977], p. 145).

Living as we do in an age of conspicuous consumption—which even plays a role in the nuclear arms race—it is certain that Girard is talking about a real phenomenon. I am convinced, however, that the "mimetic desire" he describes—desire in imitation of a rival—is a perversion of desire, not its essence, and that this perversion results from a perversion of self-validation. I am primarily concerned with a deeper level of desire, feeling certain that it is not even possible to describe "mimetic desire" adequately except in relation to that of which it is the perversion.

9. "The Republic of Science: Its Political and Economic Theory (1962)," in Marjorie Grene, ed., *Knowing and Being: Essays by Michael Polanyi* (Chicago: U of Chicago, 1969), p. 56.

10. This subject and its important philosophical and psychological implications are

examined in George B. Hogenson, *Jung's Struggle with Freud* (Notre Dame: U of Notre Dame, 1983).

11. "The Problem of Types in the History of Classical and Medieval Thought," *CW* 6, p. 52.

12. "Problem of Types," *CW* 6, p. 53.

13. "Mutual Authority," in Michael Polanyi and Harry Prosch, *Meaning* (Chicago: U of Chicago, 1975), pp. 196–97.

14. "Tacit knowing" is treated in several works by Polanyi, most thoroughly in his *Personal Knowledge*.

15. Erich Neumann's term, as cited by Alfred Plaut in his "Hungry Patients: Reflections on Ego Structure," in Gerhard Adler, ed., *Current Trends in Analytical Psychology: Proceedings of the First International Congress for Analytical Psychology* (London: Tavistock, 1961), p. 155.

16. *CW* 9.ii (2nd ed.), pp. 167–68. Though in this passage Jung also calls the self an archetype, it would seem preferable to regard the self as supraordinate to archetypes, as Michael Fordham maintains in *Children as Individuals*, rev. ed. (London: Hodder and Stoughton, 1969), pp. 27–29.

The following works germane to my discussion of the self appeared too late to be taken into account in it: J. W. T. Redfearn, *My Self: My Many Selves* (Orlando, FL: Academic, 1985); Daniel N. Stern, *The Interpersonal World of the Infant* (New York: Basic, 1985); Michael Fordham, *Exploration into Self* (Orlando, FL: Academic, 1986); and Polly Young-Eisendrath and James Hall, eds., *The Book of the Self* (New York: New York UP, 1987).

17. Douglas K. Candland et al., *Emotion* (Monterey, CA: Brooks/Cole-Wadsworth, 1977).

18. "The Psychology of Dementia Praecox," *CW* 3, p. 38.

19. Edith Jacobson, *Depression: Comparative Studies of Normal, Neurotic, and Psychotic Conditions* (New York: International UP, 1971), p. 68.

20. Thomas Gould, *Platonic Love* (New York: Free, 1963), see pp. 146, 161.

21. Fordham has described deintegration in many publications, including *The Self and Autism*. That the concept has a wide range of applicability is persuasively argued by Renaldo Maduro, "Abandonment and Deintegration of the Primary Self," *Chiron: A Review of Jungian Analysis* (1985): 131–56. Deintegration calls attention to more global movements of ego and self—for example, as King Lear goes mad on the heath.

22. See James S. Grotstein, *Splitting and Projective Identification* (New York: Aronson, 1985).

23. In *Emotion and Personality*, 2 vols. (New York: Columbia UP, 1960) 2:36–37.

24. Mikel Dufrenne, *The Phenomenology of Aesthetic Experience*, trans. Edward S. Casey et al. (Evanston, IL: Northwestern UP, 1973), pp. 10, 378.

25. My use of the terms *self*, *ego*, and *feeling* follows that of Jung, though with some differences of emphasis and some departures from his use of them. The reader may wish to compare the foregoing definitions with Jung's in *CW* 6, pp. 433–36 ("feeling"); 6, p. 425 and 9.ii (2nd ed.), pp. 3–7 ("ego"); 6, pp. 460–61, 467 (2nd ed.), pp. 238–40 and 9.ii (2nd ed.), pp. 23–35 ("self").

For further discussion of Jung's concept of feeling, see my articles in the *Journal of Analytical Psychology:* "Towards a Dynamic Concept of Feeling," 20 (1975): 18–40; "The Primacy of Feeling (I): Affectivity, the Ego, and the Feeling Function," 21 (1976): 115–33; and "The Primacy of Feeling (II): Relations among the Functions," 22 (1977): 1–16.

26. See his *Pathosophie* (Göttingen: Vandenhoeck & Ruprecht, 1956), pp. 57–86; and *Der Gestaltkreis: Theorie der Einheit von Wahrnehmen und Bewegen*, 4th ed. (Stuttgart: Thieme, 1950), pp. 183–90.

27. See Rosemary Gordon, "Losing and Finding: the Location of Archetypal Experience," *Journal of Analytical Psychology* 30 (1985): 121.

28. "The Holy Men of India," *CW* 11, p. 583.

29. "Definitions," *CW* 6, pp. 429, 433.

30. "Sermon Sixty-Seven," *On the Song of Songs*, vol. 4, trans. Irene Edmonds (Kalamazoo, MI: Cistercian, 1980), p. 6.

31. For Bernard on will and grace in this (and the preceding) paragraph, see his treatise "On Grace and Free Choice," VI.17, trans. Daniel O'Donovan, in *Treatises* (Kalamazoo, MI: Cistercian Publications, 1977) 3:73.

32. "A Review of the Complex Theory," *CW* 8 (2nd ed.), p. 96; Jolande Jacobi, *Complex/Archetype/Symbol in the Psychology of C. G. Jung*, trans. Ralph Manheim (London: Routledge, 1959), p. 9.

33. See Thomas X. Davis, trans., appendix to *William of Saint Thierry: The Mirror of Faith* (Kalamazoo, MI: Cistercian, 1979), pp. 93–94.

34. W. Zwingmann, trans. Patrick Ryan; in Ryan's *The Experience of God in the De Contemplando Deo of William of St. Thierry* (Ann Arbor, MI: UMI, 1977), p. 54; cited by Davis, pp. 94 and 95, n. 1.

35. Friedrich Heer, *The Medieval World: Europe 1100–1350*, trans. Janet Sondheimer (New York: Mentor, 1963), pp. 114–16.

36. "On the Relation of Analytical Psychology to Poetry," *CW* 15, p. 82.

37. See, for example, "Schiller's Ideas on the Type Problem," *CW* 6, p. 121.

38. *Select Library of Nicene and Post-Nicene Fathers* 10:269.

39. "Commentary on 1 Corinthians 15," trans. Martin H. Bertram, in *Luther's Works*, vol. 28, ed. Hilton C. Oswald (St. Louis: Concordia, 1973), p. 202.

40. Frederick C. Eiselen, Edwin Lewis, and David G. Downey, eds., *The Abingdon Bible Commentary* (New York: Abingdon, 1929), p. 962, citing H. Wheeler Robinson.

41. Raymond E. Brown, Joseph A. Fitzmyer, and Roland E. Murphy, eds., *The Jerome Biblical Commentary* (Englewood Cliffs, NJ: Prentice-Hall, 1968), p. 747.

42. Marteus Barth, comment on Eph. 3:14–21, in *The Anchor Bible: Ephesians* (Garden City, NY: Doubleday, 1974), p. 370.

43. Karl Rahner, *Theological Investigations* (*vol. 3*): *The Theology of the Spiritual Life*, trans. Karl-H. and Boniface Kruger (New York: Seabury, 1974), p. 332.

44. For reflections upon "The Heart of Harvey," see James Hillman's 1979 Eranos Conference lecture, published as *The Thought of the Heart* (Dallas: Spring, 1981), pp. 11–16. While reflecting upon themes in the work of Henry Corbin, Hillman

touches upon concerns similar to mine in parts of this section and the two that follow, but treats them differently.

45. *Summa Theologica*, III, q. 3, a. 1, ad 2, cited by Stephan Strasser in his *Phenomenology of Feeling: An Essay on the Phenomena of the Heart*, trans. Robert E. Wood (Pittsburgh: Duquesne UP, 1977), pp. 258 and 310, n. 16.

46. Harrison Hayford, Hershel Parker, and G. Thomas Tanselle, *Pierre, or the Ambiguities* (Evanston, IL: Northwestern UP and the Newberry Library, 1971), pp. 288–89.

47. Brown, Fitzmyer, and Murphy, *Jerome Biblical Commentary*, pp. 820–21.

48. "Lectures on Philemon," trans. Jaroslav Pelikan, in *Luther's Works*, vol. 29, ed. Jaroslav Pelikan (St. Louis: Concordia, 1968), p. 98.

49. "The First Sermon" on the Gospel of St. John, Chapter One, trans. Martin H. Bertram, in *Luther's Works*, vol. 22, ed. Jaroslav Pelikan (St. Louis: Concordia, 1957), pp. 9, 12.

50. *Select Library of Nicene and Post-Nicene Fathers* 10: 269.

51. "The Gospel for the Main Christmas Service, John 2[:1–14]," trans. John G. Kunstmann, in *Luther's Works*, vol. 52, ed. Hans J. Hillerbrand (Philadelphia: Fortress, 1974), p. 46.

52. *Grace Abounding to the Chief of Sinners*, ed. Roger Sharrock (Oxford: Clarendon, 1962), pp. 64–65.

53. *Select Library of Nicene and Post-Nicene Fathers* 51: 402–4.

54. "Scholia: Chapter Five," trans. Jacob A. O. Preus, in *Luther's Works*, vol. 25, ed. Hilton C. Oswald (St. Louis: Concordia, 1972), p. 306.

55. Oswald, *Luther's Works* 25: 369.

56. William Blake, "The Marriage of Heaven and Hell," in Geoffrey Keynes, ed., *The Complete Writings of William Blake* (London: Oxford UP, 1966), p. 154.

57. Leonard Forster, ed., *The Penguin Book of German Verse* (Baltimore: Penguin, 1959), pp. 367–68.

58. Cary F. Baynes, trans., *The I Ching or Book of Changes* [trans. of Richard Wilhelm trans.], 2 vols. (London: Routledge, 1951) 1: 169–76, and 2: 236–49.

59. Quoted by Arthur O. Lovejoy in his *The Great Chain of Being: A Study of the History of an Idea* (Cambridge, MA: Harvard UP, 1936), p. 152. The "principle of sufficient reason" is Leibniz's term; see Lovejoy, p. 145.

60. Lovejoy, *Great Chain of Being*, p. 328.

61. Quoted by Lovejoy, *Great Chain of Being*, p. 322; interpolation and clarification within brackets and parentheses are Lovejoy's.

62. See Lovejoy, *Great Chain of Being*, p. 323.

63. "The Magnificat," trans. A. T. W. Steinhaeuser, in *Luther's Works*, vol. 21, ed. Jaroslav Pelikan (St. Louis: Concordia, 1956), p. 329.

64. Lovejoy, *Great Chain of Being*, p. 325 (summarizing Schelling).

65. Lovejoy, *Great Chain of Being*, p. 326.

66. *Science and the Modern World* (New York: Macmillan, 1925), pp. 232, 258.

67. Whitehead, *Science and the Modern World*, p. 257.

68. Whitehead, *Science and the Modern World*, p. 250.

69. Whitehead, *Science and the Modern World*, p. 258. Lovejoy notes the connection between Schelling and Whitehead; see Lovejoy, *Great Chain of Being*, p. 373, n. 18.

70. In *The Origin of the Knowledge of Right and Wrong*, trans. Cecil Hague (Westminster: Constable, 1902). For a fuller edition and more recent translation, see Roderick M. Chisholm's edition (London: Routledge, 1969); Chisholm, however, throughout translates the German *richtig* as "correct" instead of "right."

71. *"Le coeur a ses raisons que la raison ne connoist point"*; see H. F. Stewart, trans., *Pascal's Pensées* (New York: Pantheon, 1950), pp. 342–43 (no. 626).

72. See Jung on "Mandalas," *CW* 9.i (2nd ed.), pp. 387–90.

73. Richard B. Onians, *The Origins of European Thought: About the Body, the Mind, the Soul, the World, Time, and Fate*, 2nd ed. (Cambridge: Cambridge UP, 1954), pp. 13–18.

74. Onians, *Origins of European thought*, p. 17.

75. Wilbur M. Urban, *Language and Reality: The Philosophy of Language and the Principles of Symbolism* (London: Allen, 1939), p. 674.

76. In *Aristotle on Emotion: A Contribution to Philosophical Psychology, Rhetoric, Poetics, Politics and Ethics* (New York: Barnes, 1975). This paragraph and the two that follow are based on his study of Aristotle's psychological and ethical theory.

77. See Fortenbaugh, *Aristotle*, pp. 12–17, 23, 29–30.

78. See Fortenbaugh, *Aristotle*, pp. 13–14.

79. See Fortenbaugh, *Aristotle*, pp. 29–30, 60–61.

80. Roger Scruton, "Emotion, Practical Knowledge and Common Culture," in Amelie O. Rorty, ed., *Explaining Emotions* (Berkeley: U of California, 1980), pp. 522–23.

81. Rorty, *Explaining Emotions*, pp. 528–30.

82. Polanyi and Prosch, *Meaning*, pp. 194–96.

83. For "The Logic of Emergence" see Polanyi, *Personal Knowledge*, pp. 393–97.

84. Several passages of Jung's in *CW* 1 are devoted to this theme, which is implicit in his analysis of feeling-toned complexes in *CW* 2. The prior history of dissociation and subsequent developments are treated in Ernest R. Hilgard, *Divided Consciousness: Multiple Controls in Human Thought and Action* (New York: Wiley, 1977).

85. *Playing and Reality* (New York: Basic, 1971), p. 12.

86. See part 1, n. 1.

87. Rosemary Gordon, *Dying and Creating: A Search for Meaning* (London: Society of Analytical Psychology, 1978), p. 30.

88. *Playing and Reality*, p. 12.

89. In Alfred Adler's *Problems of Neurosis*, ed. Philippe Mairet (New York: Cosmopolitan, 1930), p. 88–99.

90. Girard, *Violence and the Sacred*, p. 145.

91. "Jealousy, Attention, and Loss," in Rorty, *Explaining Emotions*, pp. 481–88.

Part 3

1. See especially Lenoir's albums, *Alabama Blues* (L + R, LR 4.2001), and *Down in Mississippi* (L + R LR 42.42012).

2. David Evans, *Big Road Blues: Tradition and Creativity in the Folk Blues* (Berkeley: U of California, 1982), p. 28.

3. "Killing Floor," *Chester Burnett AKA Howlin' Wolf* (Chess 60016-2). The theme is explored by many other blues artists.

4. My use of the word "transcendence" here is meant to imply Jung's account of imagination as the "transcendent [or more properly, transcending] function" bridging consciousness and unconscious psychic regions in ways responsive to the self; see Jung, "The Transcendent Function," in *CW* 8 (2nd ed.), pp. 67–91.

5. Pickens quoted in Paul Oliver, *Conversation with the Blues* (New York: Horizon, 1965), p. 170.

6. Otis Spann, "The Blues Never Die," *The Blues Never Die!* (Prestige 7719).

7. Howlin' Wolf, "I Ain't Superstitious," *Howlin' Wolf: His Greatest Sides*, vol. 1 (Chess CH-9107).

8. Otis Spann, "I Got a Feeling," *The Blues Never Die!* (Prestige 7719).

9. Johnny Copeland, "When the Rain Starts Fallin'," *Texas Twister* (Rounder 2040).

10. *Robert Johnson: King of the Delta Blues Singers* (Columbia CL 1654).

11. "Hellhound on My Trail," *Robert Johnson: King of the Delta Blues Singers* (Columbia CL 1654).

12. "Rabbit Foot Blues," *The Immortal Blind Lemon Jefferson* (Milestone 2004).

13. In Strasser's "Feeling as Basis of Knowing and Recognizing the Other as an Ego," in Magda B. Arnold, ed., *Feelings and Emotions: The Loyola Symposium* (New York: Academic, 1970), p. 306.

14. Quoted in Oliver, *Conversation*, p. 164.

15. "Banty Rooster Blues," *Charley Patton, Founder of the Delta Blues* (Yazoo L-1020).

16. "Evil is Going On" and "Back Door Man," *Chester Burnett AKA Howlin' Wolf* (Chess 60016-2).

17. Group led by George Wettling, "Serenade to a Shylock," *Jam Session at Commodore* (Commodore [78 rpm] CMS 1501), reissued in *Giants of Jazz: Jack Teagarden* (Time-Life).

18. Quoted in Oliver, *Conversation*, p. 78.

19. Jimmy Johnson, "Breaking up Somebody's Home," *Living Chicago Blues*, vol. 1 (Alligator AL 7701).

20. Snooky [Jones] and Moody [Prior, under whose names the record was issued], "Stockyard Blues," *Chicago Blues: The Early 1950's* (Blues Classics 8, BC-8).

21. "Ain't Gonna Drink No More," *Sunny Land* [sic] *Slim Plays the Rag Time Blues* (BluesWay BLS-6068).

22. William Ferris, *Blues from the Delta* (Garden City, NY: Anchor-Doubleday, 1978), pp. 107–13 ("Blues Talk"), 115–56 ("The House Party").

23. Oliver, *Conversation*, p. 9. A fascinating example of such an improvised interview-monologue is that of Buster Pickens, "Santa Fe Train," on a Flyright album under his name (FLY-LP 536), transcribed in Oliver, *Conversation*, pp. 73–74.

24. Johnny Copeland, "Don't Stop by the Creek, Son," *Texas Twister* (Rounder 2040).

25. Howlin' Wolf, "Smokestack Lightnin'," *Chester Burnett AKA Howlin' Wolf* (Chess 60016-2). Chatmon: quoted in Evans, *Big Road Blues*, p. 288. Lightning Hopkins,

"The Hearse is Backed Up to the Door," *The Legacy of the Blues*, vol. 12 (GNP Crescendo GNPS 10022).

26. Peter Guralnick, *Feel Like Going Home: Portraits in Blues & Rock 'n' Roll* (1971; New York: Vintage-Random, 1981), p. 41.

27. This aspect of the blues is emphasized by Charles Keil in *Urban Blues* (Chicago: U of Chicago, 1966).

28. See Evans, *Big Road Blues*, pp. 22–24; and Guralnick, *Feel Like Going Home*, p. 41. Since blues do not always conform to the AAB stanzaic pattern—some having such patterns as AA, AB, ABB, AAAB, ABAB, ABBA, or a combination of line patterns in one piece—it has been proposed that the basic blues stanza is a rhymed couplet, with each line divided by a caesura (see Michael Taft, *Blues Lyric Poetry: An Anthology* [New York: Garland, 1983], p. x). This would be the simplest and most comprehensive definition. Still, if by far the greatest number of blues stanzas are structured AAB, often with a variation in the second A, this must be because the AAB offers its own inherent satisfactions and provides the optimal means for achieving certain practical aesthetic ends. (For example, the repetition of A gives the singer a second to think ahead about the further progress of the song, and the listener a second to catch the first line. One repetition of A is enough for these purposes, and to repeat A a third time, say, would be to lessen the tension heightened by singing it twice.) What should be granted is that stanzas with line schemes other than AAB are not always variants upon it or departures from it; rather, such stanzas are often what they are because of the expressive potentialities of the patterns employed by them.

29. *The Boss of the Blues* (Atlantic 1234).

30. "The Marriage of Heaven and Hell," in Keynes, ed., *Complete Writings*, p. 149.

31. "They Made the Queen Welcome," *Albert King San Francisco '83* (Fantasy F-9627).

32. Valerie Wellington, *Million Dollar $ecret* [sic] (Rooster Blues R2619).

33. James Butch Cage, with Willie Thomas, "Kill That Nigger Dead" (Decca LK 4644), transcribed in Oliver, *Conversation*, p. 26.

34. Louise Kaplan, *Oneness and Separateness: from Infant to Individual* (New York: Simon, 1978). A summary of the views of Margaret S. Mahler and others.

35. Quoted in Oliver, *Conversation*, p. 2.

36. John Bowlby, *Attachment and Loss* (New York: Basic, 1969), vol. 1, *Attachment*, p. 28.

37. Robert Pete Williams, "Texas Blues," *Those Prison Blues* (Arhoolie 2015).

38. Mississippi Fred McDowell, "I Do Not Play No Rock 'n' Roll" (Capitol 0898 SM 409).

39. Johnny Copeland, "North Carolina," *Texas Twister* (Rounder 2040).

40. Muddy Waters, "Honey Bee," *More Real Folk Blues* (Chess VG 405 515020).

Part 4

1. In "The Location of Cultural Experience," *International Journal of Psycho-Analysis* 48 (1967): 368–72; as quoted by Harry J. S. Guntrip from an oral presentation—

Notes to pp. 144–53

with some differences in wording and punctuation from the published version of Winnicott's paper in Guntrip's *Psychoanalytic Theory, Therapy, and the Self* (New York: Basic, 1971), pp. 121–22.

2. For an account of Hanus Papousek's 1967 experiment see Joseph Chilton Pearce, *The Magical Child: Rediscovering Nature's Plan for Our Children* (1977; New York: Bantam-Dutton, 1980), pp. 274–75.

3. Experiment by Kalnins in 1970, cited by Pearce, *Magical Child*, p. 275.

4. In his *Expositions on the Book of Psalms*; see *Select Library of Nicene and Post-Nicene Fathers* 8 (1905): 134; Latin citation by Josef Pieper in his "Über das Phänomen des Festes," *Arbeitsgemeinschaft für Forschung des landes Nordrhein-Westfalen* 113 (1963): 19; see also J. Pieper, *In Tune With the World: A Theory of Festivity*, trans. Richard and Clara Winston (New York: Harcourt, 1965), p. 38.

5. In *Shakespeare's Festive Comedy: A Study of Dramatic Form and Its Relation to Social Custom* (1959; Cleveland and New York: Meridian-World, 1963), pp. 7–8.

6. See Jung's discussion "Concerning the Word 'Spirit,' " Section 1 of "The Phenomenology of the Spirit in Fairytales," *CW* 9.i (2nd ed.), pp. 208–14.

7. For an account of these festivals, see Frances A. Yates, *The Valois Tapestries* (London: Warburg Institute, U of London, 1959), pp. 51–108.

8. Cora Du Bois, *The People of Alor: A Social-Psychological Study of an East Indian Island*, vol. 1 (Cambridge, MA: Harvard UP, 1960), p. 148.

9. Yates, *Valois Tapestries*, p. 52.

10. Abraham Rosman and Paula G. Rubel, *Feasting with Mine Enemy: Rank and Exchange among Northwest Coast Societies* (New York: Columbia UP, 1971).

11. "Sermon Eighty-Three," in Edmonds, *On the Song of Songs*, 4:181.

12. Richard Alewyn, "Feste des Barock" in R. Alewyn et al., *Aus der Welt des Barock* (Stuttgart: Metzlersche, 1957), p. 108.

13. *CW* 3, pp. 13–14.

14. In "Acute Catatonic Schizophrenia," *Journal of Analytical Psychology*, 2 (1957): 137–52.

15. "Dementia Praecox," *CW* 3, p. 149.

16. *Saint Augustine: Confessions*, trans. R. S. Pine-Coffin (Baltimore, MD: Penguin, 1961), pp. 40–41 (Bk. I.20).

17. "Dementia Praecox," *CW* 3, pp. 147–48.

18. L[eopold] Stein, "Introducing Not-self," *Journal of Analytical Psychology* 12 (1967): 97–113. See also Michael Fordham's "Defences of the Self," *Journal of Analytical Psychology* 19 (1974): 192–99.

19. See Anne H. Rosenfeld, *The Archaeology of Affect: An NIMH [National Institute of Mental Health] Program Report* [on the research of Paul D. MacLean], U.S. Dept. of Health, Education, and Welfare, Publ. No. (ADM) 76–395 (Washington: GPO, 1976), p. 29.

20. F. S. C. Northrop, *The Meeting of East and West: An Inquiry Concerning World Understanding* (New York: Macmillan, 1946), pp. 317–18, 330–37.

21. In "A Psychological View of Conscience," *CW* 10 (2nd ed.), pp. 437–55.

22. *Ego and Archetype: Individuation and the Religious Function of the Psyche* (New York: Putnam's, 1972).

23. Pieper, "Über das Phänomen des Festes," p. 12; *In Tune With the World*, p. 20.

24. Dufrenne, *Phenomenology of Aesthetic Experience*, p. 150.

25. Dufrenne, *Phenomenology of Aesthetic Experience*, p. 150, n. 2.

26. See *Envy and Gratitude: A Study of Unconscious Sources* (New York: Basic, 1957), pp. 18–19, 45–46.

27. Paper, comment, and reply are in *Journal of Analytical Psychology* 26 (1981): 345–63.

Part 5

1. "On the Psychology of the Unconscious," *CW* 7 (2nd ed.), pp. 53–54.

2. Rollo May, *Power and Innocence: A Search for the Sources of Violence* (New York: Norton, 1972), p. 109.

3. "Location of Cultural Experience," pp. 368–72.

4. *CW* 6, p. 475.

5. Frazer, *The Golden Bough: A Study in Magic and Religion*, abridged ed. (New York: Macmillan, 1952), pp. 13–43.

6. Morton Smith, *Jesus the Magician* (San Francisco: Harper, 1978), pp. 122–23.

7. Keith Thomas, *Religion and the Decline of Magic* (New York: Scribner's, 1971), pp. 34–35.

8. John B. Walker, *Christianity: An End to Magic* (Denville, NJ: Dimension [1972]).

9. Smith, *Jesus the Magician*, pp. 60–64.

10. *Stolen Lightning* (New York: Continuum, 1982).

11. Rosman and Rubel, *Feasting with Mine Enemy*, pp. 22–23. Along similar lines, Wilfredo Pareto has observed that "banquets in honour of the dead become banquets in honour of the gods, and then again banquets in honour of saints; and then finally they go back and become merely commemorative banquets again. Forms can be changed, but it is much more difficult to suppress the banquets", in Arthur Livingston, ed., and Andrew Bongiorno and A. Livingston, trans., *The Mind and Society*, 4 vols. Vol. 2, *Theory of Residues* (New York: Harcourt, 1935), p. 607.

12. O'Keefe, *Stolen Lightning*, pp. 349–413.

13. Morris Berman, *The Reenchantment of the World* (Ithaca, NY: Cornell UP, 1981), pp. 117–26.

14. Gerardus van der Leeuw, *Religion in Essence and Manifestation*, vol. 1, trans. J. E. Turner (New York: Harper, 1963), pp. 23–36.

15. In W. Ronald D. Fairbairn, *Psychoanalytic Studies of the Personality* (London: Tavistock, 1952), pp. 66–67.

16. See Polanyi, *Personal Knowledge*.

17. Ivar Paulson in a comment on "The Notion of Magic," by Murray and Rosalie Wax, in *Current Anthropology* 4 (1963): 511.

18. Paulson, Comment on "The Notion of Magic," p. 511.

19. See *Comparative Psychology of Mental Development*, rev. ed. (New York: International UP, 1948), pp. 17–19.

20. Rosemary Gordon draws a similar distinction in "Reflections on Curing and Healing," *Journal of Analytical Psychology* 24 (1979): 207–17.

21. See Berman, *Reenchantment*, p. 132.

22. Alfred Vierkandt, "Die entwicklungspsychologische Theorie der Zauberei" (1937), in Leander Petzoldt, ed., *Magie und Religion* (Darmstadt: Wissenschaftliche Buchgesellschaft, 1978), p. 197.

23. Polanyi, *Personal Knowledge*, p. 205.

24. *The Intrapsychic Self: Feeling, Cognition, and Creativity in Health and Mental Illness* (New York: Basic, 1967), pp. 43–47.

25. *Intrapsychic Self*, pp. 84–91.

26. *Intrapsychic Self*, pp. 108–12.

27. *Intrapsychic Self*, p. 274.

28. O'Keefe, *Stolen Lightning*, pp. 85–91.

29. *How Natives Think*, trans. Lilian A. Clare (New York: Knopf [1926]), pp. 69–104.

30. Polanyi, *Personal Knowledge*, p. 101–2.

31. Barfield, *Saving the Appearances: A Study in Idolatry* (London: Faber, 1957), pp. 28–35, 133–41.

32. Adolf E. Jensen, *Myth and Cult among Primitive Peoples*, trans. Marianna T. Choldin and Wolfgang Weissleder (Chicago: U of Chicago, 1963), p. 5.

33. *Les Carnets de Lucien Lévy-Bruhl* (Paris: Presses Universitaires de Paris, 1949) pp. 60–68, 167–69.

34. Polanyi, *Personal Knowledge*, pp. 294–324.

35. See also Jung's "The Stages of Life," *CW* 8 (2nd ed.), 387–403.

36. Kenneth Burke, *A Grammar of Motives* (1945; Berkeley: U of California, 1969), pp. xv–xxii.

37. O'Keefe, *Stolen Lightning*, pp. 67–69.

38. In his *Steps to an Ecology of Mind* (New York: Ballantine, 1972), p. 410.

39. Edward C. Whitmont, "The Magic Layer of the Unconscious," *Spring* [published by The Analytical Psychology Club of New York] (1956): 58–80; "Magic and the Psychology of Compulsive States," *Journal of Analytical Psychology* 2 (1957): 3–32; "The Magical Dimension in Transference and Counter-transference," in Gerhard Adler, ed., *Current Trends in Analytical Psychology*, pp. 176–97; *Return of the Goddess* (New York: Crossroad, 1982).

40. Marija Gimbutas, *The Goddesses and Gods of Old Europe, 6500–3500 B.C.: Myths and Cult Images* (Berkeley: U of California, 1982).

41. Stephen Jay Gould, *Ontogeny and Phylogeny* (Cambridge, MA: Belknap, 1977).

42. Wolfgang Giegerich, "Ontogeny = Phylogeny?: A Fundamental Critique of Erich Neumann's Analytical Psychology," *Spring* (1975): 110–29.

43. Arieti, *Intrapsychic Self*, p. 81.

44. Dorothy Lee, "Being and Value in a Primitive Culture," *Journal of Philosophy* 46 (1949): 401–15.

45. In *Mind: An Essay on Human Feeling* (Baltimore: Johns Hopkins UP, 1982), 3: pp. 41–88.
46. Langer, *Mind*, 3:150–54.
47. See "Poetry" (longer version), in *The Complete Poems of Marianne Moore* (New York: Viking-Macmillan, 1981), pp. 266–68; in a note on the phrase, Moore indicates her debt to Yeats and her transformation of his words.
48. Langer, *Mind*, 3:51.
49. Langer, *Mind*, 3:8–9.
50. In *The Tacit Dimension* (Garden City, NY: Anchor-Doubleday, 1967), p. 4; these words are italicized in the original.
51. In his *Mind and Nature: A Necessary Unity* (New York: Dutton, 1979), pp. 14–16.
52. *Deviation into Sense: The Nature of Explanation* (London: Faber [1948]), pp. 28–29.
53. See Kerényi's *Dionysos*, trans. Ralph Manheim (Princeton: Princeton UP, 1976), pp. xxv–xxxvii.
54. In his *Persephone: Three Essays on Religion and Thought in Magna Graecia* (Oxford: Clarendon, 1971), pp. 51–52.
55. William McGuire and R. F. C. Hull, eds., *C. G. Jung Speaking: Interviews and Encounters* (Princeton: Princeton UP, 1977), p. 378.
56. Bateson, *Mind and Nature*, pp. 6–8.
57. *The Collected Earlier Poems of William Carlos Williams* (New York: New Directions [1951]), p. 200.
58. "Theses Against Occultism," *Telos*, 19 (1974): p. 9.
59. *CW* 5 (2nd ed.), pp. 414–15.
60. *One Hundred Favorite Folktales*, comp. Stith Thompson (Bloomington: Indiana UP, 1974), pp. 45–48, 113–22.
61. My attention was called to these texts by Ian Grand.
62. *The Iliad, or, the Poem of Force*, trans. Mary McCarthy (Wallingford, PA: Pendle Hill [1956]).
63. Weil, *Iliad, Poem of Force*, pp. 3–5.
64. Weil, *Iliad, Poem of Force*, p. 11.
65. Weil, *Iliad, Poem of Force*, pp. 14–15.
66. Weil, *Iliad, Poem of Force*, p. 26.
67. Weil, *Iliad, Poem of Force*, p. 27.
68. Weil, *Iliad, Poem of Force*, p. 34.
69. Weil, *Iliad, Poem of Force*, p. 36.
70. In James M. Doran's *Erroll Garner: The Most Happy Piano* (Metuchen, NJ, and London: Scarecrow Press and Institute of Jazz Studies, Rutgers University, 1985), p. 101.
71. E. Hanfmann and R. M. Jones, eds., *Neurosis and Treatment: A Holistic Theory* (New York: Wiley, 1965), chap. 8.
72. In Hanfmann and Jones, *Neurosis and Treatment*, p. 81.

73. I imagined this scene at Delphi before knowing of Joseph Eddy Fontenrose's *The Delphic Oracle: Its Responses and Operations, with a Catalogue of Responses* (Berkeley: U of California, 1978).

74. See Gibson's *The Senses Considered as Perceptual Systems* (Boston: Houghton-Mifflin, 1966), p. 286.

75. See Daniel Stern, *The First Relationship: Mother and Infant* (Cambridge, MA: Harvard UP, 1977), pp. 52–61.

76. Stern, *First Relationship*, pp. 54–58.

77. Stern, *First Relationship*, pp. 56–61.

78. Stern, *First Relationship*, p. 75.

79. Carroll E. Izard, "Emotion-Cognition Relationships and Human Development," in Carroll E. Izard, Jerome Kagan, and Robert B. Zajone, eds., *Emotions, Cognition, and Behavior* (Cambridge: Cambridge UP, 1984), p. 32.

80. Owen Barfield, *What Coleridge Thought* (Middletown, CN: Wesleyan UP, 1971), chaps. 3 and 10.

81. Johann Scheffler, "Cherubinischer Wandersmann," *Sämmtliche Poetische Werke*, ed. David A. Rosenthal (Regensburg, 1862), I, 5, aphorism I, 8; quoted in Jung, *CW* 6, p. 256.

82. Barfield, *What Coleridge Thought*, p. 145.

83. William Willeford, "Jung's Polaristic Thought in Its Historical Setting," *Analytische Psychologie* 6 (1975), 232–33.

84. Barfield, *What Coleridge Thought*, p. 148.

85. *CW* 9.i (2nd ed.), pp. 95–96.

86. In Brooke's "Jung and the Phenomenology of Guilt," *Journal of Analytical Psychology* 30 (1985): 170. Brooke's discussion of the passage is suggestive and illuminating (pp. 168–74).

87. *Religio Medici*, I.13, in *The Prose of Sir Thomas Browne*, ed. Norman J. Endicott (New York: Norton, 1967), p. 19.

88. Brooke, "Jung," p. 170.

89. In *Robert Frost: Poetry and Prose*, ed. Edward Connery Lathem and Lawrance Thompson (New York: Holt, 1972), pp. 170–71.

90. T. Berry Brazelton, Barbara Koslowski, and Mary Main, "The Origins of Reciprocity: The Early Mother-Infant Interaction," in Michael Lewis and Leonard A. Rosenblum, eds., *The Effect of the Infant on its Caregiver* (New York: Wiley, 1974), p. 68.

91. Desmond Morris, *Manwatching: A Field Guide to Human Behavior* (New York: Abrams, 1977) p. 169.

92. D. W. Winnicott, *Collected Papers: Through Paediatrics to Psycho-Analysis* (New York: Basic, 1958), chap. VIII, "Anxiety Associated with Insecurity" [1952], p. 99.

93. See Jung's "Psychology of the Child Archetype" and Kerényi's "Primordial Child in Primordial Times"; cited in part 1.

Part 6

1. *The Varieties of Religious Experience: A Study in Human Nature* (London: Longmans, 1912), p. 195.
2. James, *Varieties*, p. 150.
3. *CW* 3, p. 40, n.7; Jung quoting from Bleuler's *Affektivität, Suggestibilität, Paranoia*, 2nd ed. (Halle, 1926), p. 30.
4. Carroll E. Izard, *Human Emotions* (New York: Plenum, 1977), p. 85.
5. Magda B. Arnold, *Emotion and Personality* (New York: Columbia UP, 1960), 1: 200–201.
6. *CW* 10, pp. 338.
7. *CW* 5 (2nd ed.), p. 67.
8. *CW* 5 (2nd ed.), p. 415.
9. *CW* 13, p. 21.
10. *CW* 5 (2nd ed.), p. 67.
11. Robert Farris Thompson, *Flash of the Spirit: African and Afro-American Art and Philosophy* (New York: Random, 1983), pp. 9–16.
12. See *African Art in Motion: Icon and Act* (Los Angeles: U of California, 1974), p. 43. He focuses upon the concept in his "An Aesthetic of the Cool," *African Arts*, 7.1 (1973): 40–43.
13. Quoted by John Miller Chernoff, *African Rhythm and African Sensibility: Aesthetics and Social Action in African Musical Idioms* (Chicago: U of Chicago, 1979), pp. 106–07.
14. Chernoff, *African Rhythm*, p. 140.
15. *CW* 5 (2nd ed.), p. 137.
16. *CW* 5 (2nd ed.), pp. 133–34.
17. "Postage-Size Propaganda," *The New York Times Magazine*, February 15, 1987, p. 41.
18. On bipolar theories of emotion, see Willeford, "Primacy of Feeling (I)," p. 117; for acts of preference as expressions of a hierarchy of essential values, see Max Scheler, *Formalism in Ethics and Non-Formal Ethics of Values: A New Attempt toward the Foundation of an Ethical Personalism*, trans. Manfred S. Frings and Roger L. Funk (Evanston, IL: Northwestern UP, 1973), pp. 86–90.
19. C. K. Ogden, *Bentham's Theory of Fictions* (New York: Harcourt, 1932), pp. 87 ("Archetypation"), 94–96.
20. For an exposition of a number of these forms, see György Doczi, *The Power of Limits: Proportional Harmonies in Nature, Art and Architecture* (Boulder, CO: Shambhala, 1981).
21. See Joseph F. Rychlak, *The Psychology of Rigorous Humanism* (New York: Wiley, 1977), pp. 6–31.
22. "Dethroning the Self," *Spring* (1983), p. 55.
23. "An Inquiry into Image," *Spring* (1977), pp. 82–83.
24. *The Anxiety of Influence: A Theory of Poetry* (New York: Oxford UP, 1973), p. 7.
25. Samuels, "Dethroning the Self," p. 49.

26. Elie Humbert, "The Self and Narcissism," *Journal of Analytical Psychology* 25 (1980): 238.
27. Jung, "The Stages of Life," *CW* 8, pp. 387–403. I recommend that the reader ignore Jung's contention that children rarely have problems apart from those assimilated from their parents. One may do so because this view ignores overwhelming clinical evidence to the contrary, and because it contradicts Jung's rightful emphasis on dispositions of the emerging personality that have an individual character from the outset, relatively independently of environmental influences—as Fordham argued in *Children as Individuals* (cited in part 2.5).
28. The view of conscience implied in the last paragraphs accords with Jung, "A Psychological View of Conscience," *CW* 10, pp. 437–55.
29. "An Approach to Group Analysis," *Journal of Analytical Psychology* 4 (1959): 139–51; also in G. Adler, ed., *Current Trends in Analytical Psychology*, pp. 275–91.
30. *CW* 8 (2nd ed.), pp. 67–104.
31. W. R. Bion, *Experiences in Groups and Other Papers* (New York: Basic, 1959).
32. *CW* 8 (2nd ed.), pp. 294–95.
33. *CW* 8 (2nd ed.), pp. 417–531.
34. John Litweiler, *The Freedom Principle: Jazz after 1958* (New York: Morrow, 1984).
35. See Colwyn Trevarthen, "Communication and Cooperation in Early Infancy: A Description of Primary Intersubjectivity," in Margaret Bullowa, ed., *Before Speech: The Beginning of Interpersonal Communication* (Cambridge: Cambridge UP, 1979).
36. In his *Eleusis: Archetypal Image of Mother and Daughter*, trans. Ralph Manheim (New York: Pantheon, 1967), pp. xxvi–xxvii.
37. Kerényi, *Eleusis*, p. xxxii.
38. "The Structure of the Psyche," *CW* 8 (2nd ed.), p. 152.
39. "Psychology of the Child Archetype," *CW* 9.i (2nd ed.), pp. 152–53.
40. For myths as traditional tales, see G. S. Kirk, *The Nature of Greek Myths* (Harmondsworth, England: Penguin, 1974), pp. 27–28. For a relatively adequate definition of myth, see Lauri Honko, "The Problem of Defining Myth," in *The Myth of the State*, ed. Haralds Beizais (Stockholm: Almqvist, 1972), pp. 7–19; rpt. in *Sacred Narrative: Readings in the Theory of Myth*, ed. Alan Dundes (Berkeley: U of California, 1984), p. 49.
41. See for example, "The Structural Study of Myth," in *Structural Anthropology*, vol. 1, trans. Claire Jacobson and Brooke G. Schoepf (New York: Basic, 1963), pp. 206–31; *The Savage Mind* (Chicago: U of Chicago, 1966); "The Story of Asdiwal" and "Four Winnebago Myths," *Structural Anthropology*, vol. 2, trans. Monique Layton (New York: Basic, 1976), pp. 146–210.
42. Kerényi, *Eleusis*, p. xxviii.
43. *Art and the Creative Unconscious: Four Essays*, trans. Ralph Manheim (Princeton: Princeton UP, 1959), pp. 108–9.
44. Kerényi, *Eleusis*, p. xxxii.
45. Kirk, *Nature of Greek Myths*, p. 278.
46. Kirk, *Nature of Greek Myths*, pp. 277–86.

47. In "Der ursprüngliche Mythos im Lichte der Sympathie von Mensch und Welt," in his *Mythos und Welt* (Stuttgart: Ernst Klett, 1962), pp. 230–66.

48. Goethe quoted and briefly discussed by Otto in "Die Sprache als Mythos," *Mythos und Welt*, p. 284; my translation into English.

49. In "Ordo Amoris," *Selected Philosophical Essays*, trans. David R. Lachterman (Evanston, IL: Northwestern UP, 1973), p. 122 (italics in Lachterman's edition).

50. Otto, *Mythos und Welt*, p. 284.

51. See Joseph F. Rychlak, *Introduction to Personality and Psychotherapy: A Theory-Construction Approach* (Boston: Houghton-Mifflin, 1973), p. 4.

52. *Images and Symbols: Studies in Religious Symbolism*, trans. Philip Mairet (1961; New York: Search-Sheed, 1969), p. 59.

53. Polanyi and Prosch, *Meaning*, pp. 124–25.

54. Eliade, *Images and Symbols*, p. 59.

55. For Zeus and Hera, see Homer, *Iliad*, XIV, 346 ff.

56. *CW* 8 (2nd ed.), pp. 211–12.

57. *The Idea of the Holy: An Inquiry into the Non-Rational Factor in the Idea of the Divine and Its Relation to the Rational*, 2nd ed., trans. John W. Harvey (London: Oxford UP, 1950), pp. 25–30.

58. See Matthew Fox's Introduction to *Breakthrough: Meister Eckhart's Creation Spirituality in New Translation* [trans. M. Fox et al.] (Garden City, NY: Doubleday, 1980), p. 44.

59. See letters between Paul Evdokimov and Jung, *Harvest* (1984), pp. 6–8.

60. "Blake's 'Eye of the Imagination,' ", *Harvest* (1984), p. 40.

61. "Unitary Reality and the Creative," *Harvest* (1984), pp. 9–10.

62. *Harvest* (1984), p. 20, quoting Jung, "Medicine and Psychotherapy," *CW* 16, p. 90.

63. *Harvest* (1984), p. 25.

64. "The Incest Wound and the Marriage Archetype," *Harvest* (1984), pp. 93–95.

65. "Beyond Compensation: Modifying Jung's Approach to Dreams," *Harvest* (1984), pp. 118–20.

66. Jakob von Uexküll, *Theoretische Biologie*, 2nd ed. (1928; Frankfurt am Main: Suhrkamp, 1973), p. 57; the translation here and in the following passages is mine.

67. Uexküll, *Theoretische*, pp. 340–41.

68. Uexküll, *Theoretische*, pp. 121 22.

69. Kenneth Burke elaborates upon the dramatistic view of human motives in *A Grammar of Motives* and in his article on "Interaction: Dramatism," *International Encyclopaedia of Social Sciences*, 1968 ed.

70. See my article on "Jung's Polaristic Thought," *Analytische Psychologie* 6 (1975). See also Kenneth Burke's comments on this article in his "(Nonsymbolic) Motion/(Symbolic) Action," *Critical Inquiry* 4 (1978): 823–30.

71. Barfield, *What Coleridge Thought*, chaps. 1–4.

72. Barfield, *What Coleridge Thought*, p. 41.

73. Samuel Taylor Coleridge, *The Friend*, ed. Barbara E. Rooke (Princeton: Princeton

UP, 1969), *The Collected Works of Samuel Taylor Coleridge*, vol. 4, pt. 1, 94 n.; as quoted by Barfield in *What Coleridge Thought*, p. 31 (capitalization, typography, and punctuation normalized by Barfield).

74. Rainer Maria Rilke, *Duino Elegies*, trans. J. B. Leishman and Stephen Spender (New York: Norton, 1939), pp. 66–67.

75. Robert Grudin, *Mighty Opposites: Shakespeare and Renaissance Contrariety* (Berkeley: U of California, 1979), p. 15.

76. *Harvest* (1984), p. 11.

77. See Neumann's "Die Erfahrung der Einheitswirklichkeit und die Sympathie der Dinge," *Eranos-Jahrbuch* 24 (1955): 51–52.

78. *Harvest* (1984), p. 13.

79. See Jaffé, *Harvest* (1984), p. 13. For an opposing view, see Daniel N. Stern, "The Early Development of Schemas of Self, Other, and 'Self with Other,' " in Joseph D. Lichtenberg and Samuel Kaplan, eds., *Reflections on Self Psychology* (Hillsdale, NJ: Analytic, 1983), pp. 49–84.

80. *Shakespearean Meanings* (Princeton: Princeton UP, 1968), pp. 144–46.

81. *Poets on Fortune's Hill: Studies in Sidney, Shakespeare, Beaumont and Fletcher* (London: Faber, 1952), pp. 131–32, 135, 146.

82. *The Restoration of the Self* (New York: International UP, 1977), chap. 5.

83. *The Nature of Sympathy*, trans. Peter Heath (New Haven: Yale UP, 1954).

84. *Wesen und Formen der Sympathie*, 2nd ed. (Bonn: Cohen, 1923), pp. 16–40.

85. Scheler, *Sympathie*, pp. 23–24.

86. Spitz, *Genetic Field Theory*, p. 18.

87. See Sigfried Giedion, *The Eternal Present: A Contribution on Constancy and Change*, 2 vols. (New York: Pantheon, 1962–1964), 1: 173–92.

88. This distinction is explored by Wilhelm Worringer in his *Abstraktion und Einfühlung: Ein Beitrag zur Stilpsychologie* (1st ed., 1908); an English translation by Michael Bullock is available as *Abstraction and Empathy: A Contribution to the Psychology of Style* (New York: International UP, 1953). Worringer's views are put into illuminating perspective by Giedion in his *The Eternal Present*, 1: 40–43.

89. Much of twentieth-century depth psychology has been directly or indirectly concerned with liminal states. Cultural institutions assuming or fostering such states have been examined by a number of anthropologists, among them Victor Turner in his *The Ritual Process: Structure and Anti-Structure* (Chicago: Aldine, 1969) and *Dramas, Fields, and Metaphors: Symbolic Action in Human Society* (Ithaca: Cornell UP, 1974).

90. Helmuth Plessner, *Lachen und Weinen: Eine Untersuchung nach den Grenzen Menschlichen Verhaltens* (Bern: Francke, 1950), p. 171. The English translation, *Laughing and Crying: A Study of the Limits of Human Behavior*, trans. James S. Churchill and Marjorie Grene (Evanston, IL: Northwestern UP, 1970), p. 127, renders the German phrase as "distanceless captivation by things."

91. "Feeling as Basis of Knowing," in Arnold, *Feelings and Emotions*, pp. 299–300.

92. Strasser, "Feeling as Basis of Knowing," p. 306.

93. For "affect-ego," see Jung, "Dementia Praecox," CW 3, pp. 41–42; for "affect-object," see John Weir Perry, "Emotion and Object Relations," Journal of Analytical Psychology 15 (1970): 4.

94. Mother Courage and Her Children: A Chronicle of the Thirty Years' War, trans. Eric Bentley (New York: Grove, 1963), p. 59.

95. George Steiner's words, The Death of Tragedy (New York: Knopf, 1961), p. 354; quoted in John Fuegi's The Essential Brecht (Los Angeles: Hennessey, 1972), p. 93.

96. See Martin Buber, I and Thou, trans. Walter Kaufmann (New York: Scribner's, 1970).

97. See Jung, CW 5 (2nd ed.), p. 155.

98. See R. B. Zajonc, "Feeling and Thinking: Preferences Need No Inferences," American Psychologist 35 (1980): 151–75; R. B. Zajonc, Paula Pietromonaco, and John Bargh, "Independence and Interaction of Affect and Cognition," in Margaret Sydnor Clark and Susan T. Fiske, eds., Affect and Cognition (Hillsdale, NJ: Erlbaum, 1982), pp. 211–27; C. E. Izard, "Comments on Emotion and Cognition: Can There Be a Working Relationship?" in Clark and Fiske, Affect and Cognition, pp. 229–40.

99. According to Whitehead, "The contrast between the comparative emptiness" of sense data in the present "and the deep significance disclosed" in the mode of action "is at the root of the pathos which haunts the world. . . . Almost all pathos includes a reference to lapse of time"; in Symbolism: Its Meaning and Effect (New York: Macmillan, 1927), p. 47.

100. The Poetry of Robert Frost, ed. Edward C. Lathem (New York: Holt, 1969), p. 338; all references are to this edition.

101. Example offered by Alex Steve Hill at a meeting of Jungian analysts and trainees.

102. See especially Jung, CW 2.

103. "The Essence of Feeling: Outline of a Systematic Theory," in Martin L. Reymert, ed., Feelings and Emotions: The Wittenberg Symposium (Worcester, MA: Clark UP, 1928), p. 72. See also Willeford, "Primacy of Feeling (I and II)."

104. See Stephan Strasser, Phenomenology of Feeling (Pittsburgh: Duquesne UP, 1977), pp. 186–87.

105. Strasser, Phenomenology of Feeling, pp. 187–90.

106. For projection in the creation of consciousness, see Hogenson, Jung's Struggle with Freud, pp. 130–38.

107. John Raphael Staude, Max Scheler, 1874–1928: An Intellectual Portrait (New York: Free, 1967), p. 254.

108. M. C. Bradbrook, Themes and Conventions of Elizabethan Tragedy (1935; Cambridge: Cambridge UP, 1960), p. 240.

109. Bradbrook, Themes and Conventions, p. 247.

110. M. L. Wine, ed., Drama of the English Renaissance (New York: Modern Library, 1969), p. 405.

111. See S. H. Butcher, Aristotle's Theory of Poetry and Fine Art, 3rd ed. (London: Macmillan, 1902), pp. 123–24.

112. Physics, II.i.193b.

113. *Basic Writings of Nietzsche*, trans. and ed. Walter Kaufmann (New York: Modern Library, 1968), p. 67.

114. "Areopagitica. . .," *Works of John Milton* 4:311.

115. "Sclerotic consciousness": Erich Neumann, *The Origins and History of Consciousness*, trans. R. F. C. Hull (New York: Pantheon, 1954), pp. 384, 386.

116. In *The Collected Poems of Wallace Stevens* (1954; New York: Knopf, 1974), p. 85.

117. Jung, *CW* 5 (2nd ed.), 219.

118. Stevens, *Collected Poems*, p. 96.

119. *Dichtungen und Briefe*, ed. Walther Killy and Hans Szklenar, 2 vols. (Salzburg: Müller, 1969), I, p. 134; the translation is mine.

120. Jung, *CW* 5 (2nd ed.), p. 246 (Egyptian sun-ship); *The Sun in Art*, ed. Walter Herdeg (Zurich: Graphis, 1962), pp. 24 (vase from the Cyclades) and 102 (Fornasetti plate); Jung, *CW* 5 (2nd ed.), p. 210 (solar figures in chest or ark).

121. For the "Great Round," see Neumann's *The Great Mother: An Analysis of the Archetype*, 2nd ed., trans. Ralph Manheim (Princeton: Princeton UP, 1963), pp. 211–39.

122. *Meister Eckhart: Deutsche Predigten und Traktate*, ed. and trans. [into modern German] Josef Quint (Munich: Hanser, 1955), p. 216; trans. into English by John D. Caputo in his *The Mystical Element in Heidegger's Thought* ([Athens, OH: Ohio UP], 1978), p. 126.

123. See John Bowlby, *Attachment and Loss*. Vol. 2, *Separation: Anxiety and Anger* (New York: Basic, 1973); and Louise J. Kaplan, *Oneness and Separateness: From Infant to Individual* (New York: Simon, 1978), a summary of the views of Margaret S. Mahler and others.

124. In Hanfmann and Jones, *Neurosis and Treatment*, pp. 5–8.

125. Mircea Eliade, "Cosmogonic Myth and 'Sacred History,' " in *The Quest: History and Meaning in Religion* (Chicago: U of Chicago, 1969), pp. 72–87; rpt. in Dundes, *Sacred Narrative*, p. 149. Eliade refers his readers to T. G. H. Strehlow's "Personal Monototemism in a Polytotemic Community," in Eike Haberland, Meinhard Schuster, and Helmut Straube, eds., *Festschrift für Ad[olf] E. Jensen* 2 vols. (Munich: Renner, 1964) 2:723–54; and Strehlow's *Aranda Traditions* ([Melbourne]: Melbourne UP, 1947), pp. 35–38.

126. *Duino Elegies*, trans. J. B. Leishman and Stephen Spender (New York: Norton, 1939); all references are to this edition.

127. *Duino Elegies*, p. 117.

128. *Lao-tzu: "My Words Are Very Easy to Understand,"* lectures by Man-jan Cheng on the *Tao Teh Ching*, trans. Tam C. Gibbs (Richmond, CA: North Atlantic, 1981), pp. 102 and 75.

129. *Wordsworth: Poetical Works*, ed. Thomas Hutchinson, rev. by Ernest de Selincourt (1936; London: Oxford UP, 1973), p. 499.

130. *The Penguin Book of German Verse*, pp. 369–70; I have altered the translator's "pleasant" to "beautiful" in the third stanza.

131. *Penguin Book of German Verse*, p. 372; translator's "affluent" altered to "rich" in second half of poem.

132. In *The Poems & Letters of Andrew Marvell*, ed. H. M. Margoliouth (Oxford: Clarendon, 1927) 1:49; all references are to this edition.

133. "Dem Schicksal," *Goethes Werke* (Hamburg: Wegner, n.d.) 1: 132. For *Ungescheidenheit* and *Dumpfheit*, see Werner Danckert, *Goethe: Der mythische Urgrund seiner Weltschau* (Berlin: De Gruyter, 1951), pp. 499–502.

134. *Lao Tzu: Tao Te Ching*, trans. D. C. Lau (Baltimore: Penguin, 1963), pp. 85, 91.

135. See Lewis Hyde, *The Gift: Imagination and the Erotic Life of Property* (New York: Vintage, 1979), pp. 12–16.

136. *Argonauts of the Western Pacific: An Account of Native Enterprise and Adventure in the Archipelagoes of Melanesian New Guinea* (London: Routledge, 1922), p. 97; cited by Hyde who discusses the Kula and the theme of giving on in *The Gift*.

137. In *The Mask of Shame* (Baltimore: Johns Hopkins UP, 1981), p. 166.

138. Adam Margoshes, "Schelling, Friedrich Wilhelm Joseph von," *Encyclopedia of Philosophy*, 1967 ed.

139. Concerning the archaic nature of this mode, see Ernst Cassirer, *The Philosophy of Symbolic Forms* (New Haven: Yale UP, 1955), vol. 2, *Mythical Thought*, p. 37.

140. By Margaret Wise Brown, illus. Clement Hurd ([New York]: Harper, 1947).

141. See Renée Weber, "Field Consciousness and Field Ethics" [about physicist David Bohm], in Ken Wilber, ed., *The Holographic Paradigm and Other Paradoxes* (Boulder: New Science Library-Shambhala, 1982), pp. 35–43.

142. See L. Zinkin, "The Hologram as a Model for Analytical Psychology," *Journal of Analytical Psychology* 32 (1987): 6, 19 (esp.).

143. Jung, "Psychology of the Child Archetype," CW 9.i (2nd ed.), pp. 167–68, 170–71.

144. Jung and Kerényi, *Essays on a Science of Mythology*, pp. 105–7; cited in part 1.

145. "Individuation is practically the same as the development of consciousness out of the original state of identity"; Jung, CW 6, p. 449.

146. For reflection as the basis of "psychization" and, in turn, consciousness, see Jung, CW 8, p. 117

147. Paul Ricoeur, *Freud and Philosophy: An Essay on Interpretation* (New Haven: Yale UP, 1970), p. 542.

148. In a personal comment to me.

149. Rev. English version by Eric Bentley (New York: Evergreen Black Cat–Grove, 1966), p. 46.

Illustration Credits

1. Meister von Messkirch (?), St. *Christopher with the Christ Child.* Courtesy of the Oeffentliche Kunstsammlung Basel, Kunstmuseum.

2. Photograph by Liz Major. Courtesy of the photographer.

3. Jacob Boehme, *XL Questions concerning the soule.* London, 1647. Reprinted by permission of The Huntington Library, San Marino, California.

4. Illustration reprinted from *Psychology Today* Magazine, August 1977, p. 98. Copyright 1977 American Psychological Association.

5. Photograph courtesy of Holt, Rinehart and Winston.

6. Martin Schongauer, *La Vierge au Boisson de Roses.* Courtesy of the Paroisse St. Martin, Colmar.

7. Artwork for the poster of the 1986 Bellevue Jazz festival. Concept/design: Harper & Associates, Inc., Bellevue, WA. Photography: Jim Fagiolo, Seattle, WA. Courtesy of Harper & Associates.

8. Cover art from Albert Collins's album *Ice Pickin'.* Courtesy of Alligator Records.

9. Illustration of mother cat and kittens. Courtesy of Price/Stern/Sloan Publishers, Inc.

10. Henry Moore, "Suckling Child." © Henry Moore Foundation, 1930. Reproduced by kind permission of the Henry Moore Foundation.

11. Photograph by Vera Tenschert. Collection of John Fuegi. Reproduced by permission.

Index

Index

450

Index

Index

Index

Index

Frost, Robert, 229, 340, 347, 348, 385
fulfillment, 139
fusion, 91, 91–92, 110, 262, 323, 332, 338, 403; process of differentiation, 110–11

"Gallagher, Lenore," 86
"The Gambler" (song), 409
"The Garden" (Marvell), 403–404
"Gardner, Leah," 331, 369–70, 374
Garner, Erroll, 219
Gawain, Sir, 204
"Gayle, Linda," 56–57, 58
Generalization, 344
Gibson, James J., 223
Gift, 76, 231, 232, 297, 298; and work, 296
Giving on, 5–7, 417, 426; of life, 408, 421
"Giving Birth within a tradition" (Shorter), 315
Globalizing, 352; emotional, 352, 353, 355, 370
Gloucester, Earl of (King Lear), 204, 342, 343, 347,
God, 6, 30, 38, 41, 50, 52, 61, 63, 70, 73, 79, 165, 200, 218, 227, 228, 229; as Creator, 9; relationship with nature, 74, 229; of Becoming, 74–75; Whitehead on, 75–76; Schelling on, 76; and forgiveness, 212; and man, 301
Goethe, Johann, 57, 227, 299, 302, 317, 319, 322, 323, 380; on primordial phenomena, 305; and fate, 406
Goneril (King Lear), 31, 342
Good-enough mother, 62, 150, 225–26, 231
"Good Morning Little School Girl" (McDowell), 141
Grace, 6, 30, 32, 50, 67–68, 73, 165, 217, 232; superabundance, 68–69
Gradations, 357; of feeling, 321
Gratiano (Merchant of Venice), 308

Gratitude, 6, 158, 298; of infant-mother relationship, 260
Green Knight, 205
Grief, 50, 135, 338, 399; as response to abandonment, 24; and the blues, 134
Group [therapy]: work, 268–69, 269; disintegrating tendencies, 277, 285; dynamics of, 277, 297; making connections, 282–83; decisions, 284; exchange of opinions, 284; and fantasy, 284; dominant ear, 294
"Gubbinal" (Stevens), 381–82, 385
Guilt, 173

Habituation, 224, 224–25
Hamlet (Hamlet), 28–29, 86–87, 161–62, 255, 305, 323–24, 338; as essence, 318
Hamlet (Shakespeare): T. S. Eliot on, 86–87
Harvest, 314
Harvey, Sir William, 65
Healing: distinction betwen curing and, 175
Heart, 22, 65, 77, 78, 80, 82, 95, 98, 182, 187, 254; cool, 24; biblical, 65–66; serenity of, 69–70; and love, 77, 78; understanding, 82; reasoning of, 85, 87–88; knowledge, 87–88; blues as education of the, 98; Pascal on logic of the, 232
Hegel, 227; and dialectical procedures, 90
Héloïse: and Abelard, 263
Henry VI, Part III (Shakespeare): and community, 9
Henry V (Shakespeare), 42
Hermione, Queen (The Winter's Tale), 1, 5, 322–23, 364–67
Heteronomy: Angyal on, 394
Hierarchy: principle of, 253
Higher powers, 228, 231, 232; and connection between feeling and imagination, 223

Index

Index

Index

Index

Pascal, Blaise, 375; and heart, 80, 81, 82, 232
Passion, 343–44, 344, 345; Lear's, 346
Passionate crisis, 22, 42–43, 48, 53–54, 62, 80, 88, 196, 205, 219, 220, 223, 232, 247, 255, 338, 376–77, 378, 379, 381, 392, 414, 417; defined, 42; mitigating, 338–39
Pathic ground, 22, 48, 53–54, 58, 77, 88, 196, 254, 340, 379; defined, 41–42; of psychic life, 86; blues as expression of, 101; motivation, 376
Pathos, 135, 378
Patton, Charley, 77, 113, 117
Paul, Saint, 31, 38, 68, 125, 146, 161; and the natural man, 29; and abundance of the heart, 65, 66; and grace, 71, 72
Paulina (*The Winter's Tale*), 1, 2, 5, 12, 366
Pepper, Art, 10–11, 13–14, 261, 355; and self-division and self-deception, 10
Perception, 128; objective, 331
Perdita (*A Winter's Tale*), 366, 368; as mythical child abandoned, 417
Peripeteia, 285, 287, 288, 289, 290, 294
Perls, Fritz, 265
Perry, John A: and schizophrenic disintegration, 149; on inner psyche as dynamic matrix
Persephone: Kerényi on, 421
Perseveration, 354, 355
Persistance: of disorder, 324
Perspective, 317; partial, 328
Perturbation, 425
Perversion, 425
Piaget, Jean: and egocentricity, 19
Picasso, Pablo, 338
Pickens, Buster, 99–100
Pierce, Billie, 113
Pierce, Nat, 219

Plato, 73, 196, 258, 318; on *eros*, 40; and rationalistic theology, 75; dialectical procedures of, 90
Plenty, 303
Plessner, Helmuth, 330, 332
Plotinus, 75
Poetry, 181
Polanyi, Michael, 34, 229; and mutual authority, 35, 36; universal intent, 88; and science, 173–74; on diffuse emotional conviviality, 177; and participation, 180–81; and primitives, 181–82; tacit knowledge, 194; on creation myths, 306
Polarity, 227, 313–30, 356, 387; of *eros/logos*, 321; thinking, 377; element of relatedness, 394
Pollock, Jackson: order in chaos, 262
Polonius (*Hamlet*), 28–29
Portia (*Merchant of Venice*), 308
Possession: egoistic, 197; coercive, 198
Potlach: and festival, 147; potentiality of social and economic order to create victims, 171
Power, 166, 167, 169, 172, 215, 218, 219, 260, 261; nutrient, 165; opposite of love, 165, 235; imposed, 166; economic, 169; social, 169; politics, 171; ambiguities of, 191; magical, 205; of mother-infant bond, 326
Pound, Ezra, 259
Practice: as distinct from theory, 8
"Preaching Blues," 108
Prejudice, 87–88
The Prelude (Wordsworth), 400
Presumption, 31
Pride, 166
Primacy, 255–56
Primitive, 189–90; peoples, 199–200
"Primitive Myth in Light of the Sympathy of Man and World" (Otto), 302

Index

Index